ASTONISHING X-MEN

GHOST BOX

ASTONISHING X-MEN
GHOST BOX

Writer: **Warren Ellis**
Pencils: **Simone Bianchi**
Ink Washes: **Simone Bianchi & Andrea Silvestri**
Colors: **Simone Peruzzi**
with Christina Strain, Laura Martin, Morry Hollowell & Simone Bianchi

Ghost Boxes #1
Part 1, Pencils: **Alan Davis**
Inks: **Mark Farmer**
Colors: **Rob Schwager**
Part 2, Artist: **Adi Granov**

Ghost Boxes #2
Part 1, Artist: **Clayton Crain**
Part 2, Artist: **Kaare Andrews**

Cover Art: **Simone Bianchi, Andrea Silvestri & Simone Peruzzi**
Letterers: **Joe Caramagna & Chris Eliopoulos**
Assistant Editors: **Daniel Ketchum & Will Panzo**
Editor: **Axel Alonso**

Collection Editor: **Jennifer Grünwald**
Editorial Assistant: **Alex Starbuck**
Assistant Editors: **Cory Levine & John Denning**
Editor, Special Projects: **Mark D. Beazley**
Senior Editor, Special Projects: **Jeff Youngquist**
Senior Vice President of Sales: **David Gabriel**
Book Designer: **Michael Chatham**

Editor in Chief: **Joe Quesada**
Publisher: **Dan Buckley**
Executive Producer: **Alan Fine**

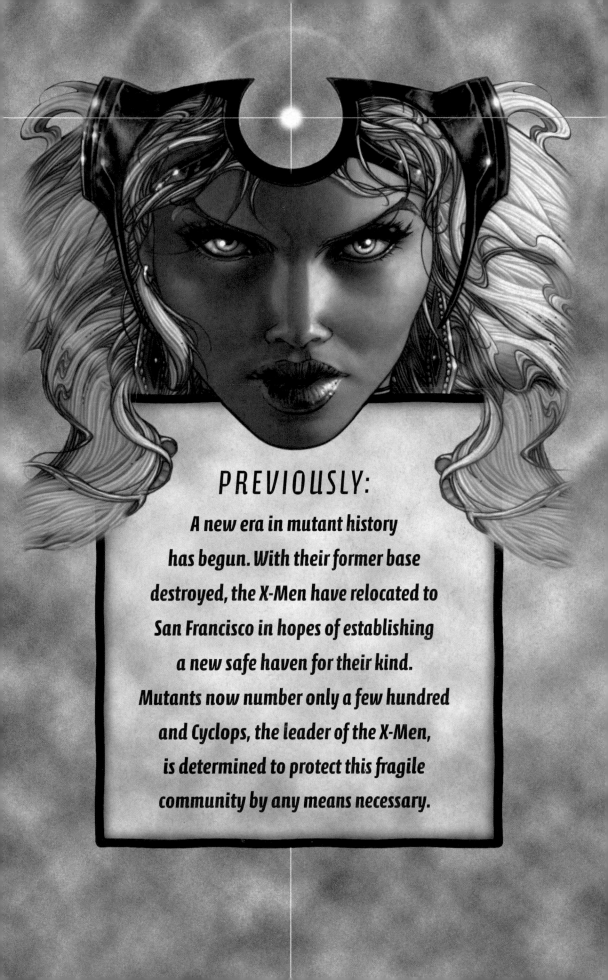

PREVIOUSLY:

A new era in mutant history
has begun. With their former base
destroyed, the X-Men have relocated to
San Francisco in hopes of establishing
a new safe haven for their kind.
Mutants now number only a few hundred
and Cyclops, the leader of the X-Men,
is determined to protect this fragile
community by any means necessary.

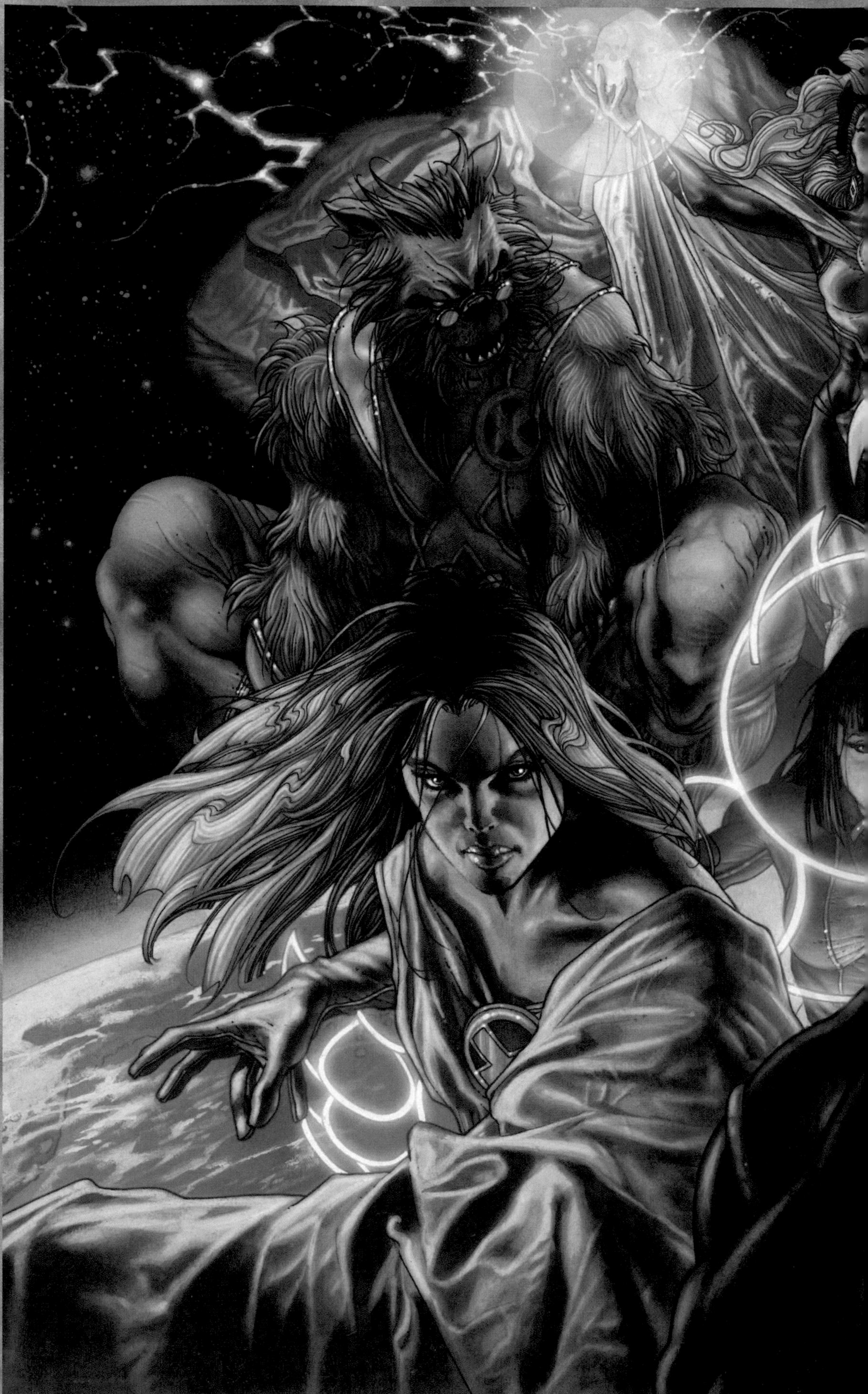

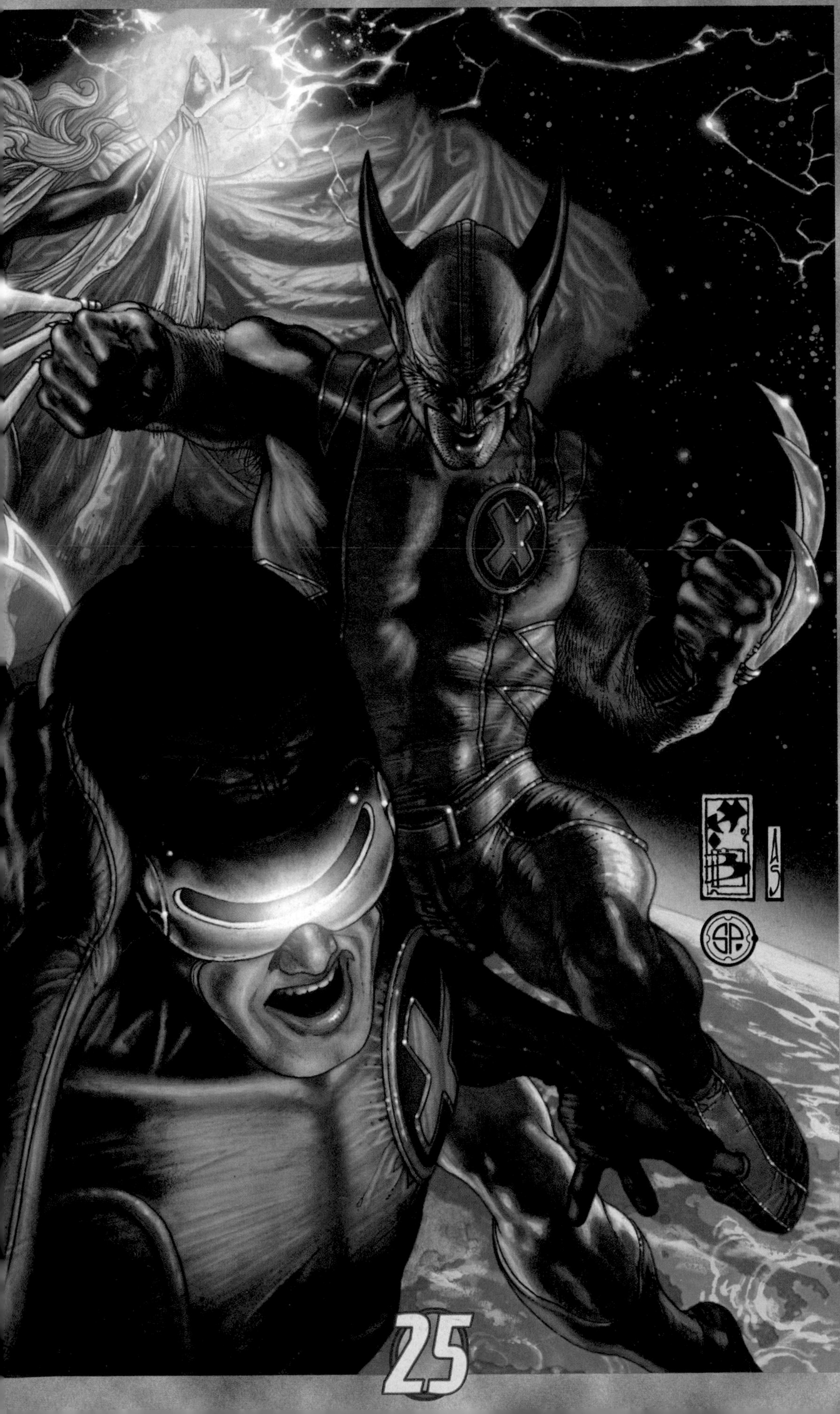
25

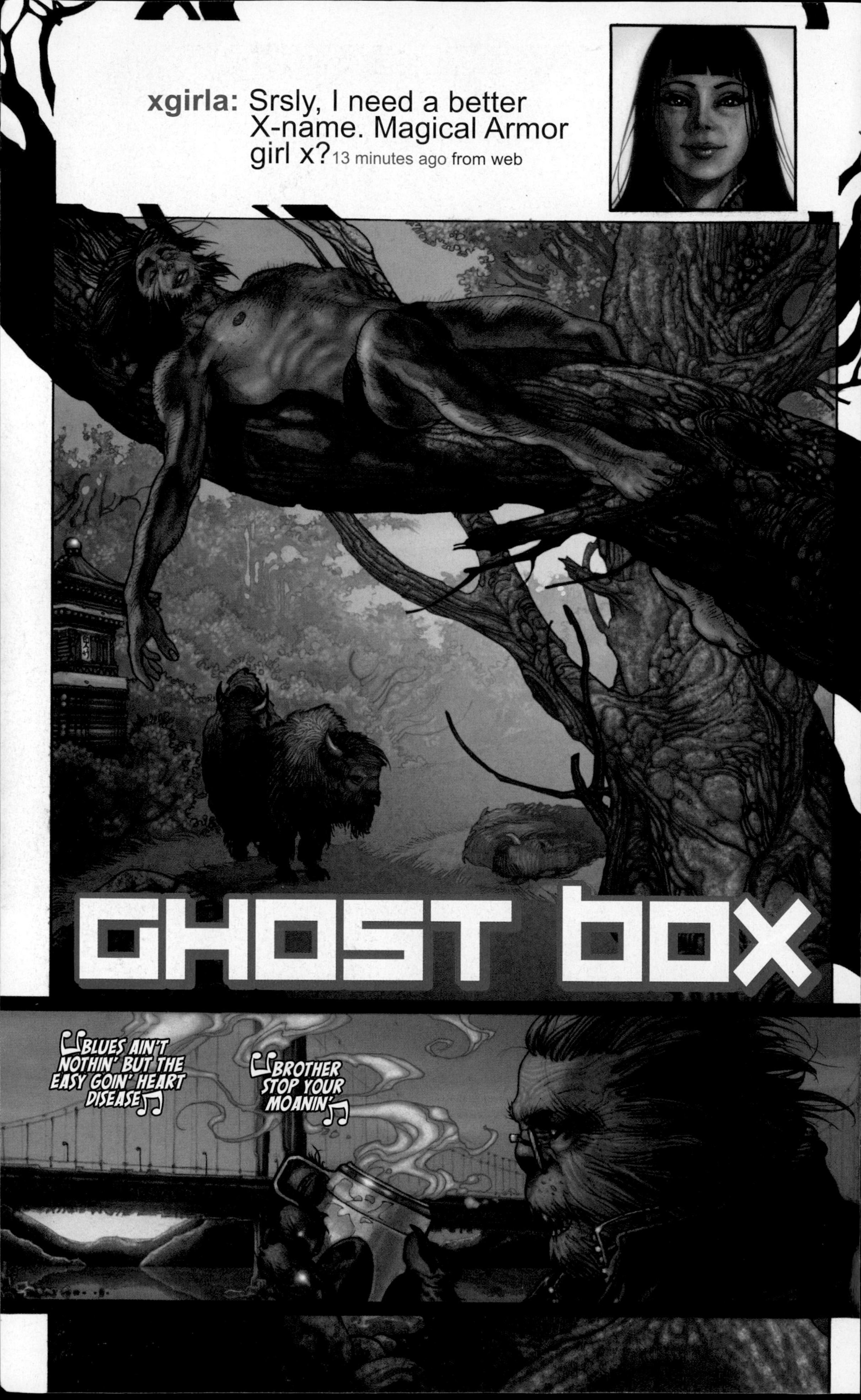
xgirla: Srsly, I need a better X-name. Magical Armor girl x? 13 minutes ago from web
GHOST BOX
BLUES AIN'T NOTHIN' BUT THE EASY GOIN' HEART DISEASE
BROTHER STOP YOUR MOANIN'

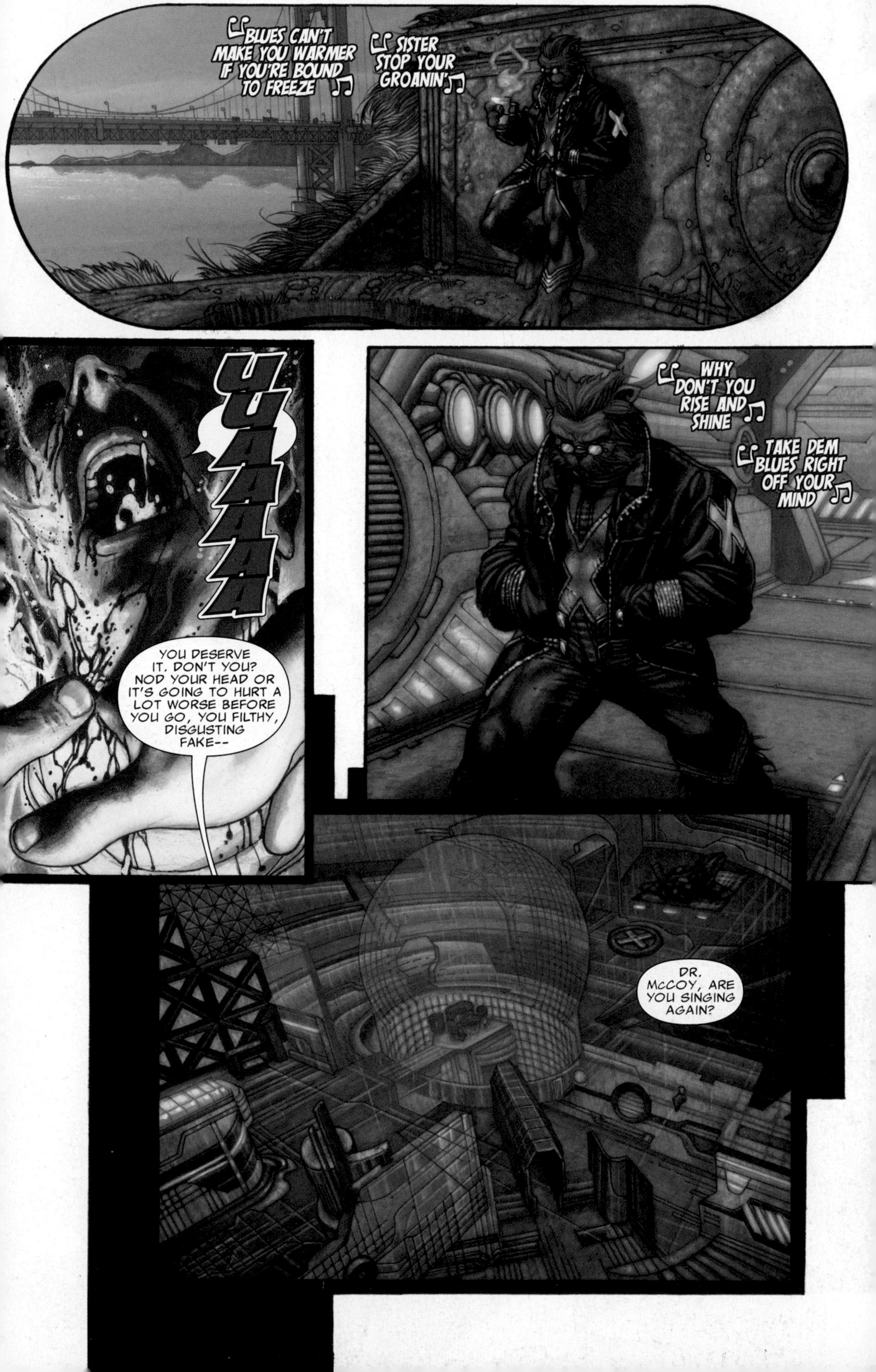
BLUES CAN'T MAKE YOU WARMER IF YOU'RE BOUND TO FREEZE
SISTER STOP YOUR GROANIN'
UUAAAAAA
YOU DESERVE IT. DON'T YOU? NOD YOUR HEAD OR IT'S GOING TO HURT A LOT WORSE BEFORE YOU GO, YOU FILTHY, DISGUSTING FAKE--
WHY DON'T YOU RISE AND SHINE
TAKE DEM BLUES RIGHT OFF YOUR MIND
DR. McCOY, ARE YOU SINGING AGAIN?

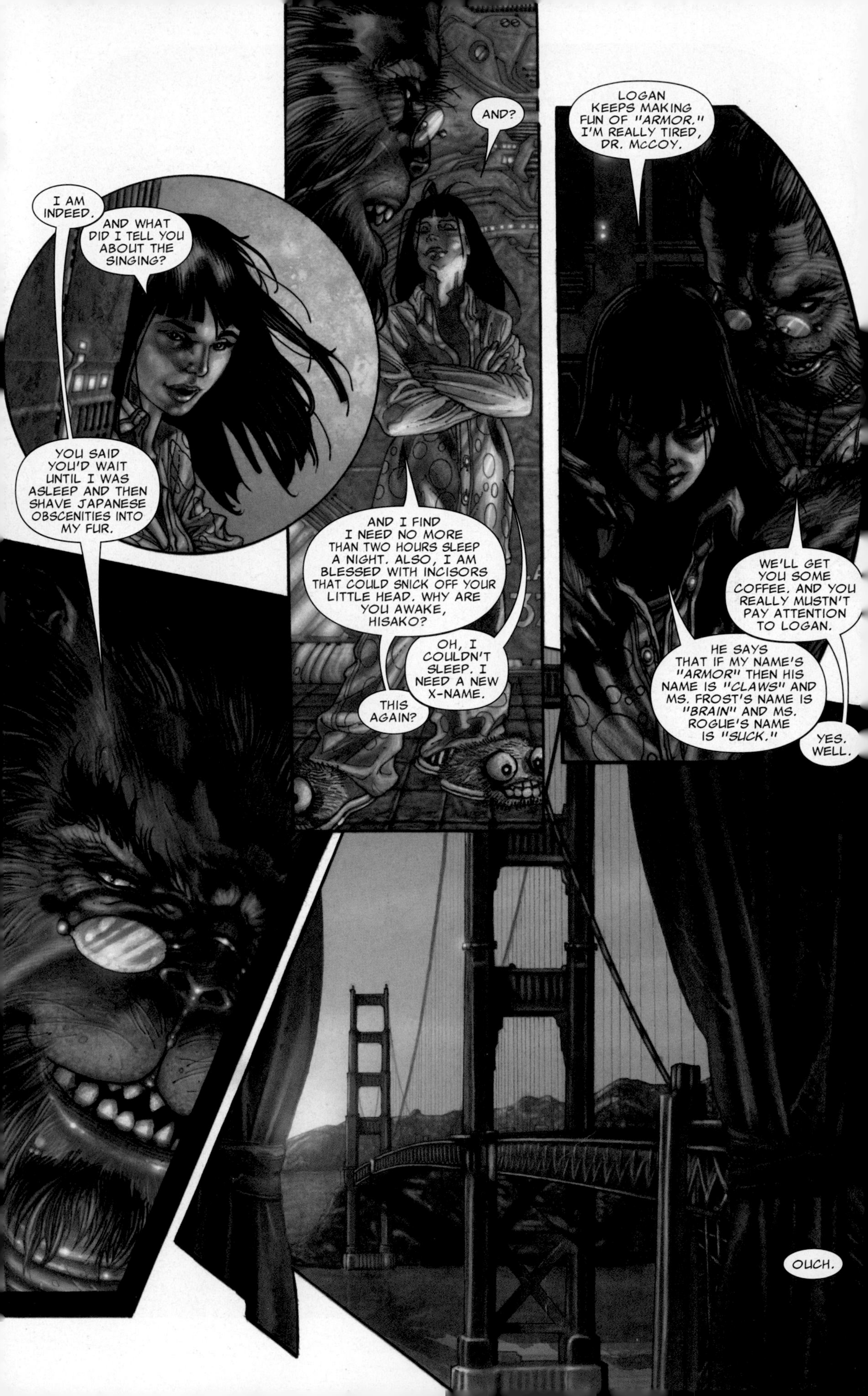
I AM INDEED.
AND WHAT DID I TELL YOU ABOUT THE SINGING?
YOU SAID YOU'D WAIT UNTIL I WAS ASLEEP AND THEN SHAVE JAPANESE OBSCENITIES INTO MY FUR.
AND?
AND I FIND I NEED NO MORE THAN TWO HOURS SLEEP A NIGHT. ALSO, I AM BLESSED WITH INCISORS THAT COULD SNICK OFF YOUR LITTLE HEAD. WHY ARE YOU AWAKE, HISAKO?
OH, I COULDN'T SLEEP. I NEED A NEW X-NAME.
THIS AGAIN?
LOGAN KEEPS MAKING FUN OF "ARMOR." I'M REALLY TIRED, DR. McCOY.
WE'LL GET YOU SOME COFFEE. AND YOU REALLY MUSTN'T PAY ATTENTION TO LOGAN.
HE SAYS THAT IF MY NAME'S "ARMOR" THEN HIS NAME IS "CLAWS" AND MS. FROST'S NAME IS "BRAIN" AND MS. ROGUE'S NAME IS "SUCK."
YES. WELL.
OUCH.

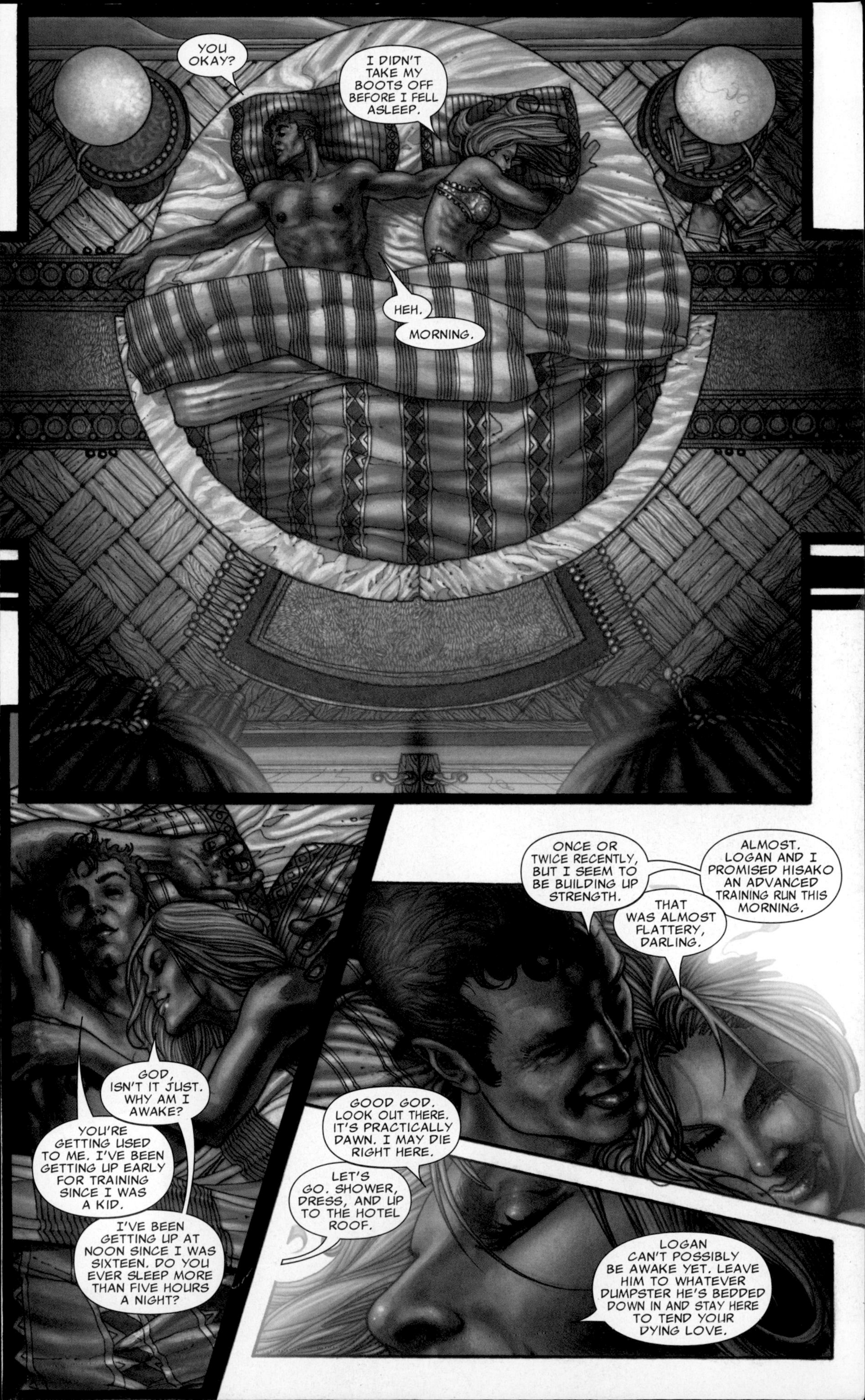
YOU OKAY?
I DIDN'T TAKE MY BOOTS OFF BEFORE I FELL ASLEEP.
HEH.
MORNING.
GOD, ISN'T IT JUST. WHY AM I AWAKE?
YOU'RE GETTING USED TO ME. I'VE BEEN GETTING UP EARLY FOR TRAINING SINCE I WAS A KID.
I'VE BEEN GETTING UP AT NOON SINCE I WAS SIXTEEN. DO YOU EVER SLEEP MORE THAN FIVE HOURS A NIGHT?
ONCE OR TWICE RECENTLY, BUT I SEEM TO BE BUILDING UP STRENGTH.
THAT WAS ALMOST FLATTERY, DARLING.
ALMOST. LOGAN AND I PROMISED HISAKO AN ADVANCED TRAINING RUN THIS MORNING.
GOOD GOD. LOOK OUT THERE. IT'S PRACTICALLY DAWN. I MAY DIE RIGHT HERE.
LET'S GO. SHOWER, DRESS, AND UP TO THE HOTEL ROOF.
LOGAN CAN'T POSSIBLY BE AWAKE YET. LEAVE HIM TO WHATEVER DUMPSTER HE'S BEDDED DOWN IN AND STAY HERE TO TEND YOUR DYING LOVE.

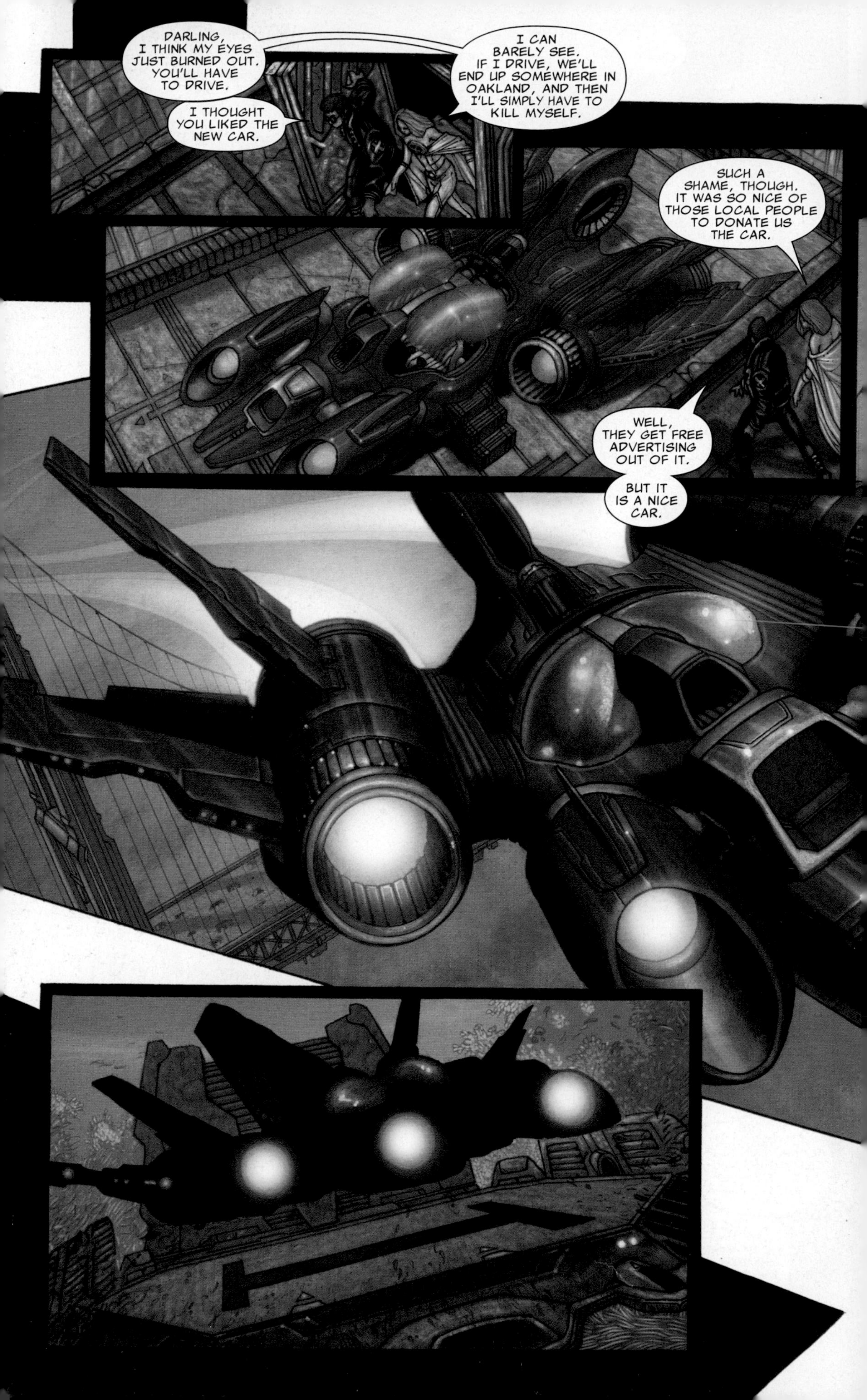
DARLING, I THINK MY EYES JUST BURNED OUT. YOU'LL HAVE TO DRIVE.
I THOUGHT YOU LIKED THE NEW CAR.
I CAN BARELY SEE. IF I DRIVE, WE'LL END UP SOMEWHERE IN OAKLAND, AND THEN I'LL SIMPLY HAVE TO KILL MYSELF.
SUCH A SHAME, THOUGH. IT WAS SO NICE OF THOSE LOCAL PEOPLE TO DONATE US THE CAR.
WELL, THEY GET FREE ADVERTISING OUT OF IT.
BUT IT IS A NICE CAR.

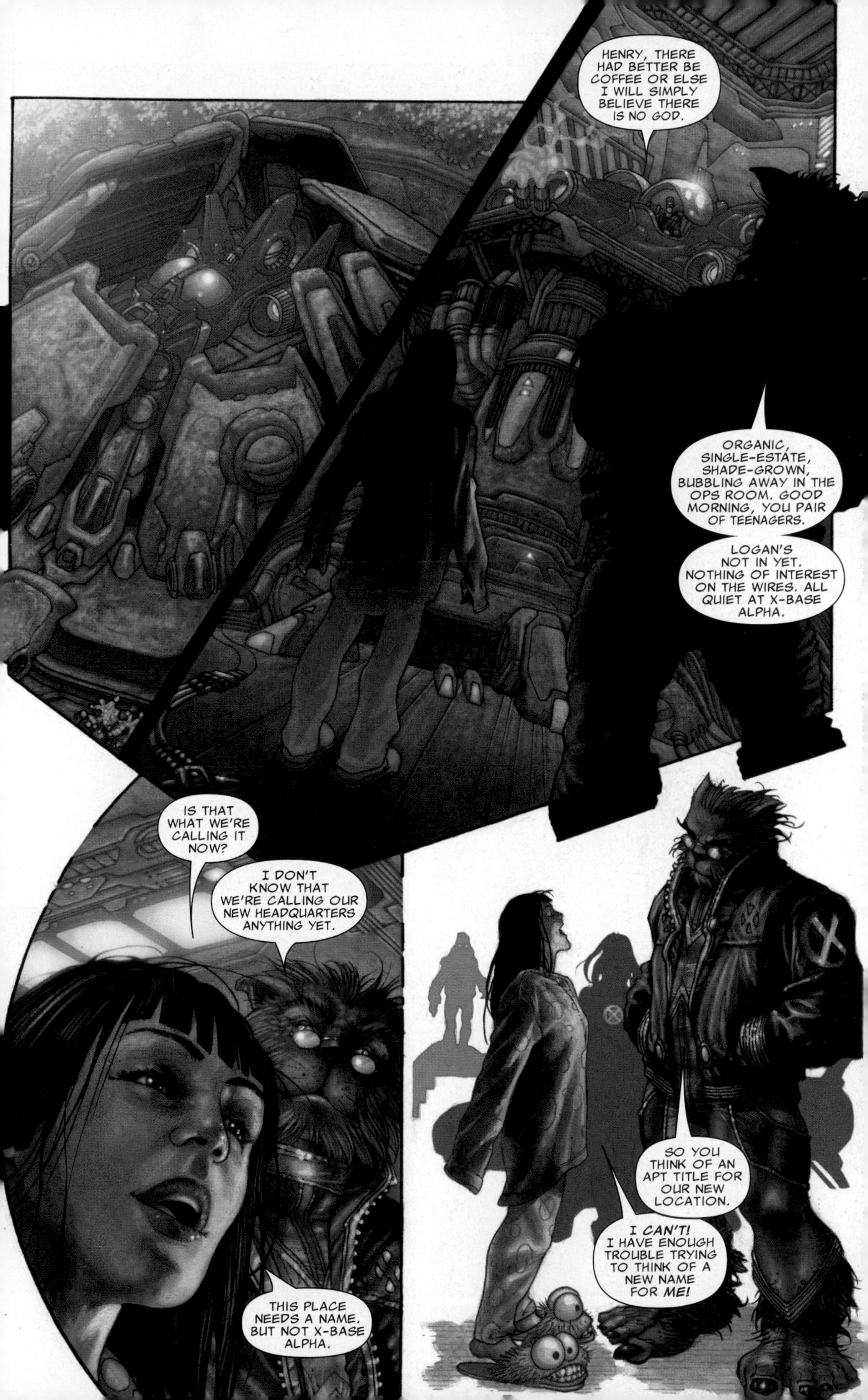
HENRY, THERE HAD BETTER BE COFFEE OR ELSE I WILL SIMPLY BELIEVE THERE IS NO GOD.
ORGANIC, SINGLE-ESTATE, SHADE-GROWN, BUBBLING AWAY IN THE OPS ROOM. GOOD MORNING, YOU PAIR OF TEENAGERS.
LOGAN'S NOT IN YET. NOTHING OF INTEREST ON THE WIRES. ALL QUIET AT X-BASE ALPHA.
IS THAT WHAT WE'RE CALLING IT NOW?
I DON'T KNOW THAT WE'RE CALLING OUR NEW HEADQUARTERS ANYTHING YET.
THIS PLACE NEEDS A NAME. BUT NOT X-BASE ALPHA.
SO YOU THINK OF AN APT TITLE FOR OUR NEW LOCATION.
I *CAN'T!* I HAVE ENOUGH TROUBLE TRYING TO THINK OF A NEW NAME FOR *ME!*

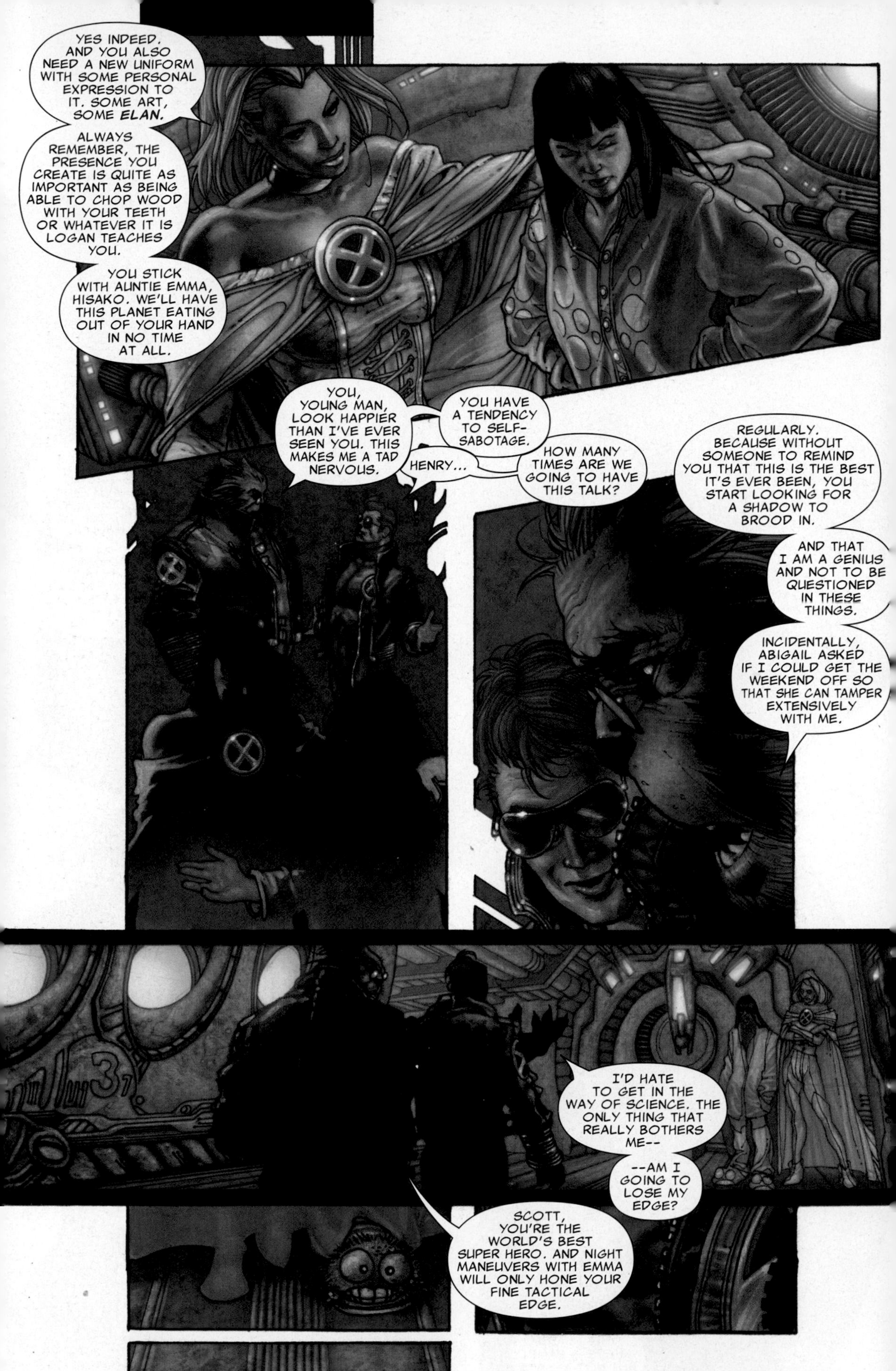
YES INDEED. AND YOU ALSO NEED A NEW UNIFORM WITH SOME PERSONAL EXPRESSION TO IT. SOME ART, SOME ELAN.
ALWAYS REMEMBER, THE PRESENCE YOU CREATE IS QUITE AS IMPORTANT AS BEING ABLE TO CHOP WOOD WITH YOUR TEETH OR WHATEVER IT IS LOGAN TEACHES YOU.
YOU STICK WITH AUNTIE EMMA, HISAKO. WE'LL HAVE THIS PLANET EATING OUT OF YOUR HAND IN NO TIME AT ALL.
YOU, YOUNG MAN, LOOK HAPPIER THAN I'VE EVER SEEN YOU. THIS MAKES ME A TAD NERVOUS.
YOU HAVE A TENDENCY TO SELF-SABOTAGE.
HENRY...
HOW MANY TIMES ARE WE GOING TO HAVE THIS TALK?
REGULARLY. BECAUSE WITHOUT SOMEONE TO REMIND YOU THAT THIS IS THE BEST IT'S EVER BEEN, YOU START LOOKING FOR A SHADOW TO BROOD IN.
AND THAT I AM A GENIUS AND NOT TO BE QUESTIONED IN THESE THINGS.
INCIDENTALLY, ABIGAIL ASKED IF I COULD GET THE WEEKEND OFF SO THAT SHE CAN TAMPER EXTENSIVELY WITH ME.
I'D HATE TO GET IN THE WAY OF SCIENCE. THE ONLY THING THAT REALLY BOTHERS ME--
--AM I GOING TO LOSE MY EDGE?
SCOTT, YOU'RE THE WORLD'S BEST SUPER HERO. AND NIGHT MANEUVERS WITH EMMA WILL ONLY HONE YOUR FINE TACTICAL EDGE.

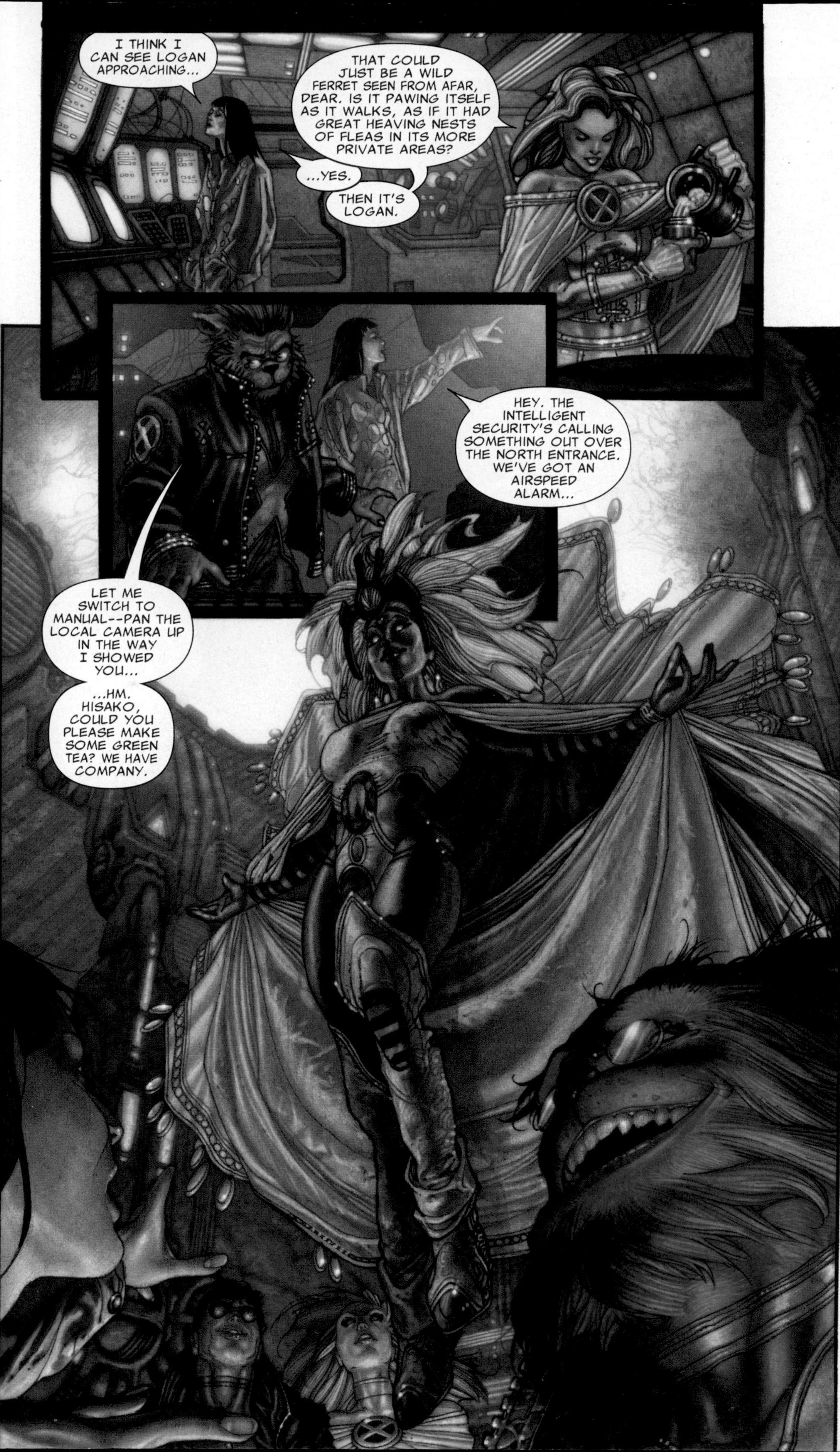
I THINK I CAN SEE LOGAN APPROACHING...
THAT COULD JUST BE A WILD FERRET SEEN FROM AFAR, DEAR. IS IT PAWING ITSELF AS IT WALKS, AS IF IT HAD GREAT HEAVING NESTS OF FLEAS IN ITS MORE PRIVATE AREAS?
...YES.
THEN IT'S LOGAN.
HEY. THE INTELLIGENT SECURITY'S CALLING SOMETHING OUT OVER THE NORTH ENTRANCE. WE'VE GOT AN AIRSPEED ALARM...
LET ME SWITCH TO MANUAL--PAN THE LOCAL CAMERA UP IN THE WAY I SHOWED YOU...
...HM. HISAKO, COULD YOU PLEASE MAKE SOME GREEN TEA? WE HAVE COMPANY.

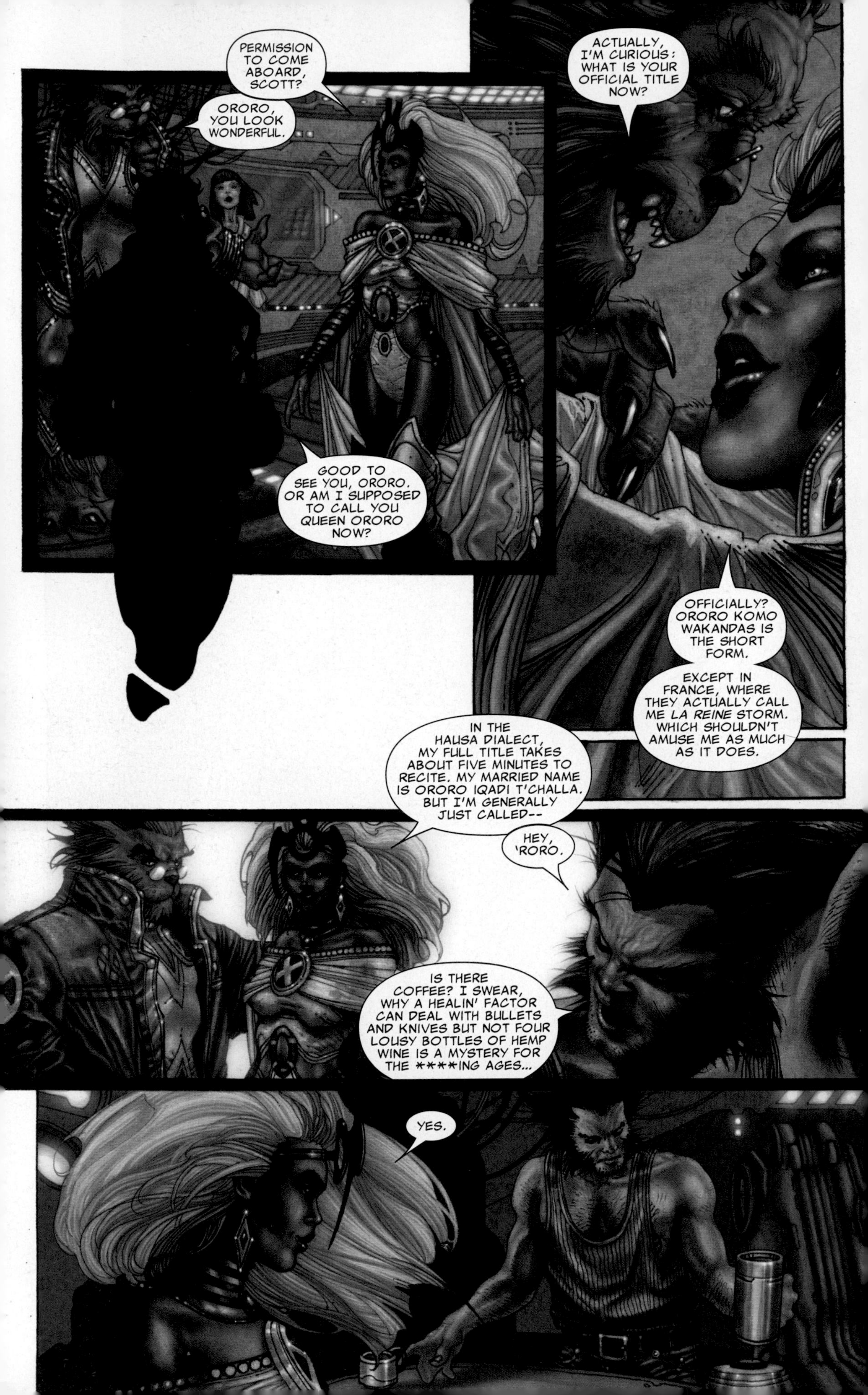
PERMISSION TO COME ABOARD, SCOTT?
ORORO, YOU LOOK WONDERFUL.
GOOD TO SEE YOU, ORORO. OR AM I SUPPOSED TO CALL YOU QUEEN ORORO NOW?
ACTUALLY, I'M CURIOUS: WHAT IS YOUR OFFICIAL TITLE NOW?
OFFICIALLY? ORORO KOMO WAKANDAS IS THE SHORT FORM.
EXCEPT IN FRANCE, WHERE THEY ACTUALLY CALL ME LA REINE STORM. WHICH SHOULDN'T AMUSE ME AS MUCH AS IT DOES.
IN THE HAUSA DIALECT, MY FULL TITLE TAKES ABOUT FIVE MINUTES TO RECITE. MY MARRIED NAME IS ORORO IQADI T'CHALLA. BUT I'M GENERALLY JUST CALLED--
HEY, 'RORO.
IS THERE COFFEE? I SWEAR, WHY A HEALIN' FACTOR CAN DEAL WITH BULLETS AND KNIVES BUT NOT FOUR LOUSY BOTTLES OF HEMP WINE IS A MYSTERY FOR THE ****ING AGES...
YES.

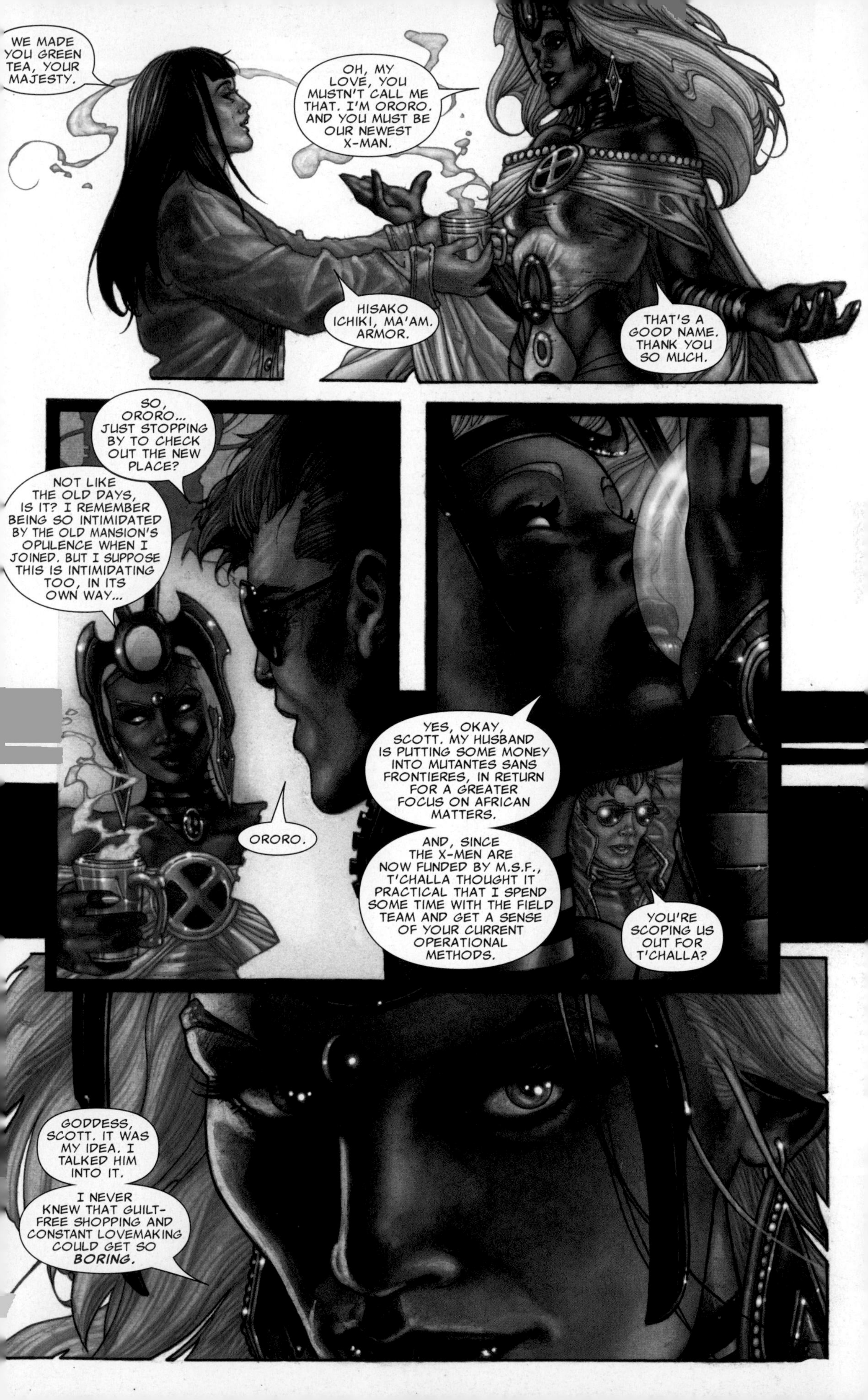
WE MADE YOU GREEN TEA, YOUR MAJESTY.
OH, MY LOVE, YOU MUSTN'T CALL ME THAT. I'M ORORO. AND YOU MUST BE OUR NEWEST X-MAN.
HISAKO ICHIKI, MA'AM. ARMOR.
THAT'S A GOOD NAME. THANK YOU SO MUCH.
SO, ORORO... JUST STOPPING BY TO CHECK OUT THE NEW PLACE?
NOT LIKE THE OLD DAYS, IS IT? I REMEMBER BEING SO INTIMIDATED BY THE OLD MANSION'S OPULENCE WHEN I JOINED. BUT I SUPPOSE THIS IS INTIMIDATING TOO, IN ITS OWN WAY...
ORORO.
YES, OKAY, SCOTT. MY HUSBAND IS PUTTING SOME MONEY INTO MUTANTES SANS FRONTIERES, IN RETURN FOR A GREATER FOCUS ON AFRICAN MATTERS.
AND, SINCE THE X-MEN ARE NOW FUNDED BY M.S.F., T'CHALLA THOUGHT IT PRACTICAL THAT I SPEND SOME TIME WITH THE FIELD TEAM AND GET A SENSE OF YOUR CURRENT OPERATIONAL METHODS.
YOU'RE SCOPING US OUT FOR T'CHALLA?
GODDESS, SCOTT. IT WAS MY IDEA. I TALKED HIM INTO IT.
I NEVER KNEW THAT GUILT-FREE SHOPPING AND CONSTANT LOVEMAKING COULD GET SO BORING.

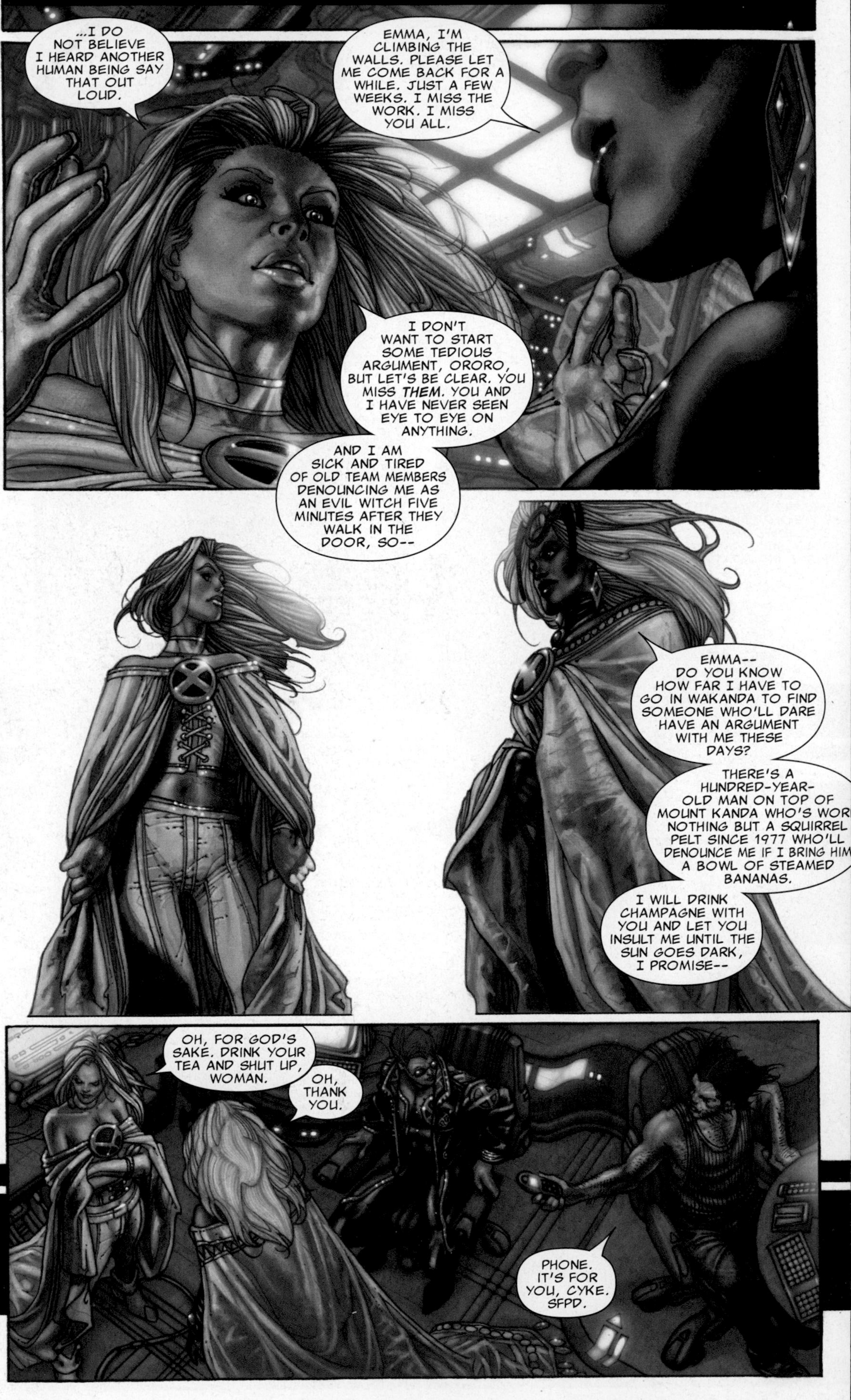

...I DO NOT BELIEVE I HEARD ANOTHER HUMAN BEING SAY THAT OUT LOUD.
EMMA, I'M CLIMBING THE WALLS. PLEASE LET ME COME BACK FOR A WHILE. JUST A FEW WEEKS. I MISS THE WORK. I MISS YOU ALL.
I DON'T WANT TO START SOME TEDIOUS ARGUMENT, ORORO, BUT LET'S BE CLEAR. YOU MISS *THEM*. YOU AND I HAVE NEVER SEEN EYE TO EYE ON ANYTHING.
AND I AM SICK AND TIRED OF OLD TEAM MEMBERS DENOUNCING ME AS AN EVIL WITCH FIVE MINUTES AFTER THEY WALK IN THE DOOR, SO--
EMMA-- DO YOU KNOW HOW FAR I HAVE TO GO IN WAKANDA TO FIND SOMEONE WHO'LL DARE HAVE AN ARGUMENT WITH ME THESE DAYS?
THERE'S A HUNDRED-YEAR-OLD MAN ON TOP OF MOUNT KANDA WHO'S WOR NOTHING BUT A SQUIRREL PELT SINCE 1977 WHO'LL DENOUNCE ME IF I BRING HIM A BOWL OF STEAMED BANANAS.
I WILL DRINK CHAMPAGNE WITH YOU AND LET YOU INSULT ME UNTIL THE SUN GOES DARK, I PROMISE--
OH, FOR GOD'S SAKE. DRINK YOUR TEA AND SHUT UP, WOMAN.
OH, THANK YOU.
PHONE. IT'S FOR YOU, CYKE. SFPD.

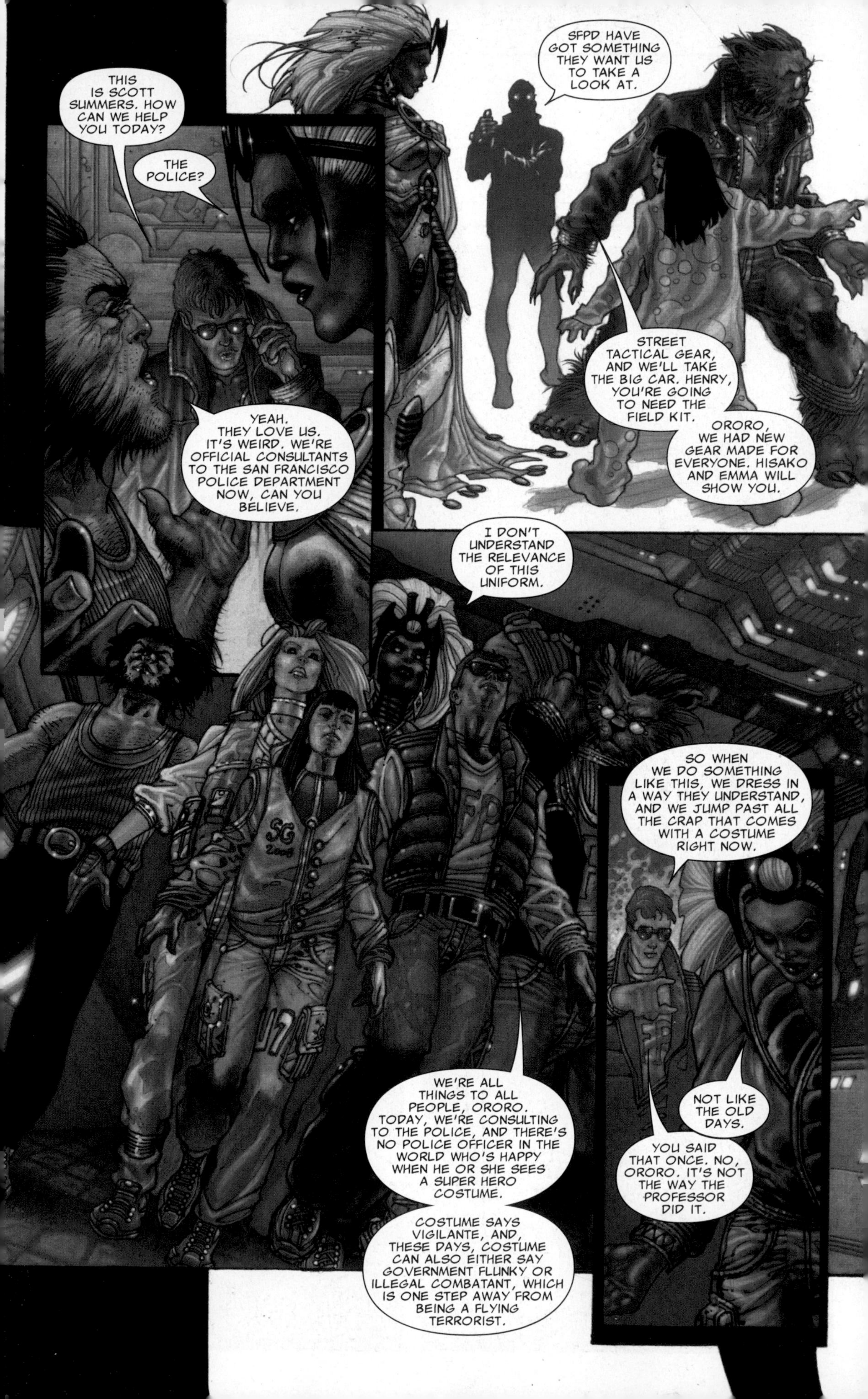
THIS IS SCOTT SUMMERS. HOW CAN WE HELP YOU TODAY?
THE POLICE?
YEAH. THEY LOVE US. IT'S WEIRD. WE'RE OFFICIAL CONSULTANTS TO THE SAN FRANCISCO POLICE DEPARTMENT NOW, CAN YOU BELIEVE.
SFPD HAVE GOT SOMETHING THEY WANT US TO TAKE A LOOK AT.
STREET TACTICAL GEAR, AND WE'LL TAKE THE BIG CAR. HENRY, YOU'RE GOING TO NEED THE FIELD KIT.
ORORO, WE HAD NEW GEAR MADE FOR EVERYONE. HISAKO AND EMMA WILL SHOW YOU.
I DON'T UNDERSTAND THE RELEVANCE OF THIS UNIFORM.
WE'RE ALL THINGS TO ALL PEOPLE, ORORO. TODAY, WE'RE CONSULTING TO THE POLICE, AND THERE'S NO POLICE OFFICER IN THE WORLD WHO'S HAPPY WHEN HE OR SHE SEES A SUPER HERO COSTUME.
COSTUME SAYS VIGILANTE, AND, THESE DAYS, COSTUME CAN ALSO EITHER SAY GOVERNMENT FLUNKY OR ILLEGAL COMBATANT, WHICH IS ONE STEP AWAY FROM BEING A FLYING TERRORIST.
SO WHEN WE DO SOMETHING LIKE THIS, WE DRESS IN A WAY THEY UNDERSTAND, AND WE JUMP PAST ALL THE CRAP THAT COMES WITH A COSTUME RIGHT NOW.
NOT LIKE THE OLD DAYS.
YOU SAID THAT ONCE. NO, ORORO. IT'S NOT THE WAY THE PROFESSOR DID IT.

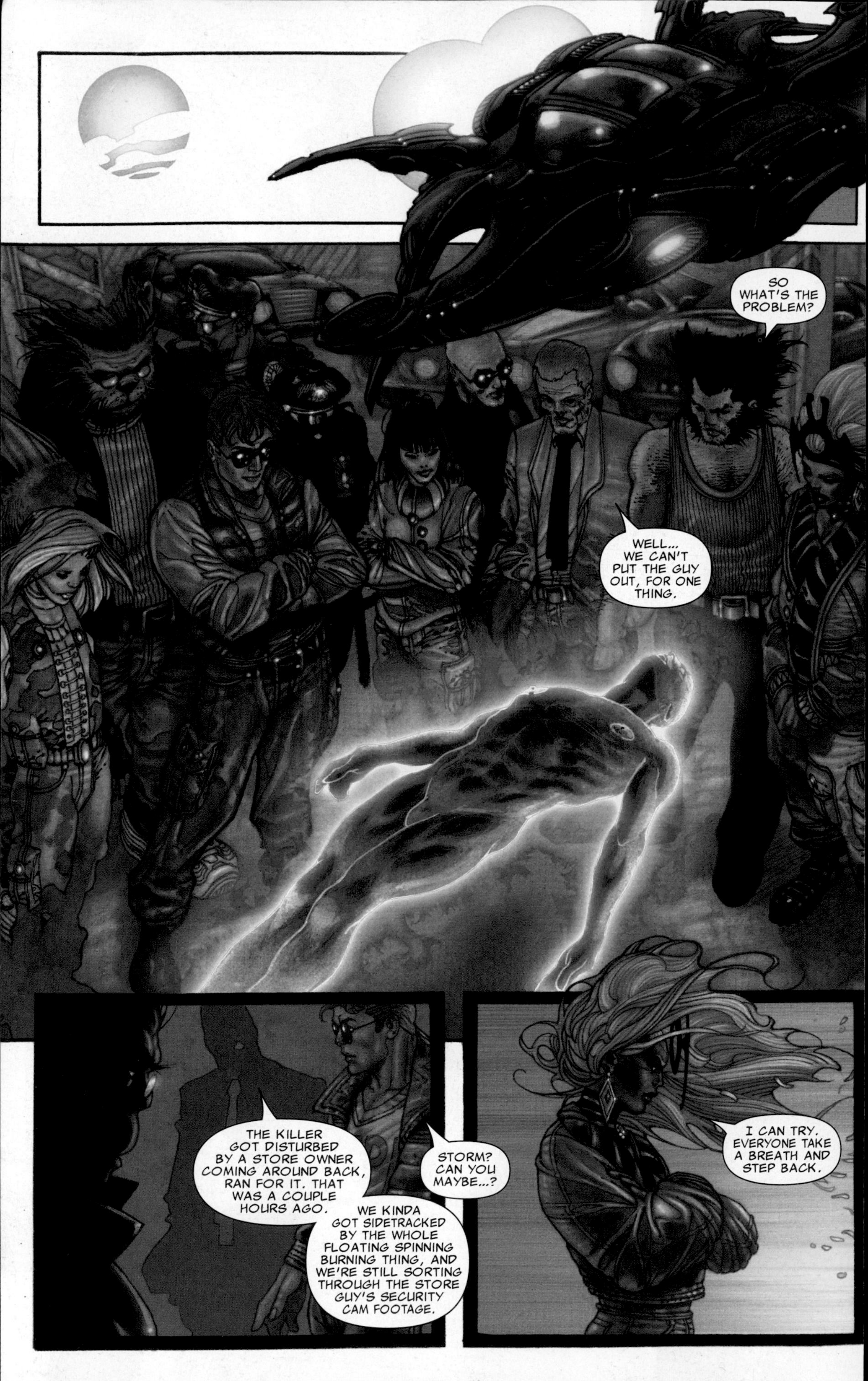
SO WHAT'S THE PROBLEM?
WELL... WE CAN'T PUT THE GUY OUT, FOR ONE THING.
THE KILLER GOT DISTURBED BY A STORE OWNER COMING AROUND BACK, RAN FOR IT. THAT WAS A COUPLE HOURS AGO.
WE KINDA GOT SIDETRACKED BY THE WHOLE FLOATING SPINNING BURNING THING, AND WE'RE STILL SORTING THROUGH THE STORE GUY'S SECURITY CAM FOOTAGE.
STORM? CAN YOU MAYBE...?
I CAN TRY. EVERYONE TAKE A BREATH AND STEP BACK.

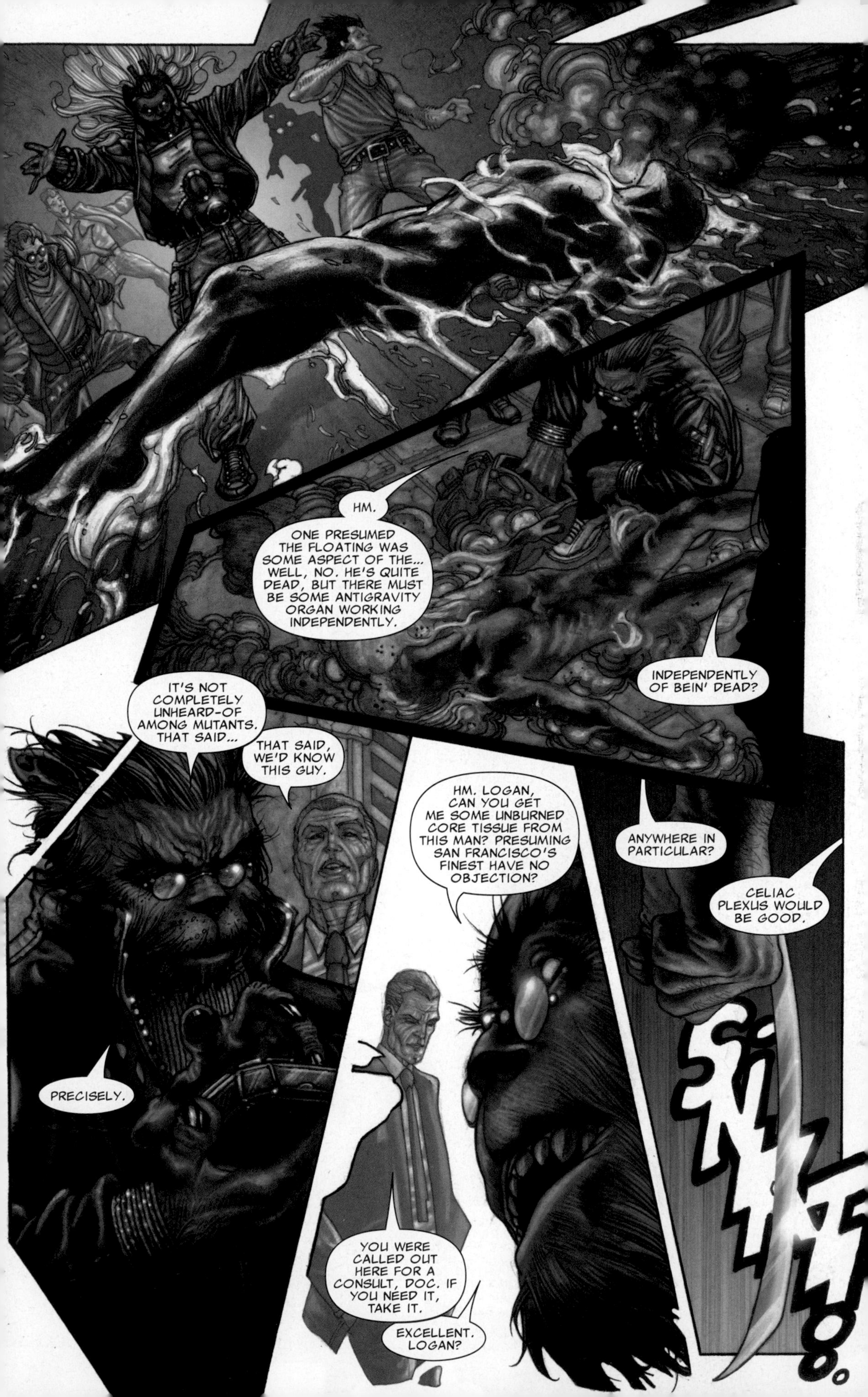
HM.
ONE PRESUMED THE FLOATING WAS SOME ASPECT OF THE... WELL, NO. HE'S QUITE DEAD, BUT THERE MUST BE SOME ANTIGRAVITY ORGAN WORKING INDEPENDENTLY.
INDEPENDENTLY OF BEIN' DEAD?
IT'S NOT COMPLETELY UNHEARD-OF AMONG MUTANTS. THAT SAID...
THAT SAID, WE'D KNOW THIS GUY.
PRECISELY.
HM. LOGAN, CAN YOU GET ME SOME UNBURNED CORE TISSUE FROM THIS MAN? PRESUMING SAN FRANCISCO'S FINEST HAVE NO OBJECTION?
YOU WERE CALLED OUT HERE FOR A CONSULT, DOC. IF YOU NEED IT, TAKE IT.
EXCELLENT. LOGAN?
ANYWHERE IN PARTICULAR?
CELIAC PLEXUS WOULD BE GOOD.
SNIKT

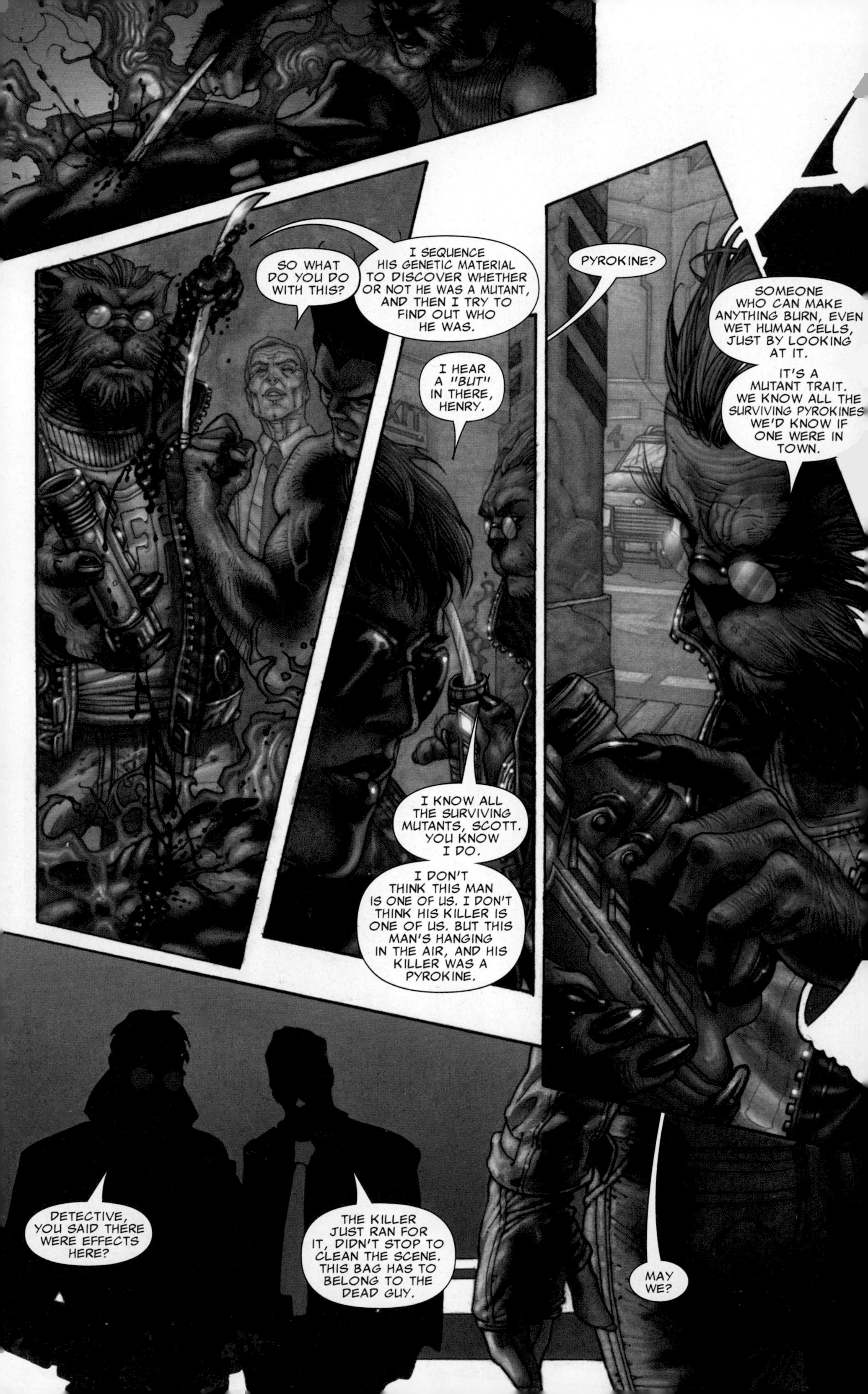
SO WHAT DO YOU DO WITH THIS?
I SEQUENCE HIS GENETIC MATERIAL TO DISCOVER WHETHER OR NOT HE WAS A MUTANT, AND THEN I TRY TO FIND OUT WHO HE WAS.
I HEAR A "BUT" IN THERE, HENRY.
I KNOW ALL THE SURVIVING MUTANTS, SCOTT. YOU KNOW I DO.
I DON'T THINK THIS MAN IS ONE OF US. I DON'T THINK HIS KILLER IS ONE OF US. BUT THIS MAN'S HANGING IN THE AIR, AND HIS KILLER WAS A PYROKINE.
PYROKINE?
SOMEONE WHO CAN MAKE ANYTHING BURN, EVEN WET HUMAN CELLS, JUST BY LOOKING AT IT.
IT'S A MUTANT TRAIT. WE KNOW ALL THE SURVIVING PYROKINES. WE'D KNOW IF ONE WERE IN TOWN.
DETECTIVE, YOU SAID THERE WERE EFFECTS HERE?
THE KILLER JUST RAN FOR IT, DIDN'T STOP TO CLEAN THE SCENE. THIS BAG HAS TO BELONG TO THE DEAD GUY.
MAY WE?

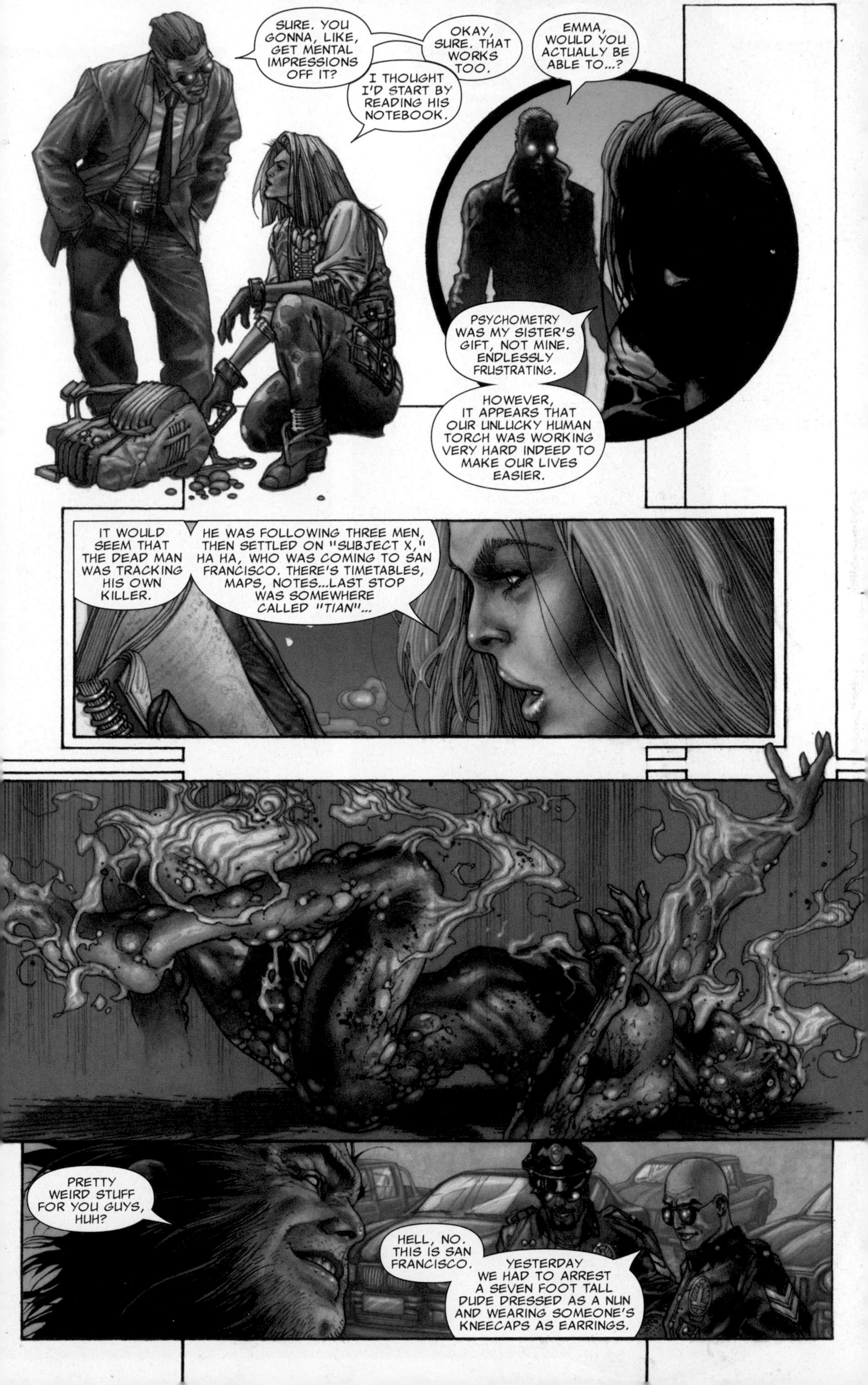
SURE. YOU GONNA, LIKE, GET MENTAL IMPRESSIONS OFF IT?
I THOUGHT I'D START BY READING HIS NOTEBOOK.
OKAY, SURE. THAT WORKS TOO.
EMMA, WOULD YOU ACTUALLY BE ABLE TO...?
PSYCHOMETRY WAS MY SISTER'S GIFT, NOT MINE. ENDLESSLY FRUSTRATING.
HOWEVER, IT APPEARS THAT OUR UNLUCKY HUMAN TORCH WAS WORKING VERY HARD INDEED TO MAKE OUR LIVES EASIER.
IT WOULD SEEM THAT THE DEAD MAN WAS TRACKING HIS OWN KILLER.
HE WAS FOLLOWING THREE MEN, THEN SETTLED ON "SUBJECT X," HA HA, WHO WAS COMING TO SAN FRANCISCO. THERE'S TIMETABLES, MAPS, NOTES...LAST STOP WAS SOMEWHERE CALLED "TIAN"...
PRETTY WEIRD STUFF FOR YOU GUYS, HUH?
HELL, NO. THIS IS SAN FRANCISCO.
YESTERDAY WE HAD TO ARREST A SEVEN FOOT TALL DUDE DRESSED AS A NUN AND WEARING SOMEONE'S KNEECAPS AS EARRINGS.

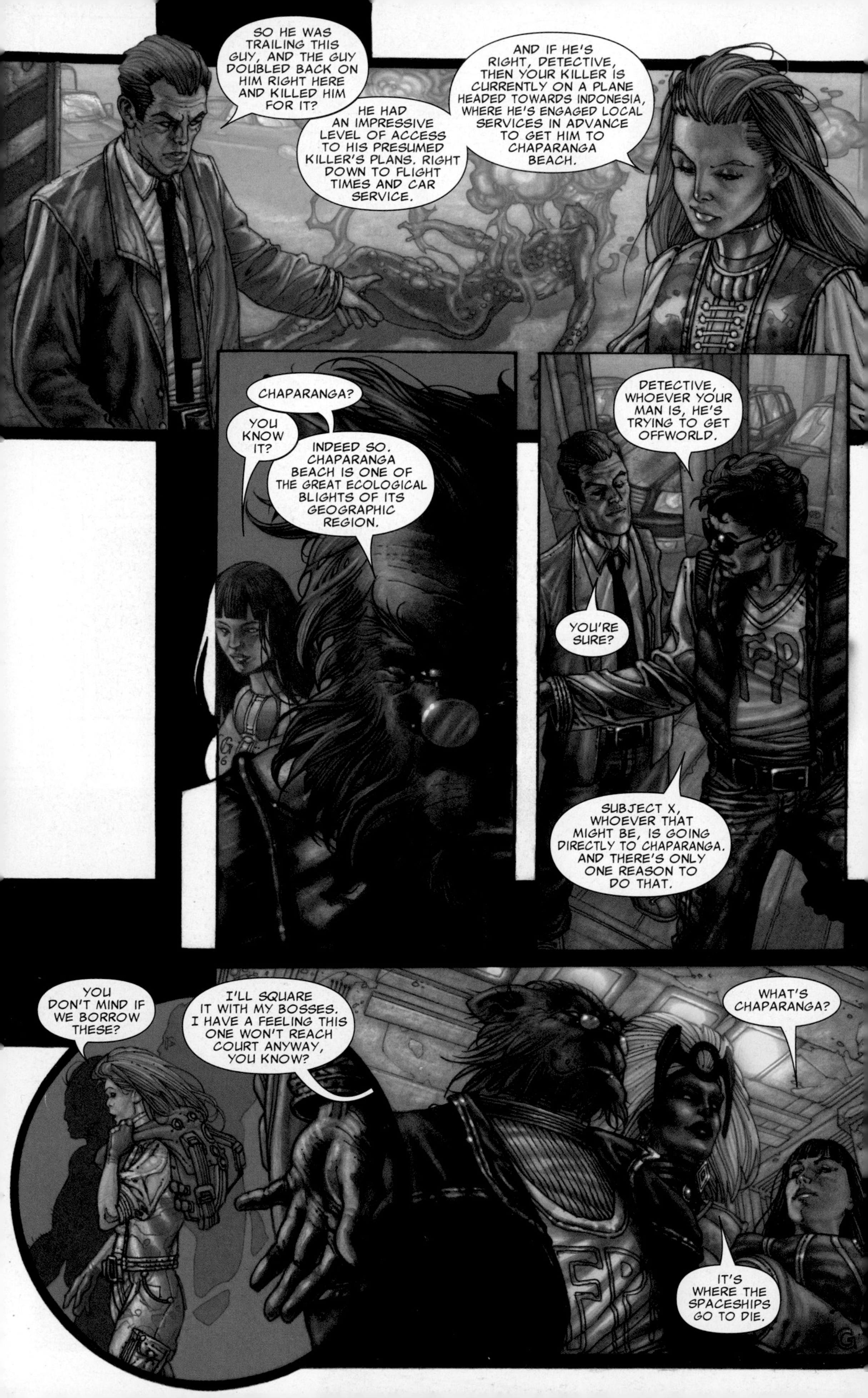
SO HE WAS TRAILING THIS GUY, AND THE GUY DOUBLED BACK ON HIM RIGHT HERE AND KILLED HIM FOR IT?
HE HAD AN IMPRESSIVE LEVEL OF ACCESS TO HIS PRESUMED KILLER'S PLANS. RIGHT DOWN TO FLIGHT TIMES AND CAR SERVICE.
AND IF HE'S RIGHT, DETECTIVE, THEN YOUR KILLER IS CURRENTLY ON A PLANE HEADED TOWARDS INDONESIA, WHERE HE'S ENGAGED LOCAL SERVICES IN ADVANCE TO GET HIM TO CHAPARANGA BEACH.
CHAPARANGA?
YOU KNOW IT?
INDEED SO. CHAPARANGA BEACH IS ONE OF THE GREAT ECOLOGICAL BLIGHTS OF ITS GEOGRAPHIC REGION.
DETECTIVE, WHOEVER YOUR MAN IS, HE'S TRYING TO GET OFFWORLD.
YOU'RE SURE?
SUBJECT X, WHOEVER THAT MIGHT BE, IS GOING DIRECTLY TO CHAPARANGA. AND THERE'S ONLY ONE REASON TO DO THAT.
YOU DON'T MIND IF WE BORROW THESE?
I'LL SQUARE IT WITH MY BOSSES. I HAVE A FEELING THIS ONE WON'T REACH COURT ANYWAY, YOU KNOW?
WHAT'S CHAPARANGA?
IT'S WHERE THE SPACESHIPS GO TO DIE.

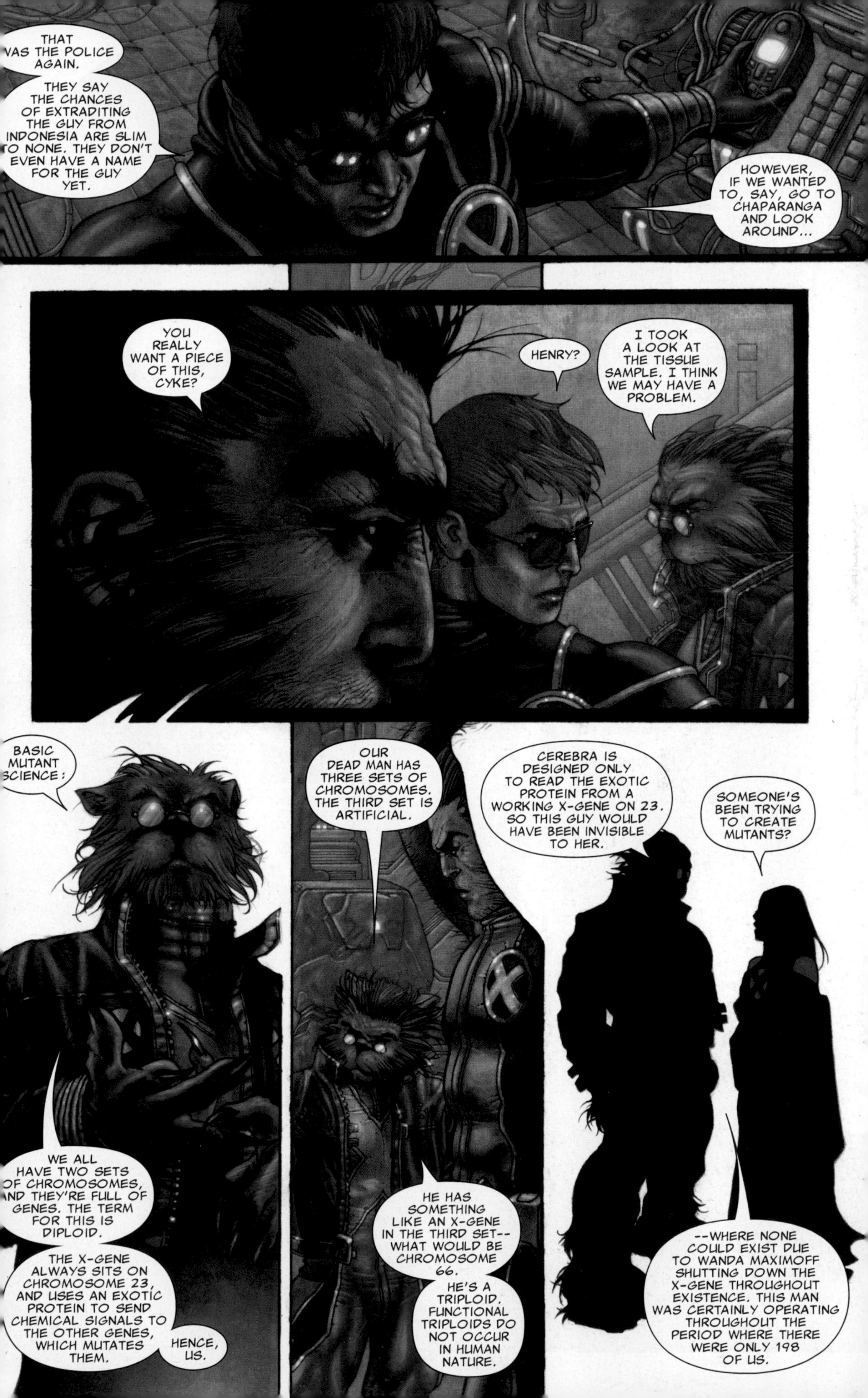
THAT VAS THE POLICE AGAIN.
THEY SAY THE CHANCES OF EXTRADITING THE GUY FROM INDONESIA ARE SLIM TO NONE. THEY DON'T EVEN HAVE A NAME FOR THE GUY YET.
HOWEVER, IF WE WANTED TO, SAY, GO TO CHAPARANGA AND LOOK AROUND...
YOU REALLY WANT A PIECE OF THIS, CYKE?
HENRY?
I TOOK A LOOK AT THE TISSUE SAMPLE. I THINK WE MAY HAVE A PROBLEM.
BASIC MUTANT SCIENCE:
WE ALL HAVE TWO SETS OF CHROMOSOMES, AND THEY'RE FULL OF GENES. THE TERM FOR THIS IS DIPLOID.
THE X-GENE ALWAYS SITS ON CHROMOSOME 23, AND USES AN EXOTIC PROTEIN TO SEND CHEMICAL SIGNALS TO THE OTHER GENES, WHICH MUTATES THEM.
HENCE, US.
OUR DEAD MAN HAS THREE SETS OF CHROMOSOMES. THE THIRD SET IS ARTIFICIAL.
HE HAS SOMETHING LIKE AN X-GENE IN THE THIRD SET--WHAT WOULD BE CHROMOSOME 66.
HE'S A TRIPLOID. FUNCTIONAL TRIPLOIDS DO NOT OCCUR IN HUMAN NATURE.
CEREBRA IS DESIGNED ONLY TO READ THE EXOTIC PROTEIN FROM A WORKING X-GENE ON 23. SO THIS GUY WOULD HAVE BEEN INVISIBLE TO HER.
SOMEONE'S BEEN TRYING TO CREATE MUTANTS?
--WHERE NONE COULD EXIST DUE TO WANDA MAXIMOFF SHUTTING DOWN THE X-GENE THROUGHOUT EXISTENCE. THIS MAN WAS CERTAINLY OPERATING THROUGHOUT THE PERIOD WHERE THERE WERE ONLY 198 OF US.

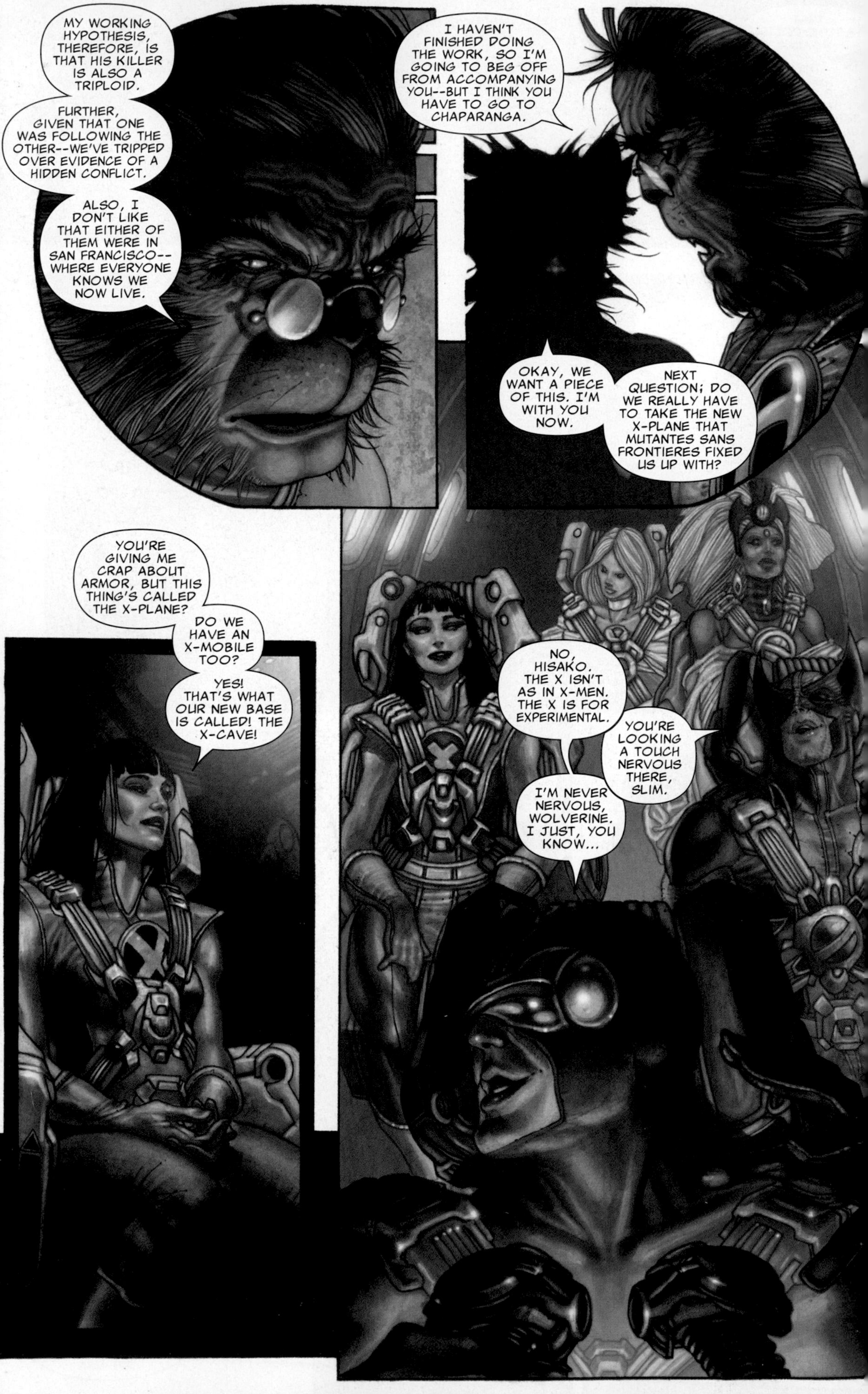
MY WORKING HYPOTHESIS, THEREFORE, IS THAT HIS KILLER IS ALSO A TRIPLOID.
FURTHER, GIVEN THAT ONE WAS FOLLOWING THE OTHER--WE'VE TRIPPED OVER EVIDENCE OF A HIDDEN CONFLICT.
ALSO, I DON'T LIKE THAT EITHER OF THEM WERE IN SAN FRANCISCO--WHERE EVERYONE KNOWS WE NOW LIVE.
I HAVEN'T FINISHED DOING THE WORK, SO I'M GOING TO BEG OFF FROM ACCOMPANYING YOU--BUT I THINK YOU HAVE TO GO TO CHAPARANGA.
OKAY, WE WANT A PIECE OF THIS. I'M WITH YOU NOW.
NEXT QUESTION; DO WE REALLY HAVE TO TAKE THE NEW X-PLANE THAT MUTANTES SANS FRONTIERES FIXED US UP WITH?
YOU'RE GIVING ME CRAP ABOUT ARMOR, BUT THIS THING'S CALLED THE X-PLANE?
DO WE HAVE AN X-MOBILE TOO?
YES! THAT'S WHAT OUR NEW BASE IS CALLED! THE X-CAVE!
NO, HISAKO. THE X ISN'T AS IN X-MEN. THE X IS FOR EXPERIMENTAL.
YOU'RE LOOKING A TOUCH NERVOUS THERE, SLIM.
I'M NEVER NERVOUS, WOLVERINE. I JUST, YOU KNOW...

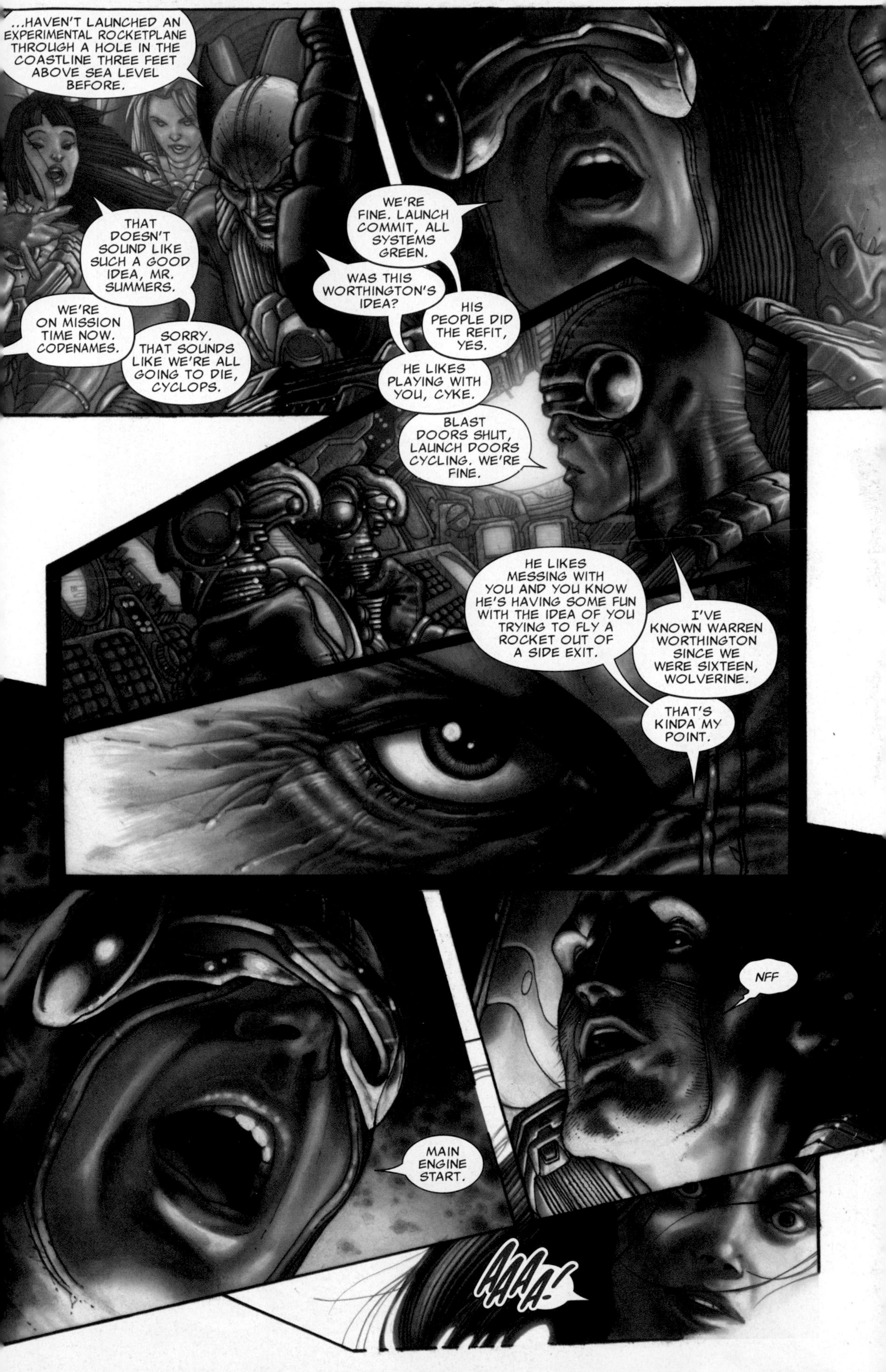
...HAVEN'T LAUNCHED AN EXPERIMENTAL ROCKETPLANE THROUGH A HOLE IN THE COASTLINE THREE FEET ABOVE SEA LEVEL BEFORE.
THAT DOESN'T SOUND LIKE SUCH A GOOD IDEA, MR. SUMMERS.
WE'RE ON MISSION TIME NOW. CODENAMES.
SORRY. THAT SOUNDS LIKE WE'RE ALL GOING TO DIE, CYCLOPS.
WE'RE FINE. LAUNCH COMMIT, ALL SYSTEMS GREEN.
WAS THIS WORTHINGTON'S IDEA?
HIS PEOPLE DID THE REFIT, YES.
HE LIKES PLAYING WITH YOU, CYKE.
BLAST DOORS SHUT, LAUNCH DOORS CYCLING. WE'RE FINE.
HE LIKES MESSING WITH YOU AND YOU KNOW HE'S HAVING SOME FUN WITH THE IDEA OF YOU TRYING TO FLY A ROCKET OUT OF A SIDE EXIT.
I'VE KNOWN WARREN WORTHINGTON SINCE WE WERE SIXTEEN, WOLVERINE.
THAT'S KINDA MY POINT.
MAIN ENGINE START.
NFF
AAAA-!

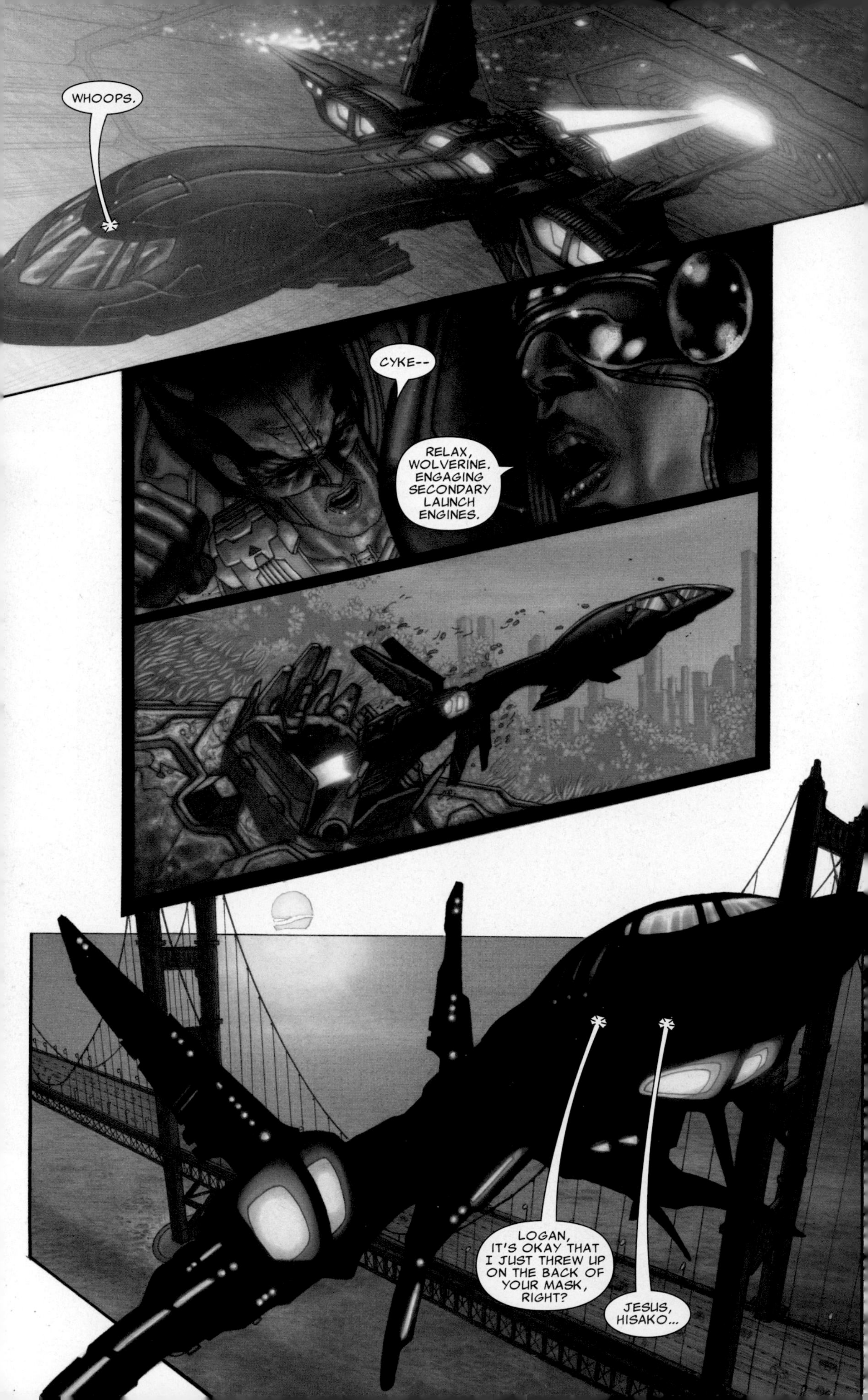
WHOOPS.
CYKE--
RELAX, WOLVERINE. ENGAGING SECONDARY LAUNCH ENGINES.
LOGAN, IT'S OKAY THAT I JUST THREW UP ON THE BACK OF YOUR MASK, RIGHT?
JESUS, HISAKO...

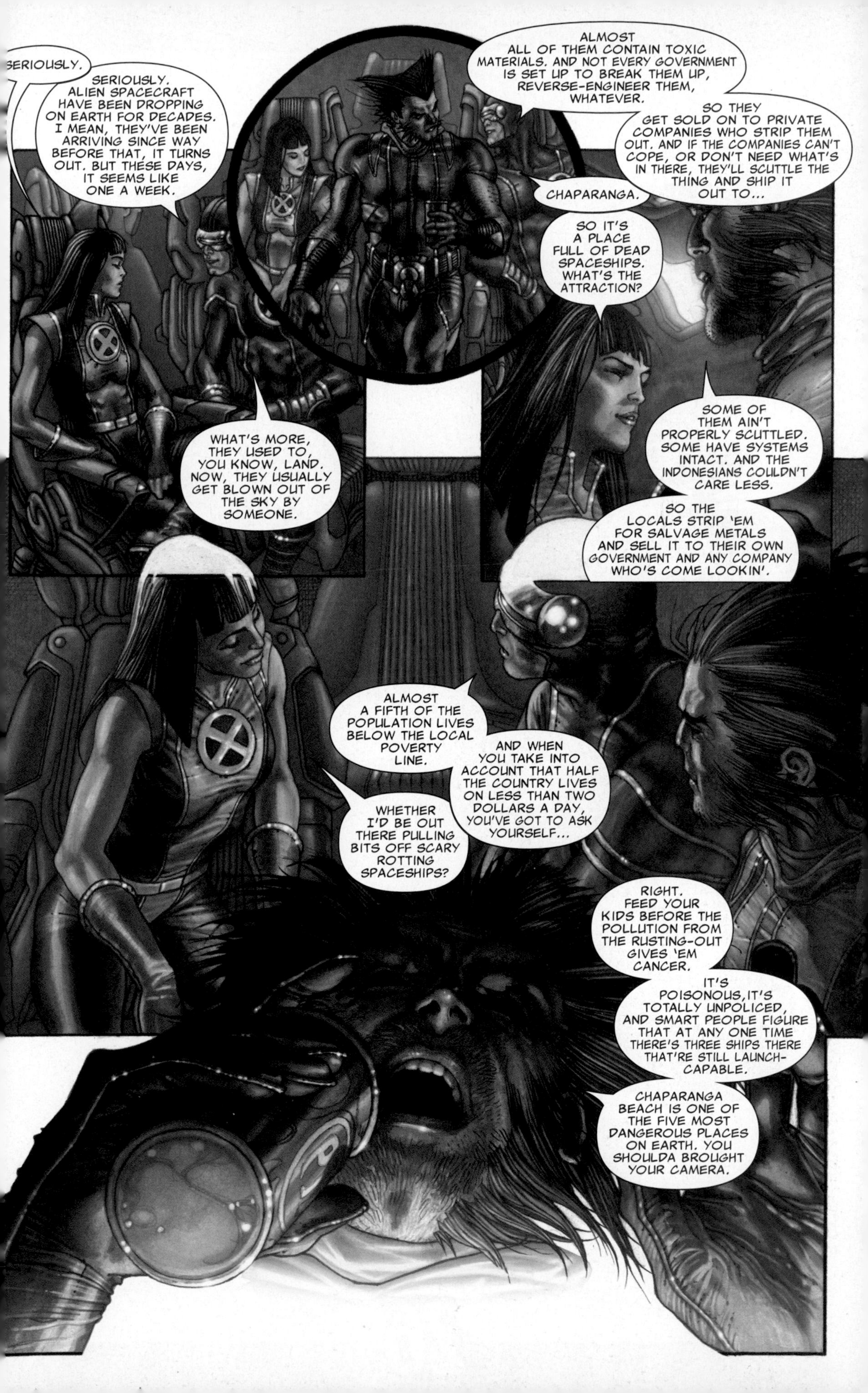
SERIOUSLY.
SERIOUSLY. ALIEN SPACECRAFT HAVE BEEN DROPPING ON EARTH FOR DECADES. I MEAN, THEY'VE BEEN ARRIVING SINCE WAY BEFORE THAT, IT TURNS OUT. BUT THESE DAYS, IT SEEMS LIKE ONE A WEEK.
ALMOST ALL OF THEM CONTAIN TOXIC MATERIALS. AND NOT EVERY GOVERNMENT IS SET UP TO BREAK THEM UP, REVERSE-ENGINEER THEM, WHATEVER.
SO THEY GET SOLD ON TO PRIVATE COMPANIES WHO STRIP THEM OUT. AND IF THE COMPANIES CAN'T COPE, OR DON'T NEED WHAT'S IN THERE, THEY'LL SCUTTLE THE THING AND SHIP IT OUT TO...
CHAPARANGA.
SO IT'S A PLACE FULL OF DEAD SPACESHIPS. WHAT'S THE ATTRACTION?
WHAT'S MORE, THEY USED TO, YOU KNOW, LAND. NOW, THEY USUALLY GET BLOWN OUT OF THE SKY BY SOMEONE.
SOME OF THEM AIN'T PROPERLY SCUTTLED. SOME HAVE SYSTEMS INTACT. AND THE INDONESIANS COULDN'T CARE LESS.
SO THE LOCALS STRIP 'EM FOR SALVAGE METALS AND SELL IT TO THEIR OWN GOVERNMENT AND ANY COMPANY WHO'S COME LOOKIN'.
ALMOST A FIFTH OF THE POPULATION LIVES BELOW THE LOCAL POVERTY LINE.
AND WHEN YOU TAKE INTO ACCOUNT THAT HALF THE COUNTRY LIVES ON LESS THAN TWO DOLLARS A DAY, YOU'VE GOT TO ASK YOURSELF...
WHETHER I'D BE OUT THERE PULLING BITS OFF SCARY ROTTING SPACESHIPS?
RIGHT. FEED YOUR KIDS BEFORE THE POLLUTION FROM THE RUSTING-OUT GIVES 'EM CANCER.
IT'S POISONOUS, IT'S TOTALLY UNPOLICED, AND SMART PEOPLE FIGURE THAT AT ANY ONE TIME THERE'S THREE SHIPS THERE THAT'RE STILL LAUNCH-CAPABLE.
CHAPARANGA BEACH IS ONE OF THE FIVE MOST DANGEROUS PLACES ON EARTH. YOU SHOULDA BROUGHT YOUR CAMERA.

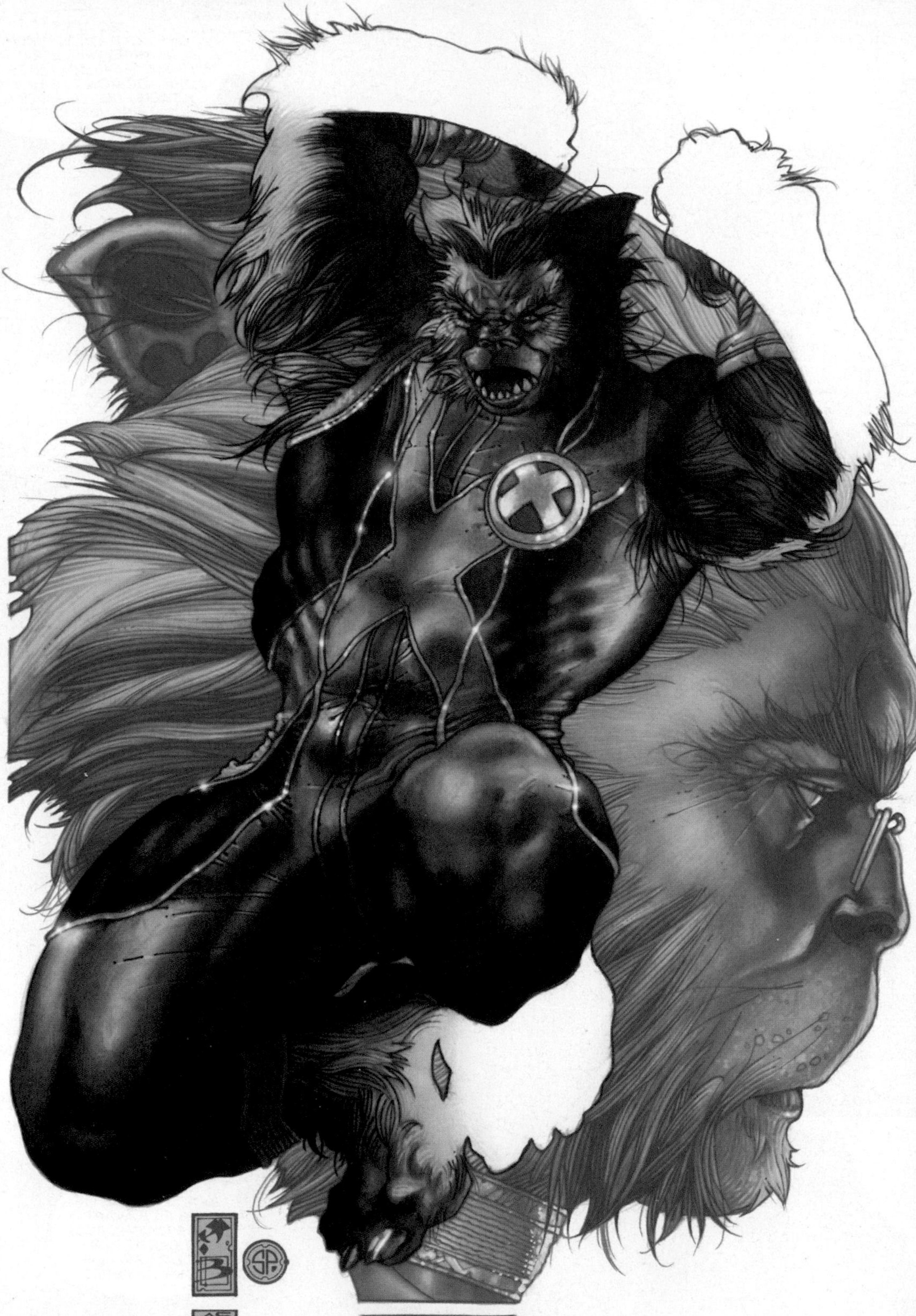

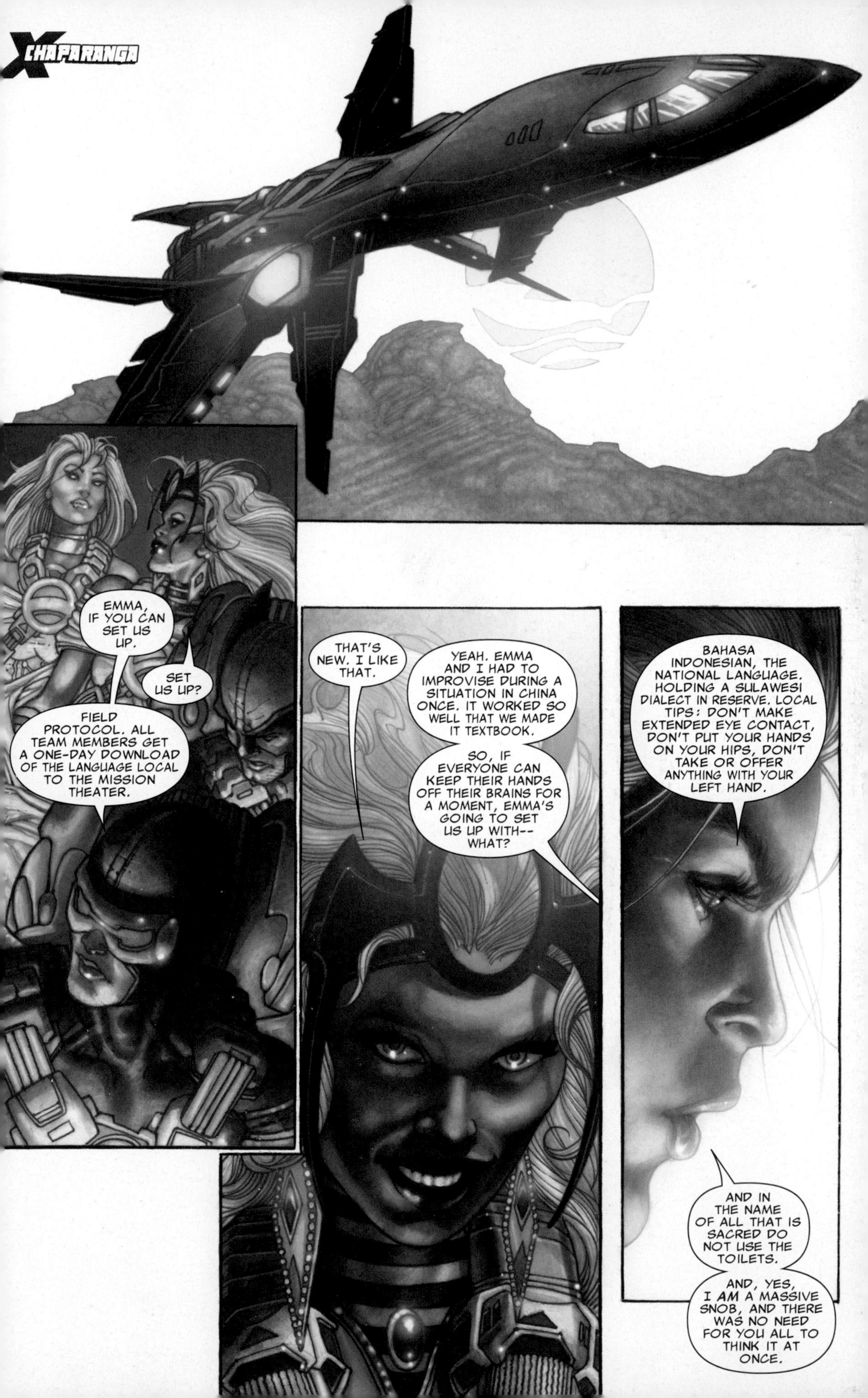
X CHAPARANGA
EMMA, IF YOU CAN SET US UP.
SET US UP?
FIELD PROTOCOL. ALL TEAM MEMBERS GET A ONE-DAY DOWNLOAD OF THE LANGUAGE LOCAL TO THE MISSION THEATER.
THAT'S NEW. I LIKE THAT.
YEAH. EMMA AND I HAD TO IMPROVISE DURING A SITUATION IN CHINA ONCE. IT WORKED SO WELL THAT WE MADE IT TEXTBOOK.
SO, IF EVERYONE CAN KEEP THEIR HANDS OFF THEIR BRAINS FOR A MOMENT, EMMA'S GOING TO SET US UP WITH-- WHAT?
BAHASA INDONESIAN, THE NATIONAL LANGUAGE. HOLDING A SULAWESI DIALECT IN RESERVE. LOCAL TIPS: DON'T MAKE EXTENDED EYE CONTACT, DON'T PUT YOUR HANDS ON YOUR HIPS, DON'T TAKE OR OFFER ANYTHING WITH YOUR LEFT HAND.
AND IN THE NAME OF ALL THAT IS SACRED DO NOT USE THE TOILETS.
AND, YES, I *AM* A MASSIVE SNOB, AND THERE WAS NO NEED FOR YOU ALL TO THINK IT AT ONCE.

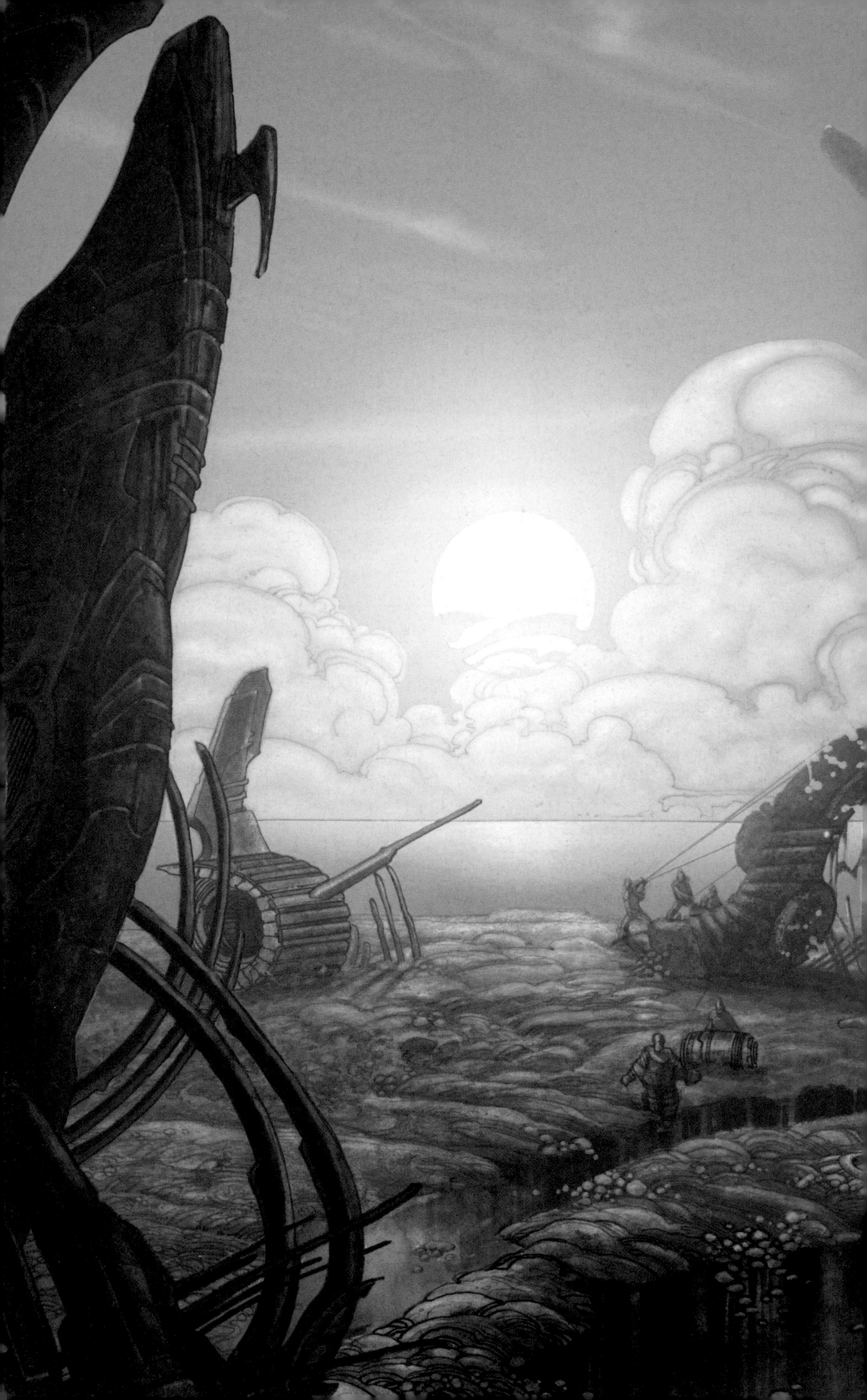

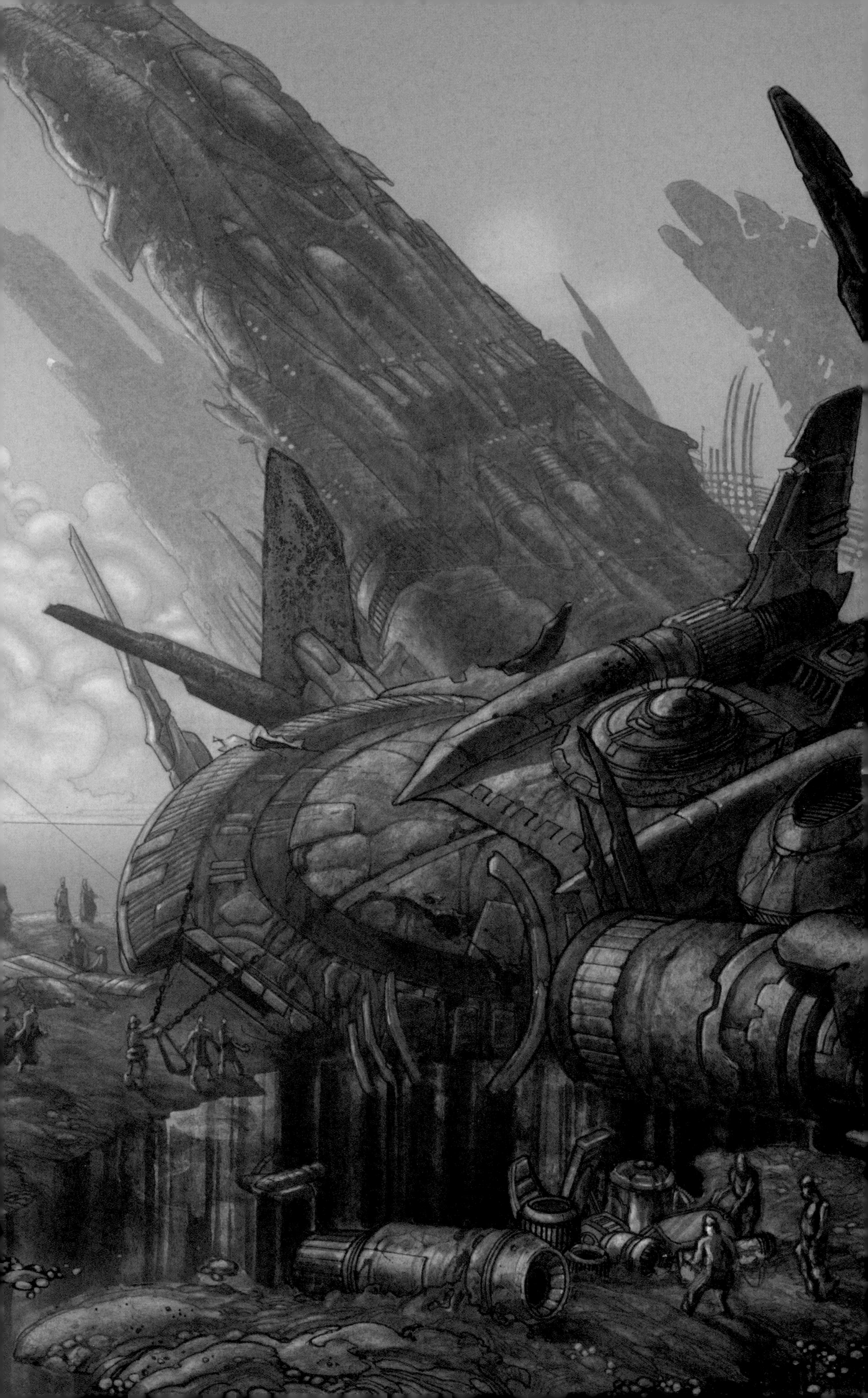

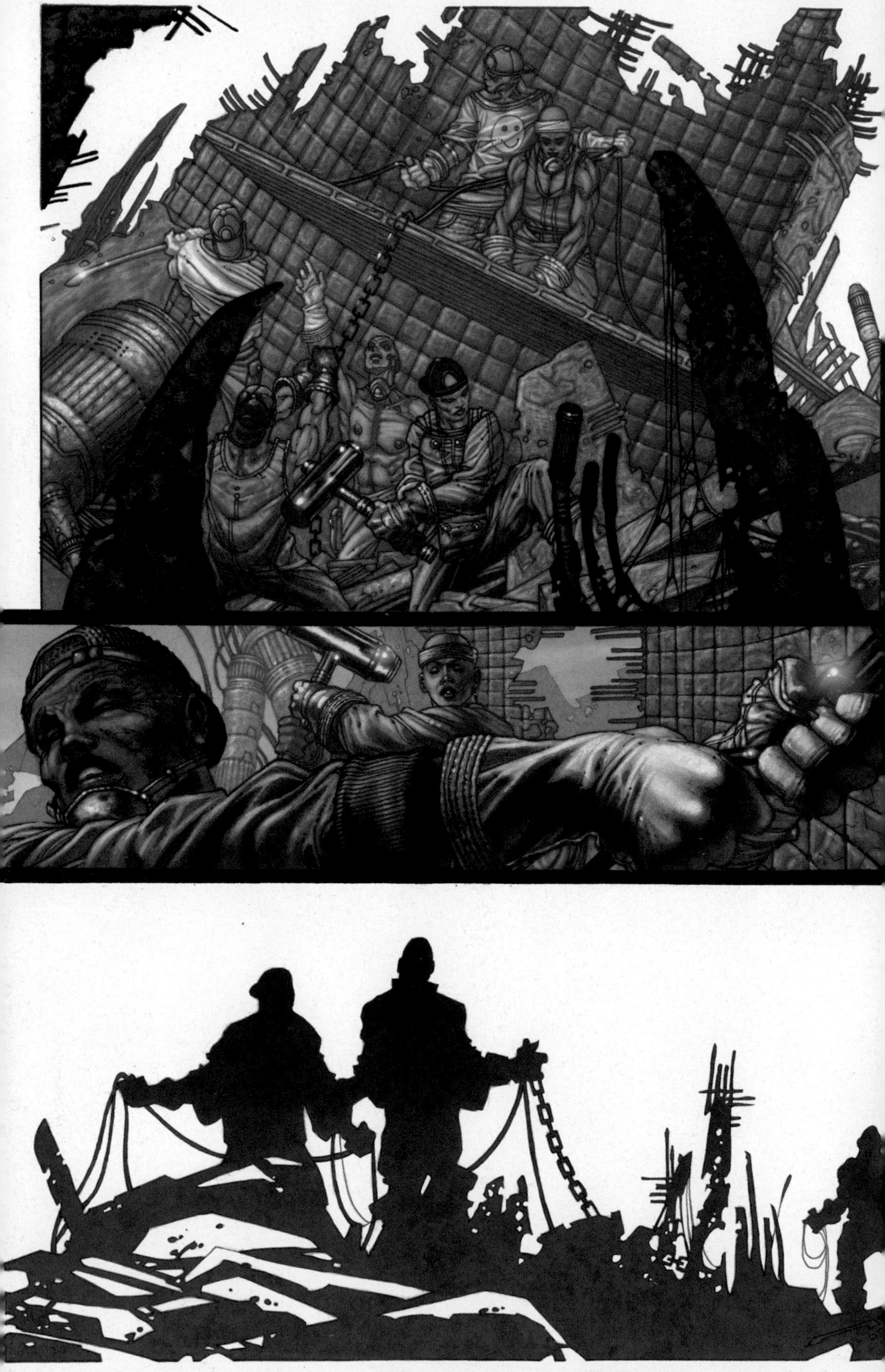

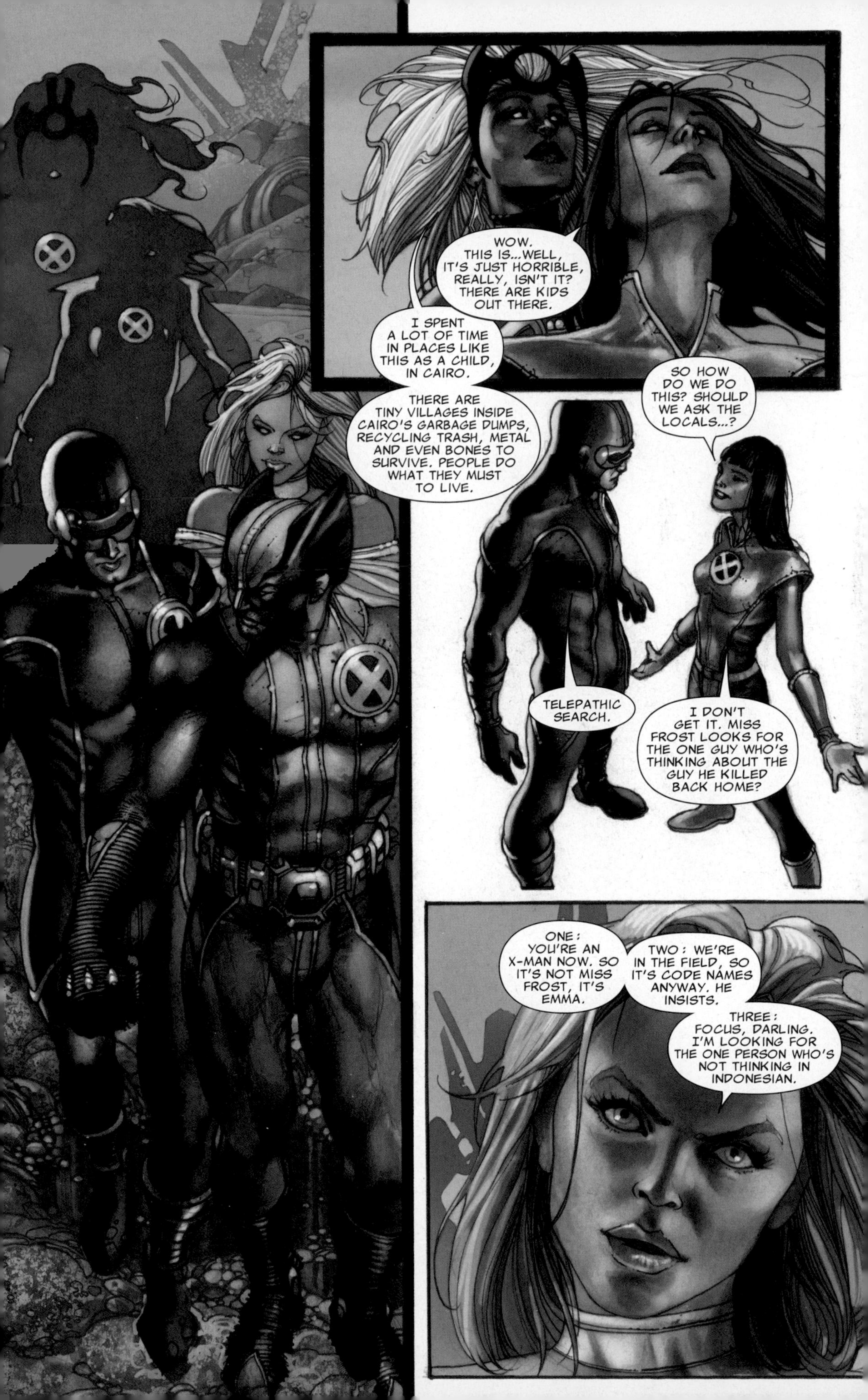
WOW. THIS IS...WELL, IT'S JUST HORRIBLE, REALLY, ISN'T IT? THERE ARE KIDS OUT THERE.
I SPENT A LOT OF TIME IN PLACES LIKE THIS AS A CHILD, IN CAIRO.
THERE ARE TINY VILLAGES INSIDE CAIRO'S GARBAGE DUMPS, RECYCLING TRASH, METAL AND EVEN BONES TO SURVIVE. PEOPLE DO WHAT THEY MUST TO LIVE.
SO HOW DO WE DO THIS? SHOULD WE ASK THE LOCALS...?
TELEPATHIC SEARCH.
I DON'T GET IT. MISS FROST LOOKS FOR THE ONE GUY WHO'S THINKING ABOUT THE GUY HE KILLED BACK HOME?
ONE: YOU'RE AN X-MAN NOW. SO IT'S NOT MISS FROST, IT'S EMMA.
TWO: WE'RE IN THE FIELD, SO IT'S CODE NAMES ANYWAY. HE INSISTS.
THREE: FOCUS, DARLING. I'M LOOKING FOR THE ONE PERSON WHO'S NOT THINKING IN INDONESIAN.

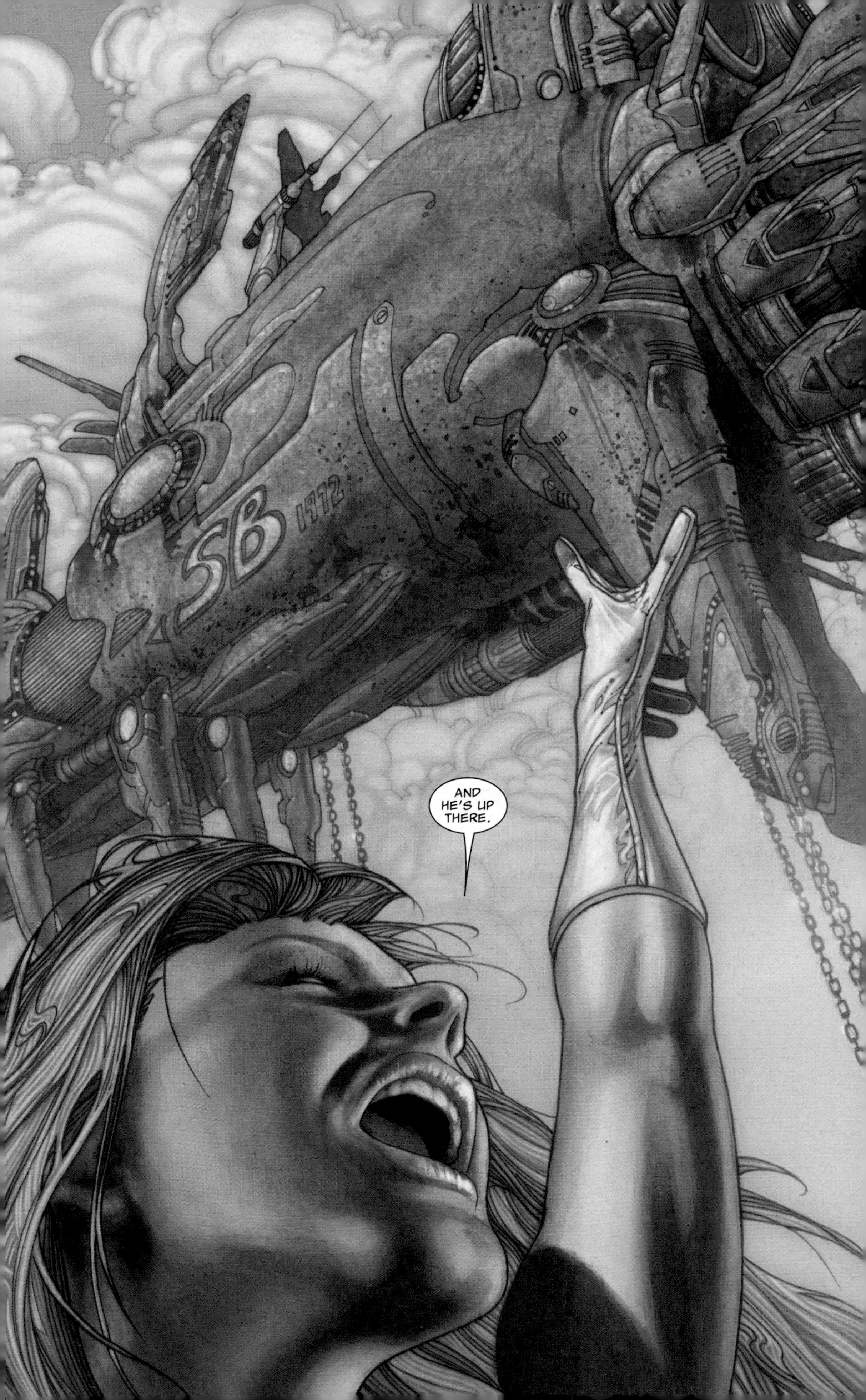

SB 1912
AND HE'S UP THERE.

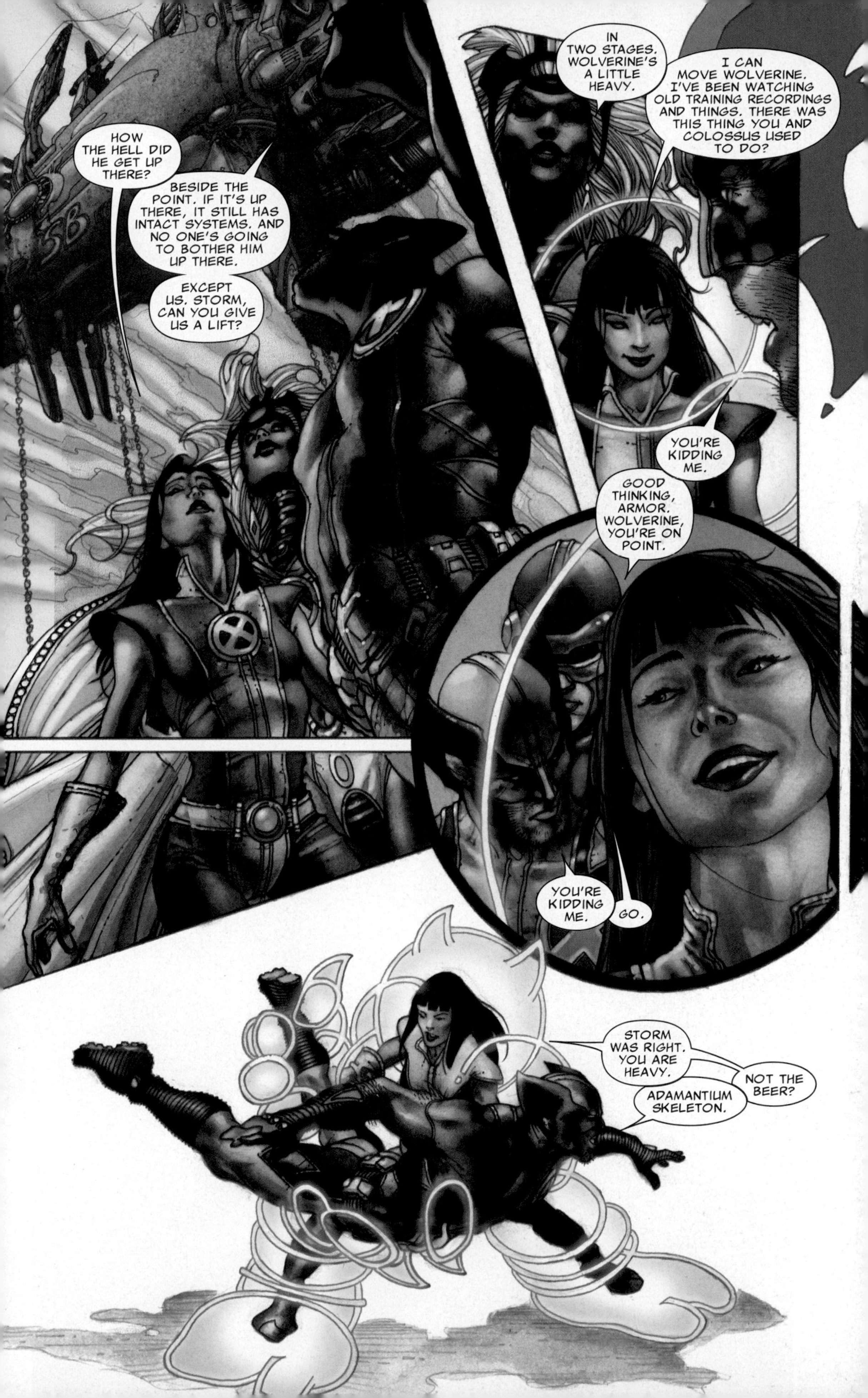
HOW THE HELL DID HE GET UP THERE?
BESIDE THE POINT. IF IT'S UP THERE, IT STILL HAS INTACT SYSTEMS. AND NO ONE'S GOING TO BOTHER HIM UP THERE.
EXCEPT US. STORM, CAN YOU GIVE US A LIFT?
IN TWO STAGES. WOLVERINE'S A LITTLE HEAVY.
I CAN MOVE WOLVERINE. I'VE BEEN WATCHING OLD TRAINING RECORDINGS AND THINGS. THERE WAS THIS THING YOU AND COLOSSUS USED TO DO?
YOU'RE KIDDING ME.
GOOD THINKING, ARMOR. WOLVERINE, YOU'RE ON POINT.
YOU'RE KIDDING ME.
GO.
STORM WAS RIGHT. YOU ARE HEAVY.
NOT THE BEER?
ADAMANTIUM SKELETON.

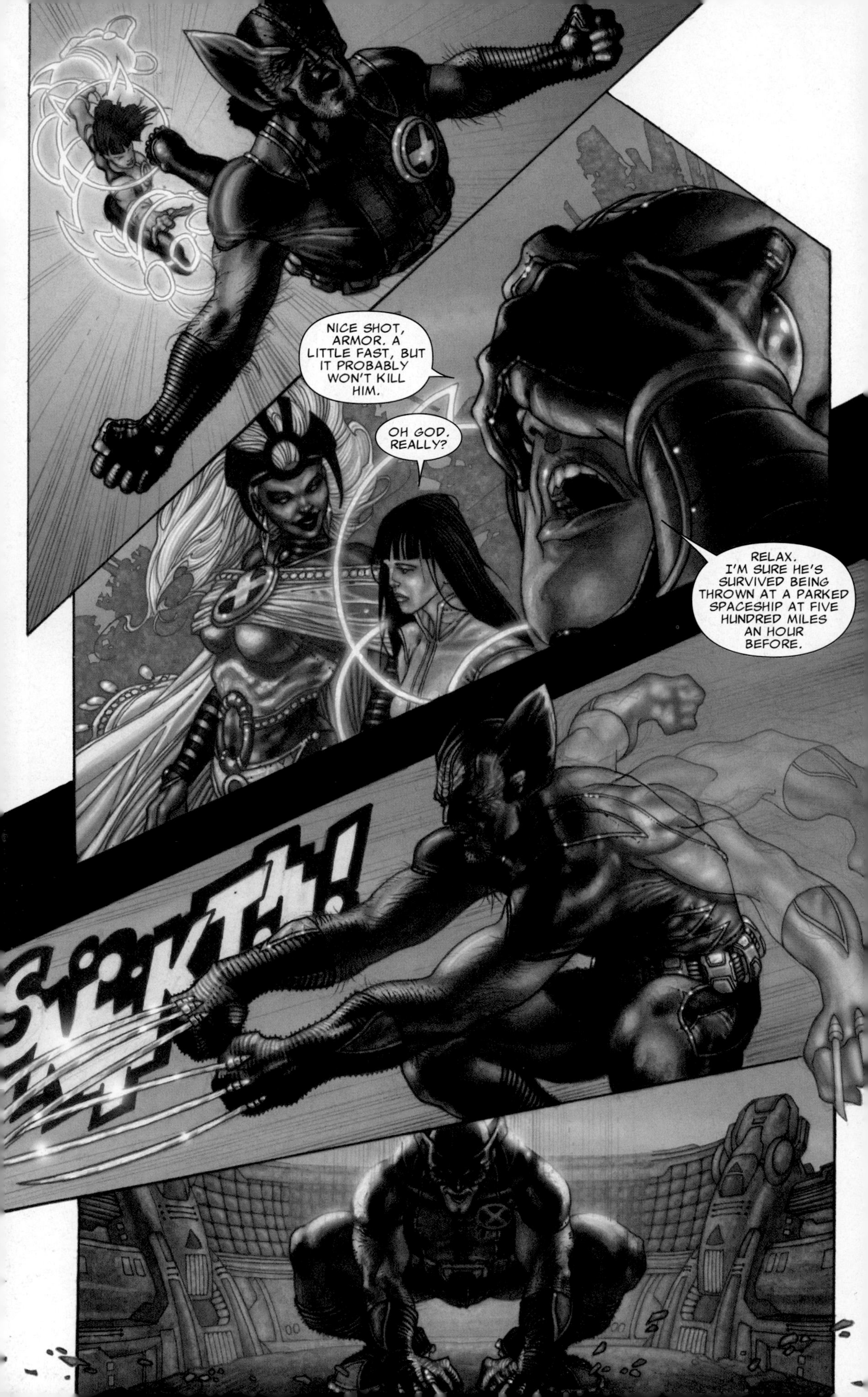
NICE SHOT, ARMOR. A LITTLE FAST, BUT IT PROBABLY WON'T KILL HIM.
OH GOD. REALLY?
RELAX. I'M SURE HE'S SURVIVED BEING THROWN AT A PARKED SPACESHIP AT FIVE HUNDRED MILES AN HOUR BEFORE.
SNIKT!

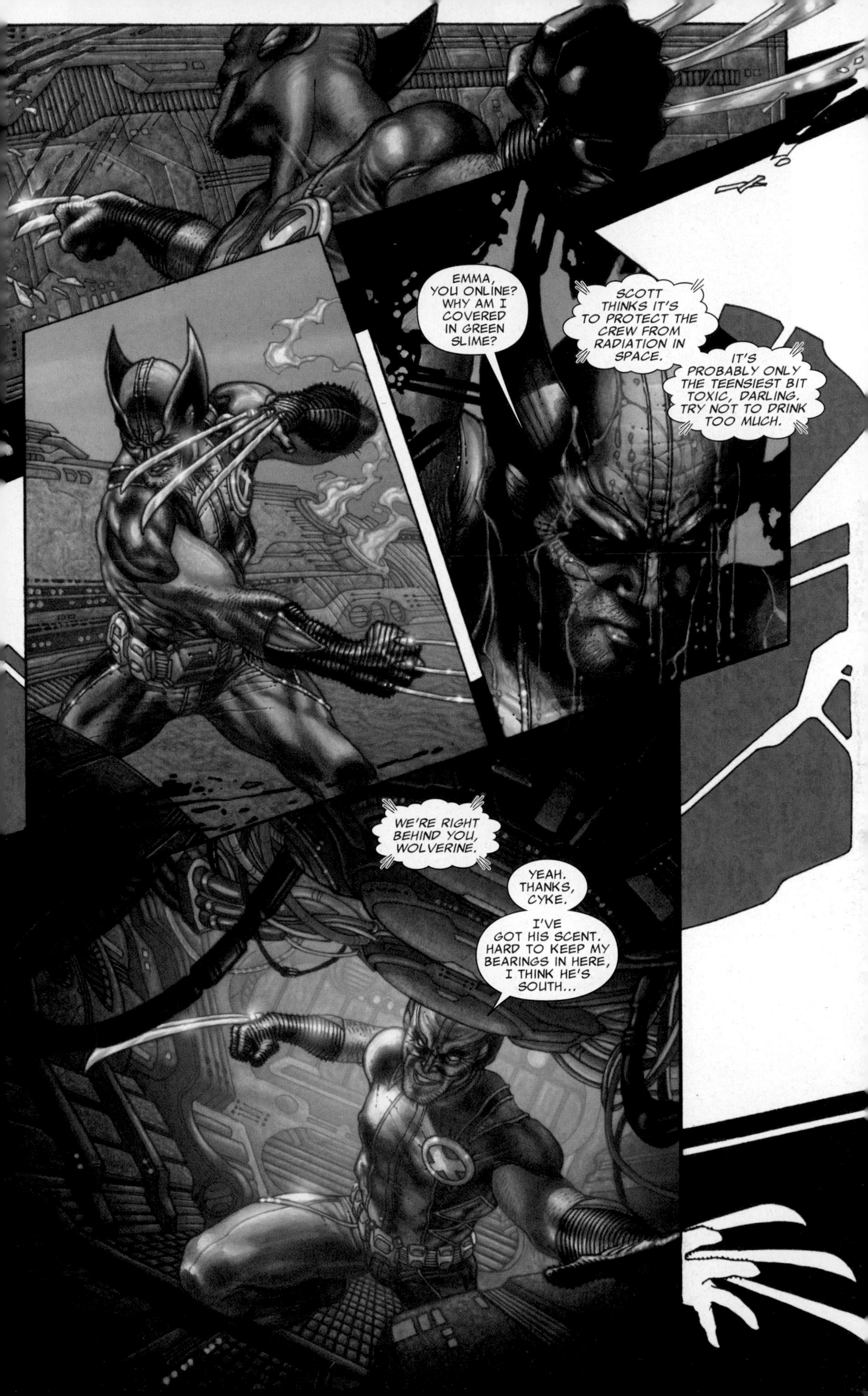
EMMA, YOU ONLINE? WHY AM I COVERED IN GREEN SLIME?
SCOTT THINKS IT'S TO PROTECT THE CREW FROM RADIATION IN SPACE.
IT'S PROBABLY ONLY THE TEENSIEST BIT TOXIC, DARLING. TRY NOT TO DRINK TOO MUCH.
WE'RE RIGHT BEHIND YOU, WOLVERINE.
YEAH. THANKS, CYKE.
I'VE GOT HIS SCENT. HARD TO KEEP MY BEARINGS IN HERE, I THINK HE'S SOUTH...

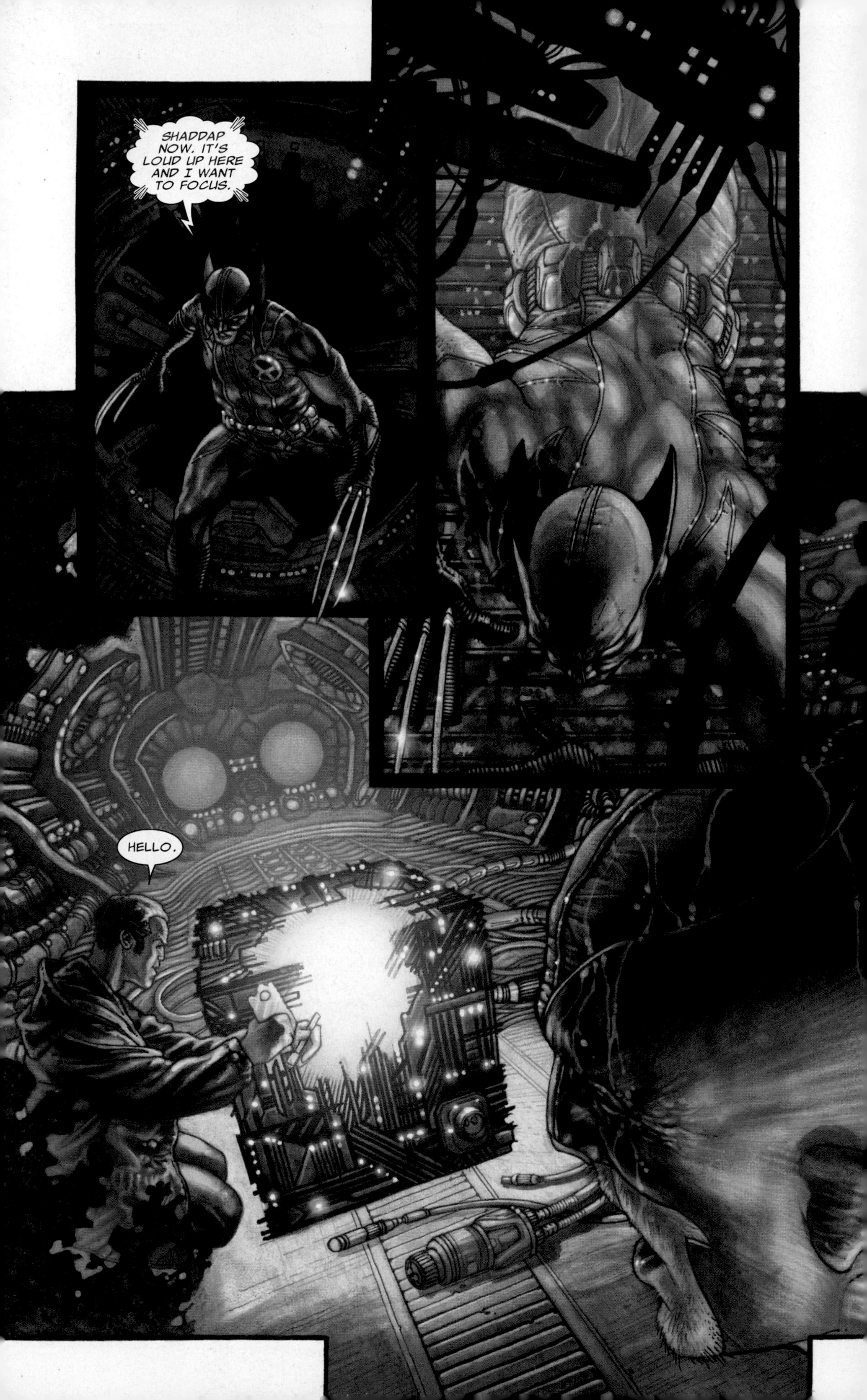
SHADDAP NOW. IT'S LOUD UP HERE AND I WANT TO FOCUS.
HELLO.

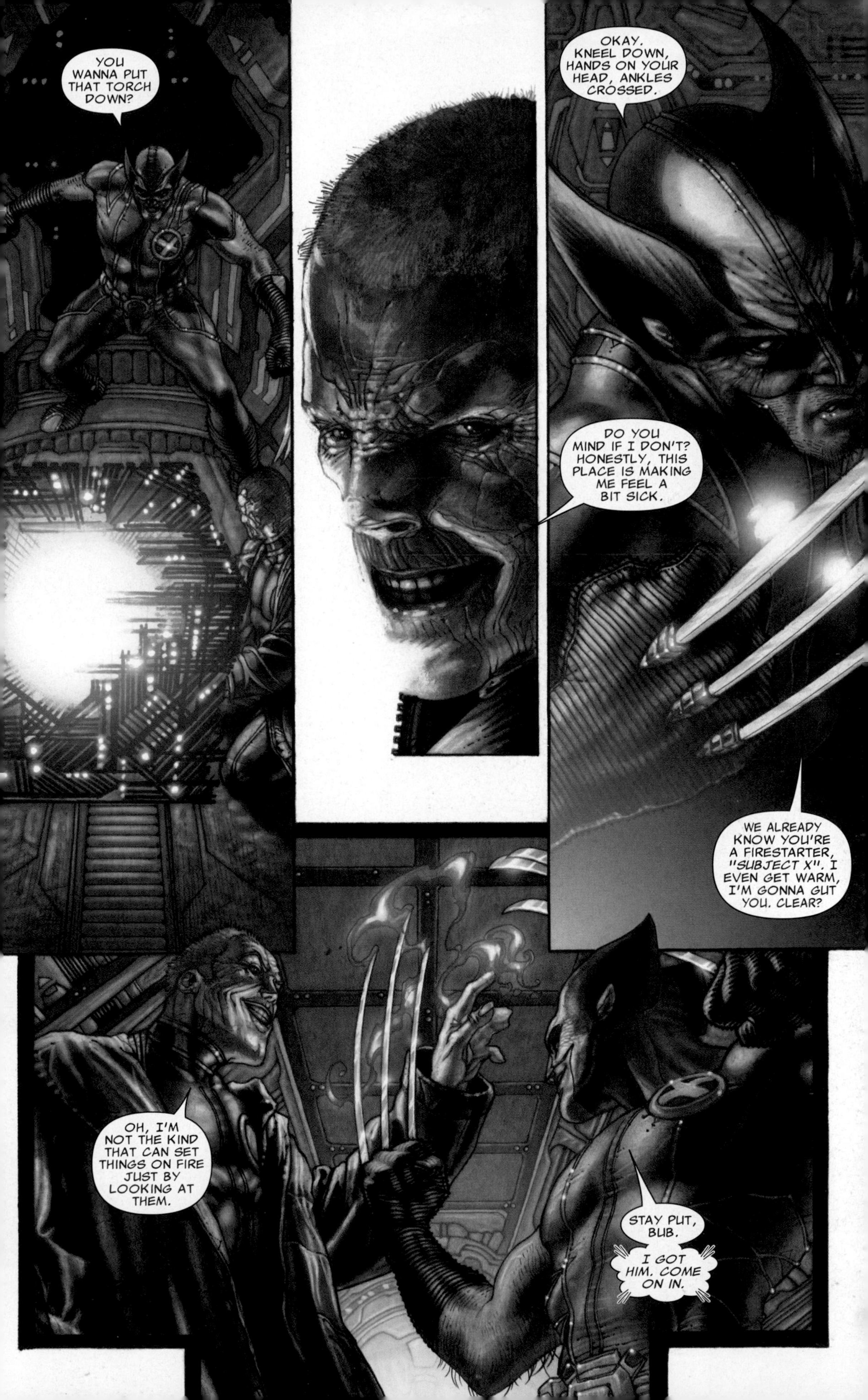
YOU WANNA PUT THAT TORCH DOWN?
OKAY. KNEEL DOWN, HANDS ON YOUR HEAD, ANKLES CROSSED.
DO YOU MIND IF I DON'T? HONESTLY, THIS PLACE IS MAKING ME FEEL A BIT SICK.
WE ALREADY KNOW YOU'RE A FIRESTARTER, "SUBJECT X". I EVEN GET WARM, I'M GONNA GUT YOU. CLEAR?
OH, I'M NOT THE KIND THAT CAN SET THINGS ON FIRE JUST BY LOOKING AT THEM.
STAY PUT, BUB.
I GOT HIM. COME ON IN.

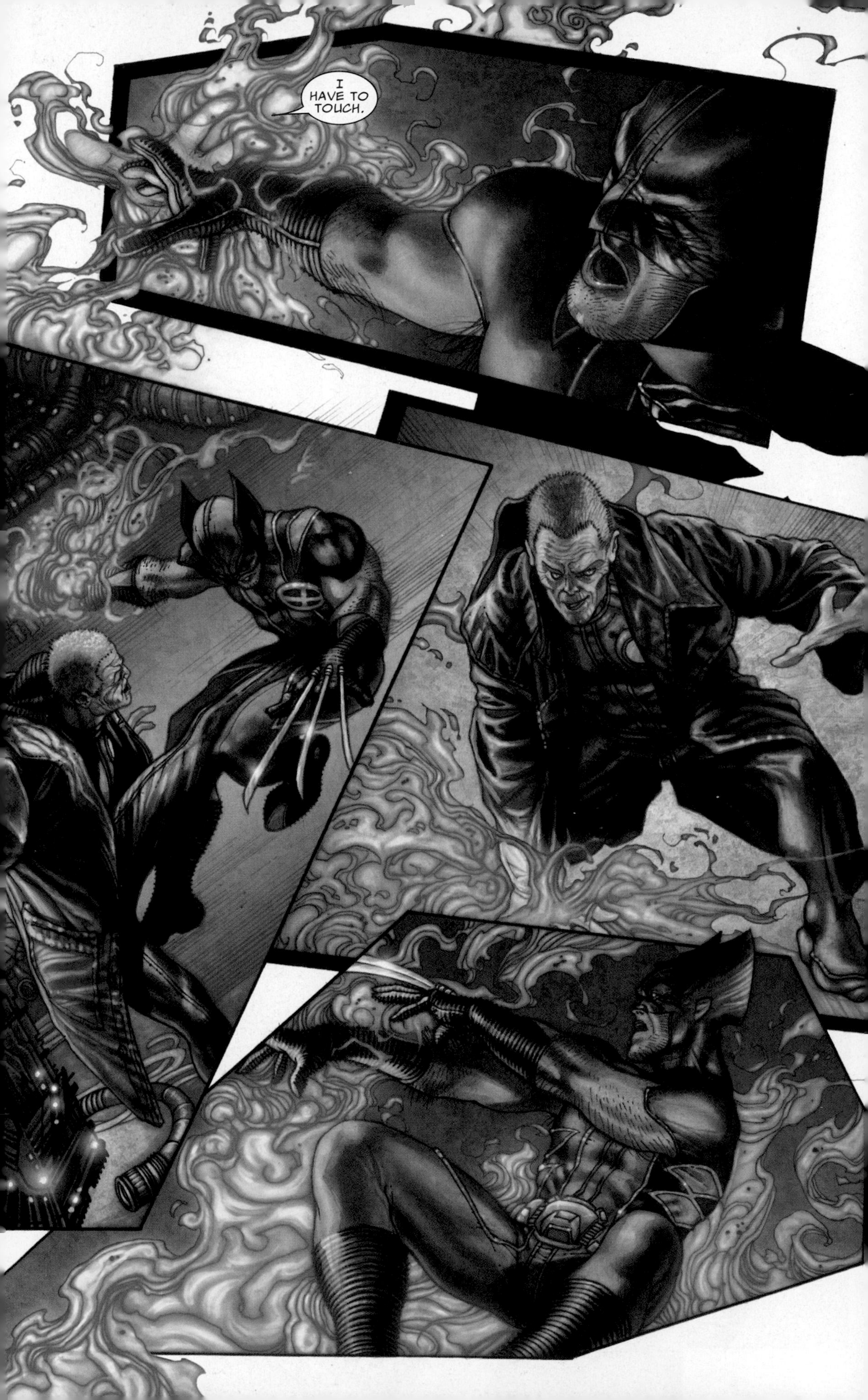
I HAVE TO TOUCH.

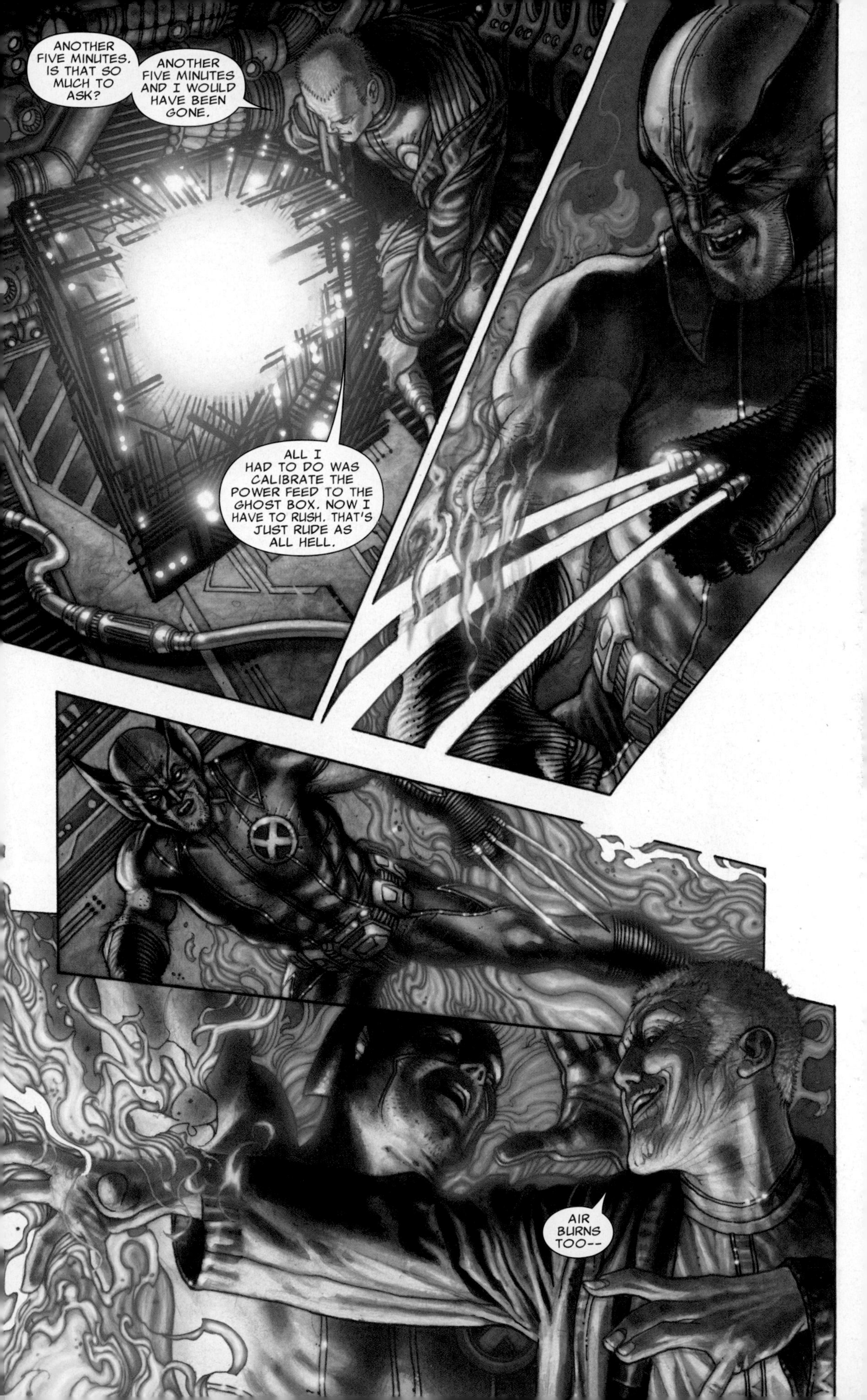
ANOTHER FIVE MINUTES. IS THAT SO MUCH TO ASK?
ANOTHER FIVE MINUTES AND I WOULD HAVE BEEN GONE.
ALL I HAD TO DO WAS CALIBRATE THE POWER FEED TO THE GHOST BOX. NOW I HAVE TO RUSH. THAT'S JUST RUDE AS ALL HELL.
AIR BURNS TOO--

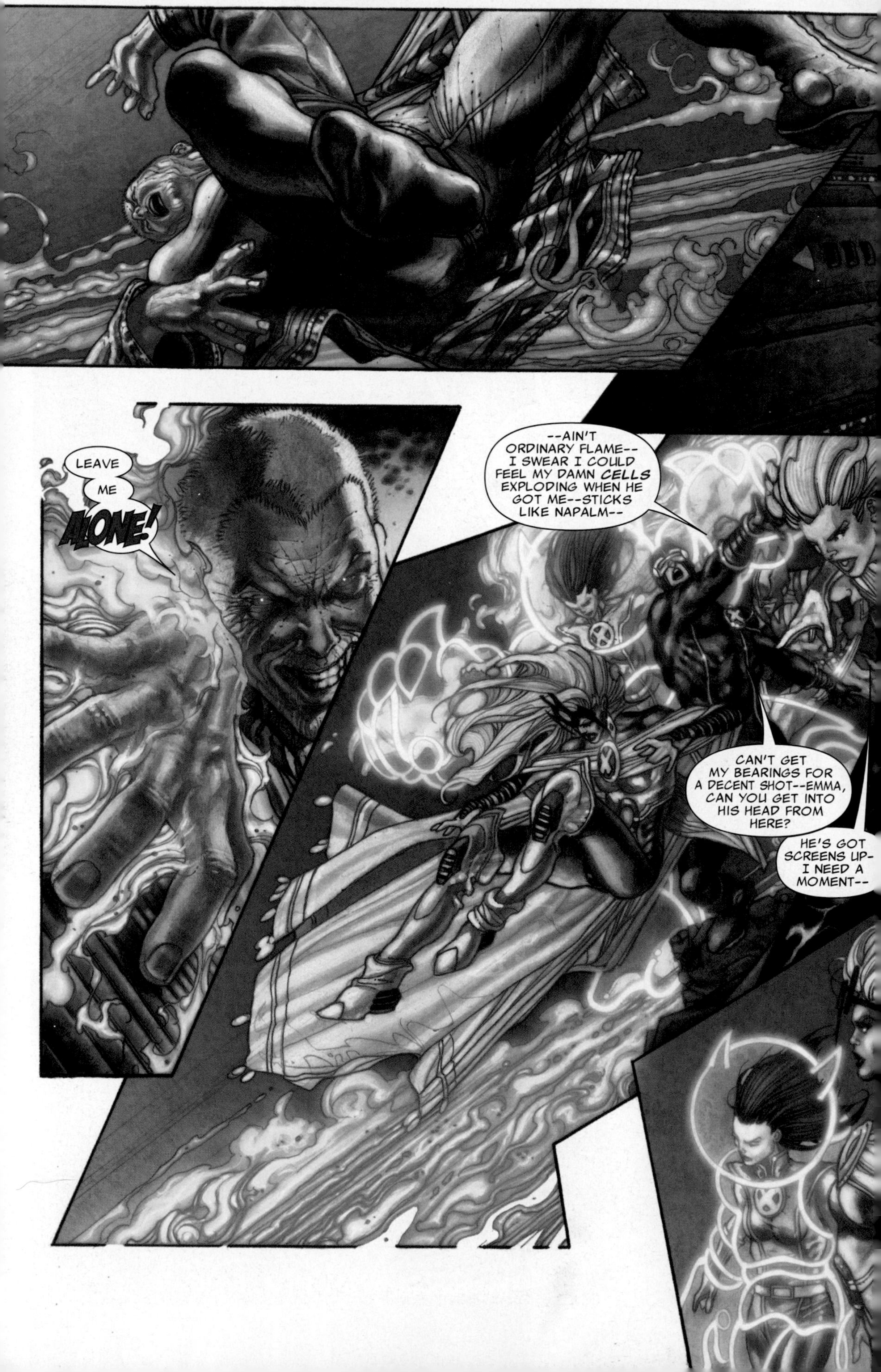
LEAVE ME ALONE!
--AIN'T ORDINARY FLAME-- I SWEAR I COULD FEEL MY DAMN CELLS EXPLODING WHEN HE GOT ME--STICKS LIKE NAPALM--
CAN'T GET MY BEARINGS FOR A DECENT SHOT--EMMA, CAN YOU GET INTO HIS HEAD FROM HERE?
HE'S GOT SCREENS UP- I NEED A MOMENT--

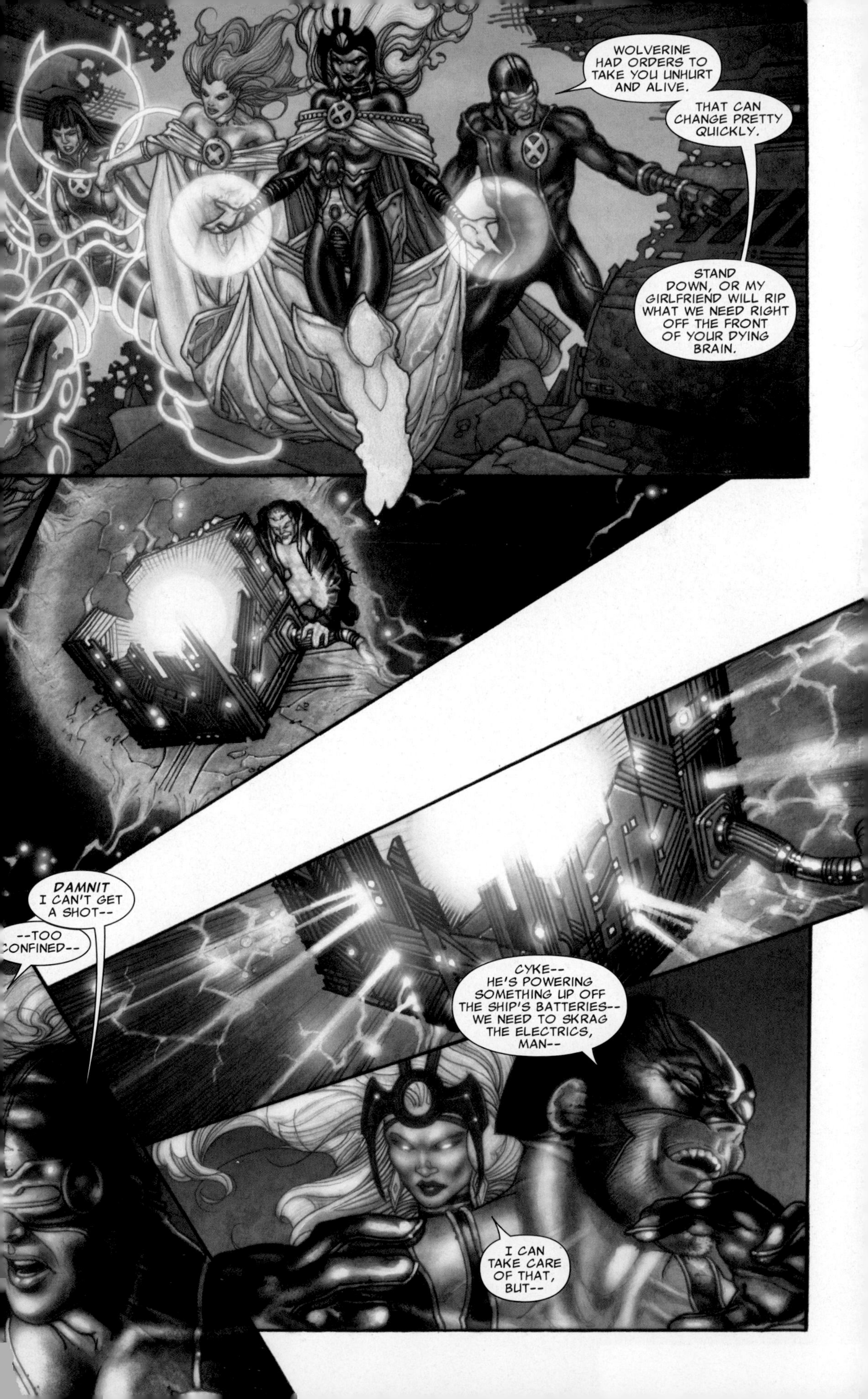
WOLVERINE HAD ORDERS TO TAKE YOU UNHURT AND ALIVE.
THAT CAN CHANGE PRETTY QUICKLY.
STAND DOWN, OR MY GIRLFRIEND WILL RIP WHAT WE NEED RIGHT OFF THE FRONT OF YOUR DYING BRAIN.
DAMNIT I CAN'T GET A SHOT--
--TOO CONFINED--
CYKE-- HE'S POWERING SOMETHING UP OFF THE SHIP'S BATTERIES-- WE NEED TO SKRAG THE ELECTRICS, MAN--
I CAN TAKE CARE OF THAT, BUT--

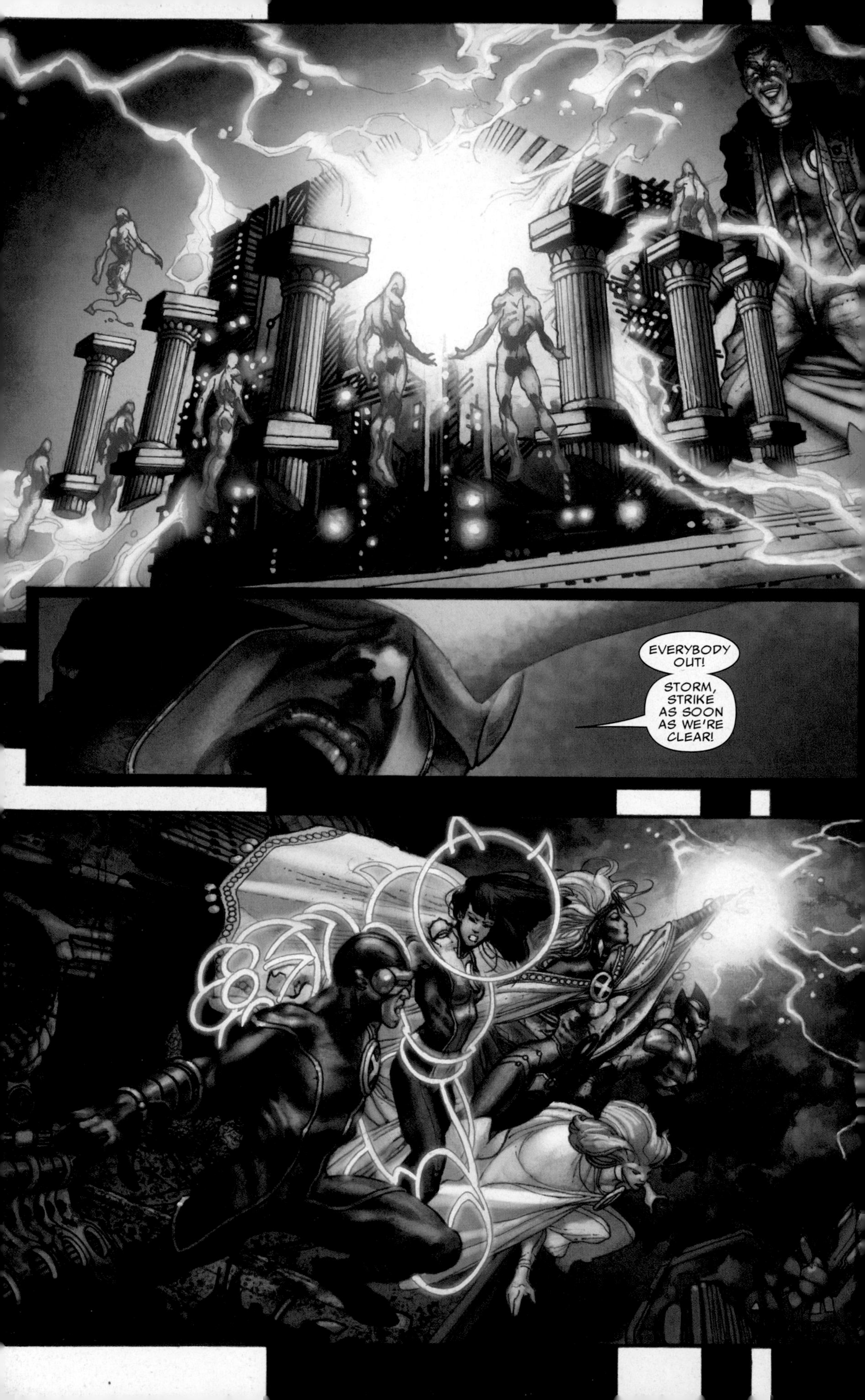
EVERYBODY OUT!
STORM, STRIKE AS SOON AS WE'RE CLEAR!

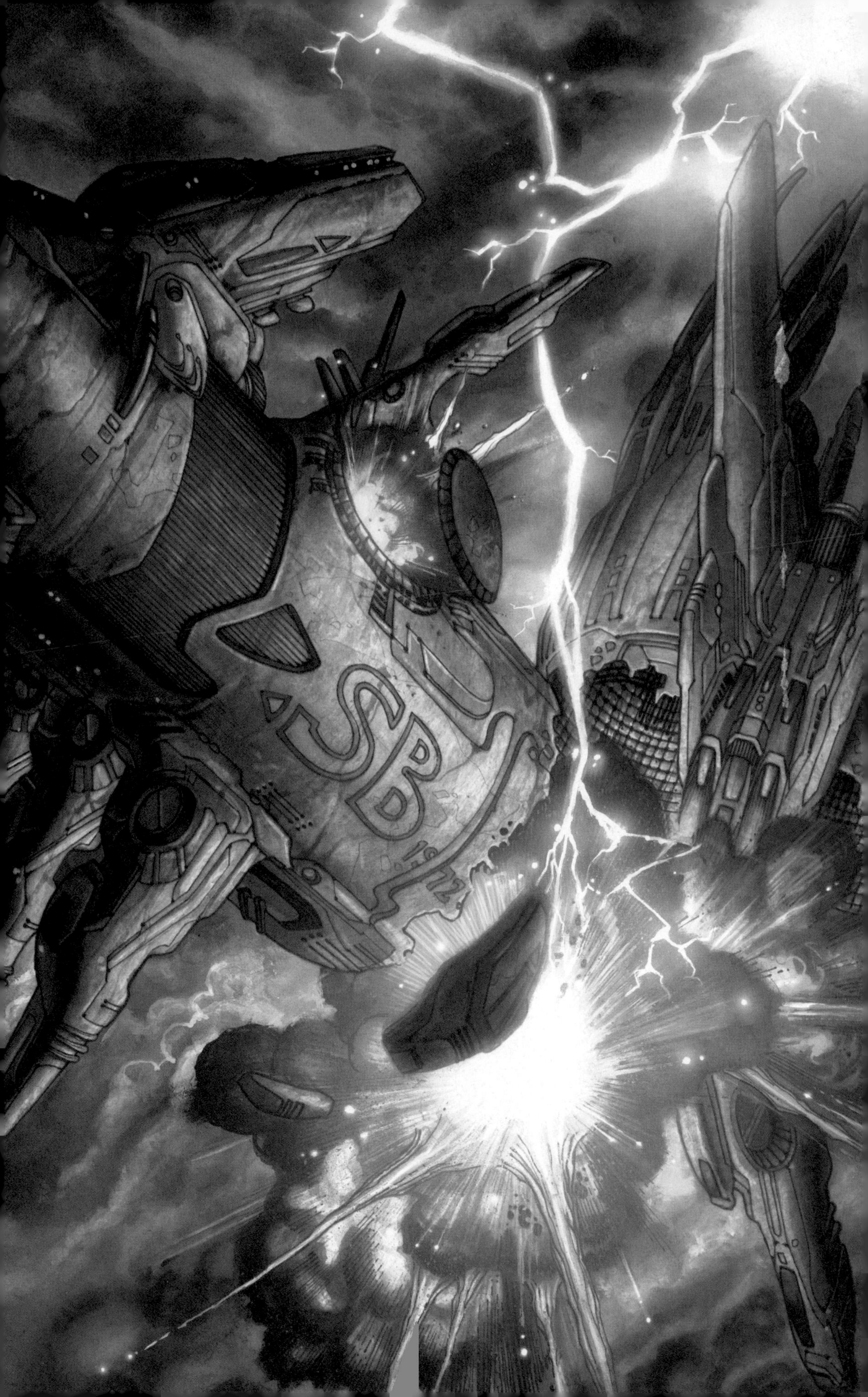

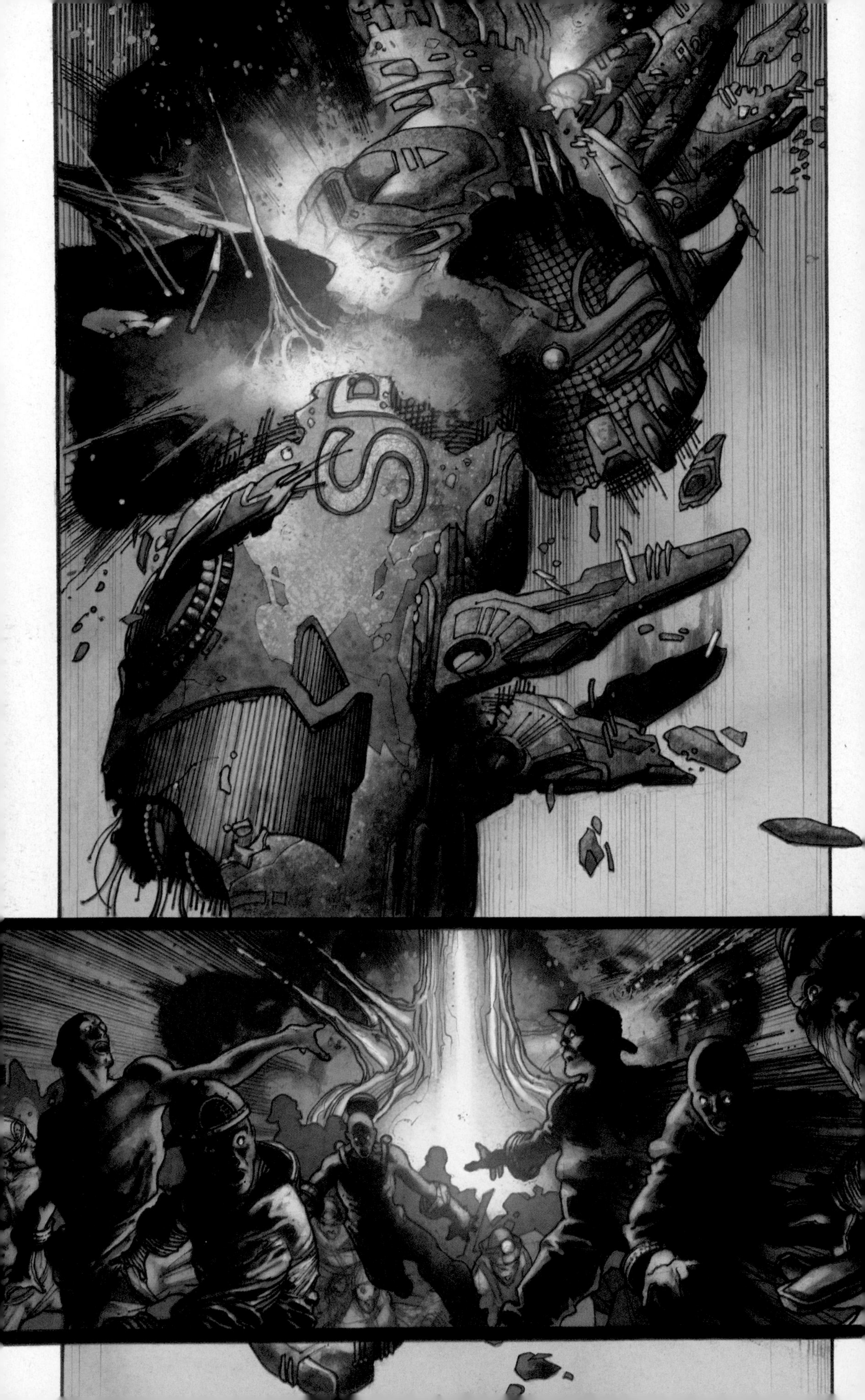

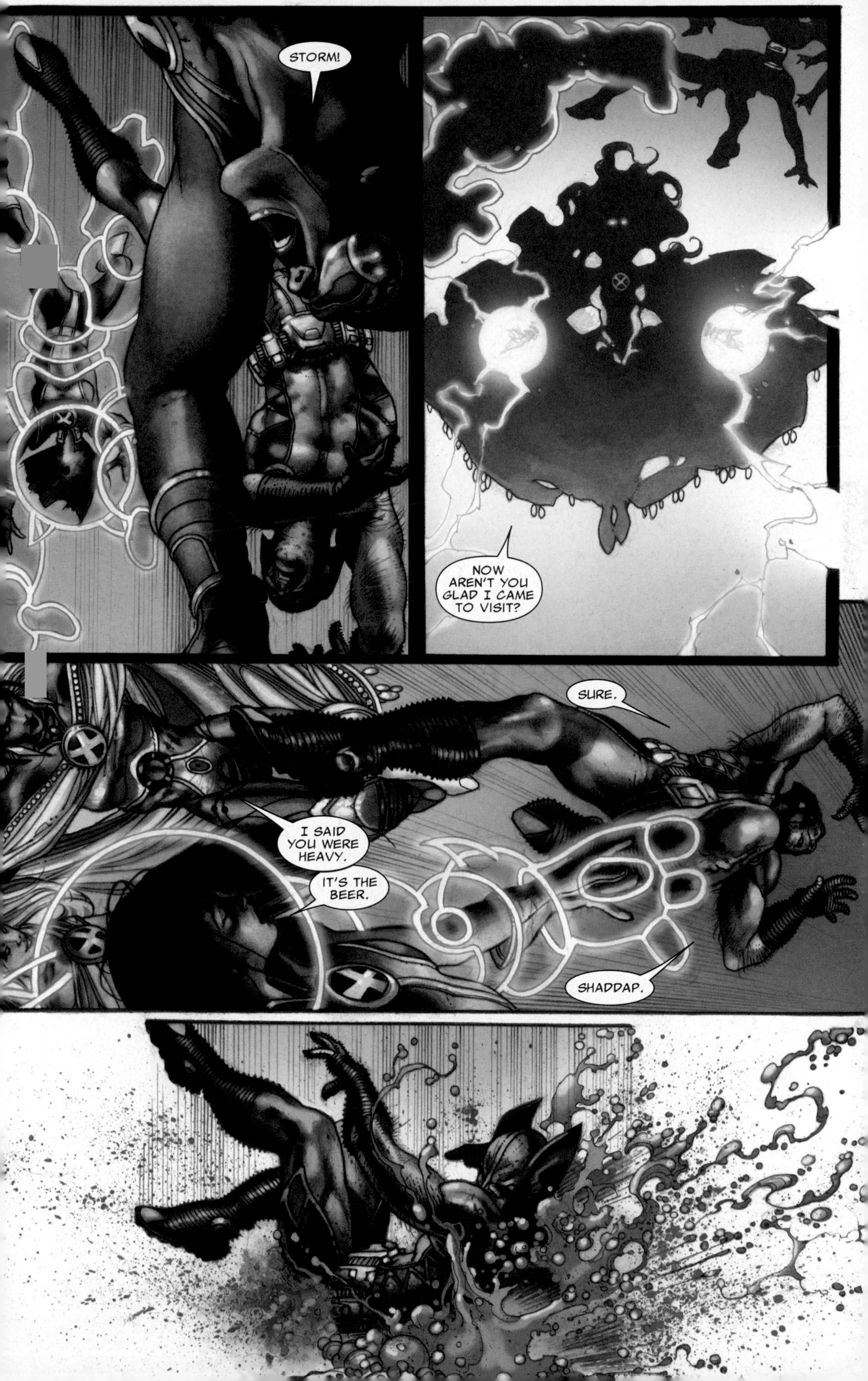
STORM!
NOW AREN'T YOU GLAD I CAME TO VISIT?
SURE.
I SAID YOU WERE HEAVY.
IT'S THE BEER.
SHADDAP.

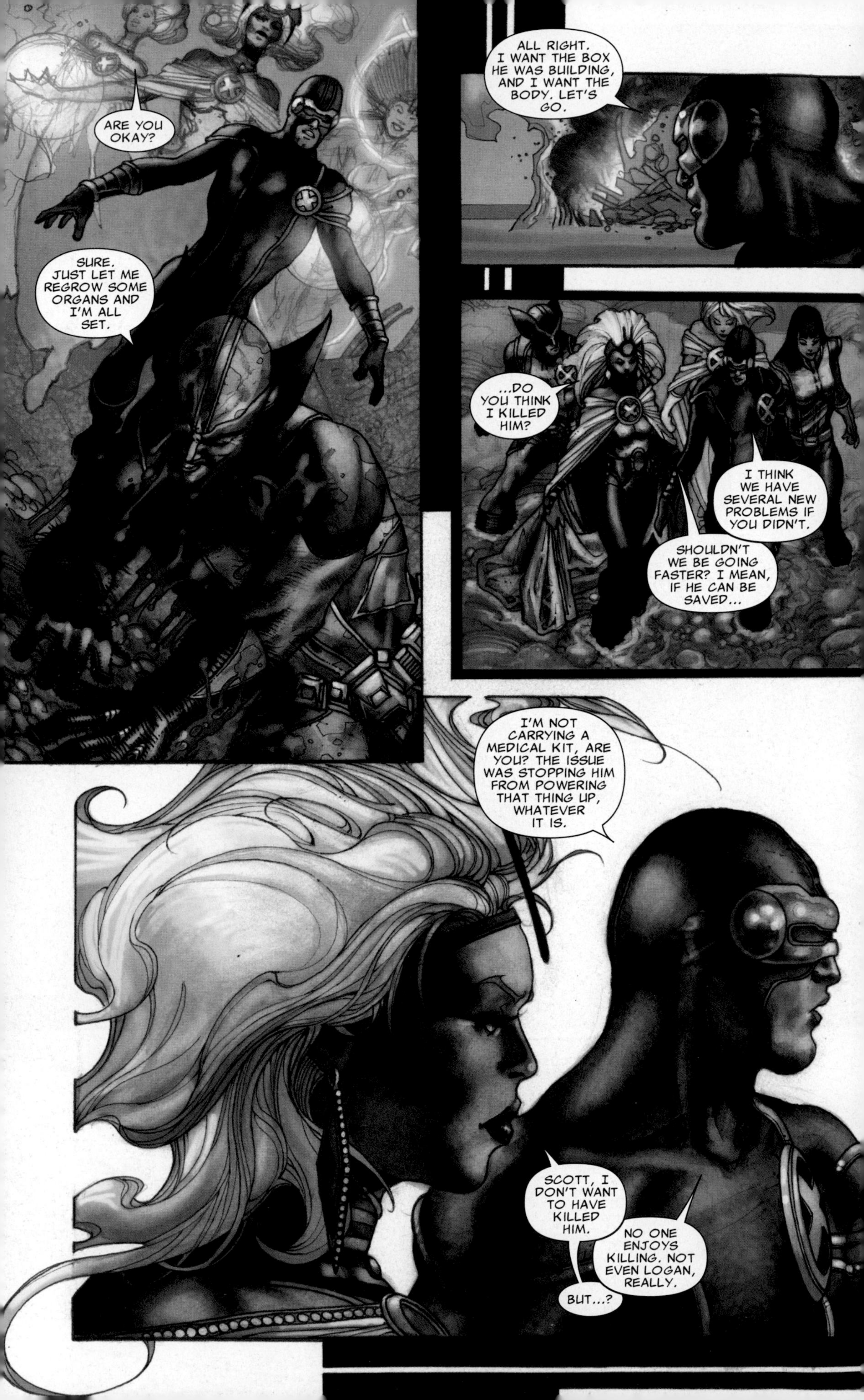
ARE YOU OKAY?
SURE. JUST LET ME REGROW SOME ORGANS AND I'M ALL SET.
ALL RIGHT. I WANT THE BOX HE WAS BUILDING, AND I WANT THE BODY. LET'S GO.
...DO YOU THINK I KILLED HIM?
I THINK WE HAVE SEVERAL NEW PROBLEMS IF YOU DIDN'T.
SHOULDN'T WE BE GOING FASTER? I MEAN, IF HE CAN BE SAVED...
I'M NOT CARRYING A MEDICAL KIT, ARE YOU? THE ISSUE WAS STOPPING HIM FROM POWERING THAT THING UP, WHATEVER IT IS.
SCOTT, I DON'T WANT TO HAVE KILLED HIM.
NO ONE ENJOYS KILLING. NOT EVEN LOGAN, REALLY.
BUT...?

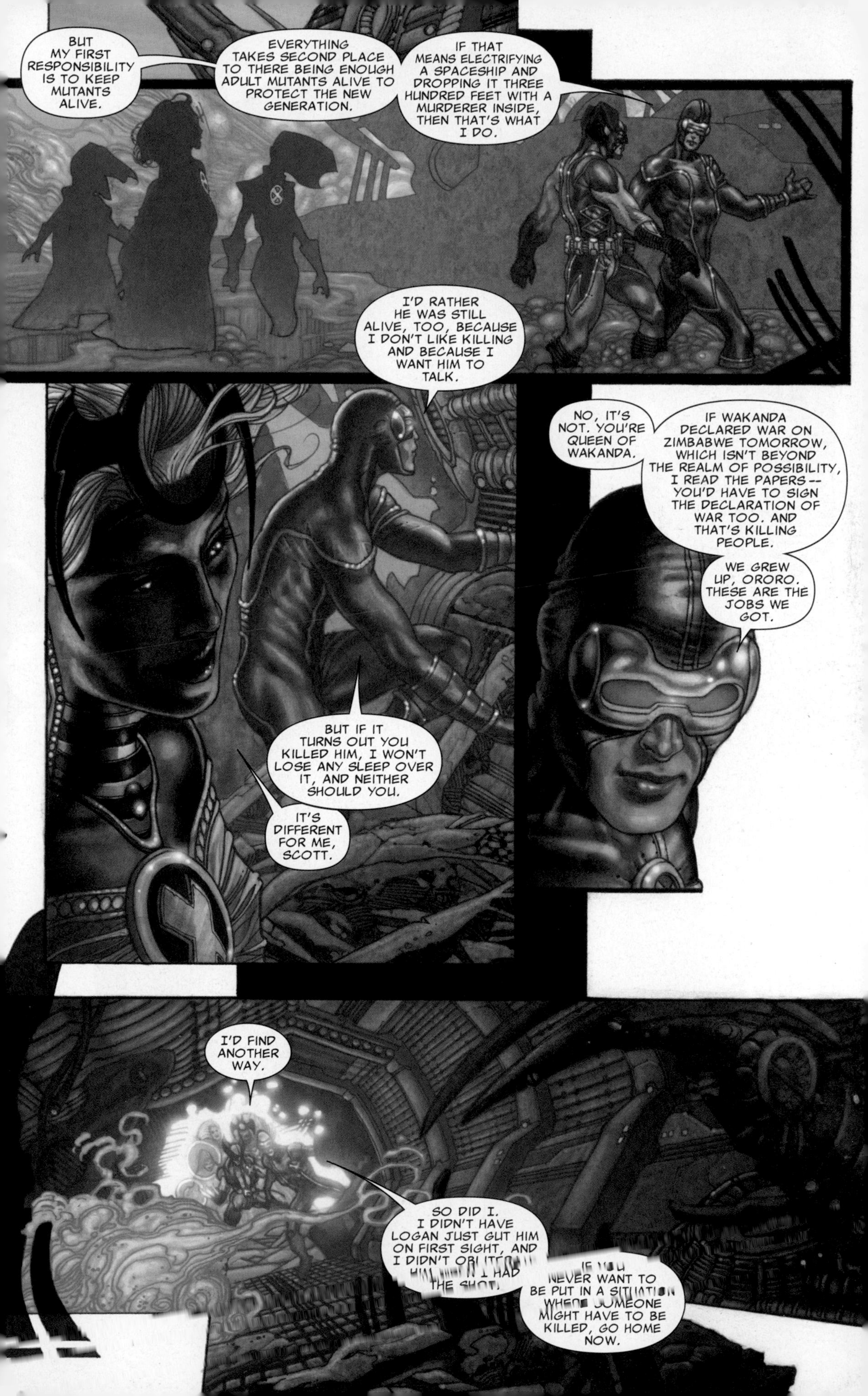
BUT MY FIRST RESPONSIBILITY IS TO KEEP MUTANTS ALIVE.
EVERYTHING TAKES SECOND PLACE TO THERE BEING ENOUGH ADULT MUTANTS ALIVE TO PROTECT THE NEW GENERATION.
IF THAT MEANS ELECTRIFYING A SPACESHIP AND DROPPING IT THREE HUNDRED FEET WITH A MURDERER INSIDE, THEN THAT'S WHAT I DO.
I'D RATHER HE WAS STILL ALIVE, TOO, BECAUSE I DON'T LIKE KILLING AND BECAUSE I WANT HIM TO TALK.
BUT IF IT TURNS OUT YOU KILLED HIM, I WON'T LOSE ANY SLEEP OVER IT, AND NEITHER SHOULD YOU.
IT'S DIFFERENT FOR ME, SCOTT.
NO, IT'S NOT. YOU'RE QUEEN OF WAKANDA.
IF WAKANDA DECLARED WAR ON ZIMBABWE TOMORROW, WHICH ISN'T BEYOND THE REALM OF POSSIBILITY, I READ THE PAPERS -- YOU'D HAVE TO SIGN THE DECLARATION OF WAR TOO. AND THAT'S KILLING PEOPLE.
WE GREW UP, ORORO. THESE ARE THE JOBS WE GOT.
I'D FIND ANOTHER WAY.
SO DID I. I DIDN'T HAVE LOGAN JUST GUT HIM ON FIRST SIGHT, AND I DIDN'T
I HAD THE
IF
NEVER WANT TO BE PUT IN A
MIGHT HAVE TO BE KILLED, GO HOME NOW.

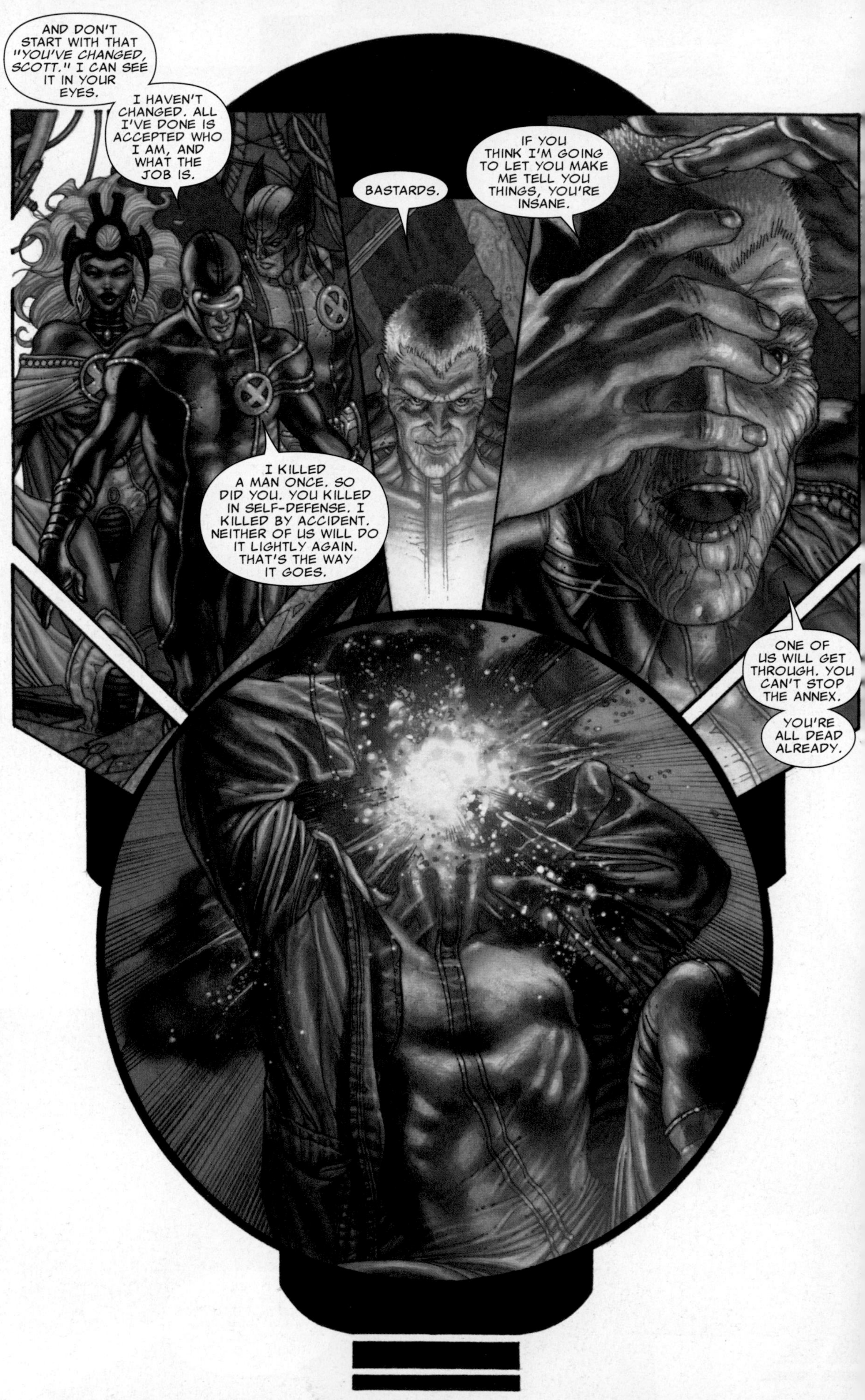
AND DON'T START WITH THAT "YOU'VE CHANGED, SCOTT." I CAN SEE IT IN YOUR EYES.
I HAVEN'T CHANGED. ALL I'VE DONE IS ACCEPTED WHO I AM, AND WHAT THE JOB IS.
I KILLED A MAN ONCE. SO DID YOU. YOU KILLED IN SELF-DEFENSE. I KILLED BY ACCIDENT. NEITHER OF US WILL DO IT LIGHTLY AGAIN. THAT'S THE WAY IT GOES.
BASTARDS.
IF YOU THINK I'M GOING TO LET YOU MAKE ME TELL YOU THINGS, YOU'RE INSANE.
ONE OF US WILL GET THROUGH. YOU CAN'T STOP THE ANNEX.
YOU'RE ALL DEAD ALREADY.

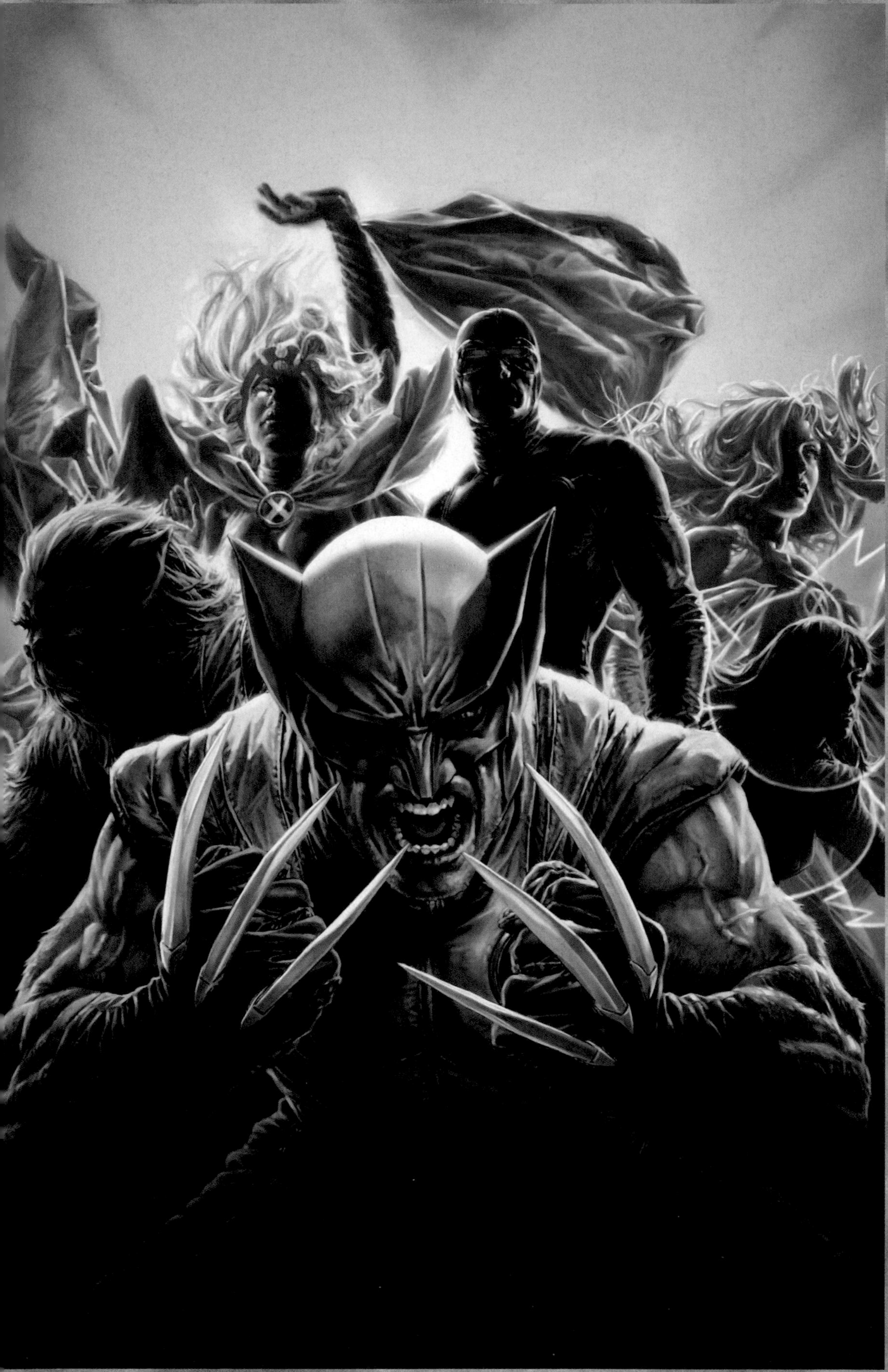

Astonishing X-Men #25 Variant by Lee Bermejo

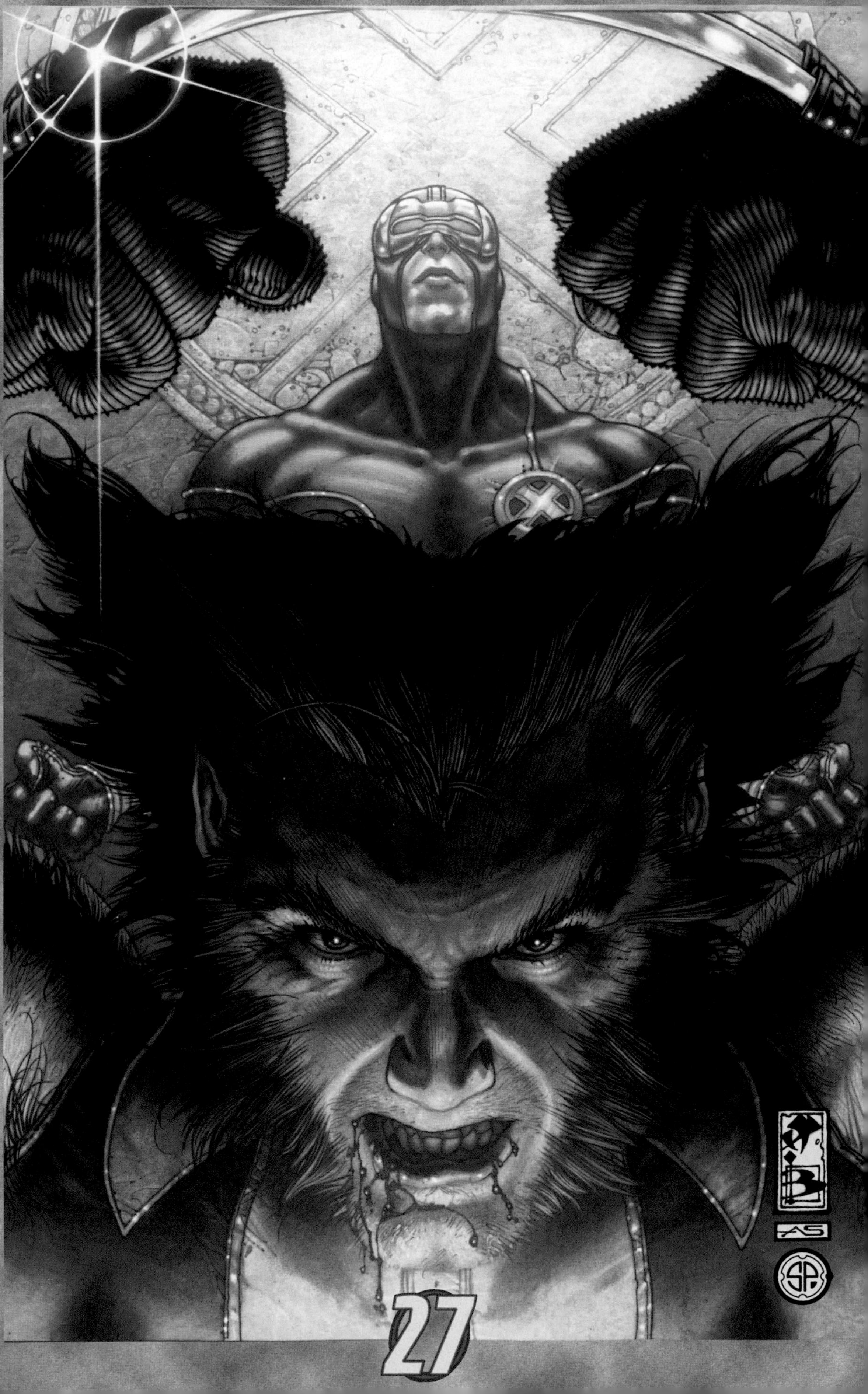
27

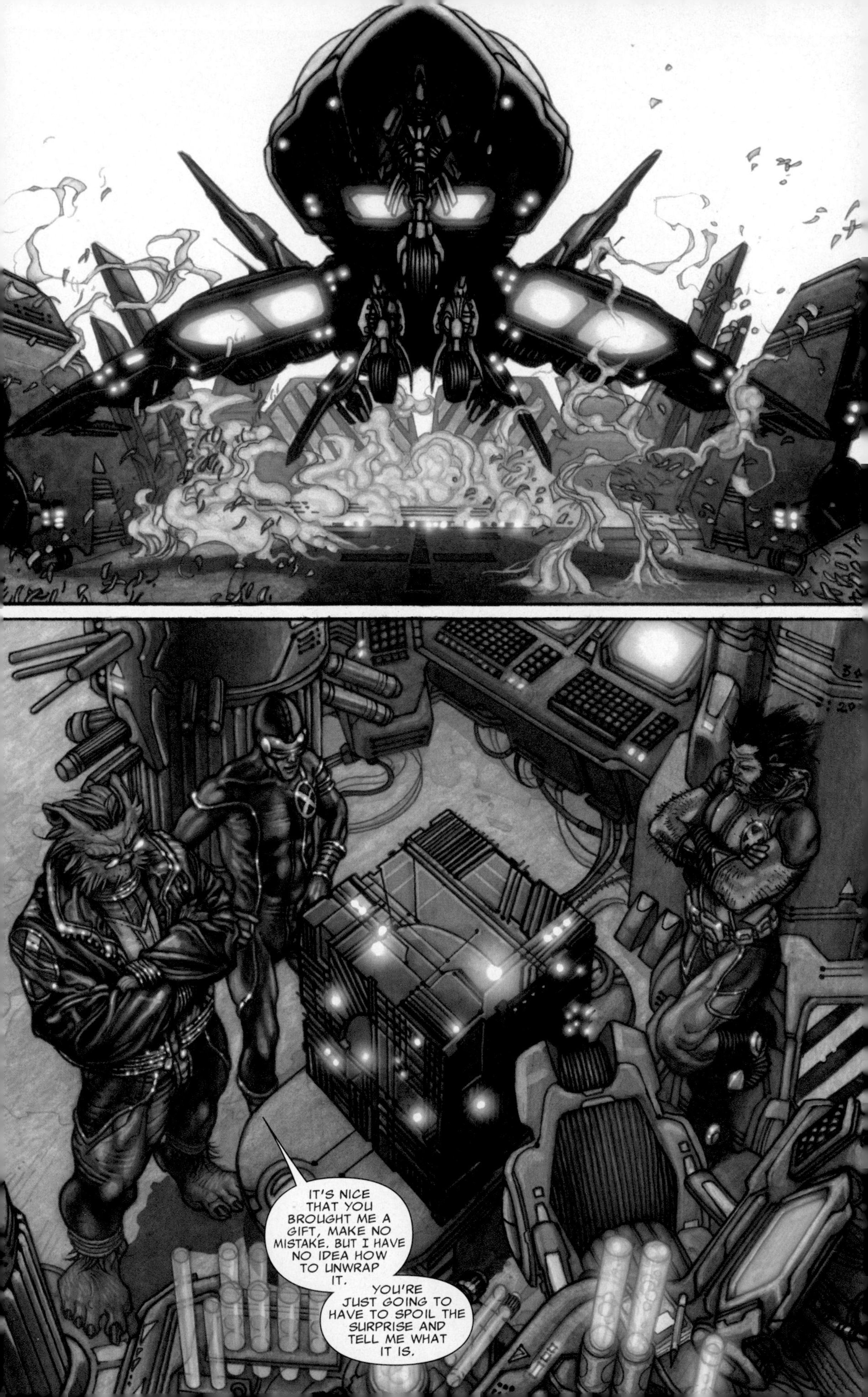
IT'S NICE THAT YOU BROUGHT ME A GIFT, MAKE NO MISTAKE. BUT I HAVE NO IDEA HOW TO UNWRAP IT.
YOU'RE JUST GOING TO HAVE TO SPOIL THE SURPRISE AND TELL ME WHAT IT IS.

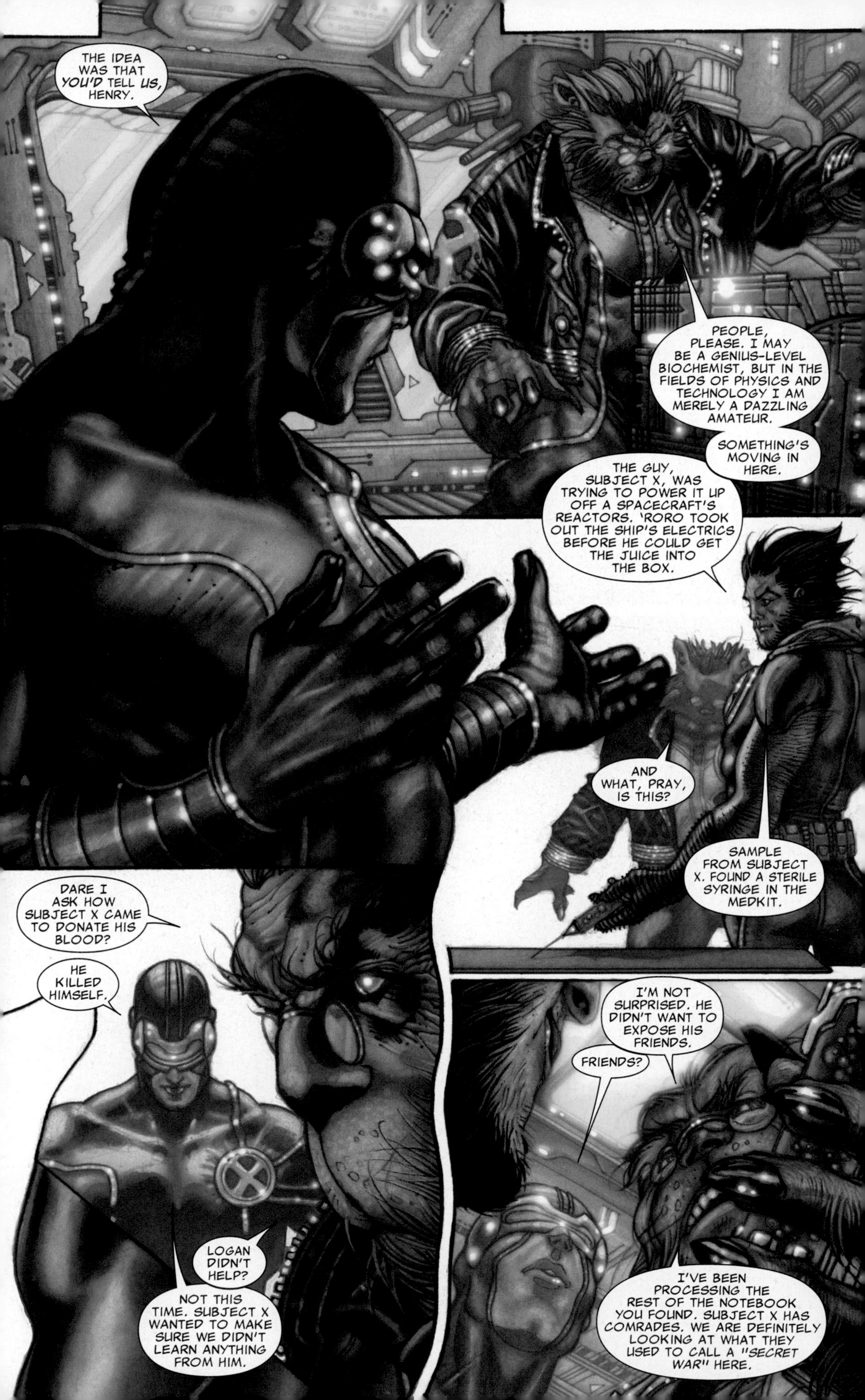
THE IDEA WAS THAT YOU'D TELL US, HENRY.
PEOPLE, PLEASE. I MAY BE A GENIUS-LEVEL BIOCHEMIST, BUT IN THE FIELDS OF PHYSICS AND TECHNOLOGY I AM MERELY A DAZZLING AMATEUR.
SOMETHING'S MOVING IN HERE.
THE GUY, SUBJECT X, WAS TRYING TO POWER IT UP OFF A SPACECRAFT'S REACTORS. 'RORO TOOK OUT THE SHIP'S ELECTRICS BEFORE HE COULD GET THE JUICE INTO THE BOX.
AND WHAT, PRAY, IS THIS?
SAMPLE FROM SUBJECT X. FOUND A STERILE SYRINGE IN THE MEDKIT.
DARE I ASK HOW SUBJECT X CAME TO DONATE HIS BLOOD?
HE KILLED HIMSELF.
I'M NOT SURPRISED. HE DIDN'T WANT TO EXPOSE HIS FRIENDS.
FRIENDS?
LOGAN DIDN'T HELP?
NOT THIS TIME. SUBJECT X WANTED TO MAKE SURE WE DIDN'T LEARN ANYTHING FROM HIM.
I'VE BEEN PROCESSING THE REST OF THE NOTEBOOK YOU FOUND. SUBJECT X HAS COMRADES. WE ARE DEFINITELY LOOKING AT WHAT THEY USED TO CALL A "SECRET WAR" HERE.

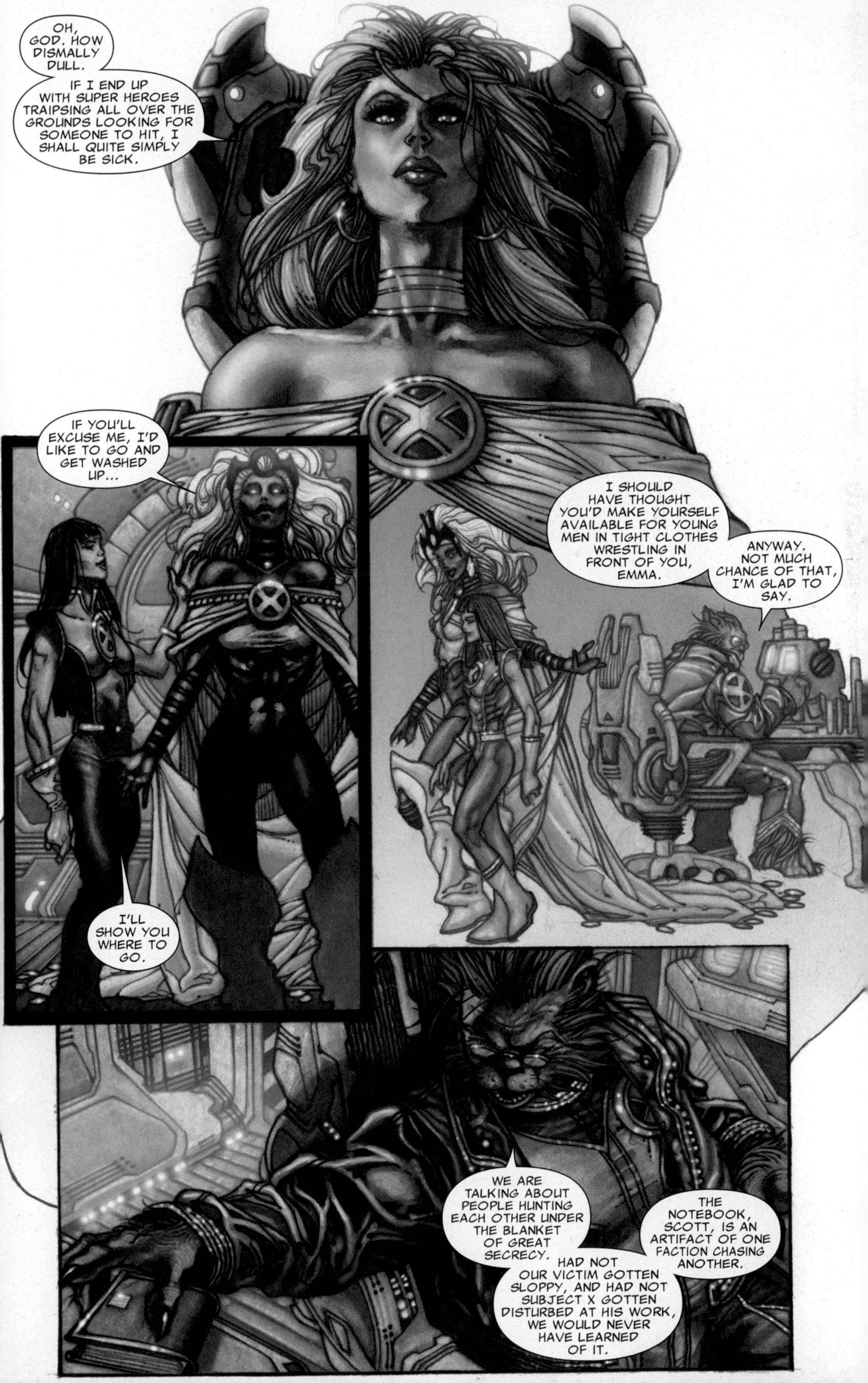
OH, GOD. HOW DISMALLY DULL.
IF I END UP WITH SUPER HEROES TRAIPSING ALL OVER THE GROUNDS LOOKING FOR SOMEONE TO HIT, I SHALL QUITE SIMPLY BE SICK.
IF YOU'LL EXCUSE ME, I'D LIKE TO GO AND GET WASHED UP...
I'LL SHOW YOU WHERE TO GO.
I SHOULD HAVE THOUGHT YOU'D MAKE YOURSELF AVAILABLE FOR YOUNG MEN IN TIGHT CLOTHES WRESTLING IN FRONT OF YOU, EMMA.
ANYWAY. NOT MUCH CHANCE OF THAT, I'M GLAD TO SAY.
WE ARE TALKING ABOUT PEOPLE HUNTING EACH OTHER UNDER THE BLANKET OF GREAT SECRECY.
THE NOTEBOOK, SCOTT, IS AN ARTIFACT OF ONE FACTION CHASING ANOTHER.
HAD NOT OUR VICTIM GOTTEN SLOPPY, AND HAD NOT SUBJECT X GOTTEN DISTURBED AT HIS WORK, WE WOULD NEVER HAVE LEARNED OF IT.

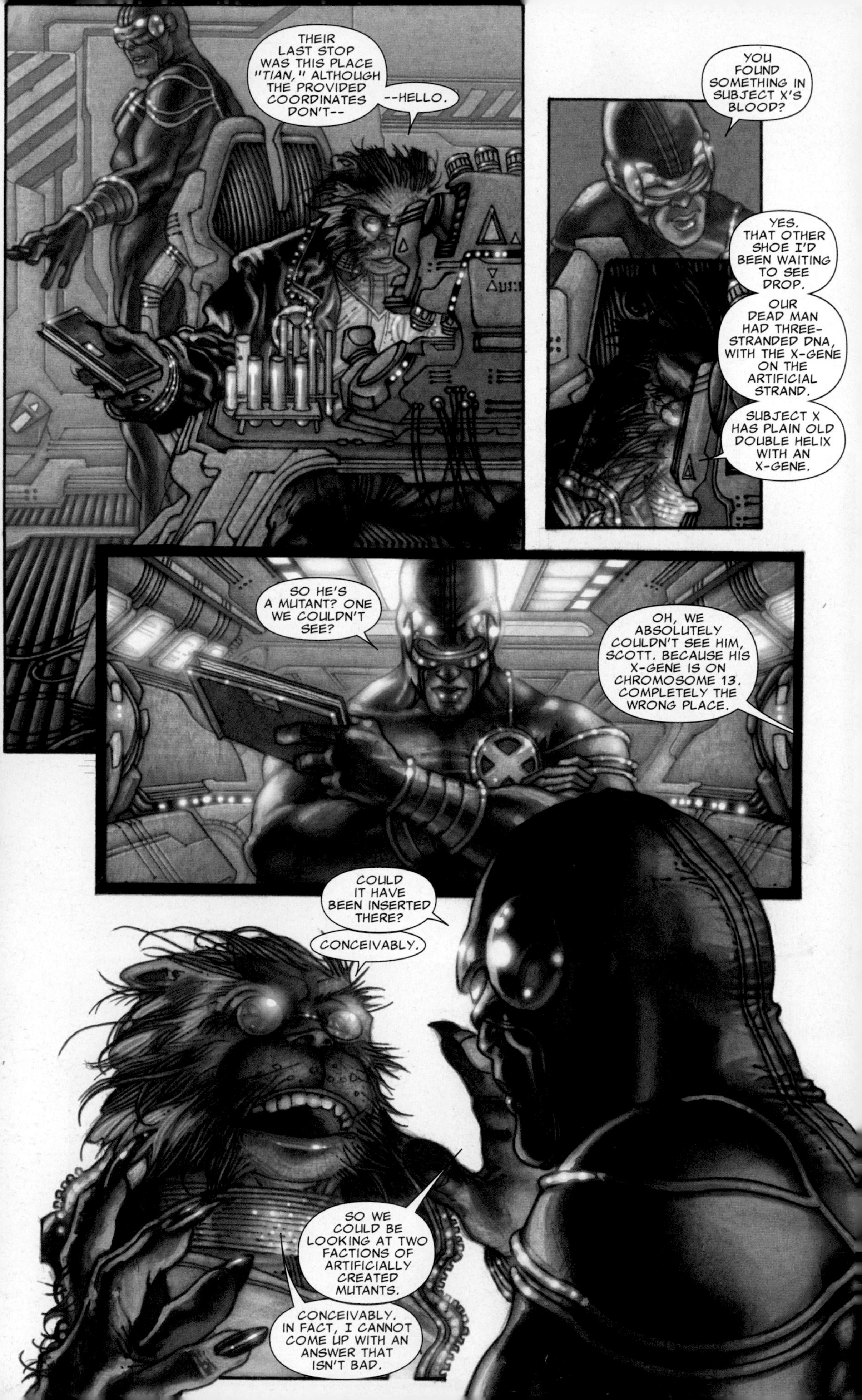
THEIR LAST STOP WAS THIS PLACE "TIAN," ALTHOUGH THE PROVIDED COORDINATES DON'T--
--HELLO.
YOU FOUND SOMETHING IN SUBJECT X'S BLOOD?
YES. THAT OTHER SHOE I'D BEEN WAITING TO SEE DROP.
OUR DEAD MAN HAD THREE-STRANDED DNA, WITH THE X-GENE ON THE ARTIFICIAL STRAND.
SUBJECT X HAS PLAIN OLD DOUBLE HELIX WITH AN X-GENE.
SO HE'S A MUTANT? ONE WE COULDN'T SEE?
OH, WE ABSOLUTELY COULDN'T SEE HIM, SCOTT. BECAUSE HIS X-GENE IS ON CHROMOSOME 13. COMPLETELY THE WRONG PLACE.
COULD IT HAVE BEEN INSERTED THERE?
CONCEIVABLY.
SO WE COULD BE LOOKING AT TWO FACTIONS OF ARTIFICIALLY CREATED MUTANTS.
CONCEIVABLY. IN FACT, I CANNOT COME UP WITH AN ANSWER THAT ISN'T BAD.

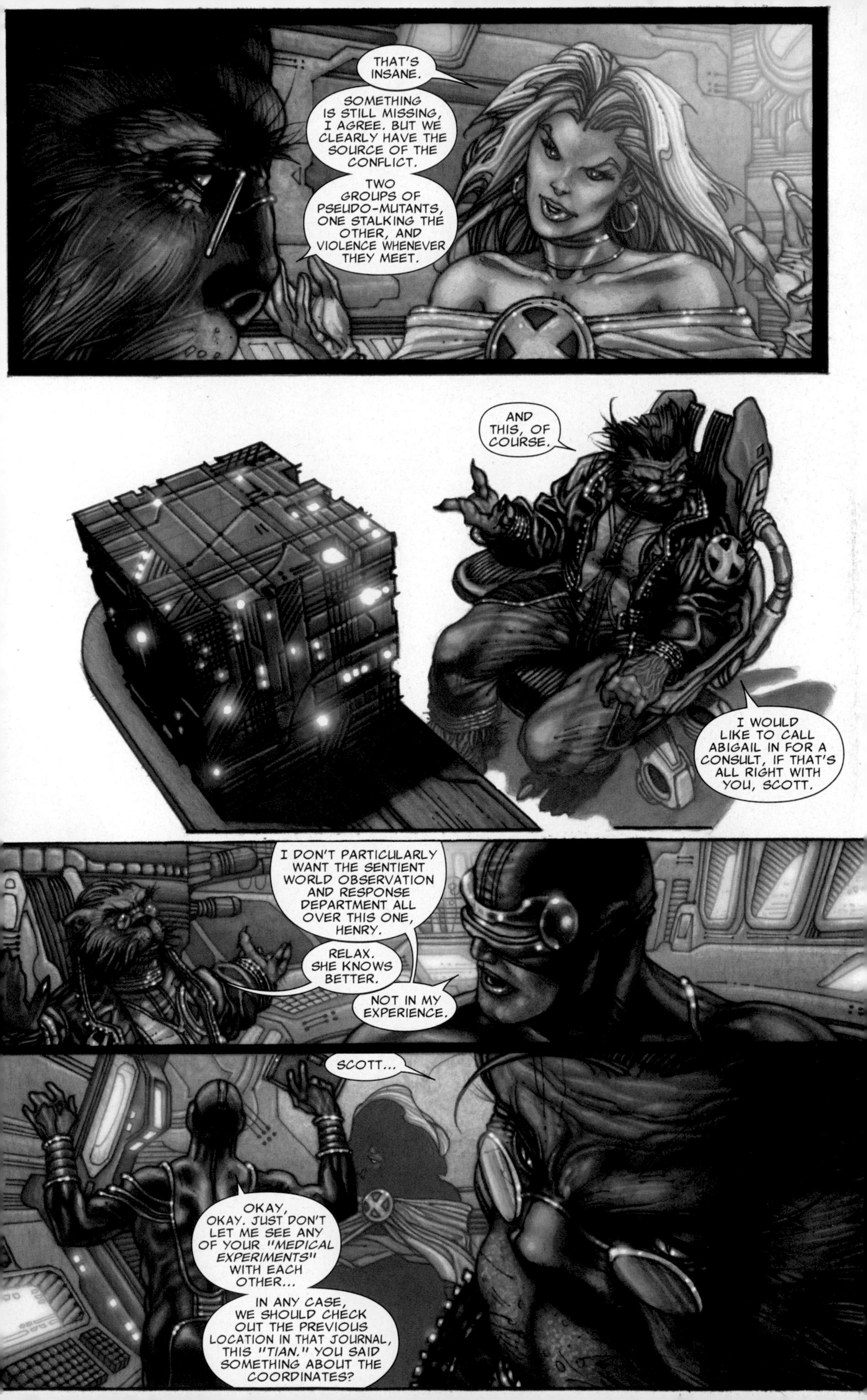
THAT'S INSANE.
SOMETHING IS STILL MISSING, I AGREE. BUT WE CLEARLY HAVE THE SOURCE OF THE CONFLICT.
TWO GROUPS OF PSEUDO-MUTANTS, ONE STALKING THE OTHER, AND VIOLENCE WHENEVER THEY MEET.
AND THIS, OF COURSE.
I WOULD LIKE TO CALL ABIGAIL IN FOR A CONSULT, IF THAT'S ALL RIGHT WITH YOU, SCOTT.
I DON'T PARTICULARLY WANT THE SENTIENT WORLD OBSERVATION AND RESPONSE DEPARTMENT ALL OVER THIS ONE, HENRY.
RELAX. SHE KNOWS BETTER.
NOT IN MY EXPERIENCE.
SCOTT...
OKAY, OKAY. JUST DON'T LET ME SEE ANY OF YOUR "MEDICAL EXPERIMENTS" WITH EACH OTHER...
IN ANY CASE, WE SHOULD CHECK OUT THE PREVIOUS LOCATION IN THAT JOURNAL, THIS "TIAN." YOU SAID SOMETHING ABOUT THE COORDINATES?

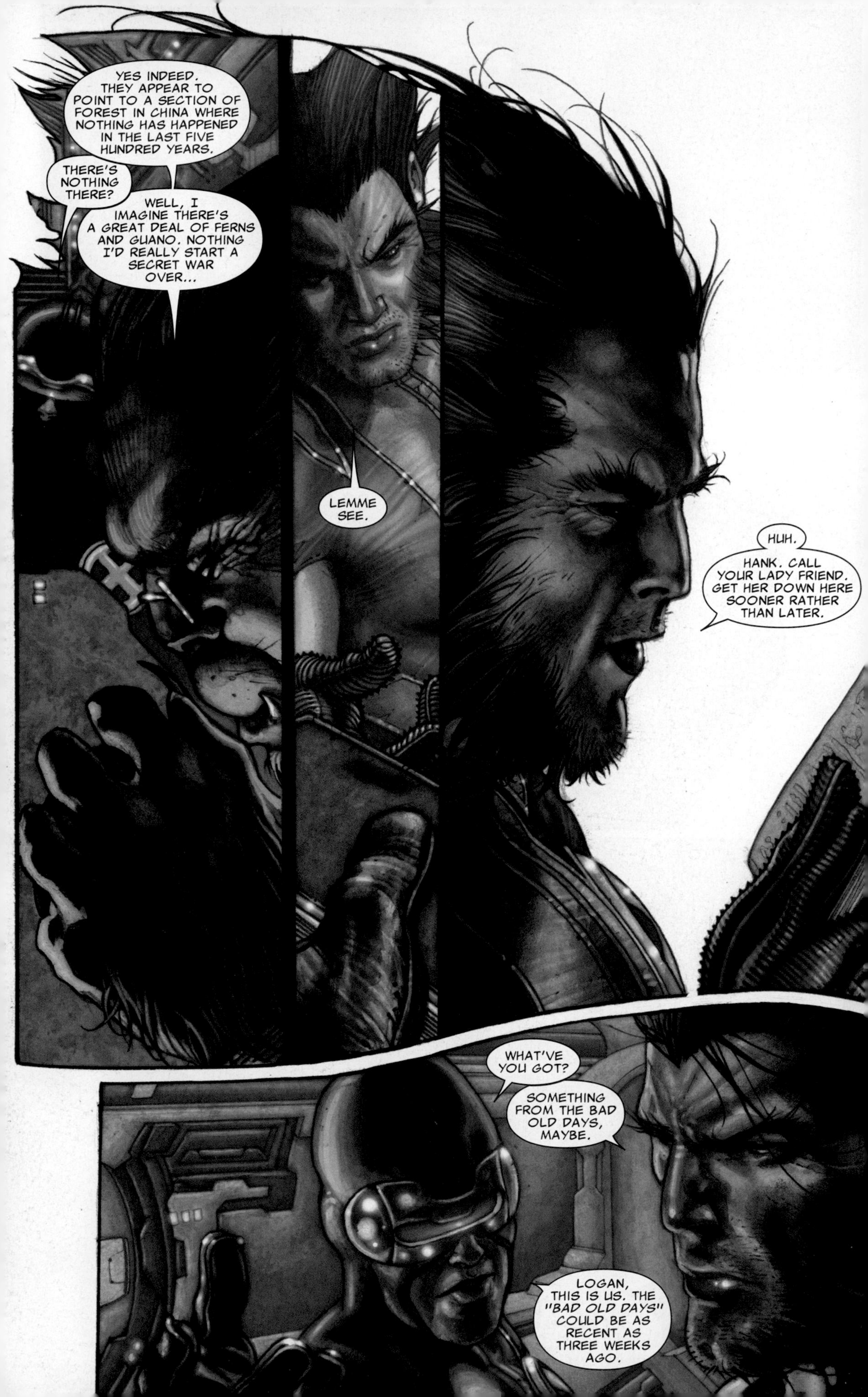
YES INDEED. THEY APPEAR TO POINT TO A SECTION OF FOREST IN CHINA WHERE NOTHING HAS HAPPENED IN THE LAST FIVE HUNDRED YEARS.
THERE'S NOTHING THERE?
WELL, I IMAGINE THERE'S A GREAT DEAL OF FERNS AND GUANO. NOTHING I'D REALLY START A SECRET WAR OVER...
LEMME SEE.
HUH.
HANK. CALL YOUR LADY FRIEND. GET HER DOWN HERE SOONER RATHER THAN LATER.
WHAT'VE YOU GOT?
SOMETHING FROM THE BAD OLD DAYS, MAYBE.
LOGAN, THIS IS US. THE "BAD OLD DAYS" COULD BE AS RECENT AS THREE WEEKS AGO.

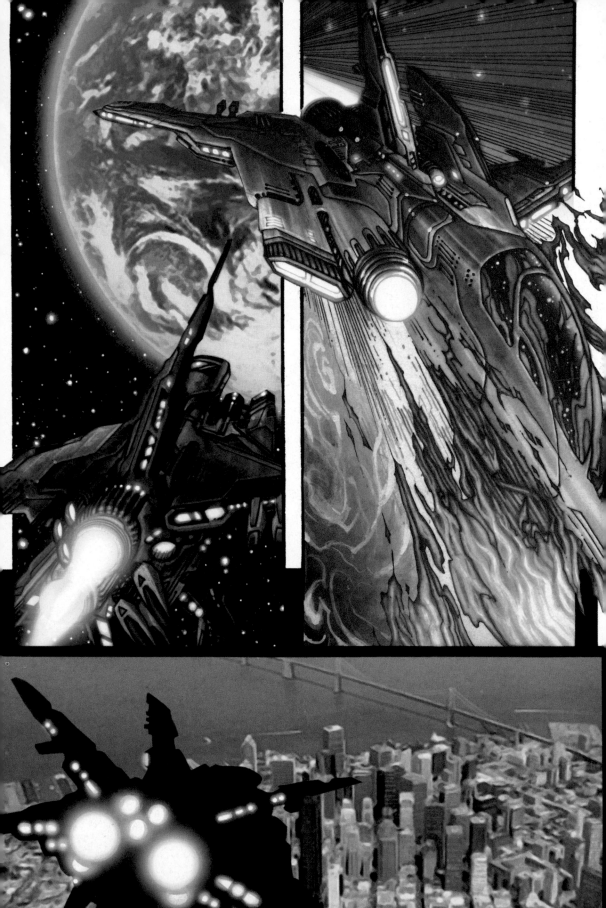

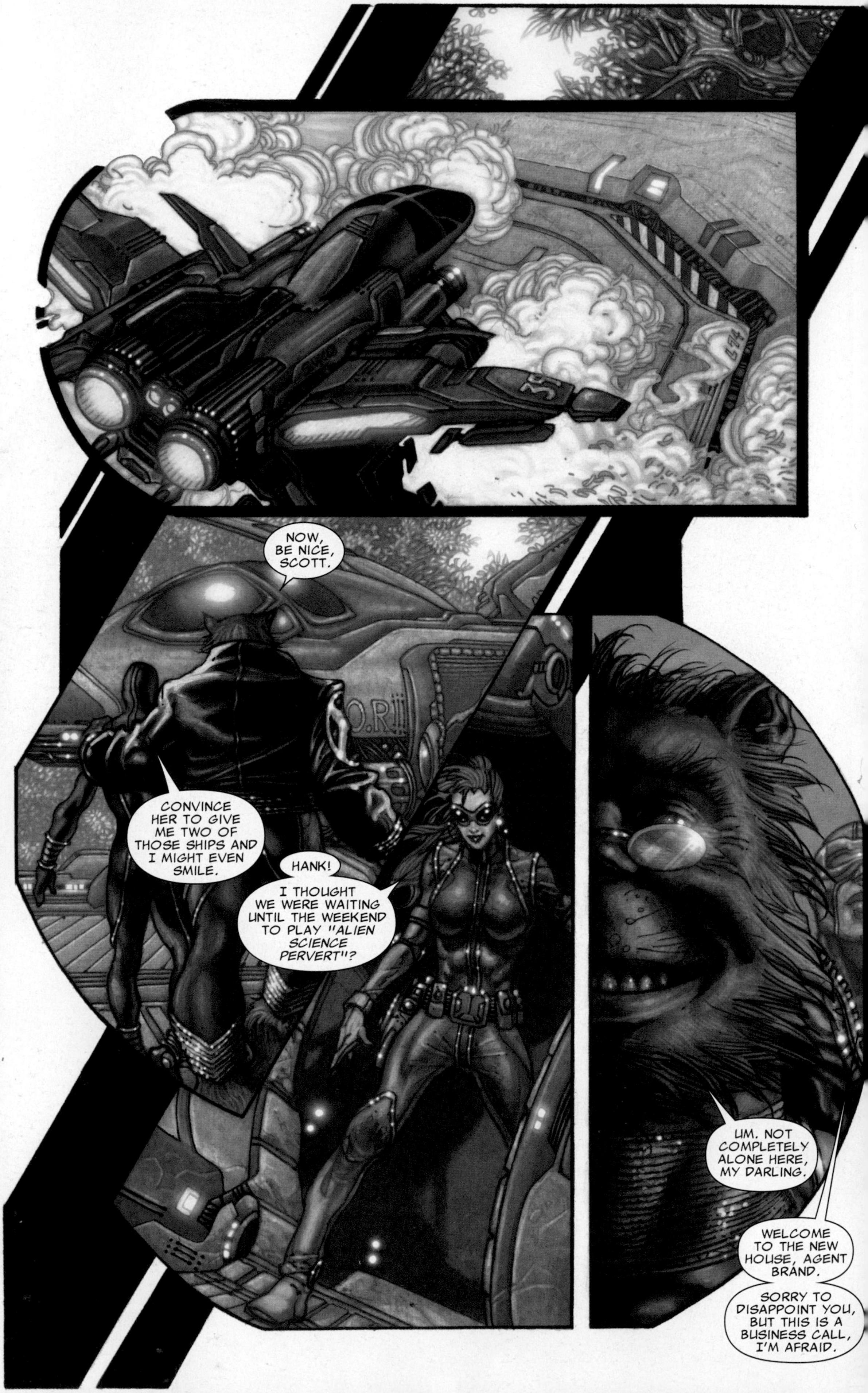
NOW, BE NICE, SCOTT.
CONVINCE HER TO GIVE ME TWO OF THOSE SHIPS AND I MIGHT EVEN SMILE.
HANK!
I THOUGHT WE WERE WAITING UNTIL THE WEEKEND TO PLAY "ALIEN SCIENCE PERVERT"?
UM. NOT COMPLETELY ALONE HERE, MY DARLING.
WELCOME TO THE NEW HOUSE, AGENT BRAND.
SORRY TO DISAPPOINT YOU, BUT THIS IS A BUSINESS CALL, I'M AFRAID.

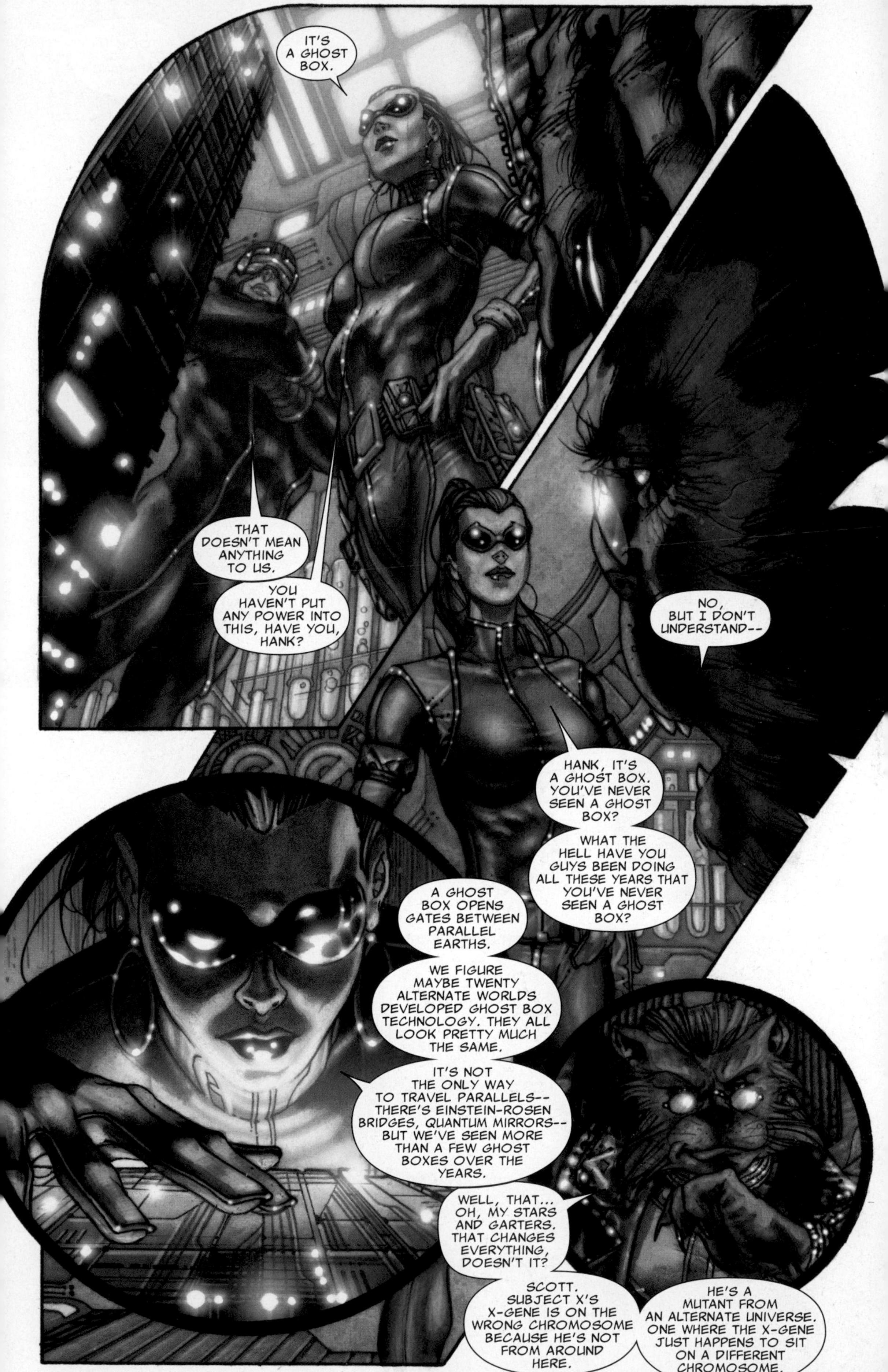
IT'S A GHOST BOX.
THAT DOESN'T MEAN ANYTHING TO US.
YOU HAVEN'T PUT ANY POWER INTO THIS, HAVE YOU, HANK?
NO, BUT I DON'T UNDERSTAND--
HANK, IT'S A GHOST BOX. YOU'VE NEVER SEEN A GHOST BOX?
WHAT THE HELL HAVE YOU GUYS BEEN DOING ALL THESE YEARS THAT YOU'VE NEVER SEEN A GHOST BOX?
A GHOST BOX OPENS GATES BETWEEN PARALLEL EARTHS.
WE FIGURE MAYBE TWENTY ALTERNATE WORLDS DEVELOPED GHOST BOX TECHNOLOGY. THEY ALL LOOK PRETTY MUCH THE SAME.
IT'S NOT THE ONLY WAY TO TRAVEL PARALLELS-- THERE'S EINSTEIN-ROSEN BRIDGES, QUANTUM MIRRORS-- BUT WE'VE SEEN MORE THAN A FEW GHOST BOXES OVER THE YEARS.
WELL, THAT... OH, MY STARS AND GARTERS. THAT CHANGES EVERYTHING, DOESN'T IT?
SCOTT. SUBJECT X'S X-GENE IS ON THE WRONG CHROMOSOME BECAUSE HE'S NOT FROM AROUND HERE.
HE'S A MUTANT FROM AN ALTERNATE UNIVERSE. ONE WHERE THE X-GENE JUST HAPPENS TO SIT ON A DIFFERENT CHROMOSOME.

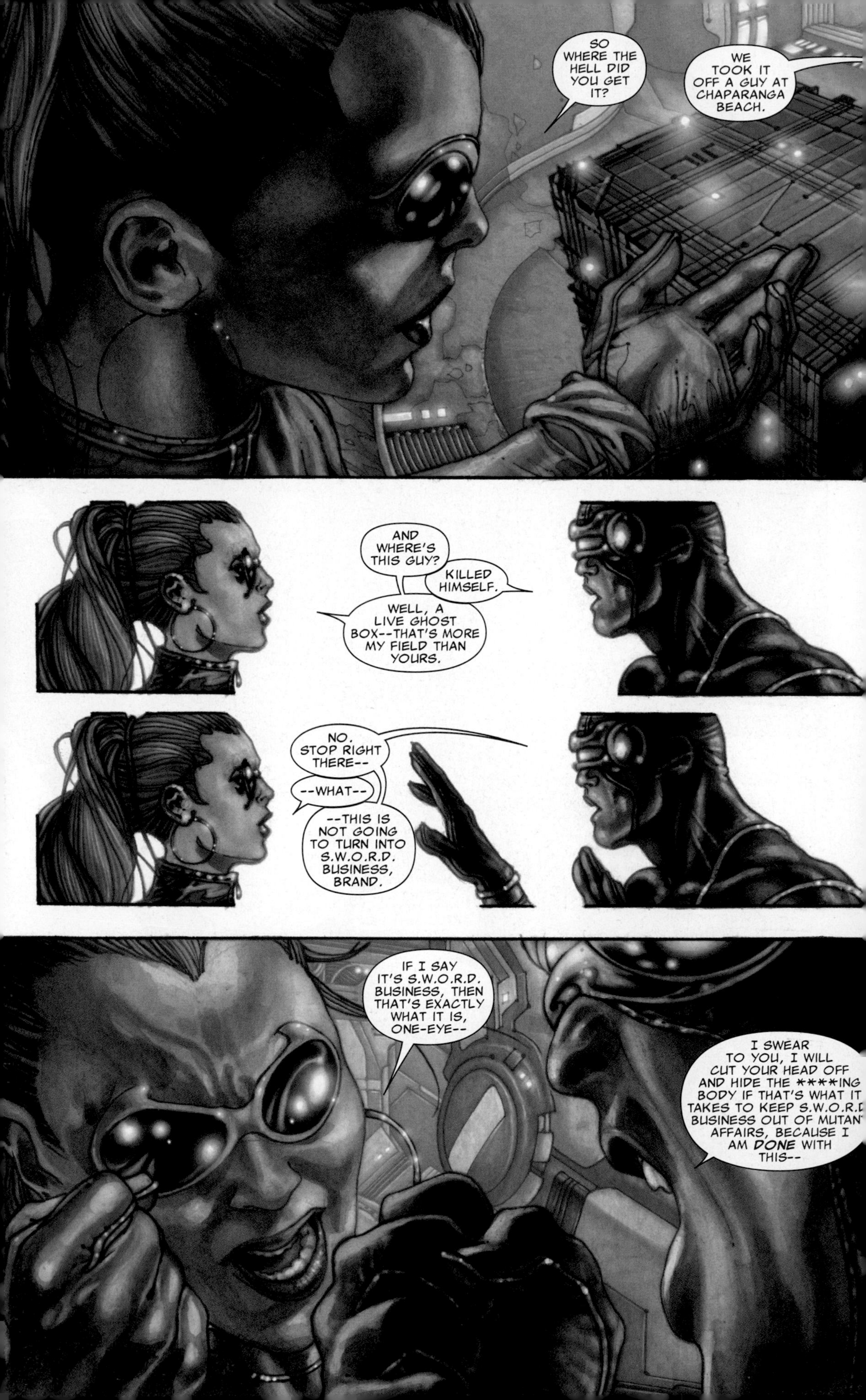

SO WHERE THE HELL DID YOU GET IT?
WE TOOK IT OFF A GUY AT CHAPARANGA BEACH.
AND WHERE'S THIS GUY?
KILLED HIMSELF.
WELL, A LIVE GHOST BOX--THAT'S MORE MY FIELD THAN YOURS.
NO. STOP RIGHT THERE--
--WHAT--
--THIS IS NOT GOING TO TURN INTO S.W.O.R.D. BUSINESS, BRAND.
IF I SAY IT'S S.W.O.R.D. BUSINESS, THEN THAT'S EXACTLY WHAT IT IS, ONE-EYE--
I SWEAR TO YOU, I WILL CUT YOUR HEAD OFF AND HIDE THE ****ING BODY IF THAT'S WHAT IT TAKES TO KEEP S.W.O.R.D BUSINESS OUT OF MUTANT AFFAIRS, BECAUSE I AM *DONE* WITH THIS--

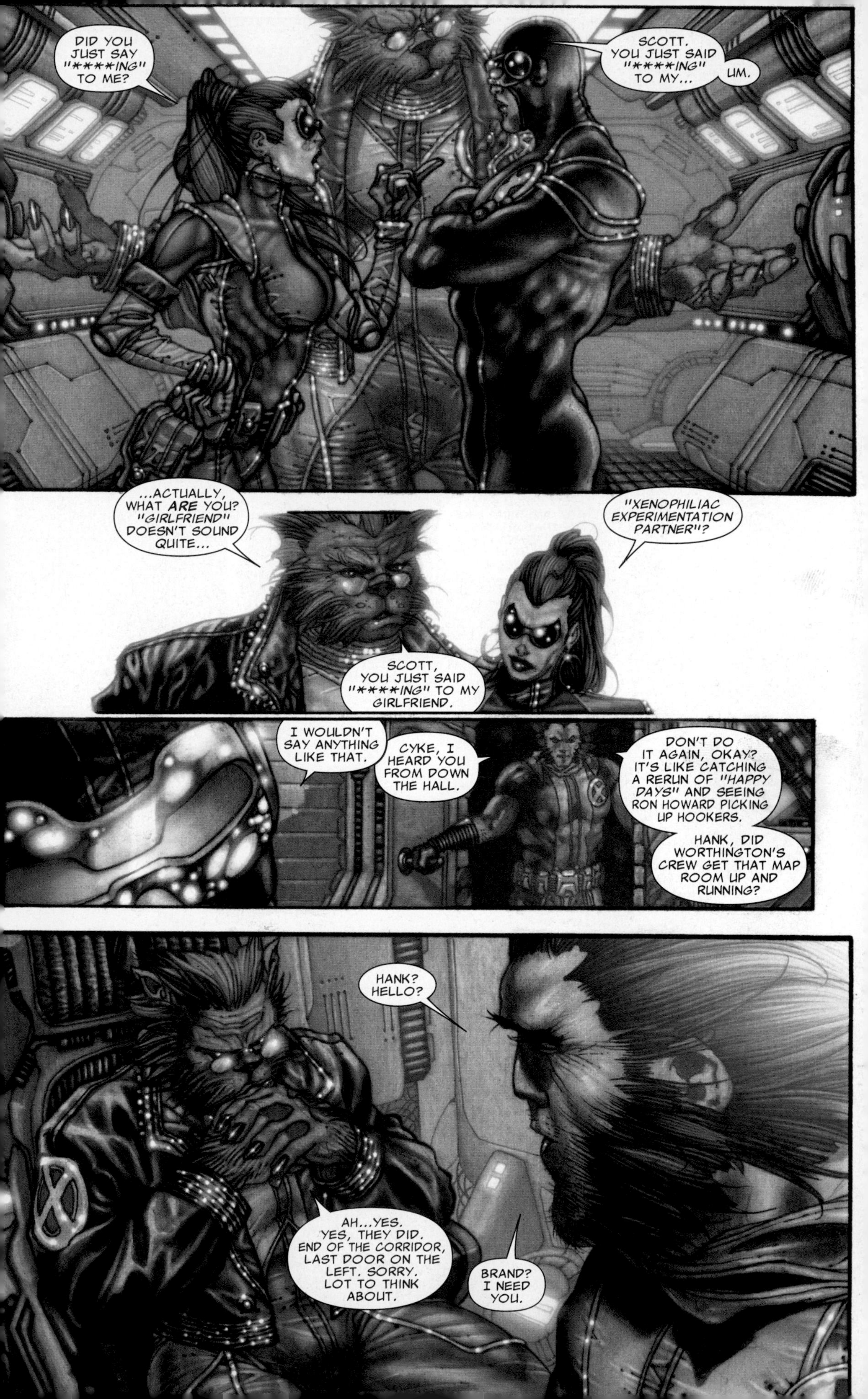
DID YOU JUST SAY "****ING" TO ME?
SCOTT. YOU JUST SAID "****ING" TO MY...
UM.
...ACTUALLY, WHAT *ARE* YOU? "GIRLFRIEND" DOESN'T SOUND QUITE...
"XENOPHILIAC EXPERIMENTATION PARTNER"?
SCOTT, YOU JUST SAID "****ING" TO MY GIRLFRIEND.
I WOULDN'T SAY ANYTHING LIKE THAT.
CYKE, I HEARD YOU FROM DOWN THE HALL.
DON'T DO IT AGAIN, OKAY? IT'S LIKE CATCHING A RERUN OF "HAPPY DAYS" AND SEEING RON HOWARD PICKING UP HOOKERS.
HANK, DID WORTHINGTON'S CREW GET THAT MAP ROOM UP AND RUNNING?
HANK? HELLO?
AH...YES. YES, THEY DID. END OF THE CORRIDOR, LAST DOOR ON THE LEFT. SORRY. LOT TO THINK ABOUT.
BRAND? I NEED YOU.

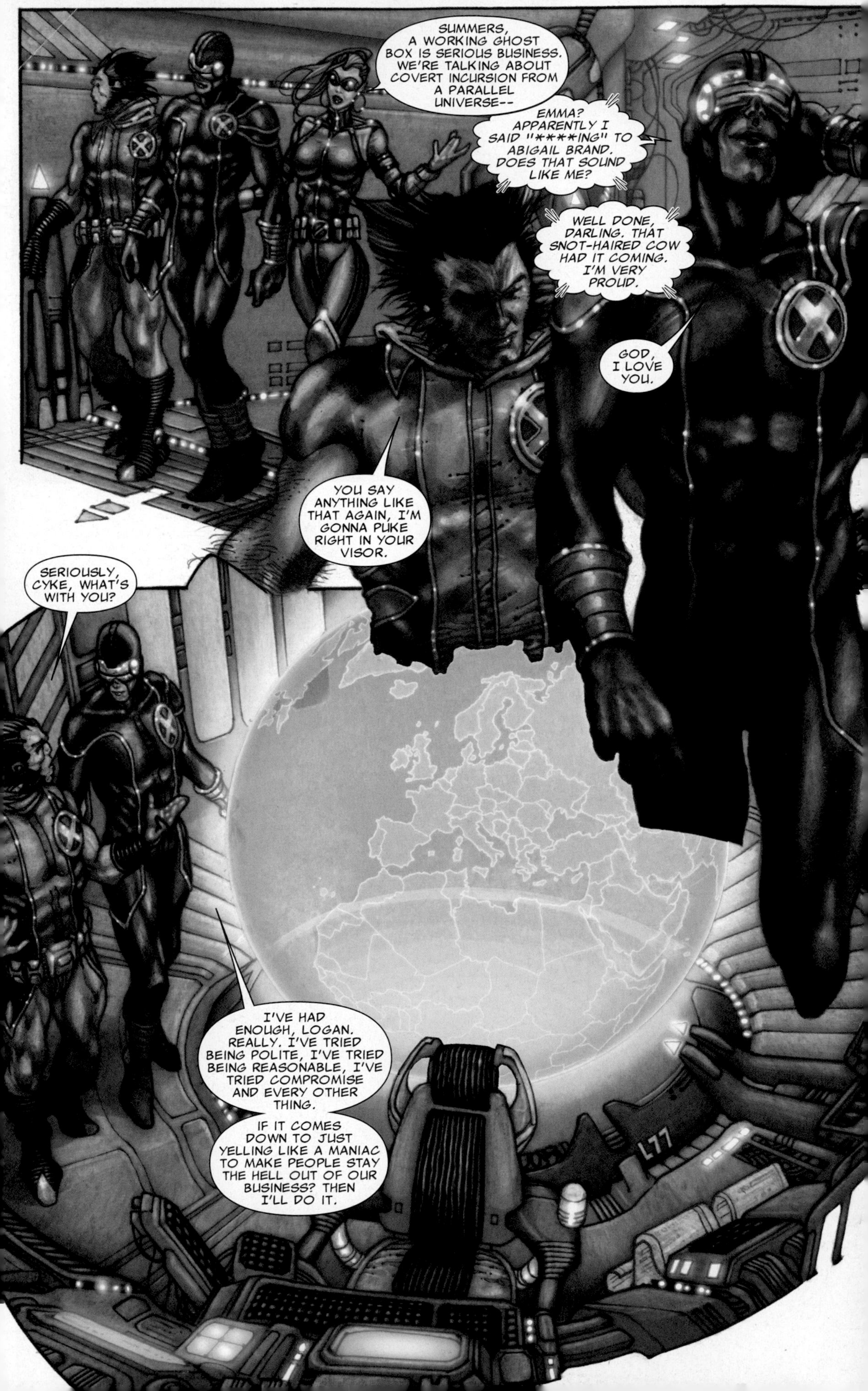
SUMMERS, A WORKING GHOST BOX IS SERIOUS BUSINESS. WE'RE TALKING ABOUT COVERT INCURSION FROM A PARALLEL UNIVERSE--
EMMA? APPARENTLY I SAID "****ING" TO ABIGAIL BRAND. DOES THAT SOUND LIKE ME?
WELL DONE, DARLING. THAT SNOT-HAIRED COW HAD IT COMING. I'M VERY PROUD.
GOD, I LOVE YOU.
YOU SAY ANYTHING LIKE THAT AGAIN, I'M GONNA PUKE RIGHT IN YOUR VISOR.
SERIOUSLY, CYKE, WHAT'S WITH YOU?
I'VE HAD ENOUGH, LOGAN. REALLY. I'VE TRIED BEING POLITE, I'VE TRIED BEING REASONABLE, I'VE TRIED COMPROMISE AND EVERY OTHER THING.
IF IT COMES DOWN TO JUST YELLING LIKE A MANIAC TO MAKE PEOPLE STAY THE HELL OUT OF OUR BUSINESS? THEN I'LL DO IT.
L77

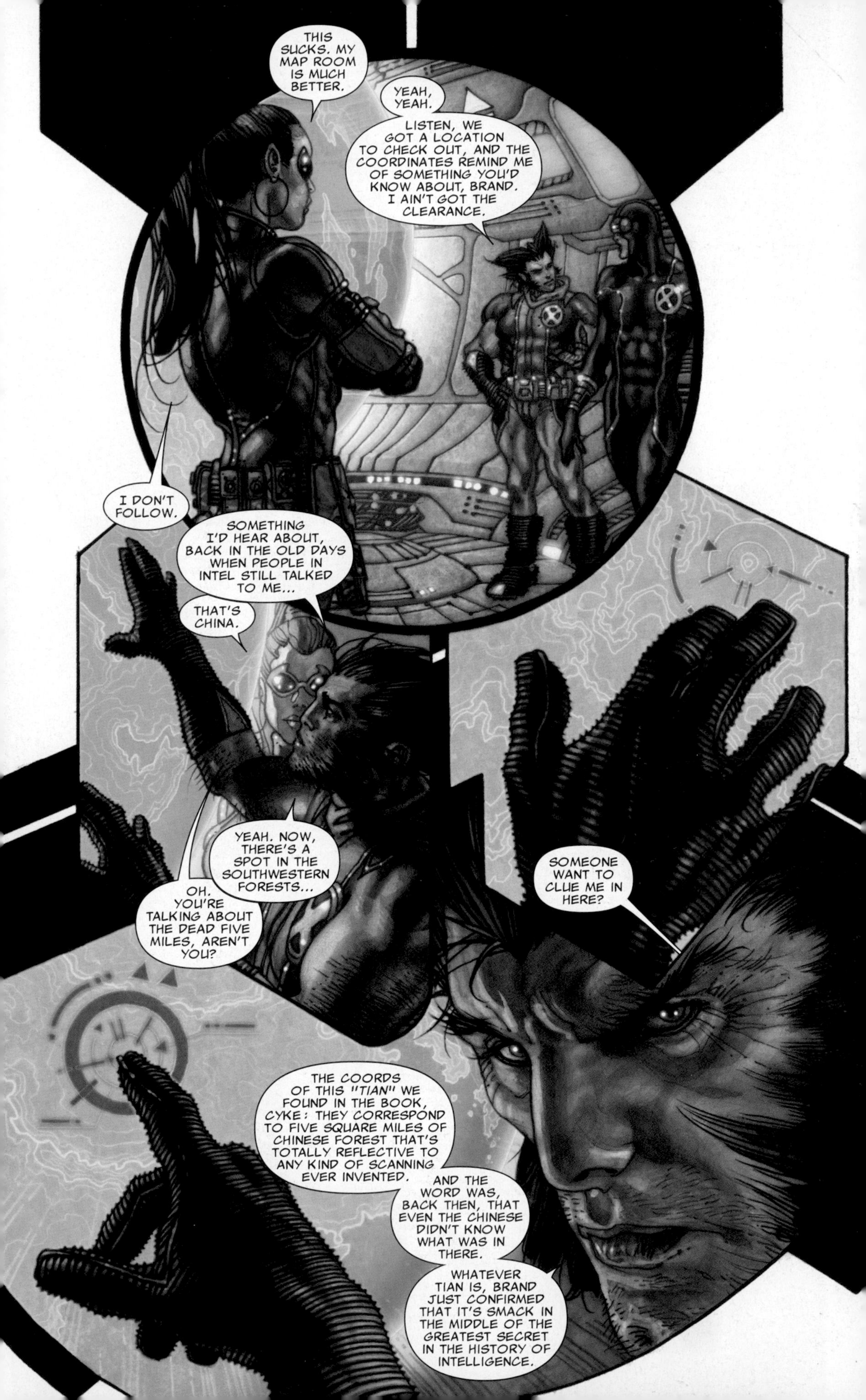
THIS SUCKS. MY MAP ROOM IS MUCH BETTER.
YEAH, YEAH.
LISTEN, WE GOT A LOCATION TO CHECK OUT, AND THE COORDINATES REMIND ME OF SOMETHING YOU'D KNOW ABOUT, BRAND. I AIN'T GOT THE CLEARANCE.
I DON'T FOLLOW.
SOMETHING I'D HEAR ABOUT, BACK IN THE OLD DAYS WHEN PEOPLE IN INTEL STILL TALKED TO ME...
THAT'S CHINA.
YEAH. NOW, THERE'S A SPOT IN THE SOUTHWESTERN FORESTS...
OH. YOU'RE TALKING ABOUT THE DEAD FIVE MILES, AREN'T YOU?
SOMEONE WANT TO CLUE ME IN HERE?
THE COORDS OF THIS "TIAN" WE FOUND IN THE BOOK, CYKE: THEY CORRESPOND TO FIVE SQUARE MILES OF CHINESE FOREST THAT'S TOTALLY REFLECTIVE TO ANY KIND OF SCANNING EVER INVENTED.
AND THE WORD WAS, BACK THEN, THAT EVEN THE CHINESE DIDN'T KNOW WHAT WAS IN THERE.
WHATEVER TIAN IS, BRAND JUST CONFIRMED THAT IT'S SMACK IN THE MIDDLE OF THE GREATEST SECRET IN THE HISTORY OF INTELLIGENCE.

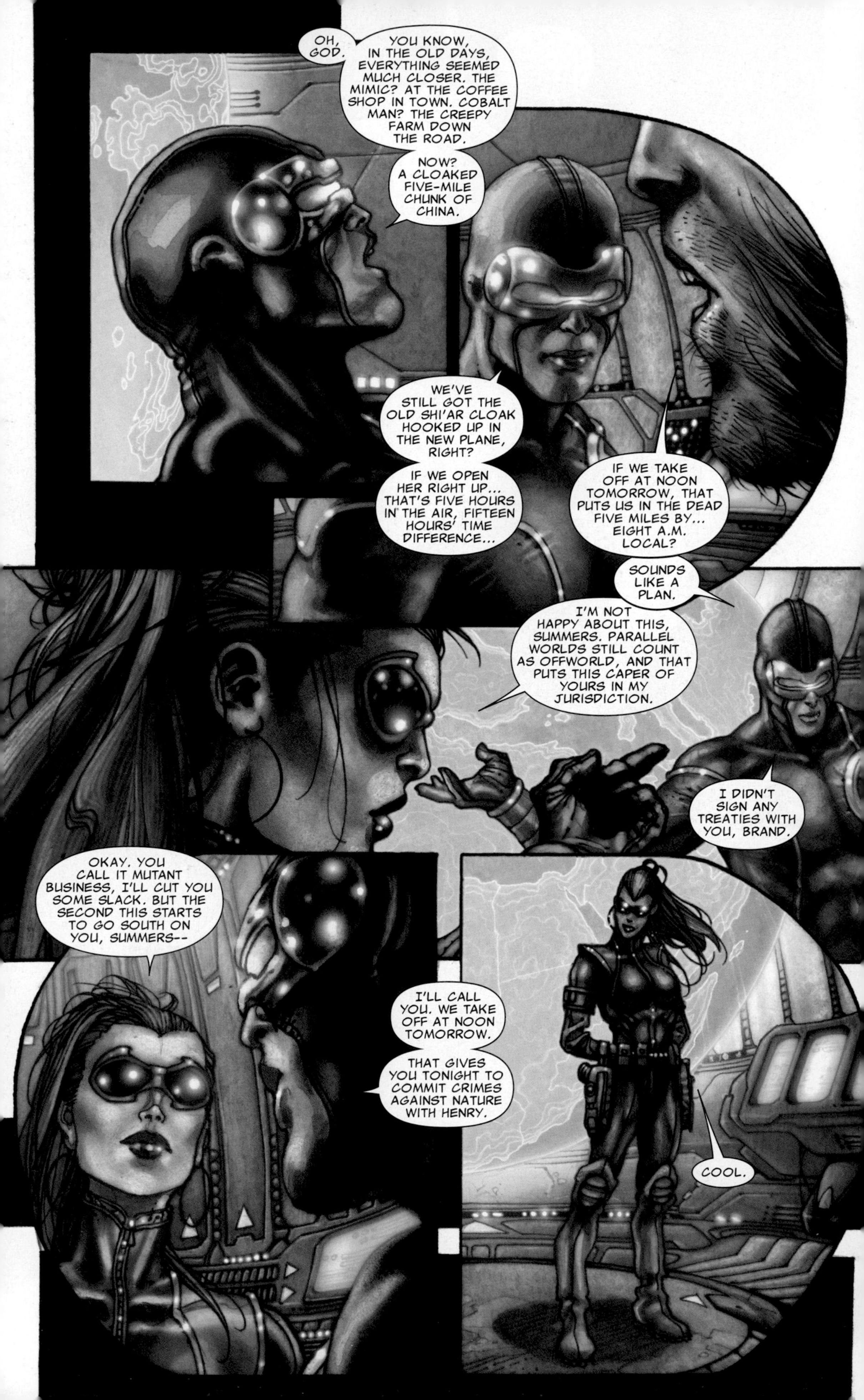
OH, GOD.
YOU KNOW, IN THE OLD DAYS, EVERYTHING SEEMED MUCH CLOSER. THE MIMIC? AT THE COFFEE SHOP IN TOWN. COBALT MAN? THE CREEPY FARM DOWN THE ROAD.
NOW? A CLOAKED FIVE-MILE CHUNK OF CHINA.
WE'VE STILL GOT THE OLD SHI'AR CLOAK HOOKED UP IN THE NEW PLANE, RIGHT?
IF WE OPEN HER RIGHT UP... THAT'S FIVE HOURS IN THE AIR, FIFTEEN HOURS' TIME DIFFERENCE...
IF WE TAKE OFF AT NOON TOMORROW, THAT PUTS US IN THE DEAD FIVE MILES BY... EIGHT A.M. LOCAL?
SOUNDS LIKE A PLAN.
I'M NOT HAPPY ABOUT THIS, SUMMERS. PARALLEL WORLDS STILL COUNT AS OFFWORLD, AND THAT PUTS THIS CAPER OF YOURS IN MY JURISDICTION.
I DIDN'T SIGN ANY TREATIES WITH YOU, BRAND.
OKAY. YOU CALL IT MUTANT BUSINESS, I'LL CUT YOU SOME SLACK. BUT THE SECOND THIS STARTS TO GO SOUTH ON YOU, SUMMERS--
I'LL CALL YOU. WE TAKE OFF AT NOON TOMORROW.
THAT GIVES YOU TONIGHT TO COMMIT CRIMES AGAINST NATURE WITH HENRY.
COOL.

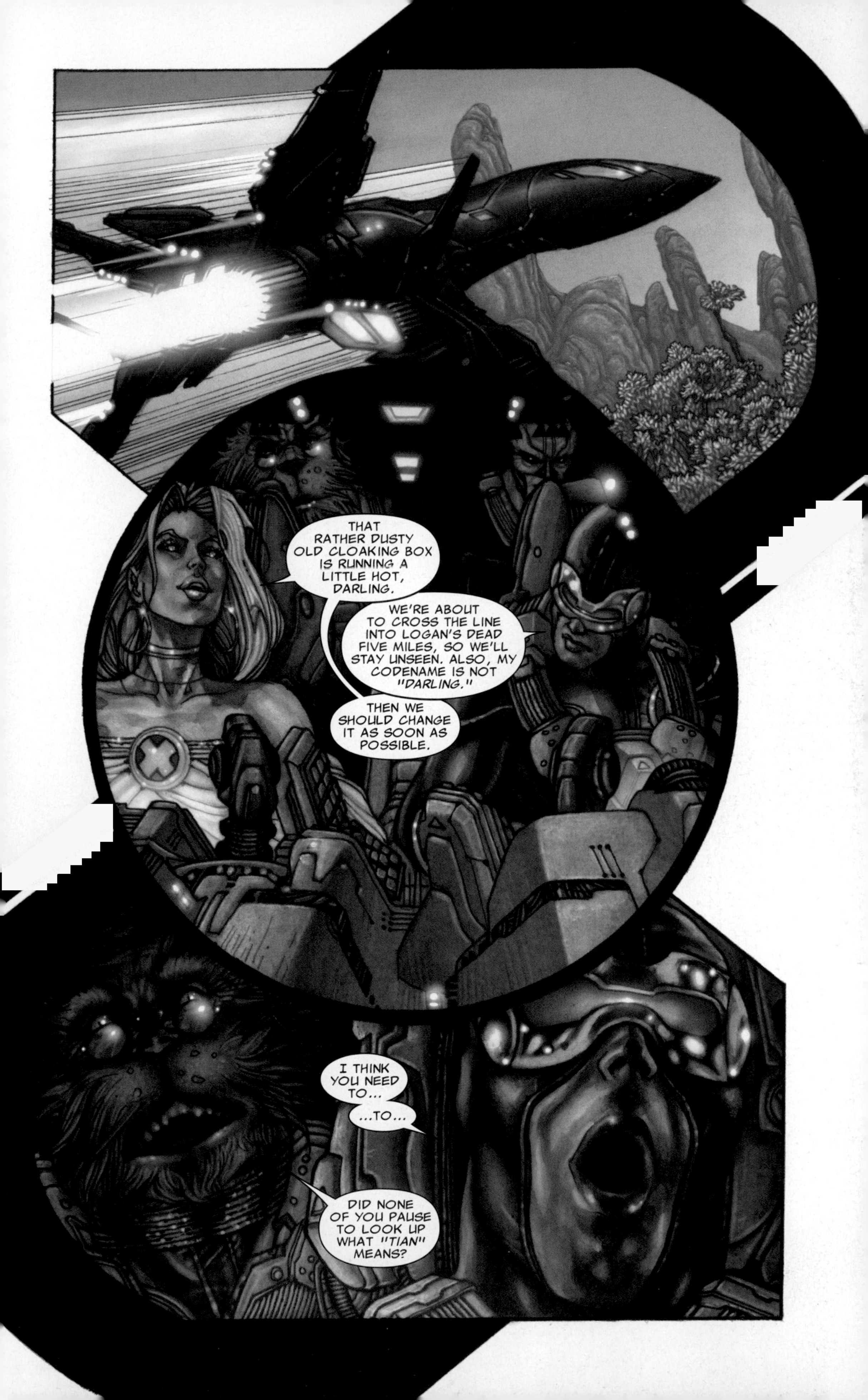
THAT RATHER DUSTY OLD CLOAKING BOX IS RUNNING A LITTLE HOT, DARLING.
WE'RE ABOUT TO CROSS THE LINE INTO LOGAN'S DEAD FIVE MILES, SO WE'LL STAY UNSEEN. ALSO, MY CODENAME IS NOT "DARLING."
THEN WE SHOULD CHANGE IT AS SOON AS POSSIBLE.
I THINK YOU NEED TO...
...TO...
DID NONE OF YOU PAUSE TO LOOK UP WHAT "TIAN" MEANS?

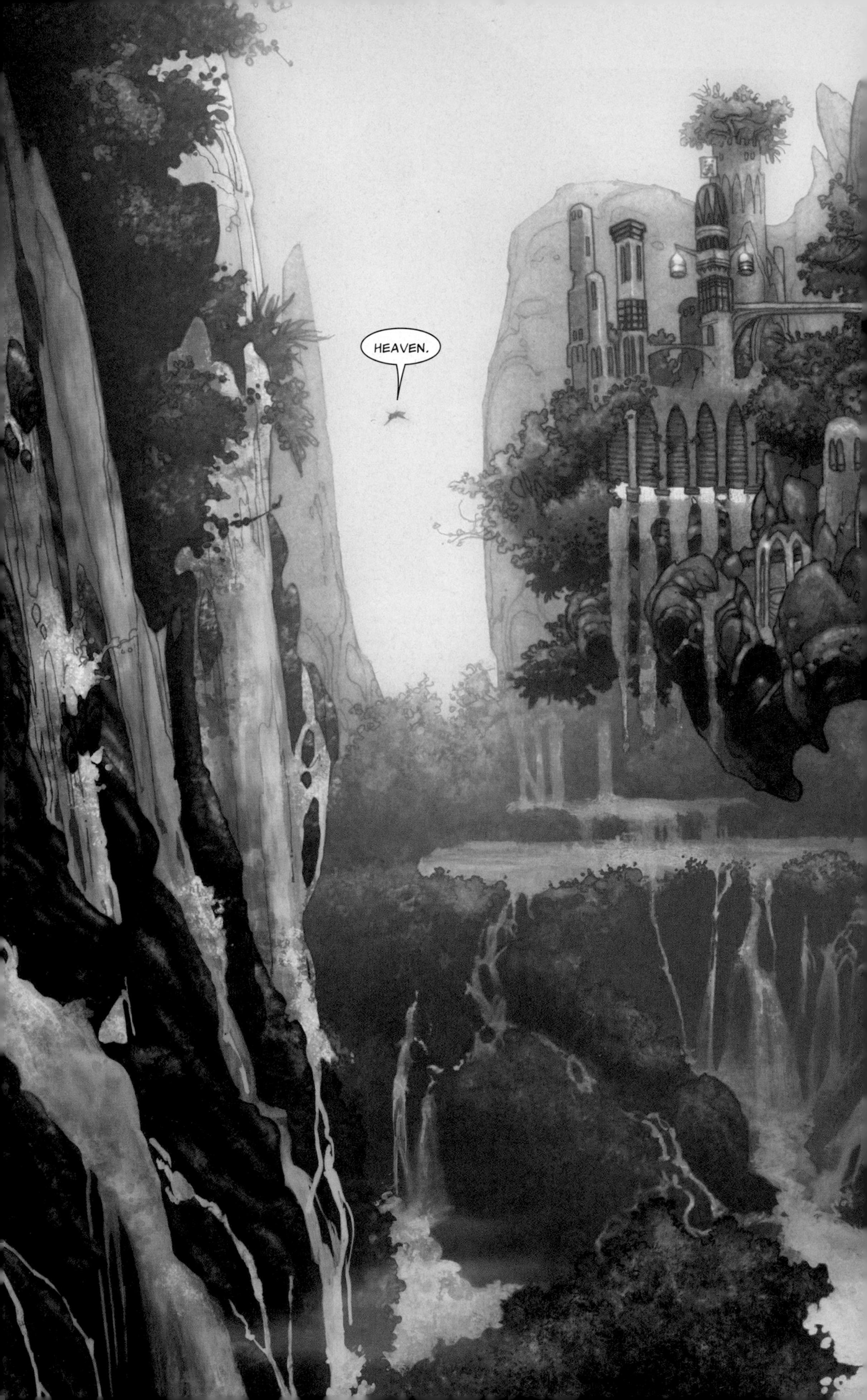
HEAVEN.

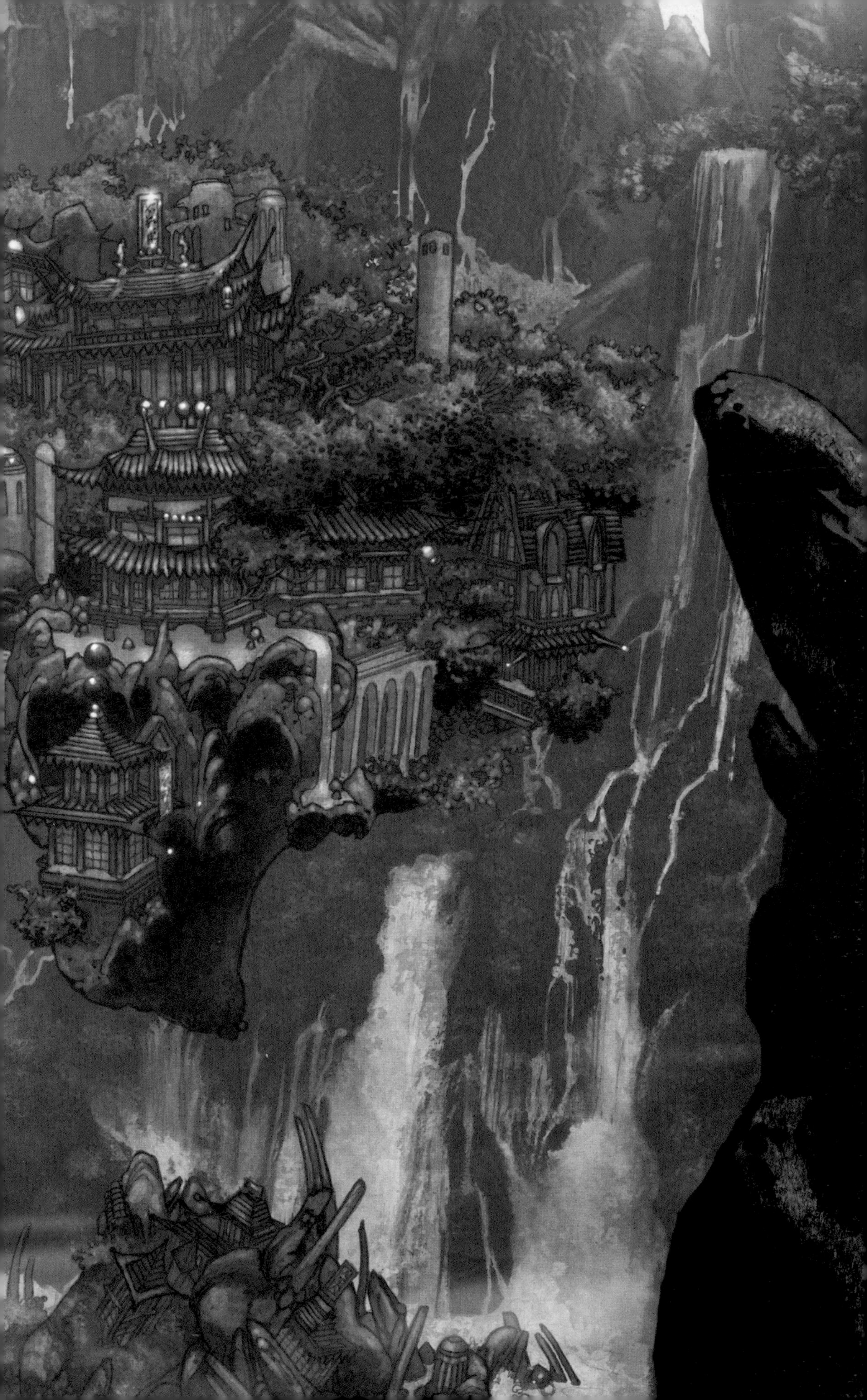

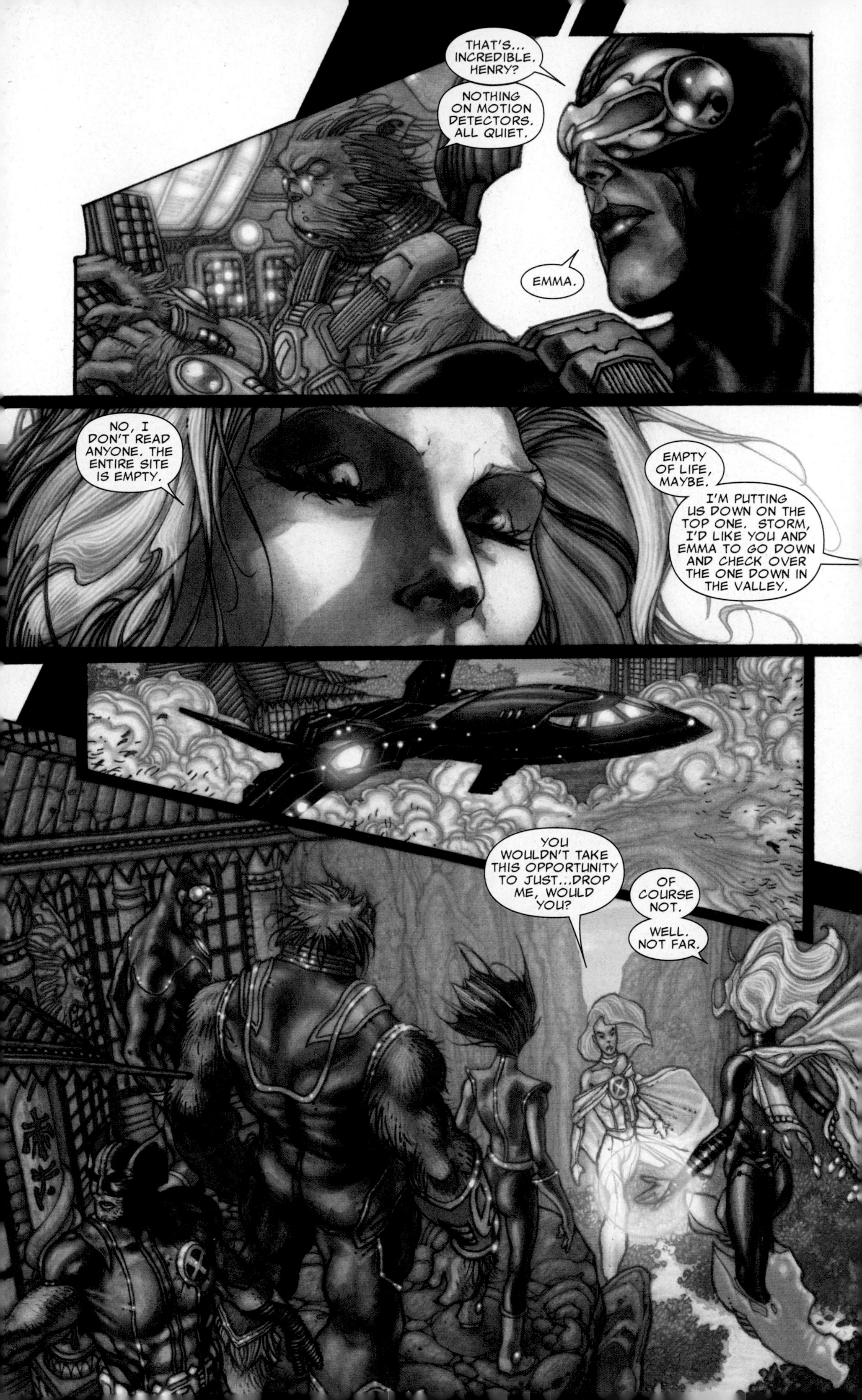
THAT'S... INCREDIBLE. HENRY?
NOTHING ON MOTION DETECTORS. ALL QUIET.
EMMA.
NO, I DON'T READ ANYONE. THE ENTIRE SITE IS EMPTY.
EMPTY OF LIFE, MAYBE.
I'M PUTTING US DOWN ON THE TOP ONE. STORM, I'D LIKE YOU AND EMMA TO GO DOWN AND CHECK OVER THE ONE DOWN IN THE VALLEY.
YOU WOULDN'T TAKE THIS OPPORTUNITY TO JUST...DROP ME, WOULD YOU?
OF COURSE NOT.
WELL. NOT FAR.

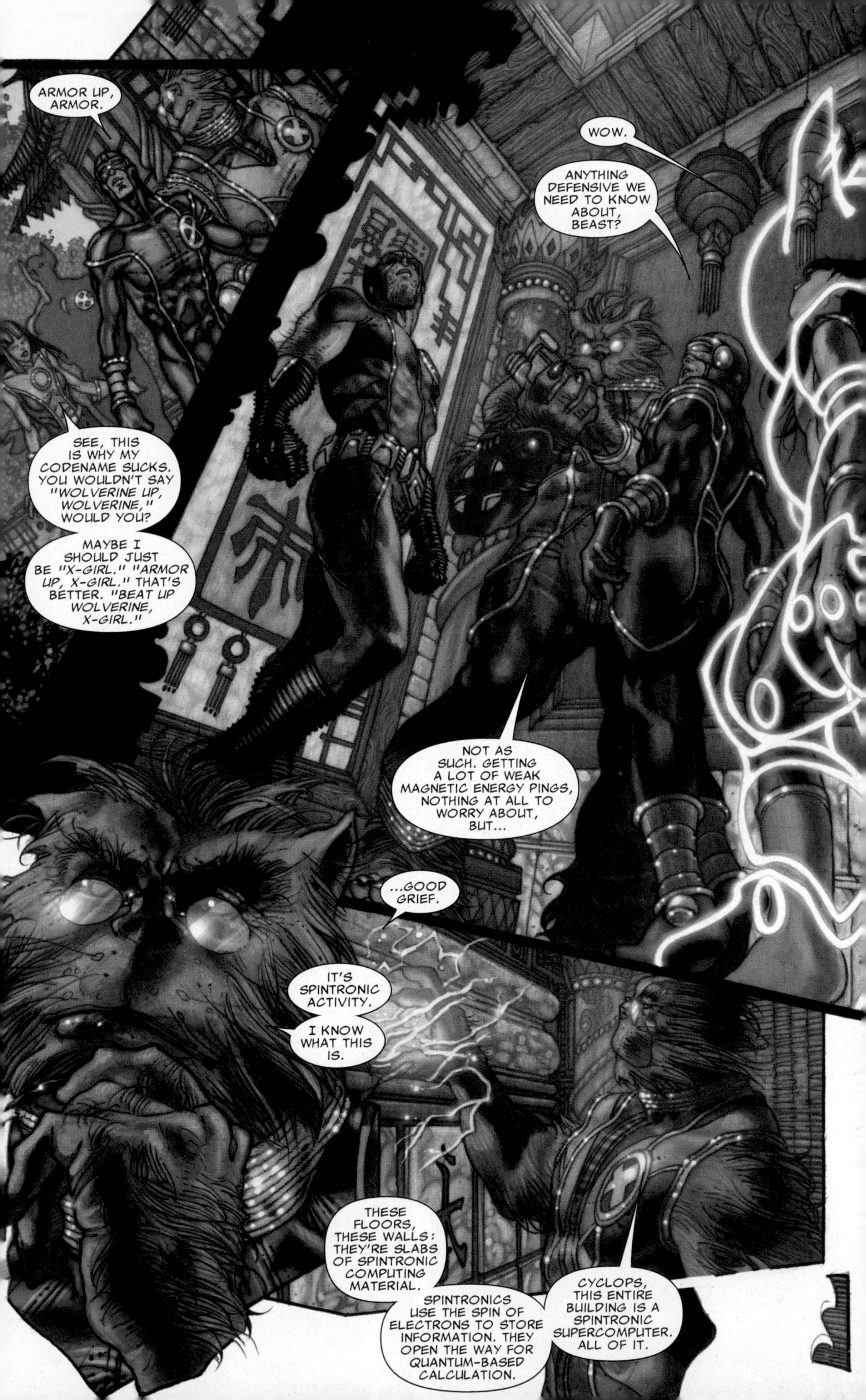
ARMOR UP, ARMOR.
SEE, THIS IS WHY MY CODENAME SUCKS. YOU WOULDN'T SAY "WOLVERINE UP, WOLVERINE," WOULD YOU?
MAYBE I SHOULD JUST BE "X-GIRL." "ARMOR UP, X-GIRL." THAT'S BETTER. "BEAT UP WOLVERINE, X-GIRL."
WOW.
ANYTHING DEFENSIVE WE NEED TO KNOW ABOUT, BEAST?
NOT AS SUCH. GETTING A LOT OF WEAK MAGNETIC ENERGY PINGS, NOTHING AT ALL TO WORRY ABOUT, BUT...
...GOOD GRIEF.
IT'S SPINTRONIC ACTIVITY.
I KNOW WHAT THIS IS.
THESE FLOORS, THESE WALLS: THEY'RE SLABS OF SPINTRONIC COMPUTING MATERIAL.
SPINTRONICS USE THE SPIN OF ELECTRONS TO STORE INFORMATION. THEY OPEN THE WAY FOR QUANTUM-BASED CALCULATION.
CYCLOPS, THIS ENTIRE BUILDING IS A SPINTRONIC SUPERCOMPUTER. ALL OF IT.

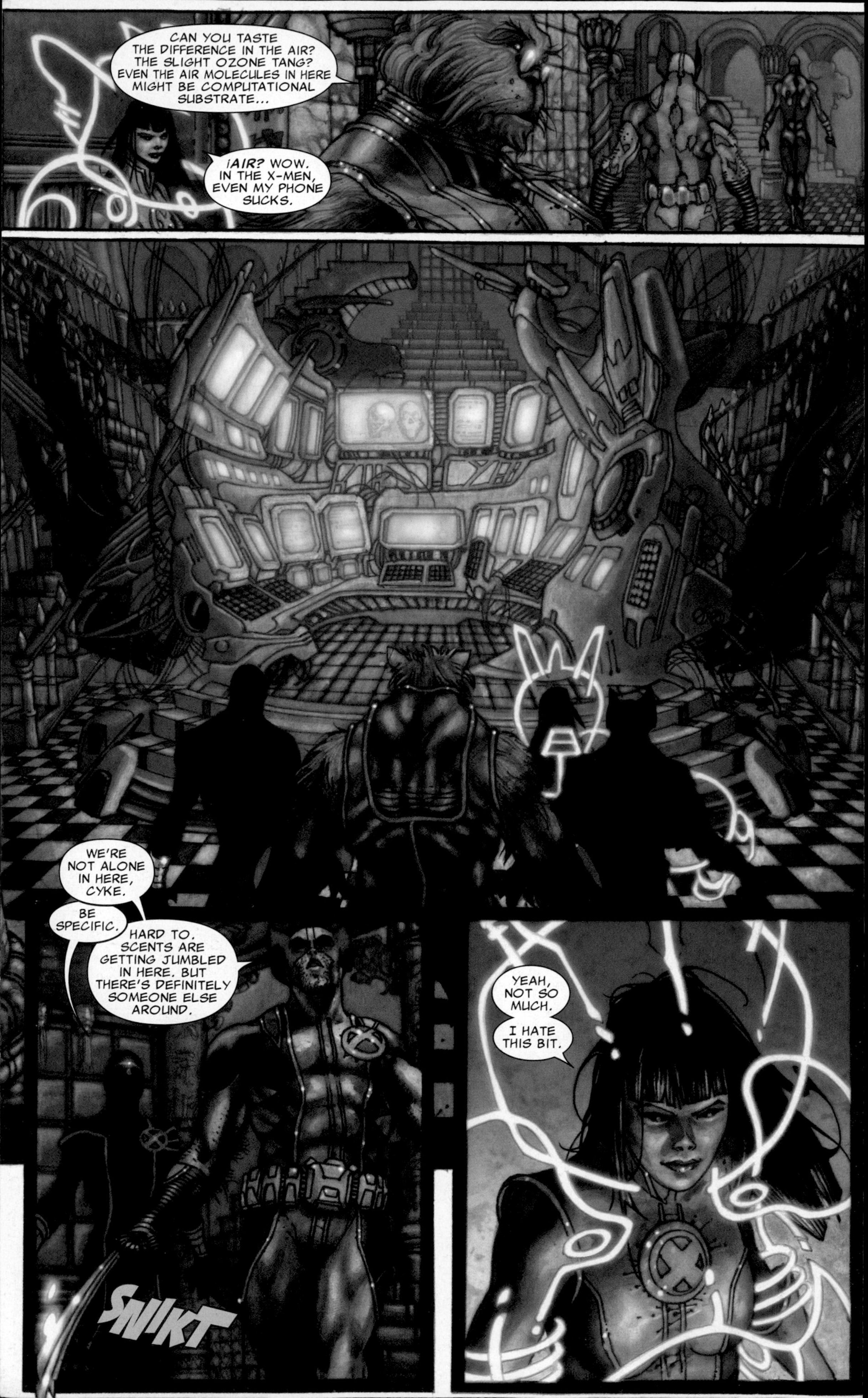
CAN YOU TASTE THE DIFFERENCE IN THE AIR? THE SLIGHT OZONE TANG? EVEN THE AIR MOLECULES IN HERE MIGHT BE COMPUTATIONAL SUBSTRATE...
¡AIR? WOW. IN THE X-MEN, EVEN MY PHONE SUCKS.
WE'RE NOT ALONE IN HERE, CYKE.
BE SPECIFIC.
HARD TO. SCENTS ARE GETTING JUMBLED IN HERE. BUT THERE'S DEFINITELY SOMEONE ELSE AROUND.
SNIKT
YEAH, NOT SO MUCH.
I HATE THIS BIT.

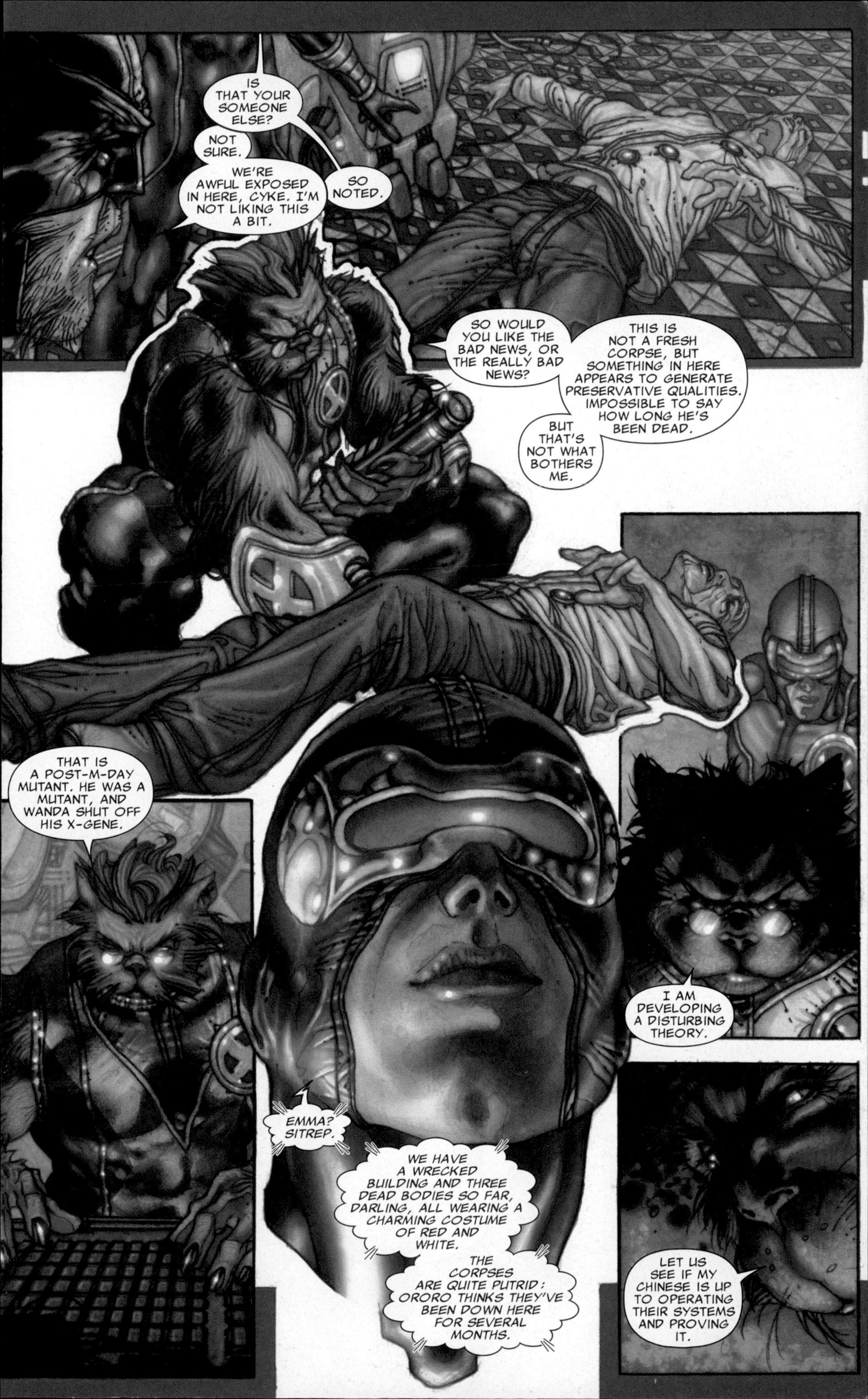
IS THAT YOUR SOMEONE ELSE?
NOT SURE.
WE'RE AWFUL EXPOSED IN HERE, CYKE. I'M NOT LIKING THIS A BIT.
SO NOTED.
SO WOULD YOU LIKE THE BAD NEWS, OR THE REALLY BAD NEWS?
THIS IS NOT A FRESH CORPSE, BUT SOMETHING IN HERE APPEARS TO GENERATE PRESERVATIVE QUALITIES. IMPOSSIBLE TO SAY HOW LONG HE'S BEEN DEAD.
BUT THAT'S NOT WHAT BOTHERS ME.
THAT IS A POST-M-DAY MUTANT. HE WAS A MUTANT, AND WANDA SHUT OFF HIS X-GENE.
I AM DEVELOPING A DISTURBING THEORY.
EMMA? SITREP.
WE HAVE A WRECKED BUILDING AND THREE DEAD BODIES SO FAR, DARLING, ALL WEARING A CHARMING COSTUME OF RED AND WHITE.
THE CORPSES ARE QUITE PUTRID; ORORO THINKS THEY'VE BEEN DOWN HERE FOR SEVERAL MONTHS.
LET US SEE IF MY CHINESE IS UP TO OPERATING THEIR SYSTEMS AND PROVING IT.

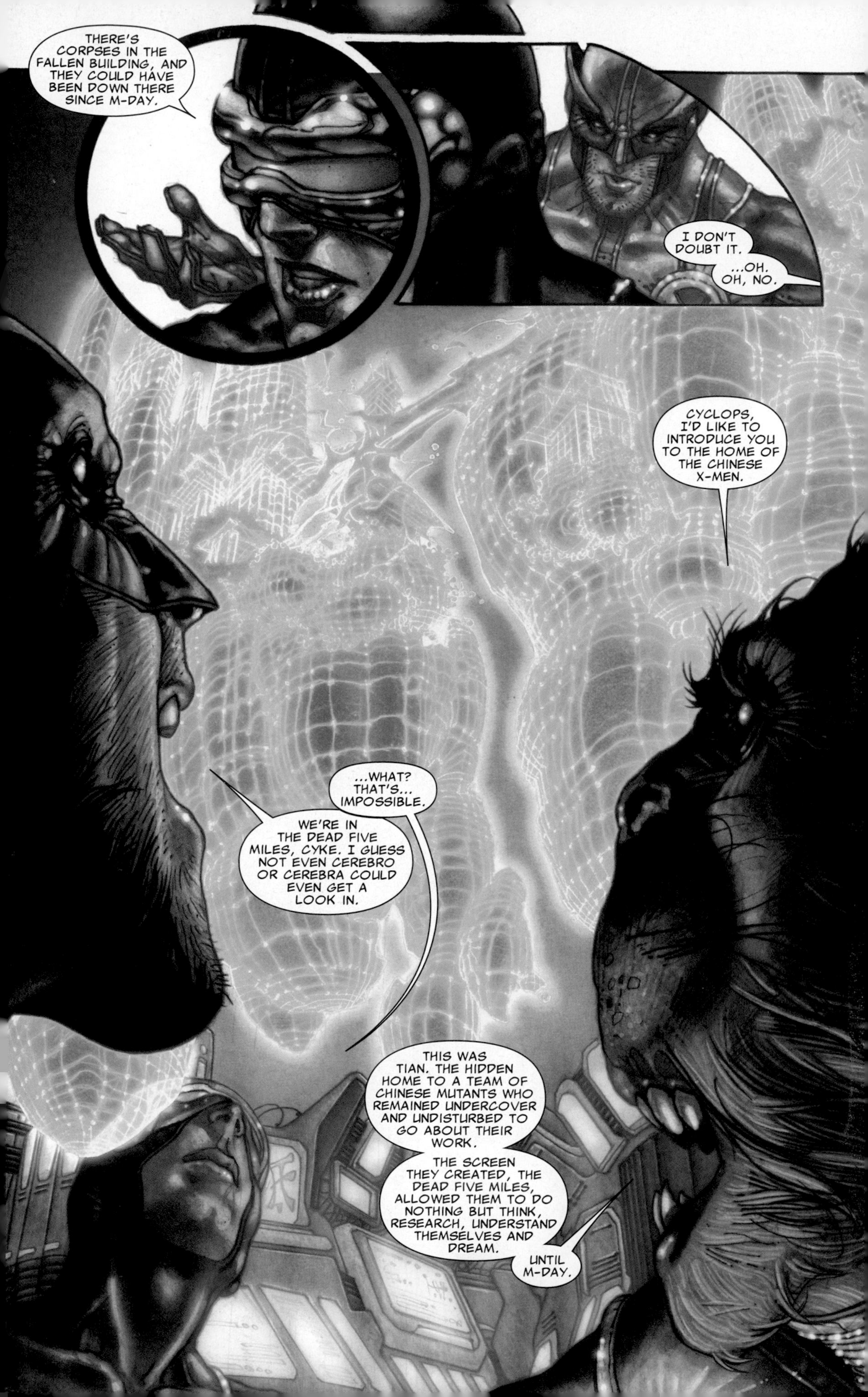
THERE'S CORPSES IN THE FALLEN BUILDING, AND THEY COULD HAVE BEEN DOWN THERE SINCE M-DAY.
I DON'T DOUBT IT.
...OH. OH, NO.
CYCLOPS, I'D LIKE TO INTRODUCE YOU TO THE HOME OF THE CHINESE X-MEN.
...WHAT? THAT'S... IMPOSSIBLE.
WE'RE IN THE DEAD FIVE MILES, CYKE. I GUESS NOT EVEN CEREBRO OR CEREBRA COULD EVEN GET A LOOK IN.
THIS WAS TIAN. THE HIDDEN HOME TO A TEAM OF CHINESE MUTANTS WHO REMAINED UNDERCOVER AND UNDISTURBED TO GO ABOUT THEIR WORK.
THE SCREEN THEY CREATED, THE DEAD FIVE MILES, ALLOWED THEM TO DO NOTHING BUT THINK, RESEARCH, UNDERSTAND THEMSELVES AND DREAM.
UNTIL M-DAY.

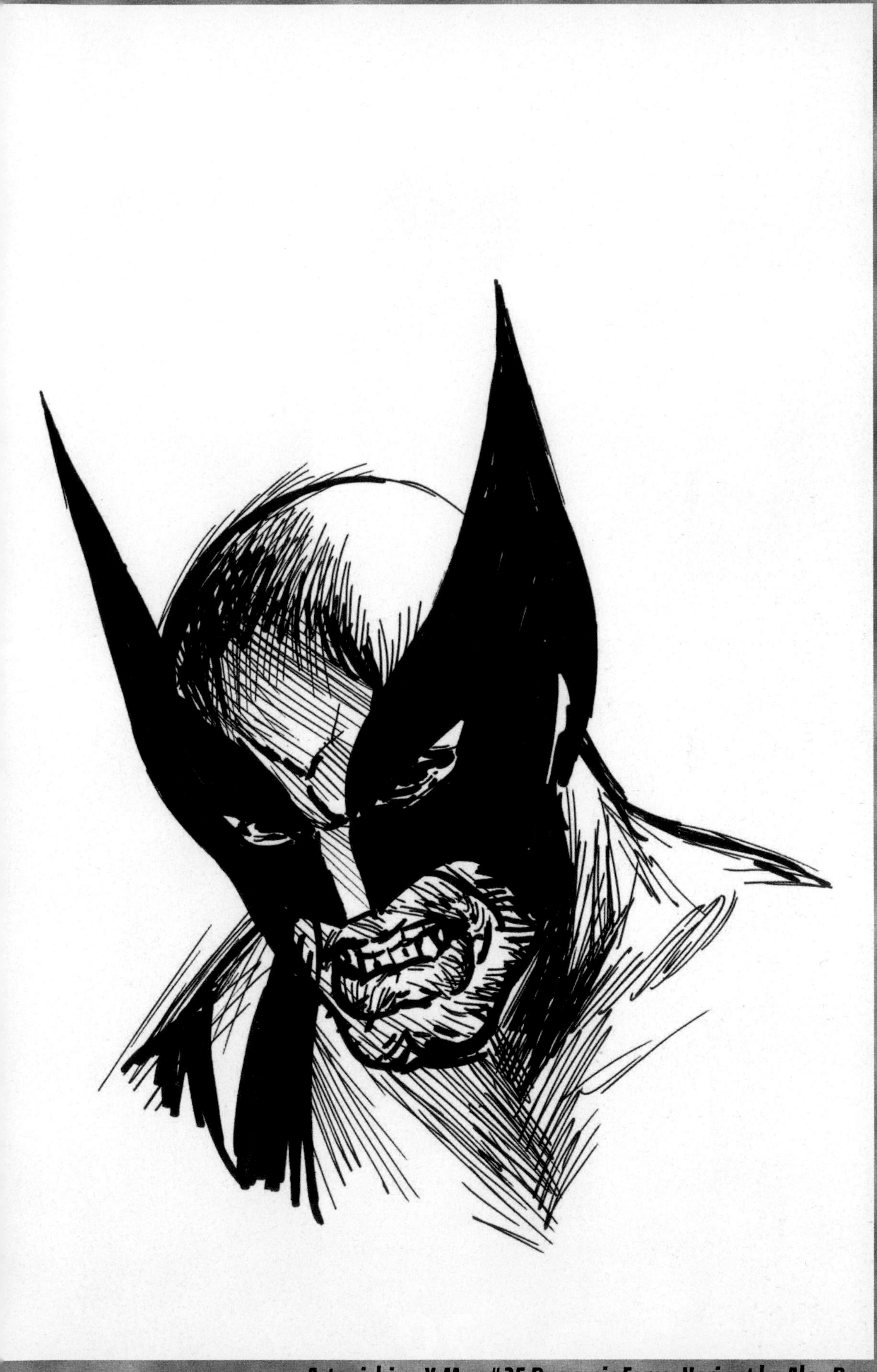

Astonishing X-Men #25 Dynamic Forces Variant by Alex Ross

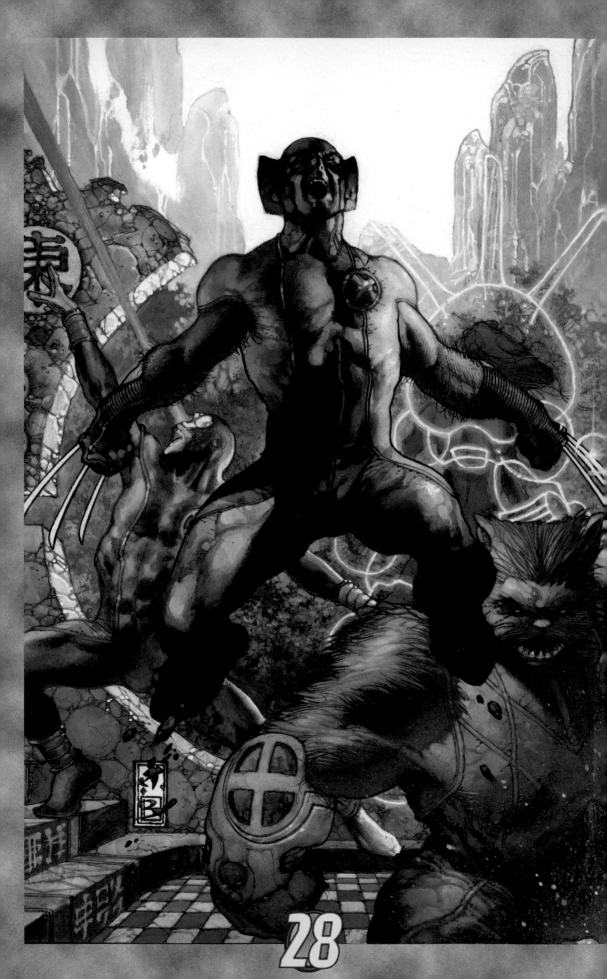

28

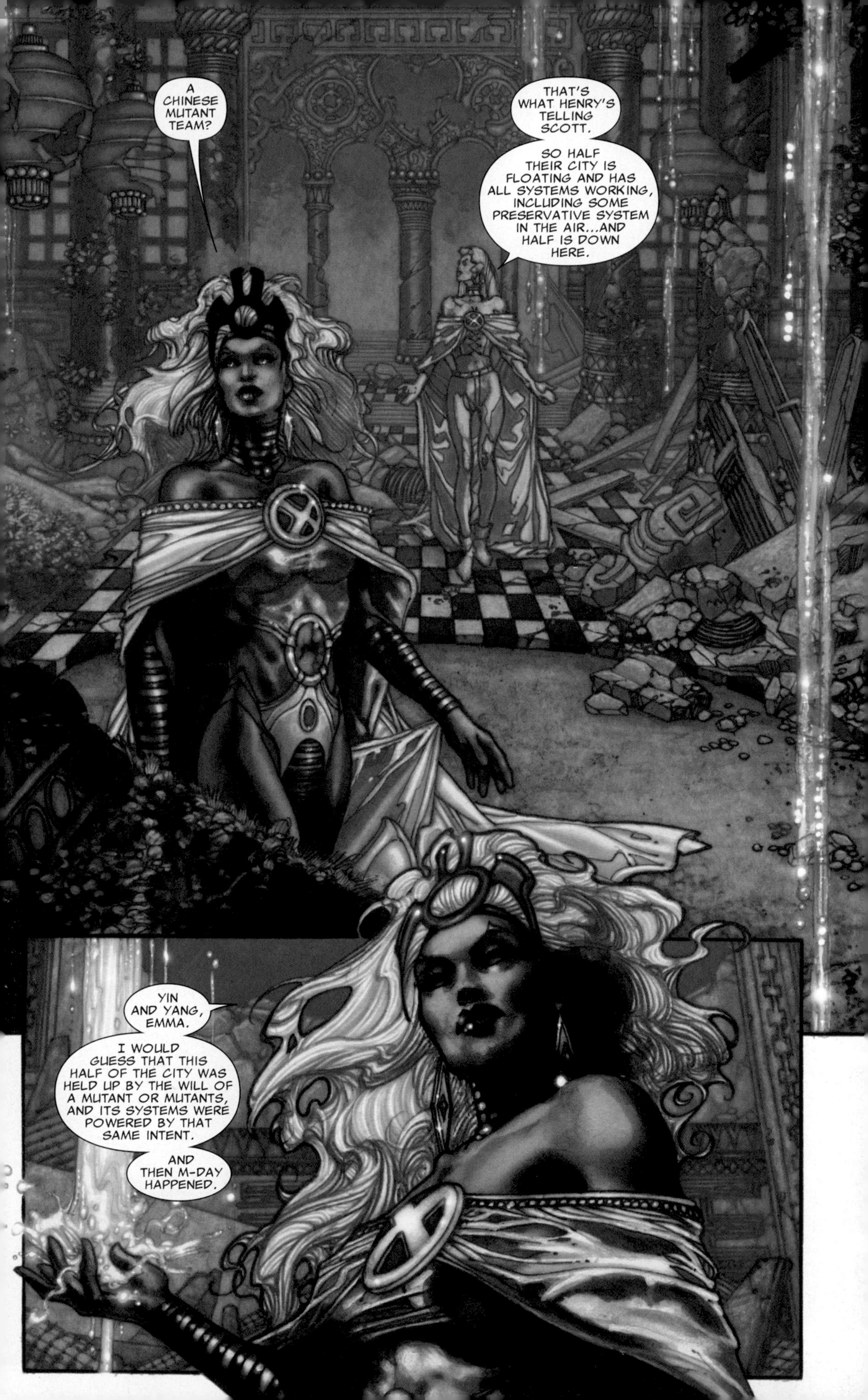

A CHINESE MUTANT TEAM?
THAT'S WHAT HENRY'S TELLING SCOTT.
SO HALF THEIR CITY IS FLOATING AND HAS ALL SYSTEMS WORKING, INCLUDING SOME PRESERVATIVE SYSTEM IN THE AIR...AND HALF IS DOWN HERE.
YIN AND YANG, EMMA.
I WOULD GUESS THAT THIS HALF OF THE CITY WAS HELD UP BY THE WILL OF A MUTANT OR MUTANTS, AND ITS SYSTEMS WERE POWERED BY THAT SAME INTENT.
AND THEN M-DAY HAPPENED.

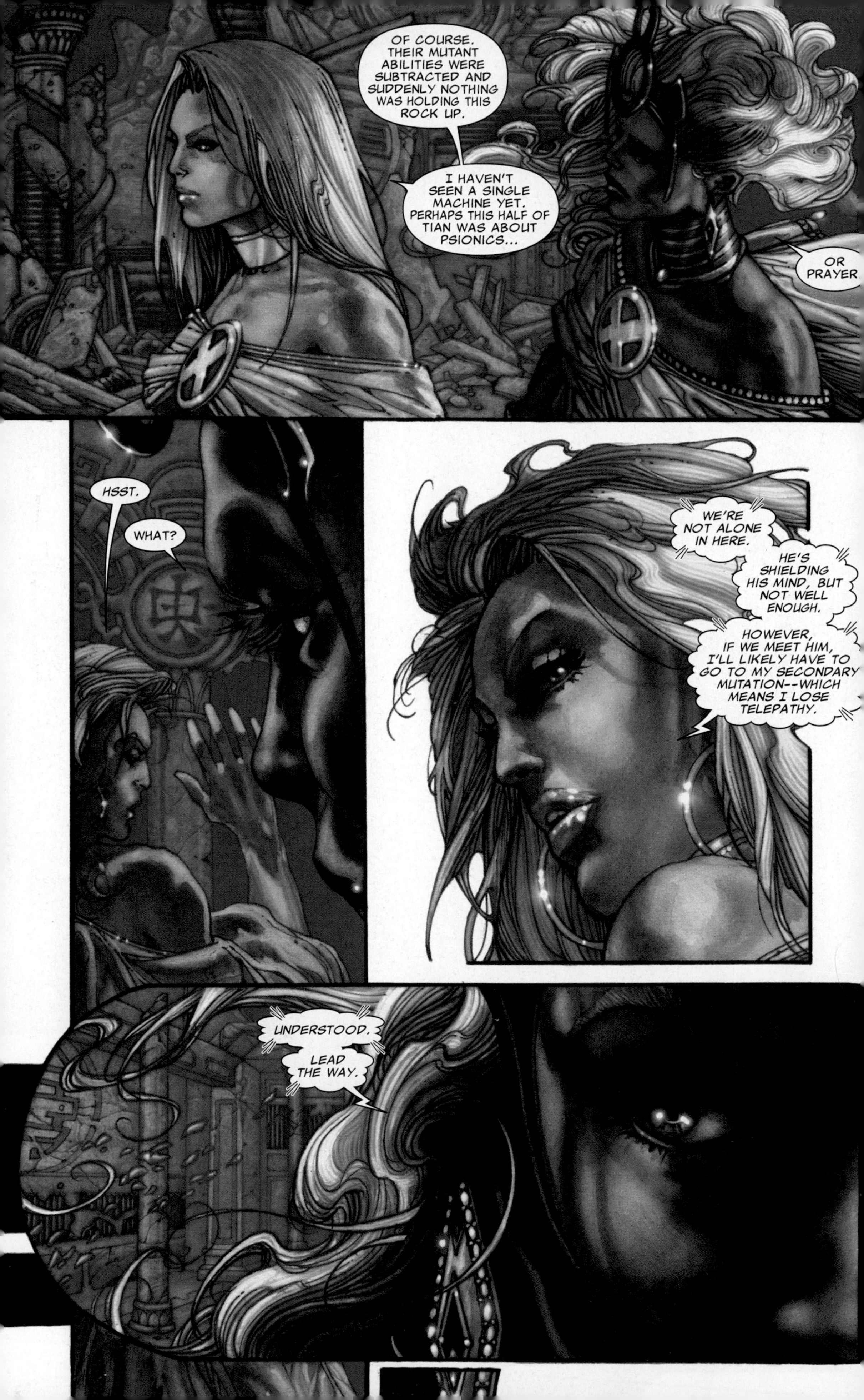
OF COURSE. THEIR MUTANT ABILITIES WERE SUBTRACTED AND SUDDENLY NOTHING WAS HOLDING THIS ROCK UP.
I HAVEN'T SEEN A SINGLE MACHINE YET. PERHAPS THIS HALF OF TIAN WAS ABOUT PSIONICS...
OR PRAYER
HSST.
WHAT?
WE'RE NOT ALONE IN HERE.
HE'S SHIELDING HIS MIND, BUT NOT WELL ENOUGH.
HOWEVER, IF WE MEET HIM, I'LL LIKELY HAVE TO GO TO MY SECONDARY MUTATION--WHICH MEANS I LOSE TELEPATHY.
UNDERSTOOD.
LEAD THE WAY.

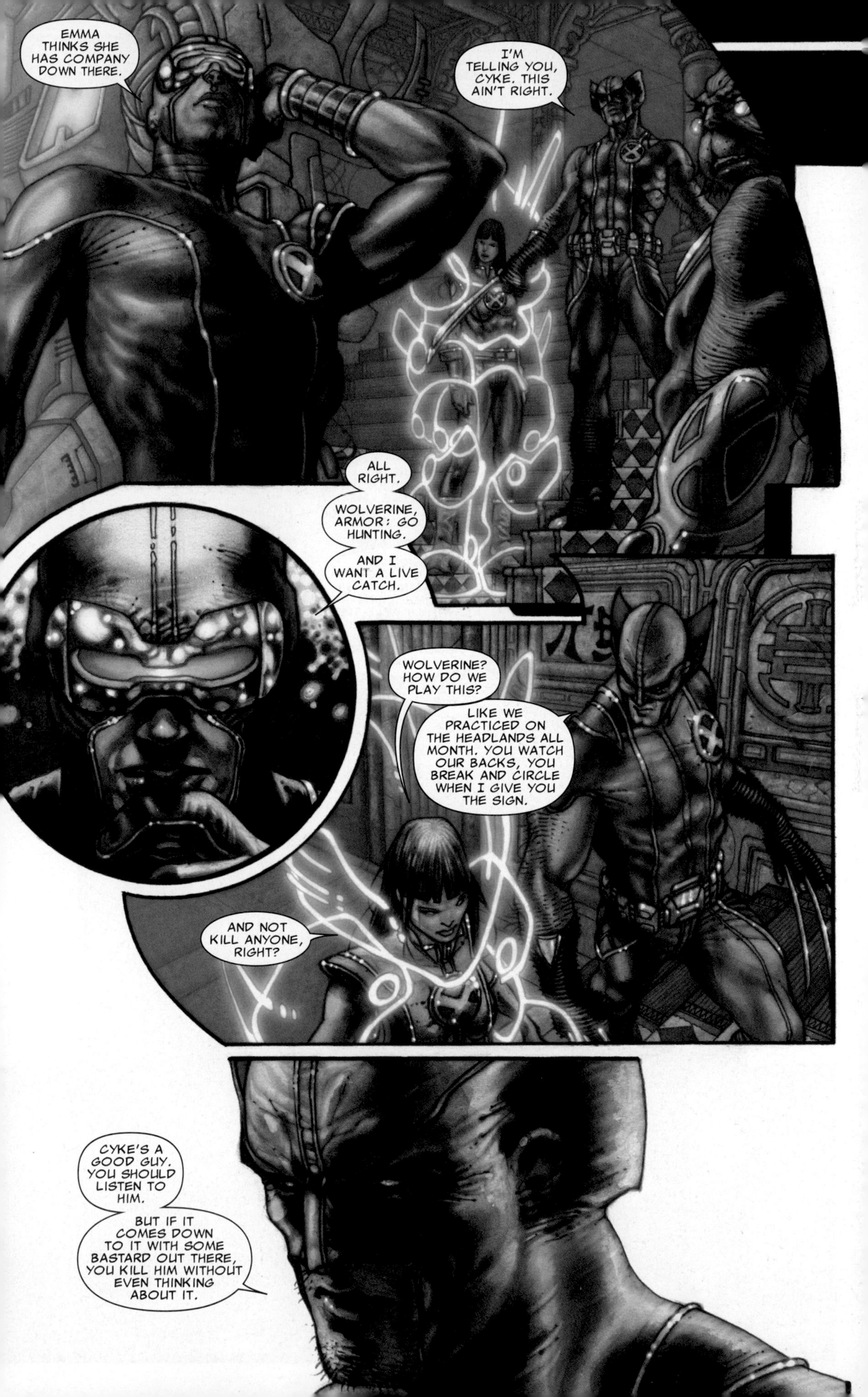
EMMA THINKS SHE HAS COMPANY DOWN THERE.
I'M TELLING YOU, CYKE. THIS AIN'T RIGHT.
ALL RIGHT.
WOLVERINE, ARMOR: GO HUNTING.
AND I WANT A LIVE CATCH.
WOLVERINE? HOW DO WE PLAY THIS?
LIKE WE PRACTICED ON THE HEADLANDS ALL MONTH. YOU WATCH OUR BACKS, YOU BREAK AND CIRCLE WHEN I GIVE YOU THE SIGN.
AND NOT KILL ANYONE, RIGHT?
CYKE'S A GOOD GUY. YOU SHOULD LISTEN TO HIM.
BUT IF IT COMES DOWN TO IT WITH SOME BASTARD OUT THERE, YOU KILL HIM WITHOUT EVEN THINKING ABOUT IT.

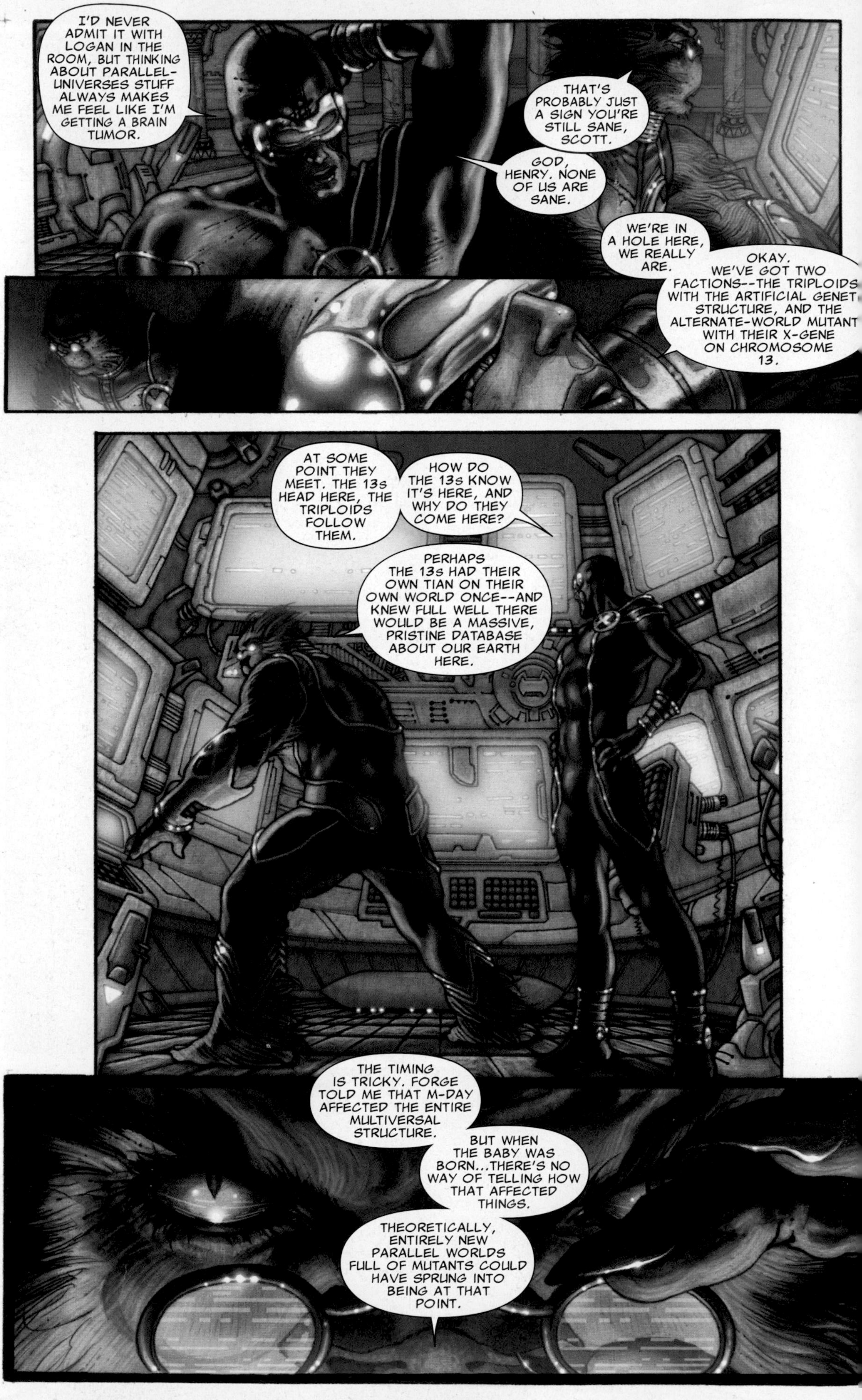
I'D NEVER ADMIT IT WITH LOGAN IN THE ROOM, BUT THINKING ABOUT PARALLEL-UNIVERSES STUFF ALWAYS MAKES ME FEEL LIKE I'M GETTING A BRAIN TUMOR.
THAT'S PROBABLY JUST A SIGN YOU'RE STILL SANE, SCOTT.
GOD, HENRY. NONE OF US ARE SANE.
WE'RE IN A HOLE HERE, WE REALLY ARE.
OKAY. WE'VE GOT TWO FACTIONS--THE TRIPLOIDS WITH THE ARTIFICIAL GENET STRUCTURE, AND THE ALTERNATE-WORLD MUTANT WITH THEIR X-GENE ON CHROMOSOME 13.
AT SOME POINT THEY MEET. THE 13s HEAD HERE, THE TRIPLOIDS FOLLOW THEM.
HOW DO THE 13s KNOW IT'S HERE, AND WHY DO THEY COME HERE?
PERHAPS THE 13s HAD THEIR OWN TIAN ON THEIR OWN WORLD ONCE--AND KNEW FULL WELL THERE WOULD BE A MASSIVE, PRISTINE DATABASE ABOUT OUR EARTH HERE.
THE TIMING IS TRICKY. FORGE TOLD ME THAT M-DAY AFFECTED THE ENTIRE MULTIVERSAL STRUCTURE.
BUT WHEN THE BABY WAS BORN...THERE'S NO WAY OF TELLING HOW THAT AFFECTED THINGS.
THEORETICALLY, ENTIRELY NEW PARALLEL WORLDS FULL OF MUTANTS COULD HAVE SPRUNG INTO BEING AT THAT POINT.

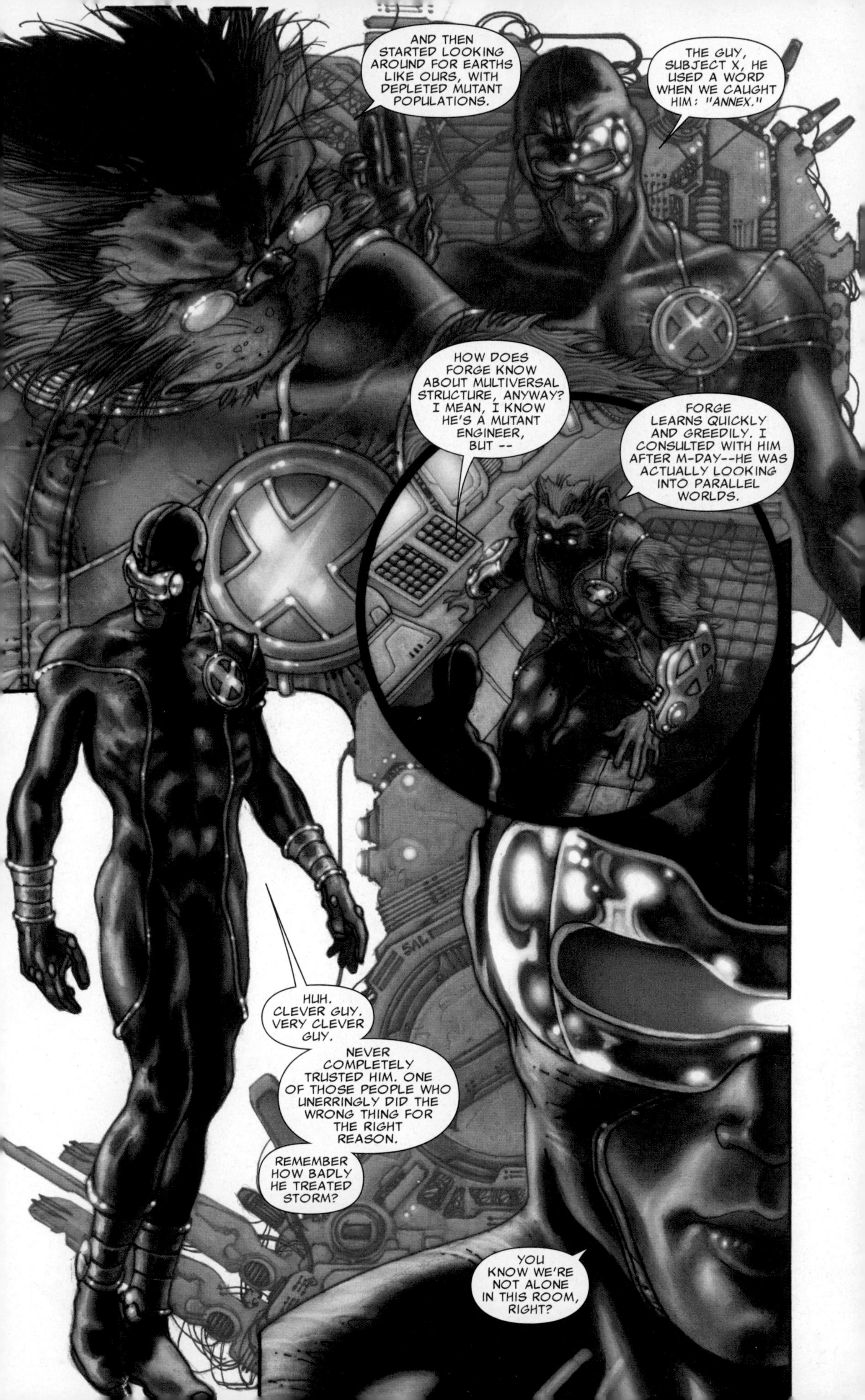
AND THEN STARTED LOOKING AROUND FOR EARTHS LIKE OURS, WITH DEPLETED MUTANT POPULATIONS.
THE GUY, SUBJECT X, HE USED A WORD WHEN WE CAUGHT HIM: "ANNEX."
HOW DOES FORGE KNOW ABOUT MULTIVERSAL STRUCTURE, ANYWAY? I MEAN, I KNOW HE'S A MUTANT ENGINEER, BUT --
FORGE LEARNS QUICKLY AND GREEDILY. I CONSULTED WITH HIM AFTER M-DAY--HE WAS ACTUALLY LOOKING INTO PARALLEL WORLDS.
HUH. CLEVER GUY. VERY CLEVER GUY.
NEVER COMPLETELY TRUSTED HIM. ONE OF THOSE PEOPLE WHO UNERRINGLY DID THE WRONG THING FOR THE RIGHT REASON.
REMEMBER HOW BADLY HE TREATED STORM?
YOU KNOW WE'RE NOT ALONE IN THIS ROOM, RIGHT?

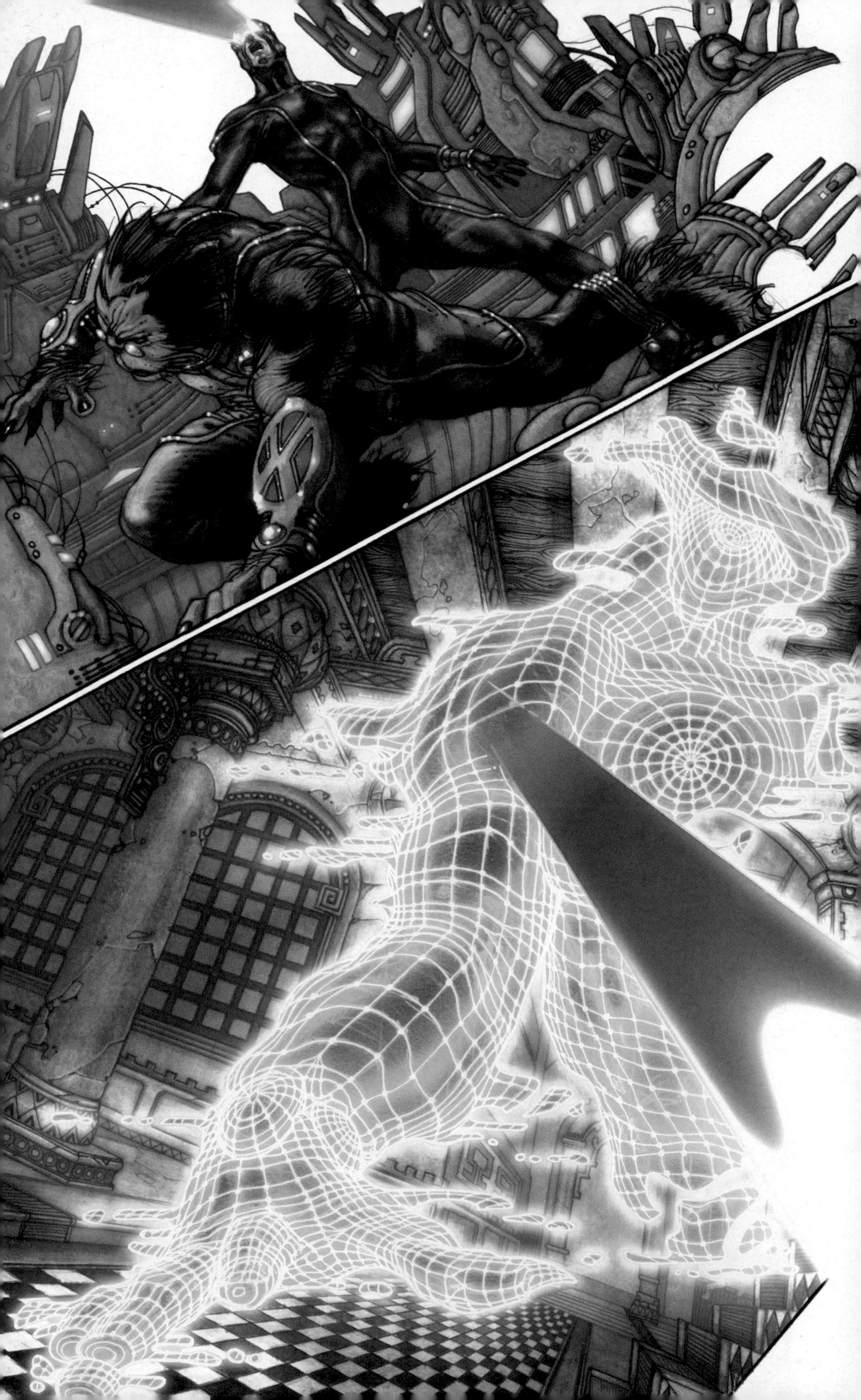

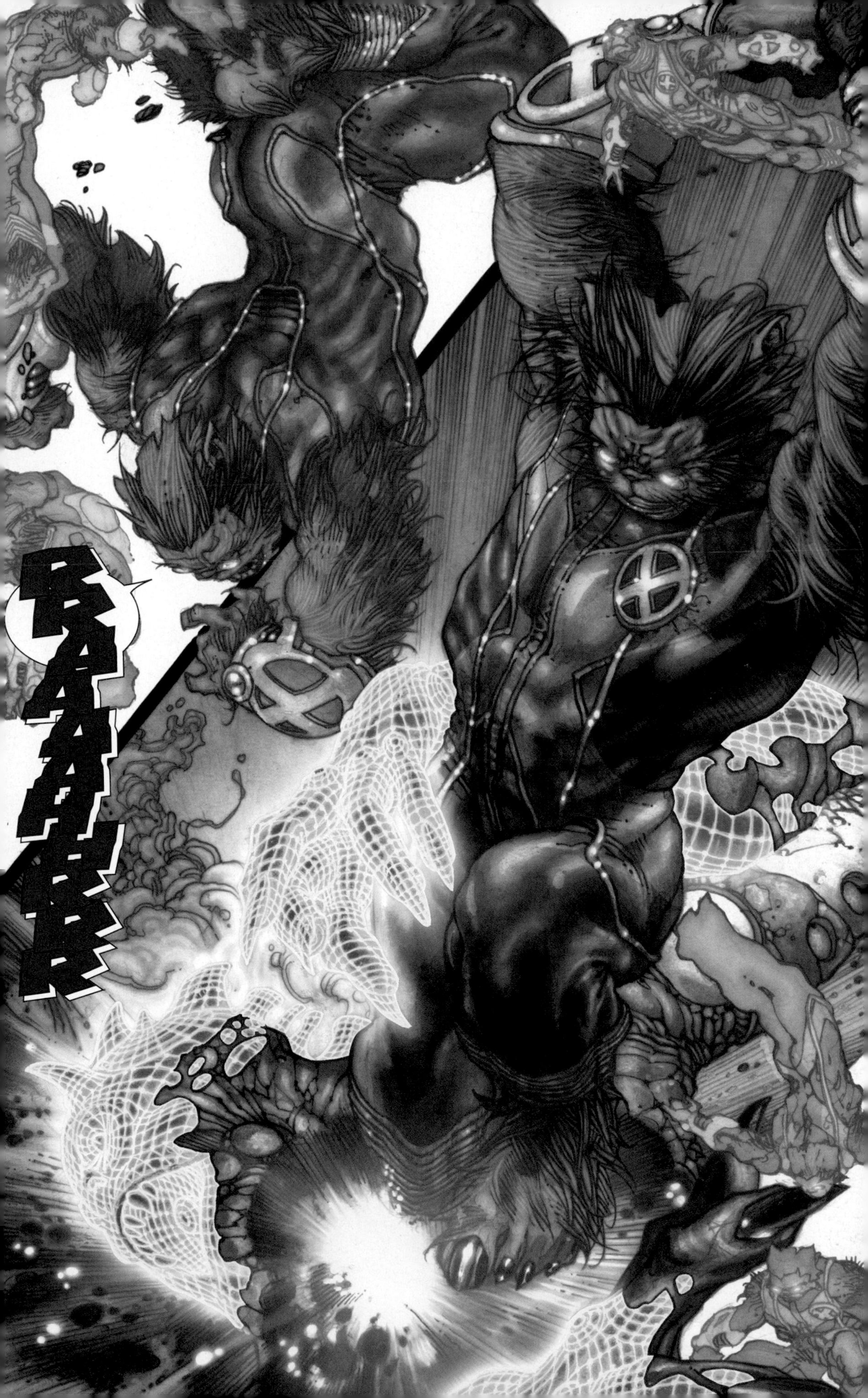
RAAAAHRRR

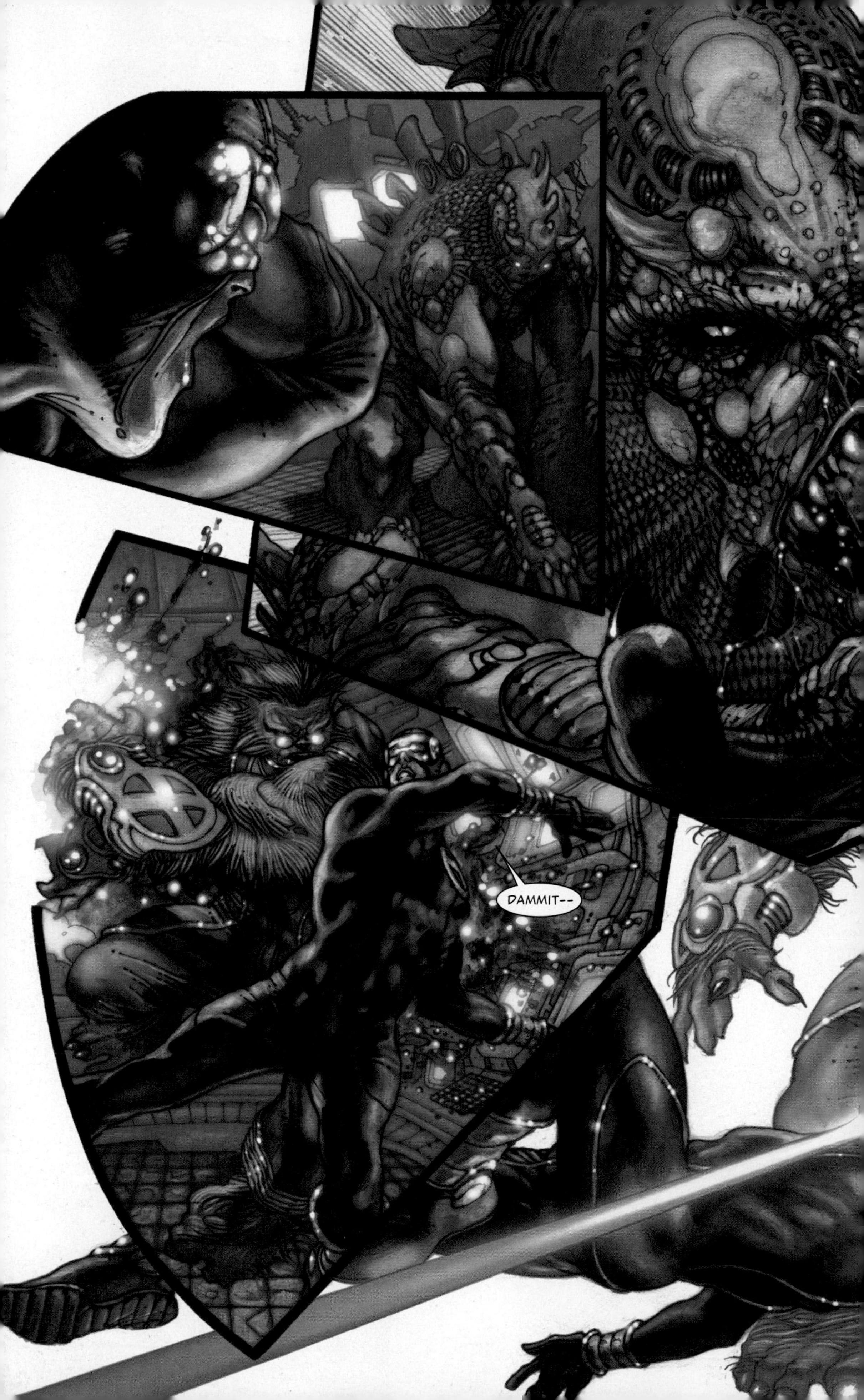
DAMMIT--

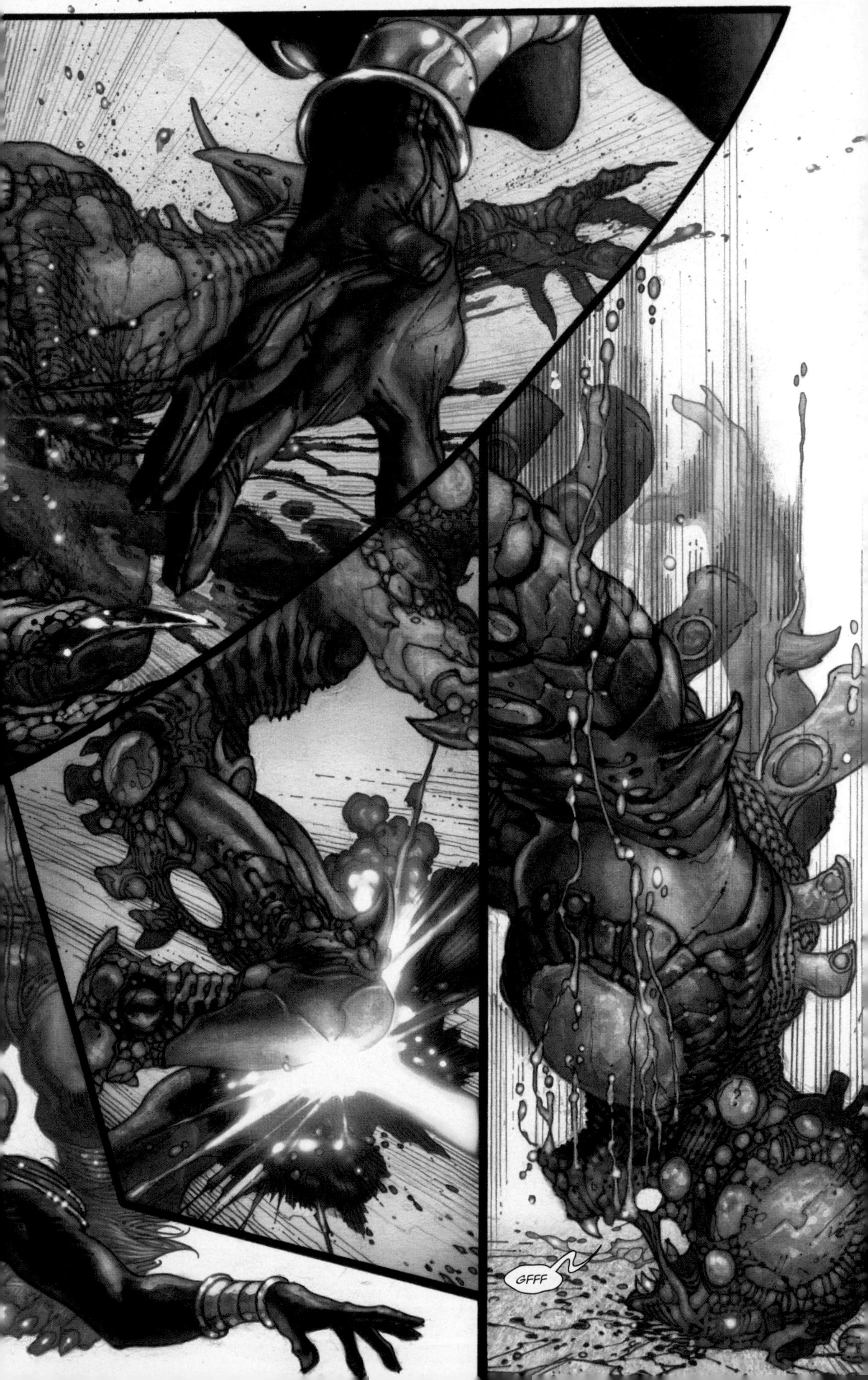
GFFF

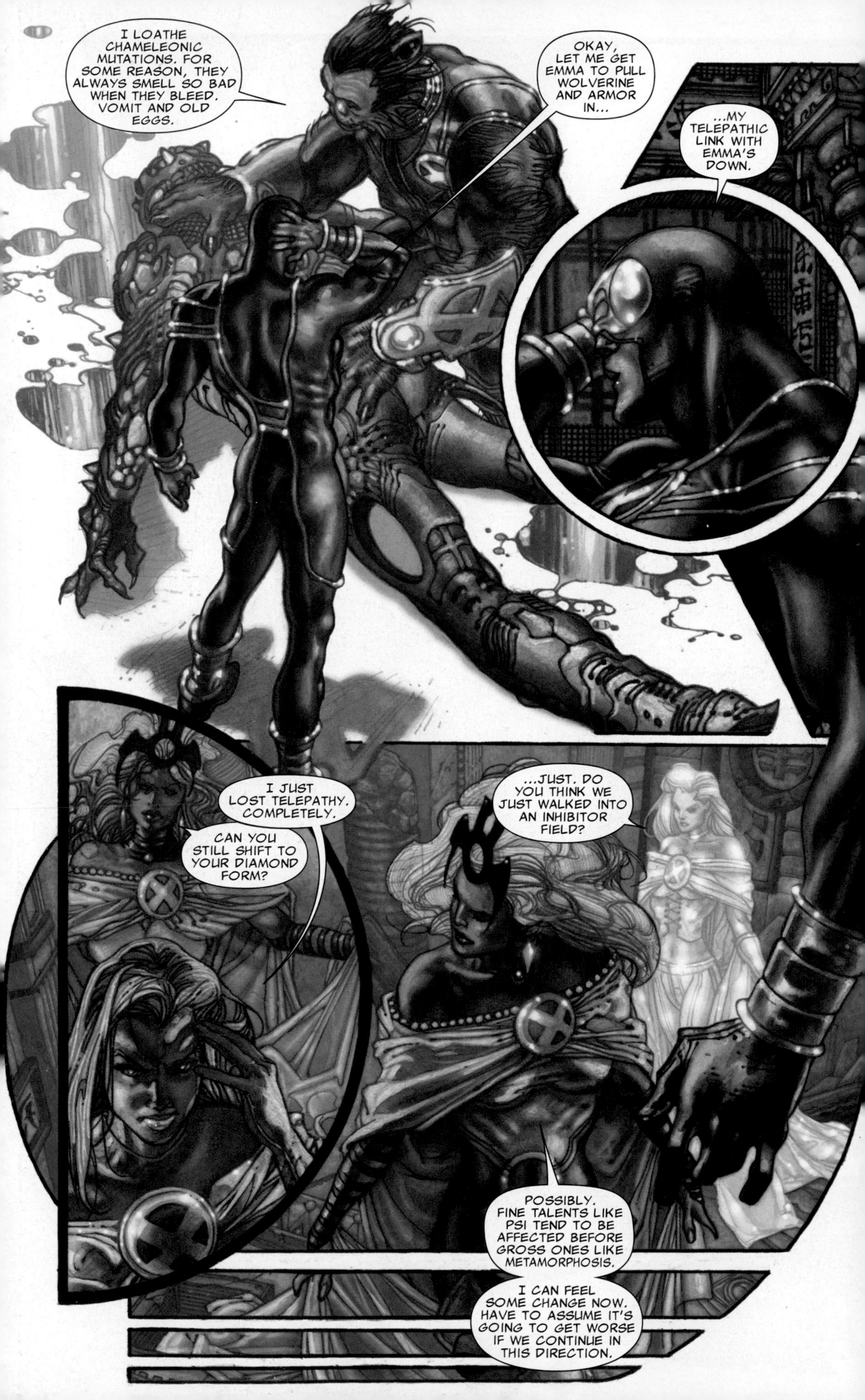
I LOATHE CHAMELEONIC MUTATIONS. FOR SOME REASON, THEY ALWAYS SMELL SO BAD WHEN THEY BLEED. VOMIT AND OLD EGGS.
OKAY, LET ME GET EMMA TO PULL WOLVERINE AND ARMOR IN...
...MY TELEPATHIC LINK WITH EMMA'S DOWN.
I JUST LOST TELEPATHY. COMPLETELY.
CAN YOU STILL SHIFT TO YOUR DIAMOND FORM?
...JUST. DO YOU THINK WE JUST WALKED INTO AN INHIBITOR FIELD?
POSSIBLY. FINE TALENTS LIKE PSI TEND TO BE AFFECTED BEFORE GROSS ONES LIKE METAMORPHOSIS.
I CAN FEEL SOME CHANGE NOW. HAVE TO ASSUME IT'S GOING TO GET WORSE IF WE CONTINUE IN THIS DIRECTION.

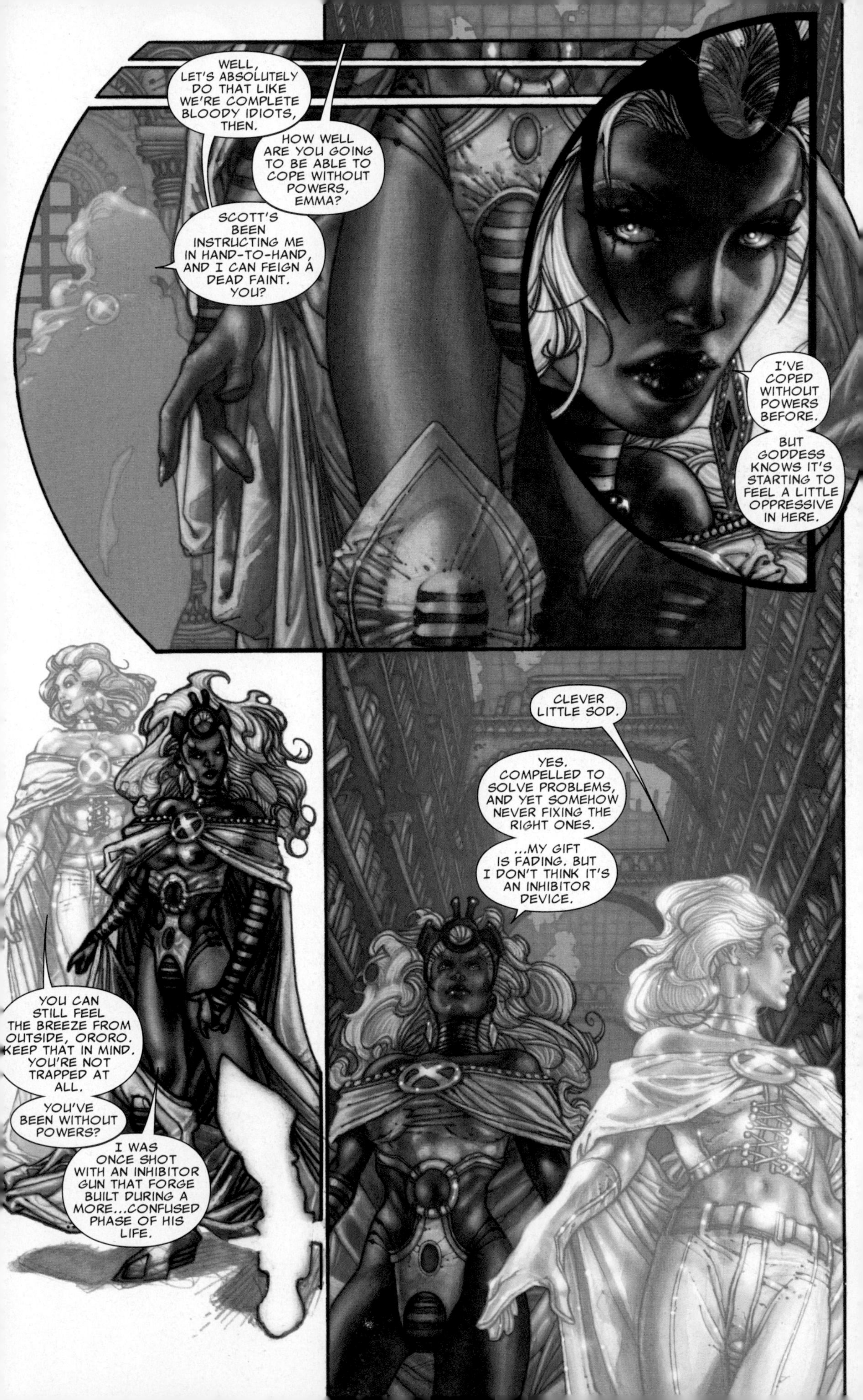
WELL, LET'S ABSOLUTELY DO THAT LIKE WE'RE COMPLETE BLOODY IDIOTS, THEN.
HOW WELL ARE YOU GOING TO BE ABLE TO COPE WITHOUT POWERS, EMMA?
SCOTT'S BEEN INSTRUCTING ME IN HAND-TO-HAND, AND I CAN FEIGN A DEAD FAINT. YOU?
I'VE COPED WITHOUT POWERS BEFORE.
BUT GODDESS KNOWS IT'S STARTING TO FEEL A LITTLE OPPRESSIVE IN HERE.
YOU CAN STILL FEEL THE BREEZE FROM OUTSIDE, ORORO. KEEP THAT IN MIND. YOU'RE NOT TRAPPED AT ALL.
YOU'VE BEEN WITHOUT POWERS?
I WAS ONCE SHOT WITH AN INHIBITOR GUN THAT FORGE BUILT DURING A MORE...CONFUSED PHASE OF HIS LIFE.
CLEVER LITTLE SOD.
YES. COMPELLED TO SOLVE PROBLEMS, AND YET SOMEHOW NEVER FIXING THE RIGHT ONES.
...MY GIFT IS FADING. BUT I DON'T THINK IT'S AN INHIBITOR DEVICE.

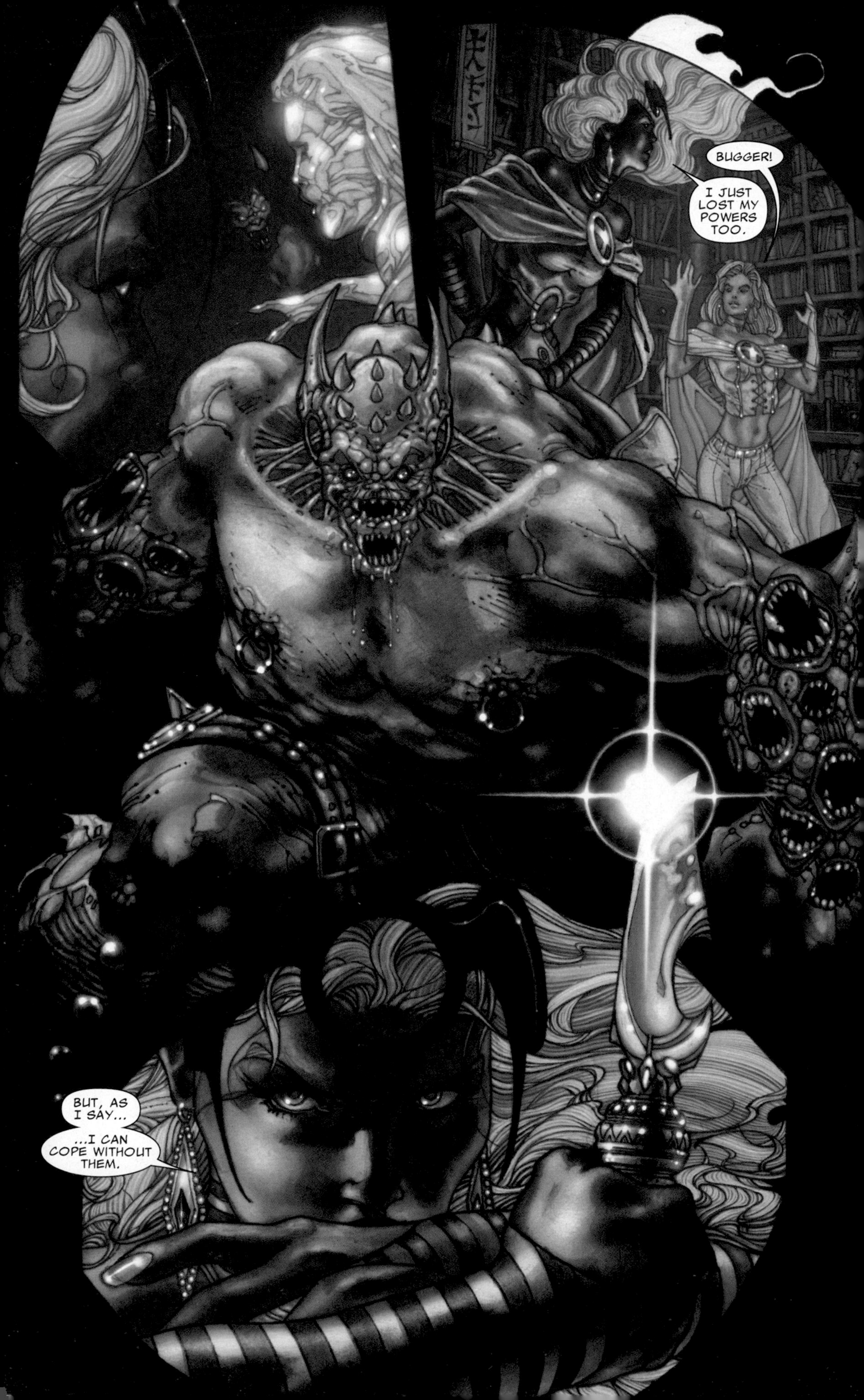
BUGGER!
I JUST LOST MY POWERS TOO.
BUT, AS I SAY...
...I CAN COPE WITHOUT THEM.

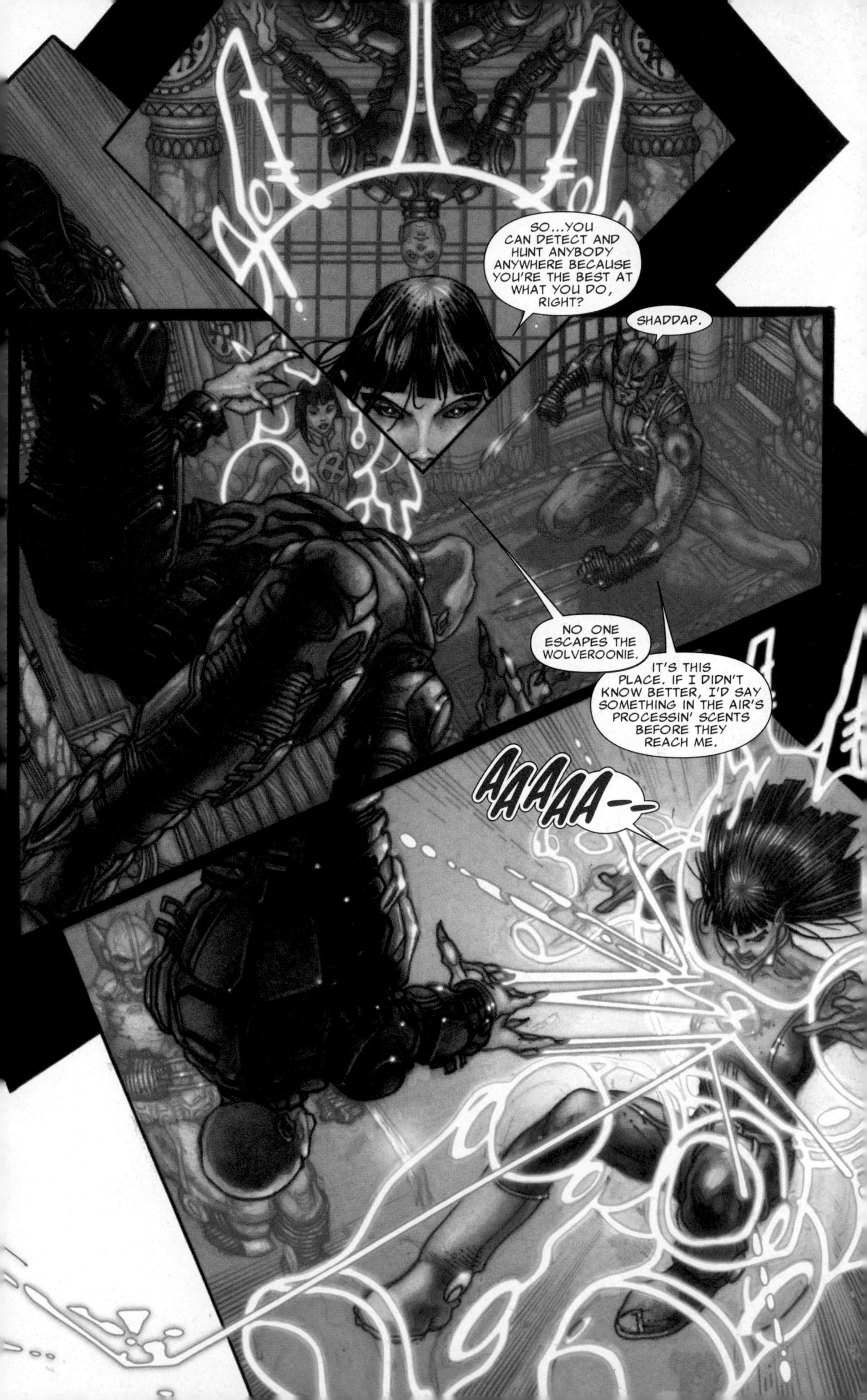
SO...YOU CAN DETECT AND HUNT ANYBODY ANYWHERE BECAUSE YOU'RE THE BEST AT WHAT YOU DO, RIGHT?
SHADDAP.
NO ONE ESCAPES THE WOLVEROONIE.
IT'S THIS PLACE. IF I DIDN'T KNOW BETTER, I'D SAY SOMETHING IN THE AIR'S PROCESSIN' SCENTS BEFORE THEY REACH ME.
AAAAAA--

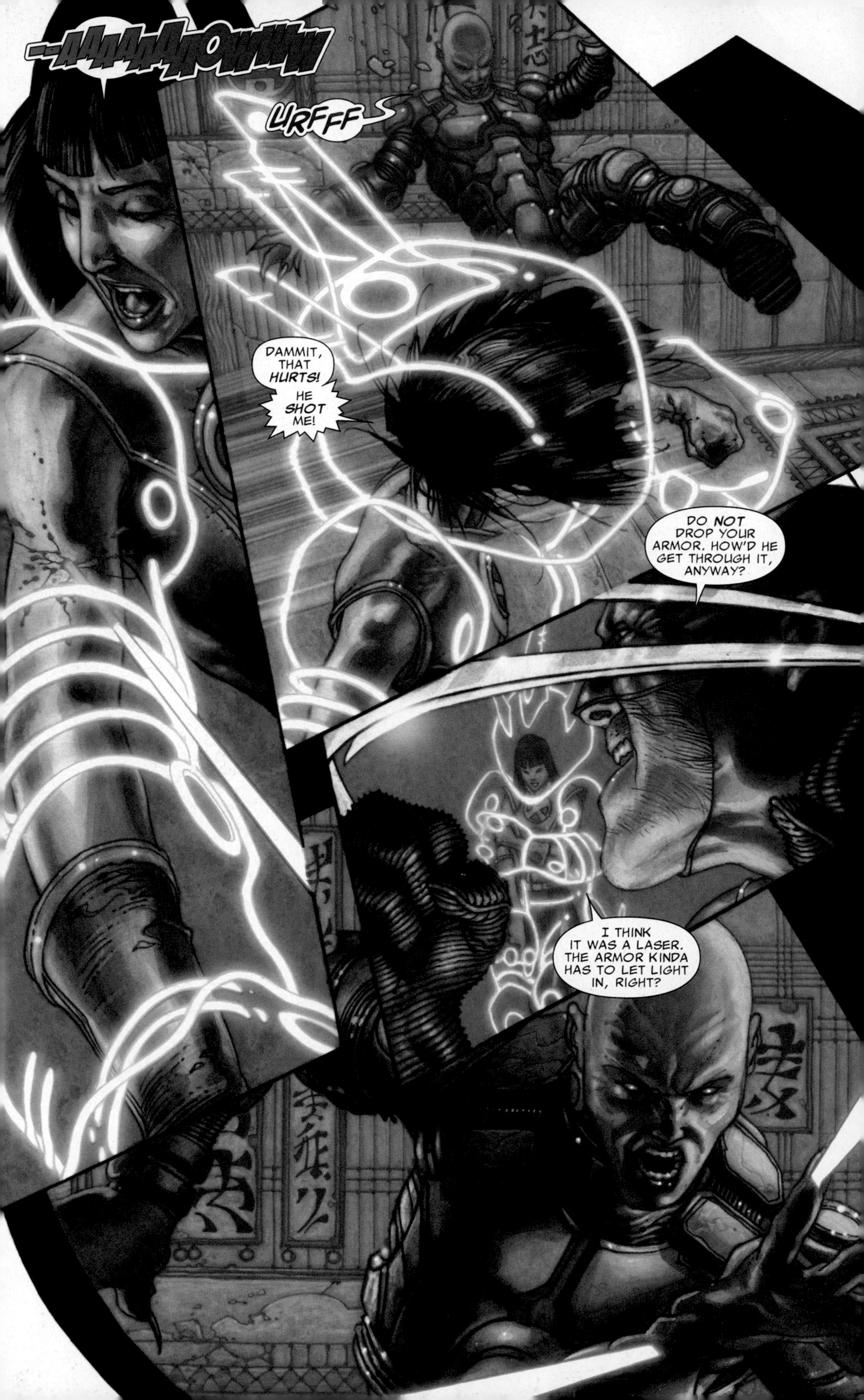
--AAAAAAAAOWWWW
URFFF
DAMMIT, THAT HURTS!
HE SHOT ME!
DO NOT DROP YOUR ARMOR. HOW'D HE GET THROUGH IT, ANYWAY?
I THINK IT WAS A LASER. THE ARMOR KINDA HAS TO LET LIGHT IN, RIGHT?

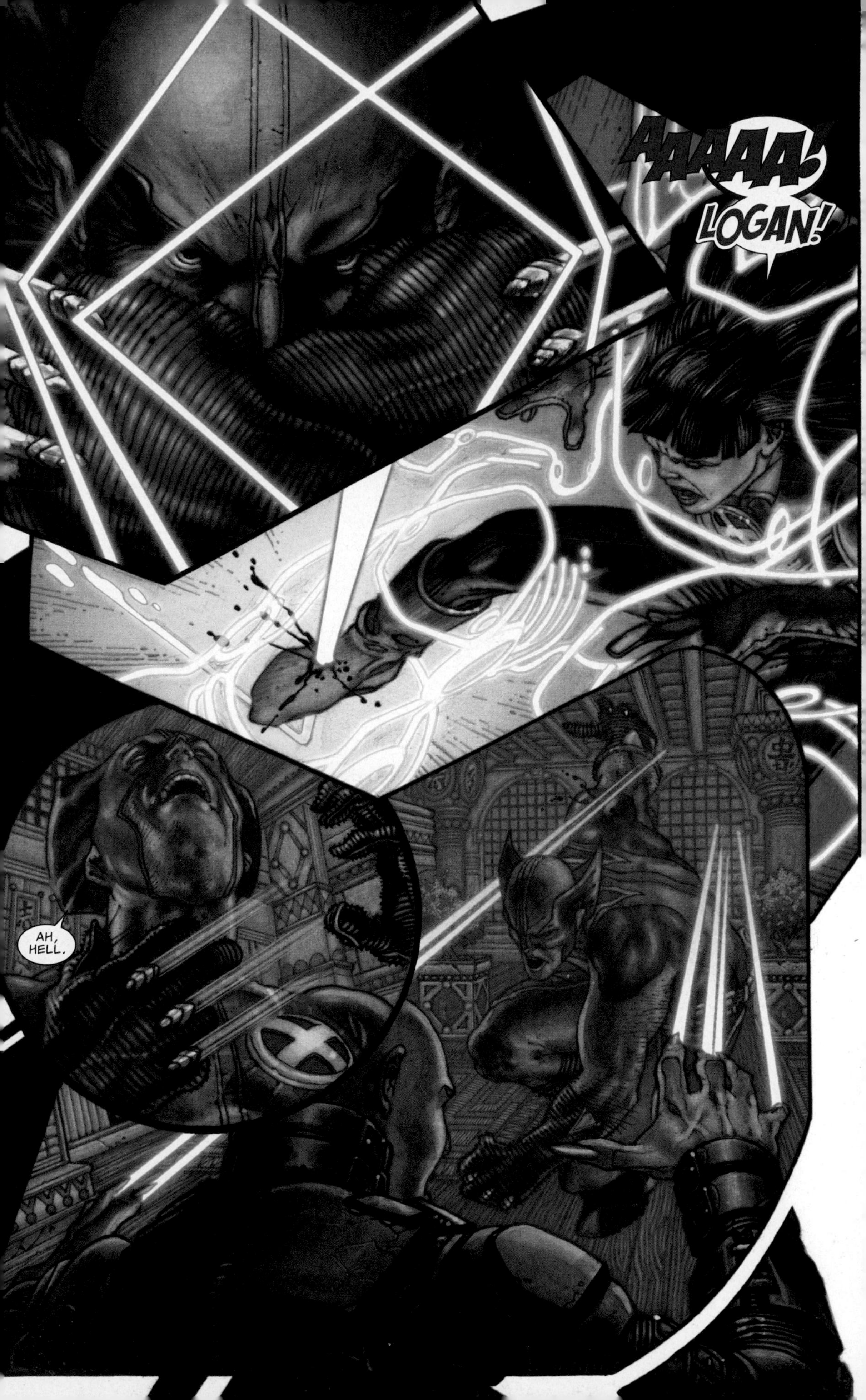
AAAAA!
LOGAN!
AH, HELL.

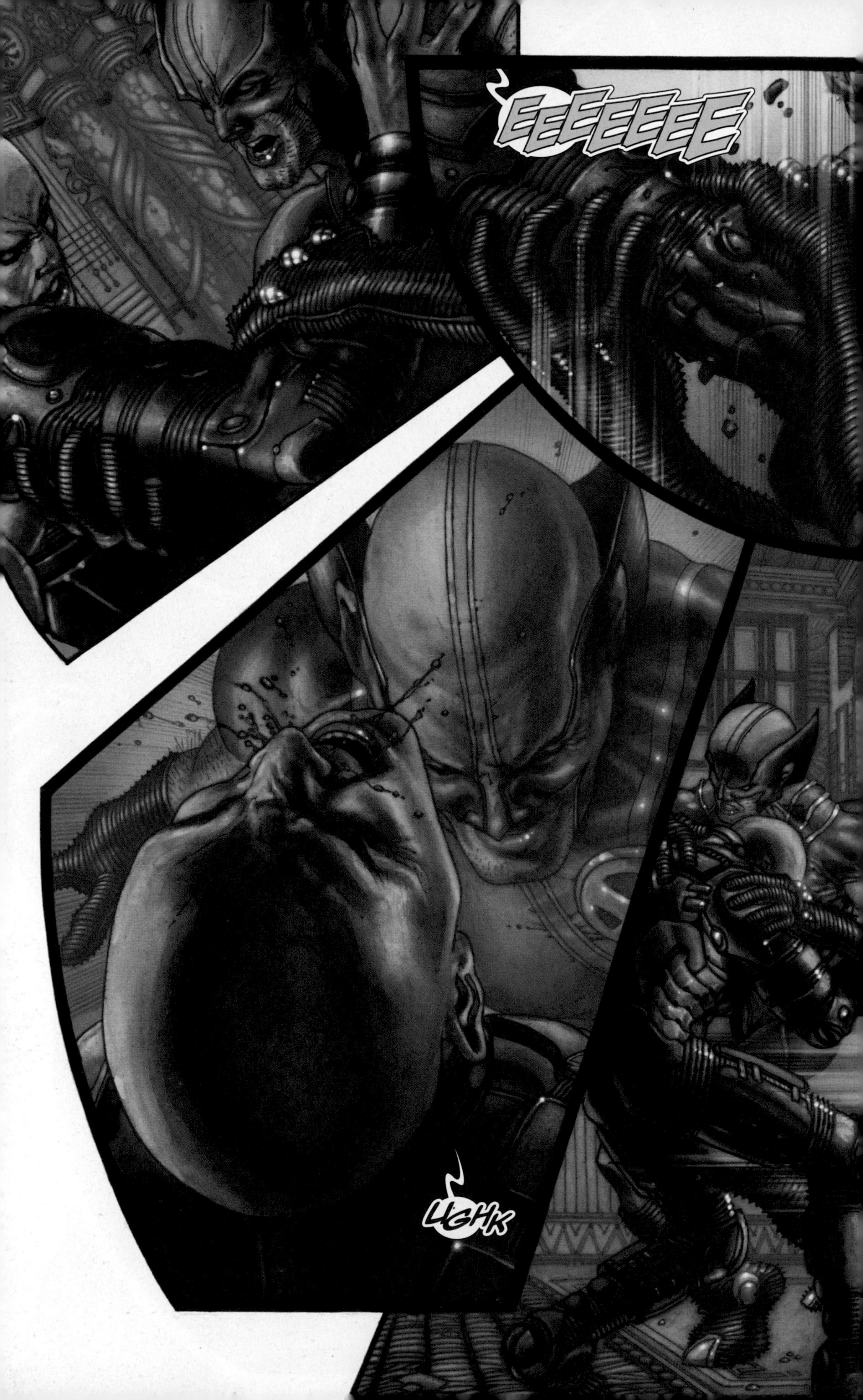
EEEEEEE
UGHK

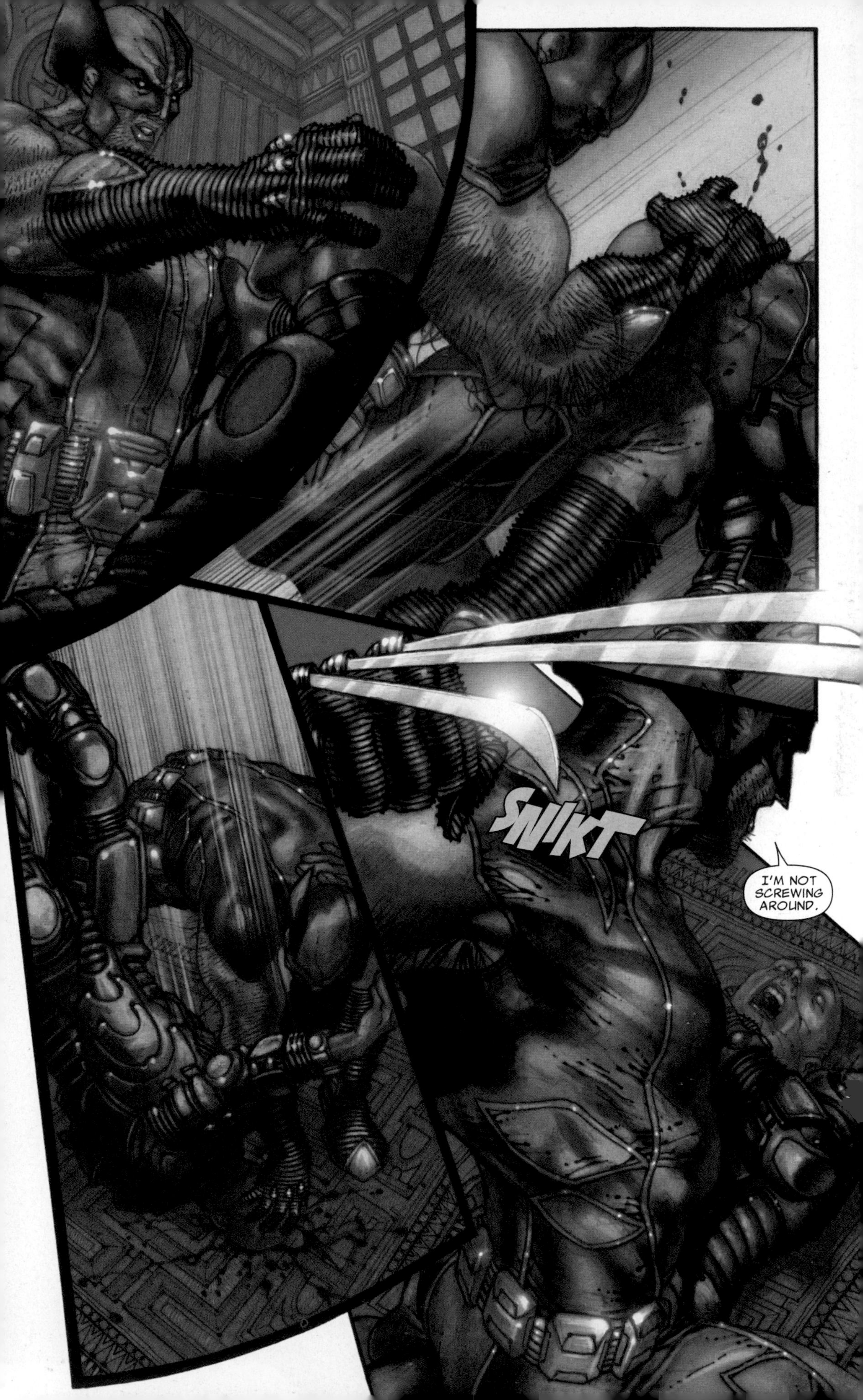
SNIKT
I'M NOT SCREWING AROUND.

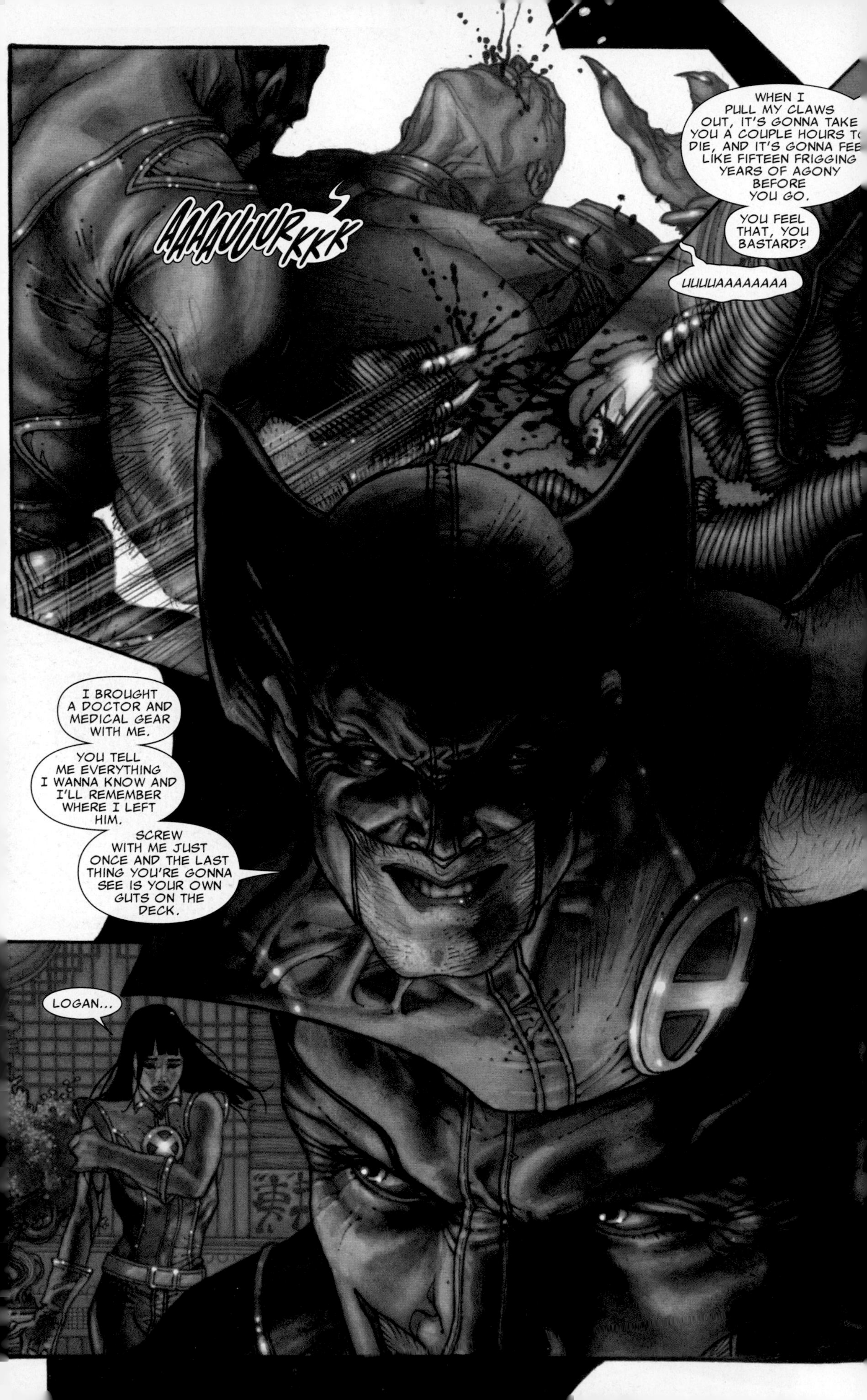
AAAAUUUURKKK
WHEN I PULL MY CLAWS OUT, IT'S GONNA TAKE YOU A COUPLE HOURS TO DIE, AND IT'S GONNA FEEL LIKE FIFTEEN FRIGGING YEARS OF AGONY BEFORE YOU GO.
YOU FEEL THAT, YOU BASTARD?
UUUUAAAAAAAA
I BROUGHT A DOCTOR AND MEDICAL GEAR WITH ME.
YOU TELL ME EVERYTHING I WANNA KNOW AND I'LL REMEMBER WHERE I LEFT HIM.
SCREW WITH ME JUST ONCE AND THE LAST THING YOU'RE GONNA SEE IS YOUR OWN GUTS ON THE DECK.
LOGAN...

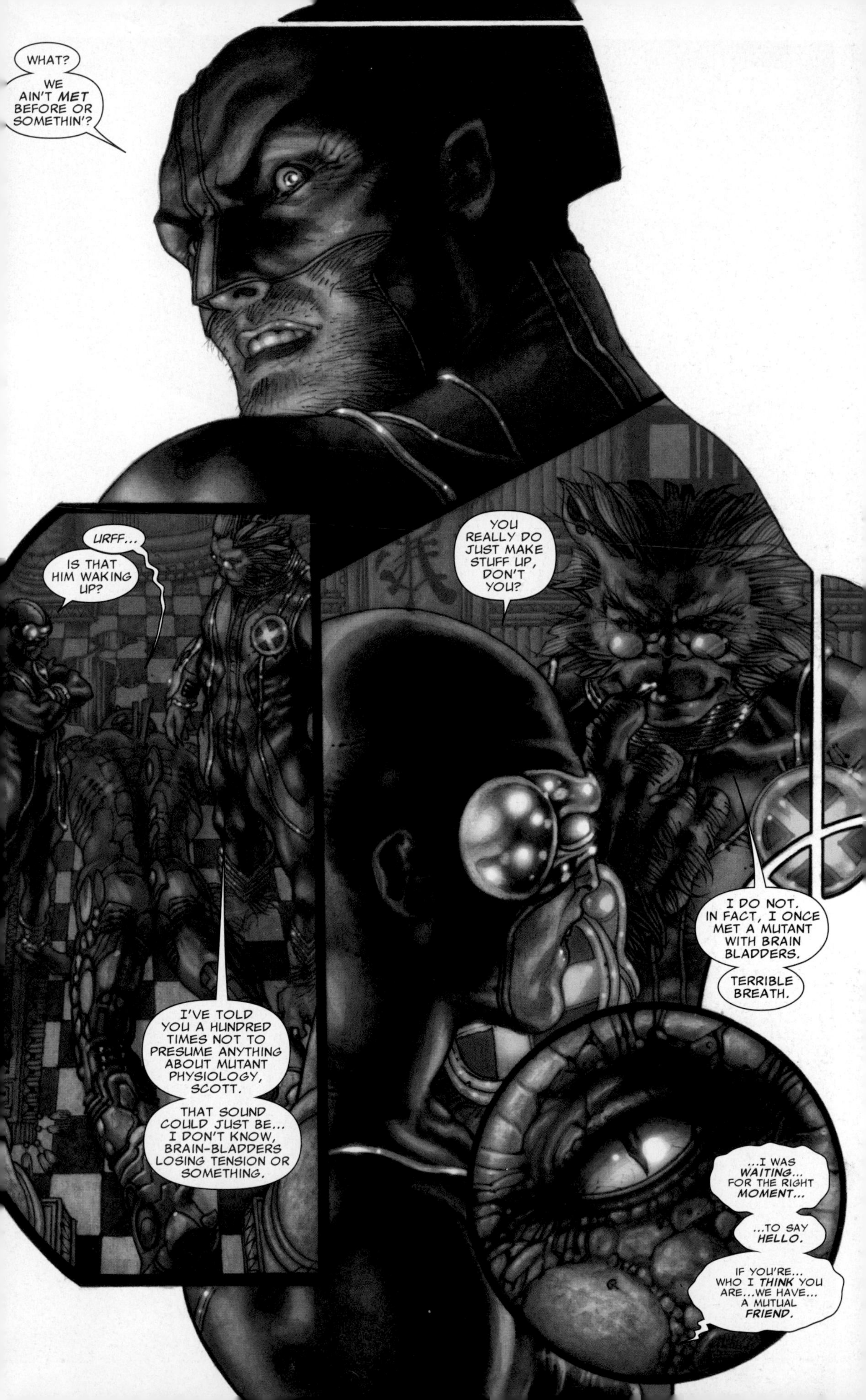
WHAT?
WE AIN'T *MET* BEFORE OR SOMETHIN'?
URFF...
IS THAT HIM WAKING UP?
I'VE TOLD YOU A HUNDRED TIMES NOT TO PRESUME ANYTHING ABOUT MUTANT PHYSIOLOGY, SCOTT.
THAT SOUND COULD JUST BE... I DON'T KNOW, BRAIN-BLADDERS LOSING TENSION OR SOMETHING.
YOU REALLY DO JUST MAKE STUFF UP, DON'T YOU?
I DO NOT. IN FACT, I ONCE MET A MUTANT WITH BRAIN BLADDERS.
TERRIBLE BREATH.
...I WAS *WAITING*... FOR THE RIGHT *MOMENT*...
...TO SAY *HELLO*.
IF YOU'RE... WHO I *THINK* YOU ARE...WE HAVE... A MUTUAL *FRIEND*.

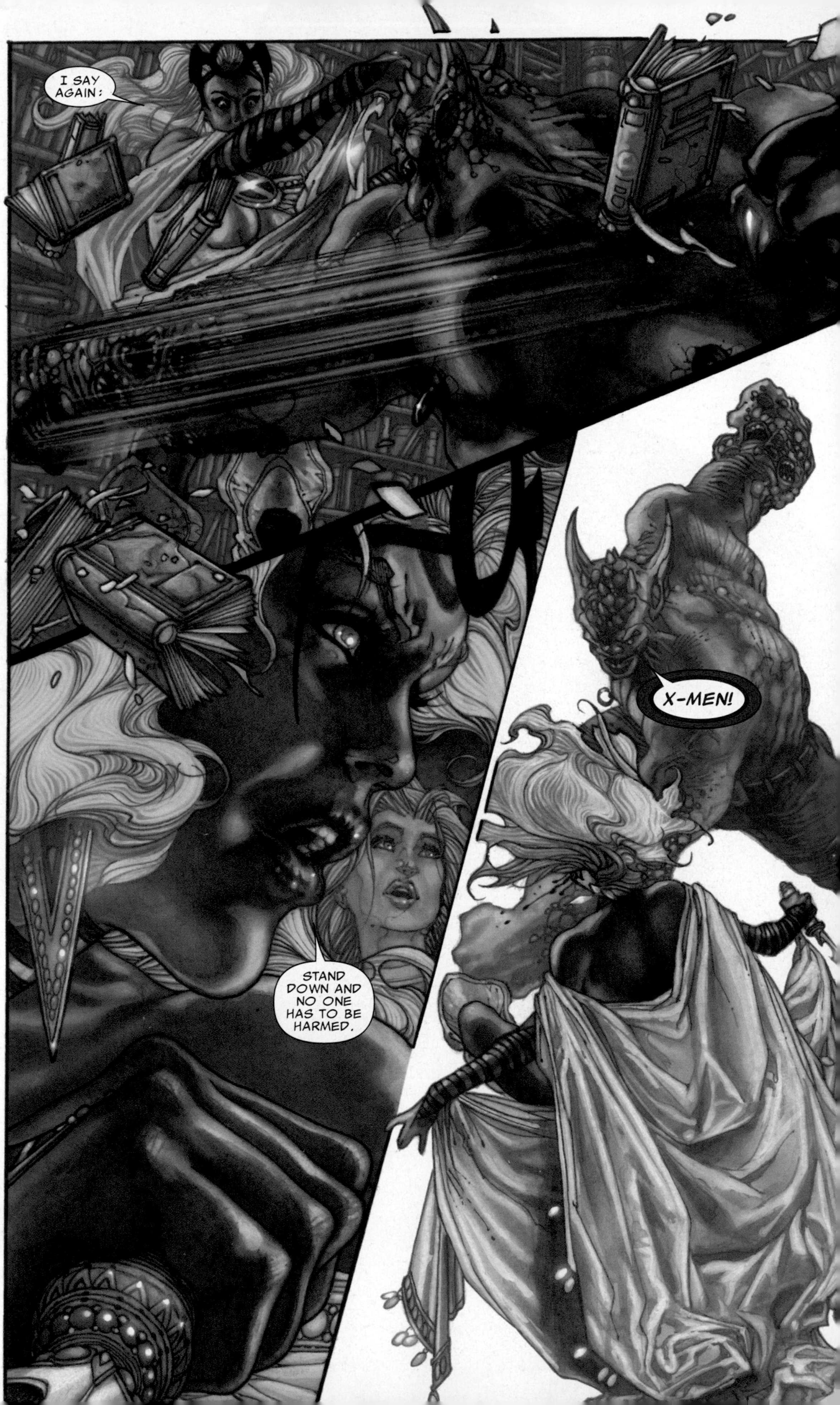
I SAY AGAIN:
STAND DOWN AND NO ONE HAS TO BE HARMED.
X-MEN!

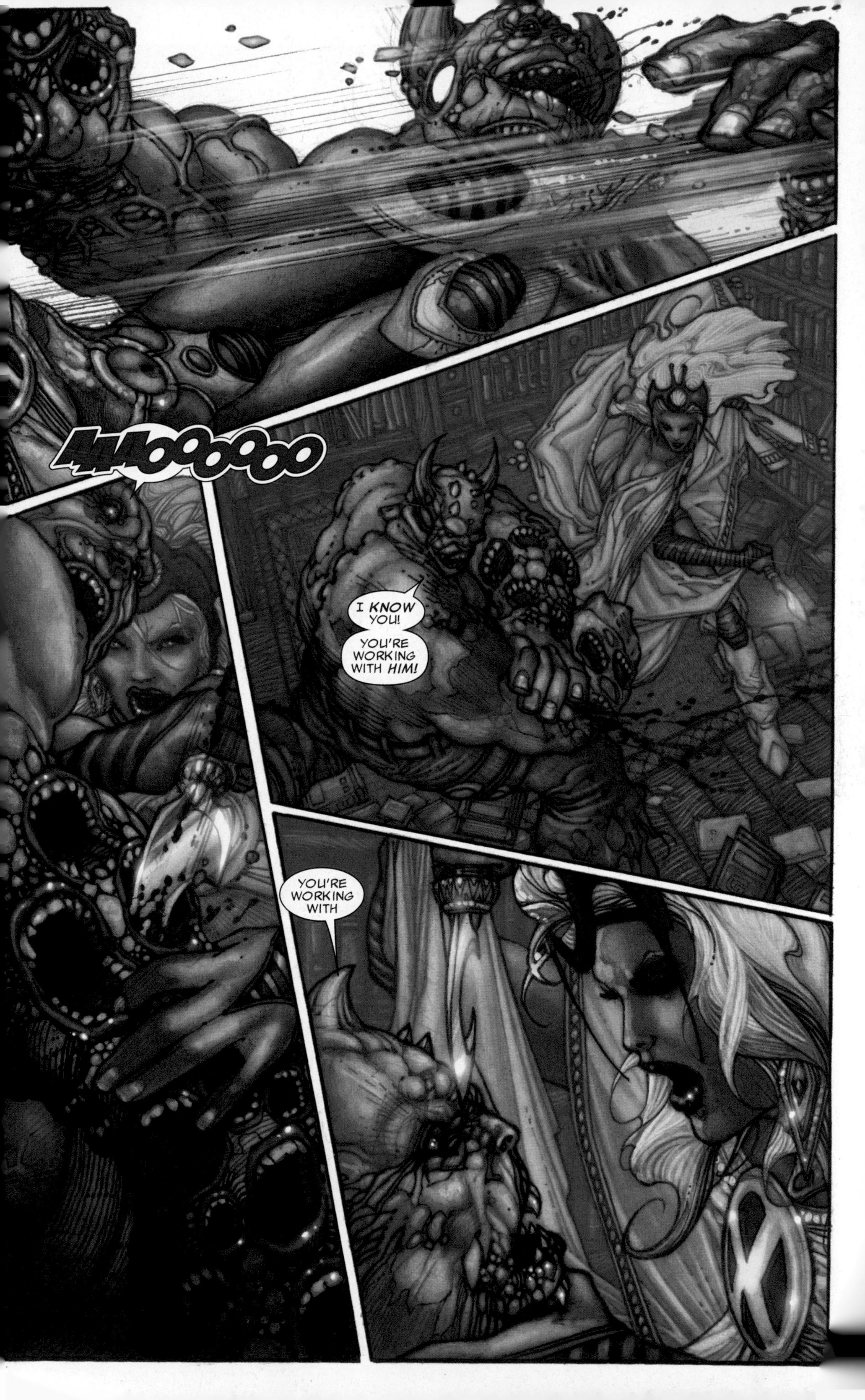
AHOOOOOO
I KNOW YOU!
YOU'RE WORKING WITH HIM!
YOU'RE WORKING WITH

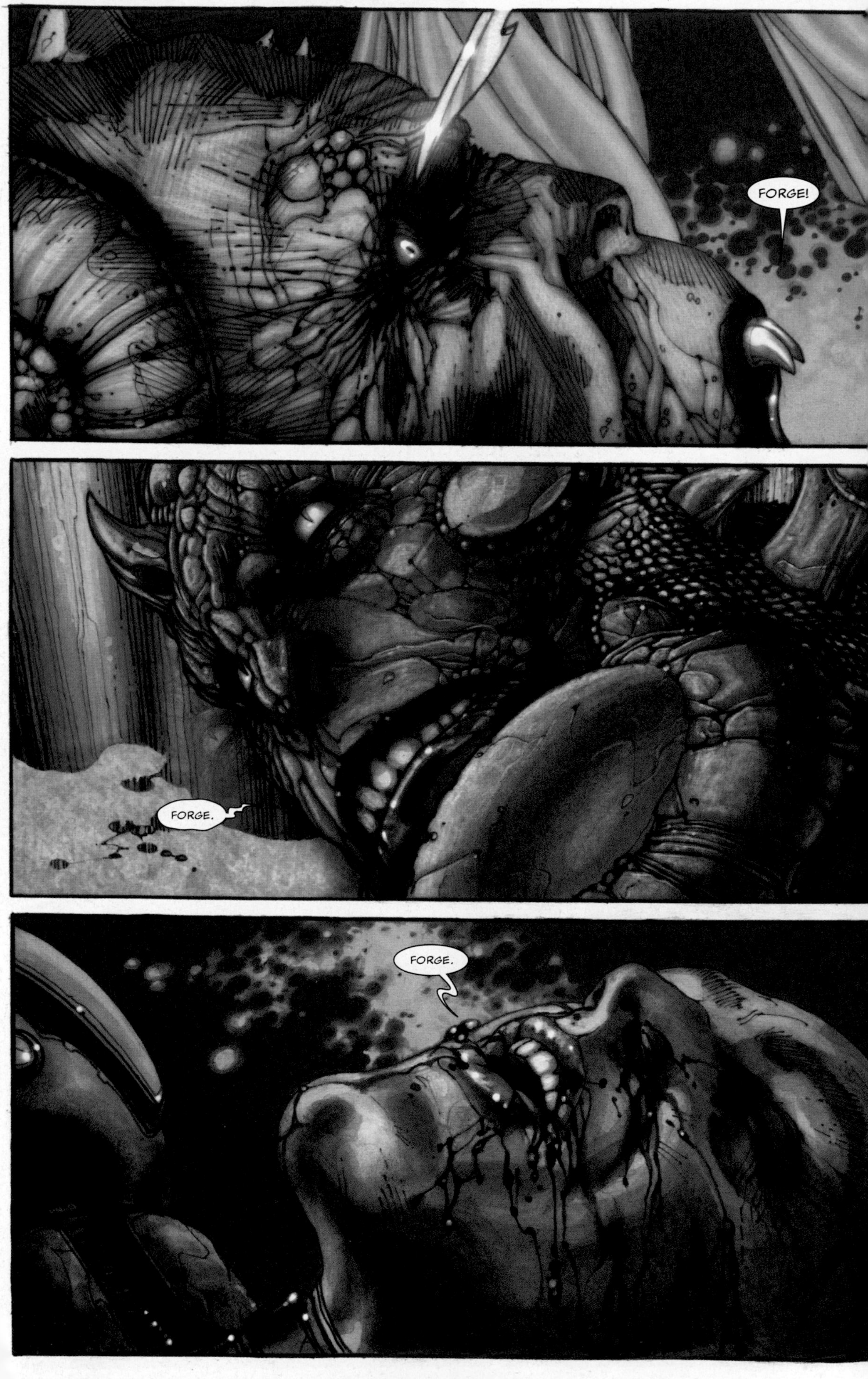
FORGE!
FORGE.
FORGE.

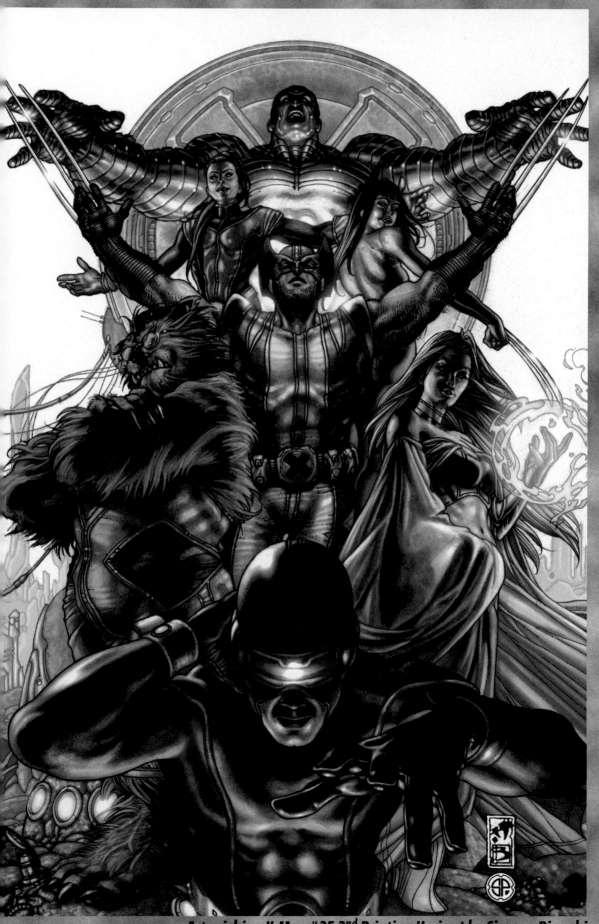

Astonishing X-Men #25 2nd Printing Variant by Simone Bianchi

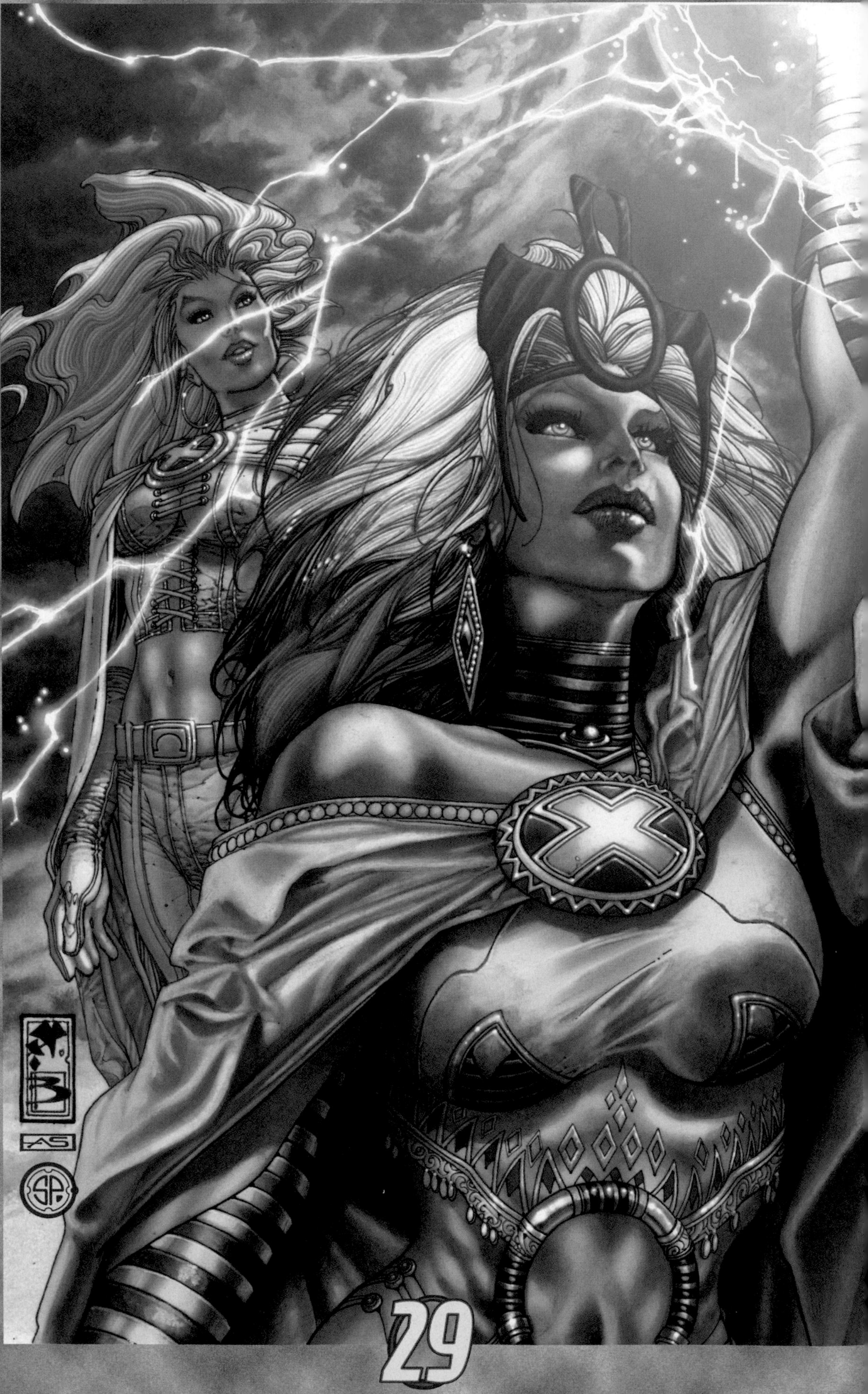
29

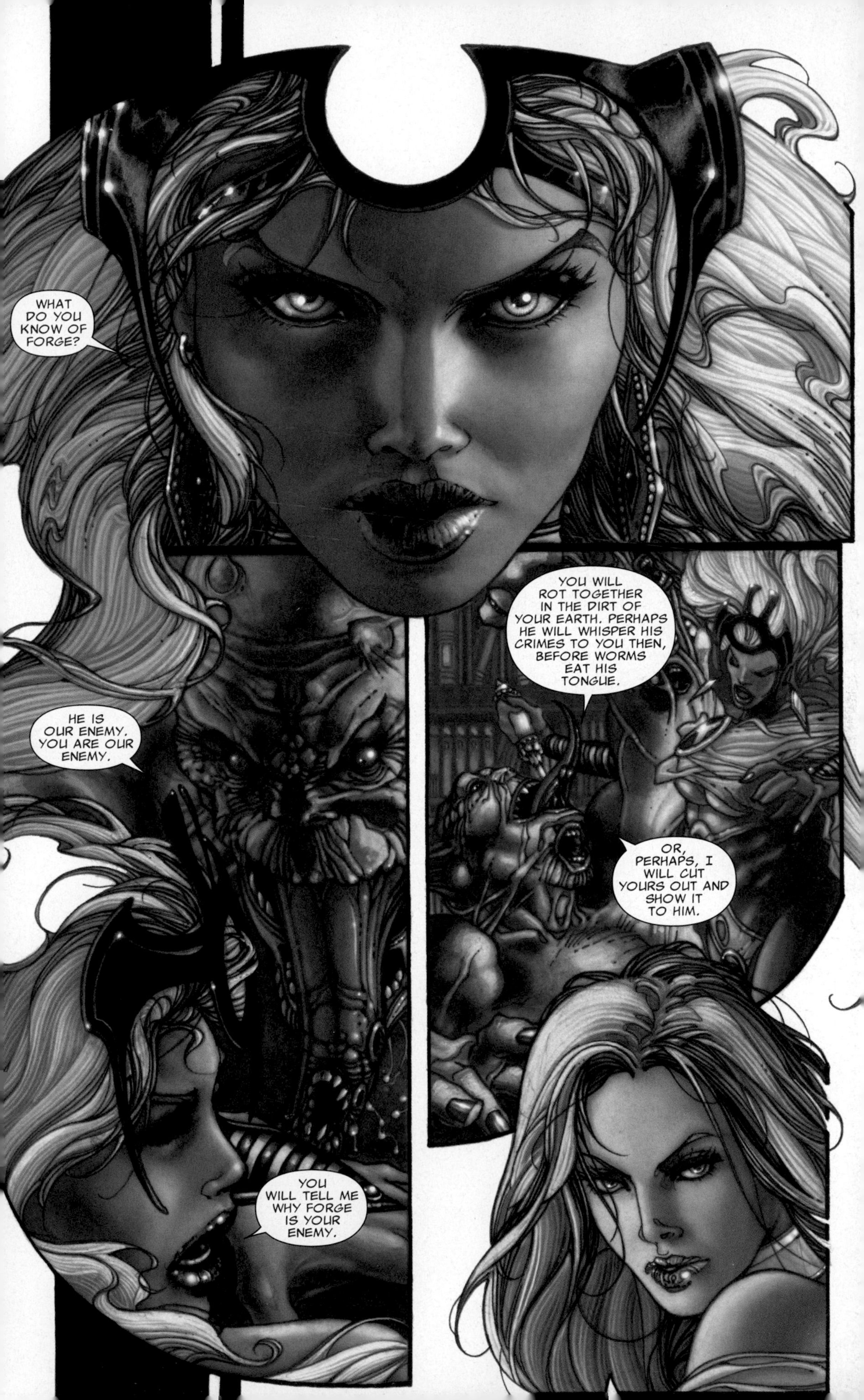
WHAT DO YOU KNOW OF FORGE?
HE IS OUR ENEMY. YOU ARE OUR ENEMY.
YOU WILL TELL ME WHY FORGE IS YOUR ENEMY.
YOU WILL ROT TOGETHER IN THE DIRT OF YOUR EARTH. PERHAPS HE WILL WHISPER HIS CRIMES TO YOU THEN, BEFORE WORMS EAT HIS TONGUE.
OR, PERHAPS, I WILL CUT YOURS OUT AND SHOW IT TO HIM.

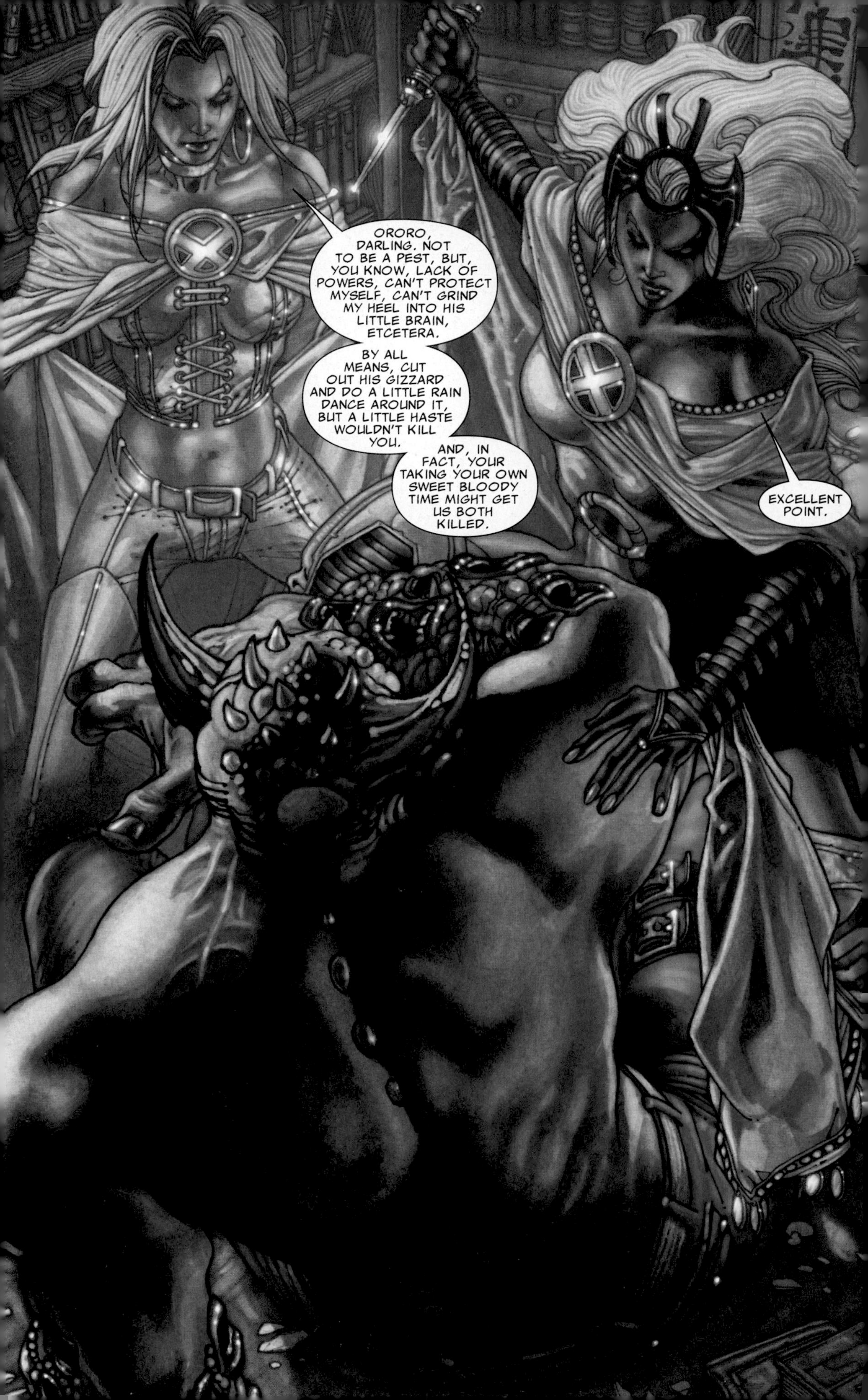
ORORO, DARLING. NOT TO BE A PEST, BUT, YOU KNOW, LACK OF POWERS, CAN'T PROTECT MYSELF, CAN'T GRIND MY HEEL INTO HIS LITTLE BRAIN, ETCETERA.
BY ALL MEANS, CUT OUT HIS GIZZARD AND DO A LITTLE RAIN DANCE AROUND IT, BUT A LITTLE HASTE WOULDN'T KILL YOU.
AND, IN FACT, YOUR TAKING YOUR OWN SWEET BLOODY TIME MIGHT GET US BOTH KILLED.
EXCELLENT POINT.

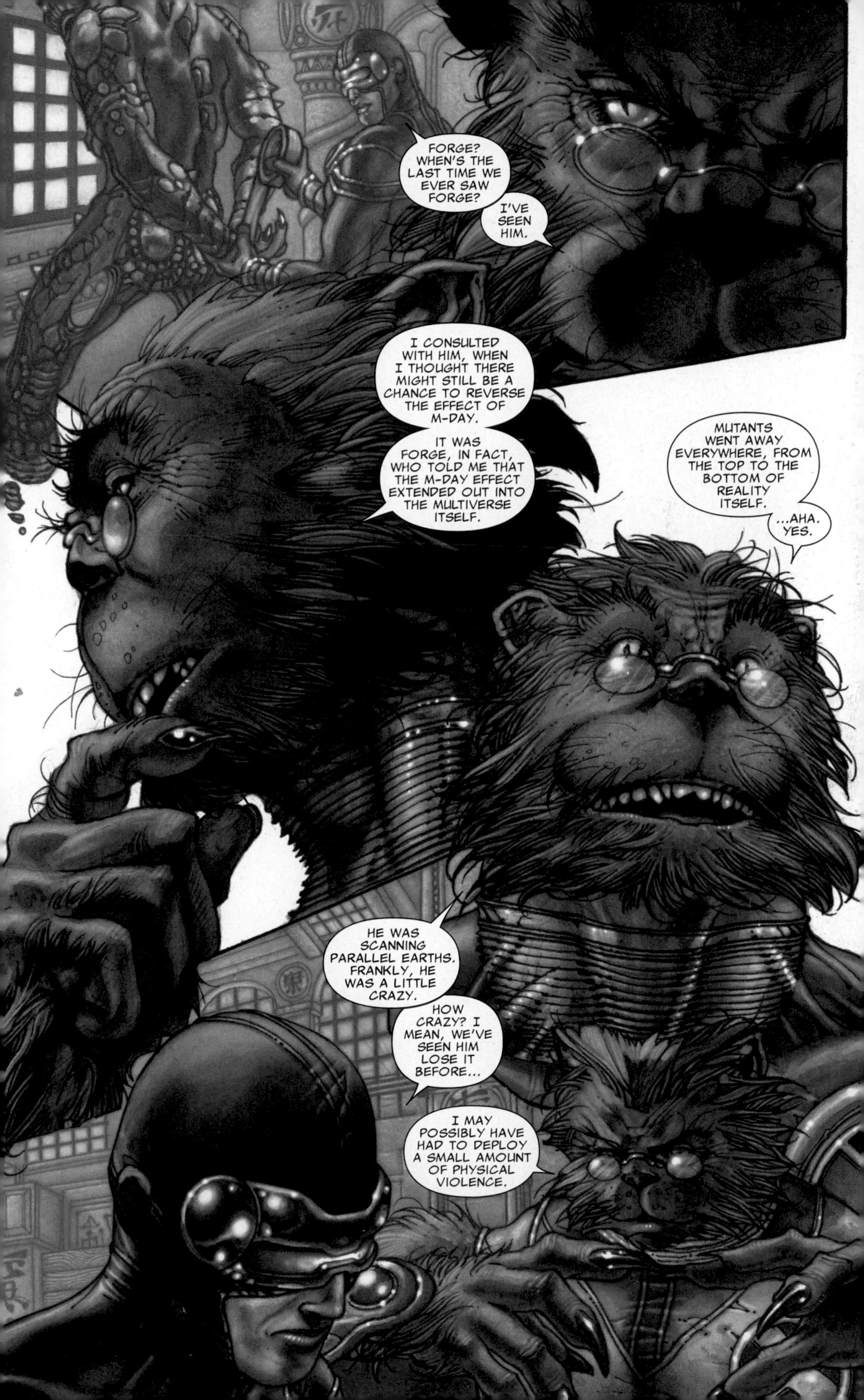
FORGE? WHEN'S THE LAST TIME WE EVER SAW FORGE?
I'VE SEEN HIM.
I CONSULTED WITH HIM, WHEN I THOUGHT THERE MIGHT STILL BE A CHANCE TO REVERSE THE EFFECT OF M-DAY.
IT WAS FORGE, IN FACT, WHO TOLD ME THAT THE M-DAY EFFECT EXTENDED OUT INTO THE MULTIVERSE ITSELF.
MUTANTS WENT AWAY EVERYWHERE, FROM THE TOP TO THE BOTTOM OF REALITY ITSELF.
...AHA. YES.
HE WAS SCANNING PARALLEL EARTHS. FRANKLY, HE WAS A LITTLE CRAZY.
HOW CRAZY? I MEAN, WE'VE SEEN HIM LOSE IT BEFORE...
I MAY POSSIBLY HAVE HAD TO DEPLOY A SMALL AMOUNT OF PHYSICAL VIOLENCE.

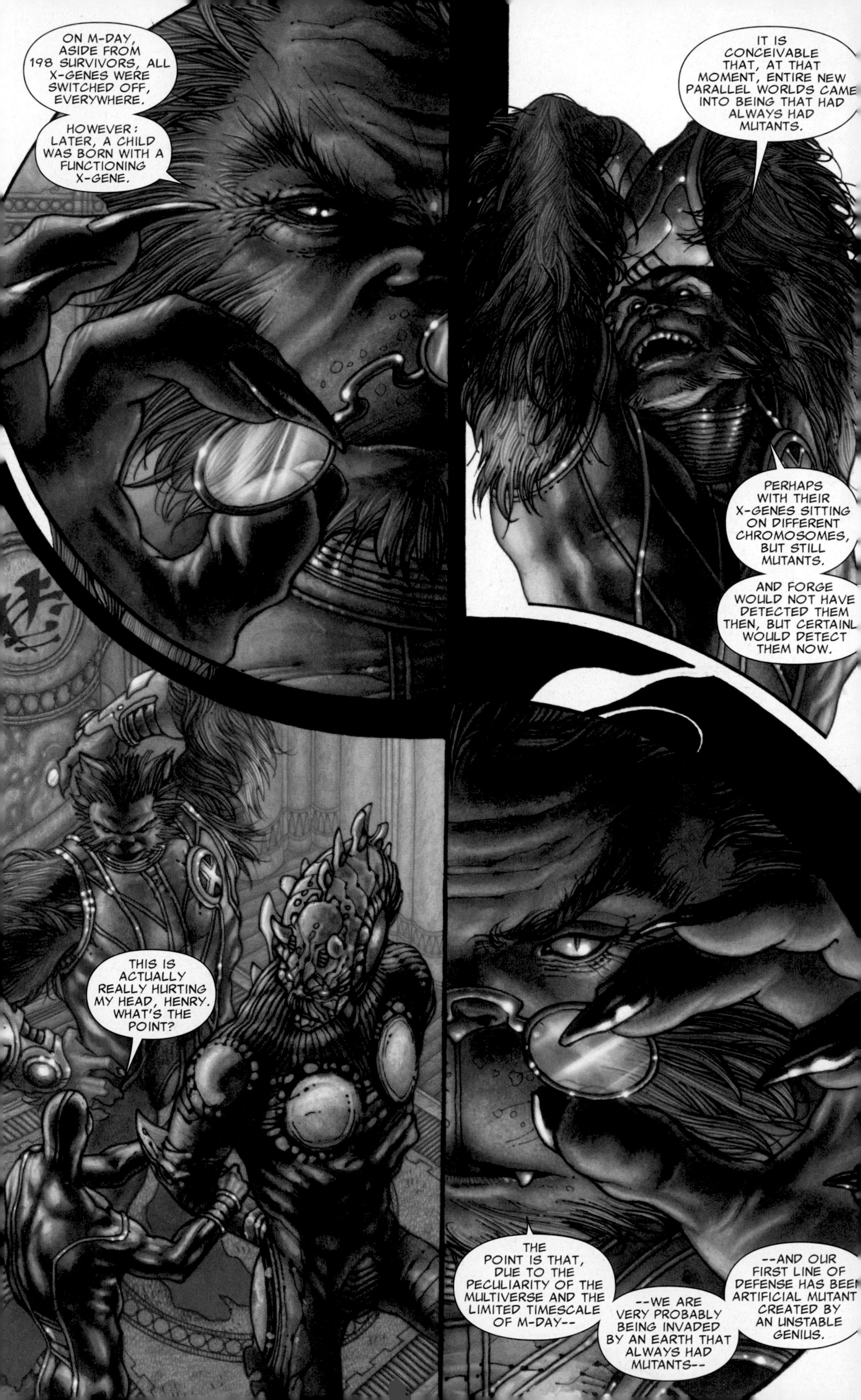
ON M-DAY, ASIDE FROM 198 SURVIVORS, ALL X-GENES WERE SWITCHED OFF, EVERYWHERE.
HOWEVER: LATER, A CHILD WAS BORN WITH A FUNCTIONING X-GENE.
IT IS CONCEIVABLE THAT, AT THAT MOMENT, ENTIRE NEW PARALLEL WORLDS CAME INTO BEING THAT HAD ALWAYS HAD MUTANTS.
PERHAPS WITH THEIR X-GENES SITTING ON DIFFERENT CHROMOSOMES, BUT STILL MUTANTS.
AND FORGE WOULD NOT HAVE DETECTED THEM THEN, BUT CERTAINL WOULD DETECT THEM NOW.
THIS IS ACTUALLY REALLY HURTING MY HEAD, HENRY. WHAT'S THE POINT?
THE POINT IS THAT, DUE TO THE PECULIARITY OF THE MULTIVERSE AND THE LIMITED TIMESCALE OF M-DAY--
--WE ARE VERY PROBABLY BEING INVADED BY AN EARTH THAT ALWAYS HAD MUTANTS--
--AND OUR FIRST LINE OF DEFENSE HAS BEE ARTIFICIAL MUTANT CREATED BY AN UNSTABLE GENIUS.

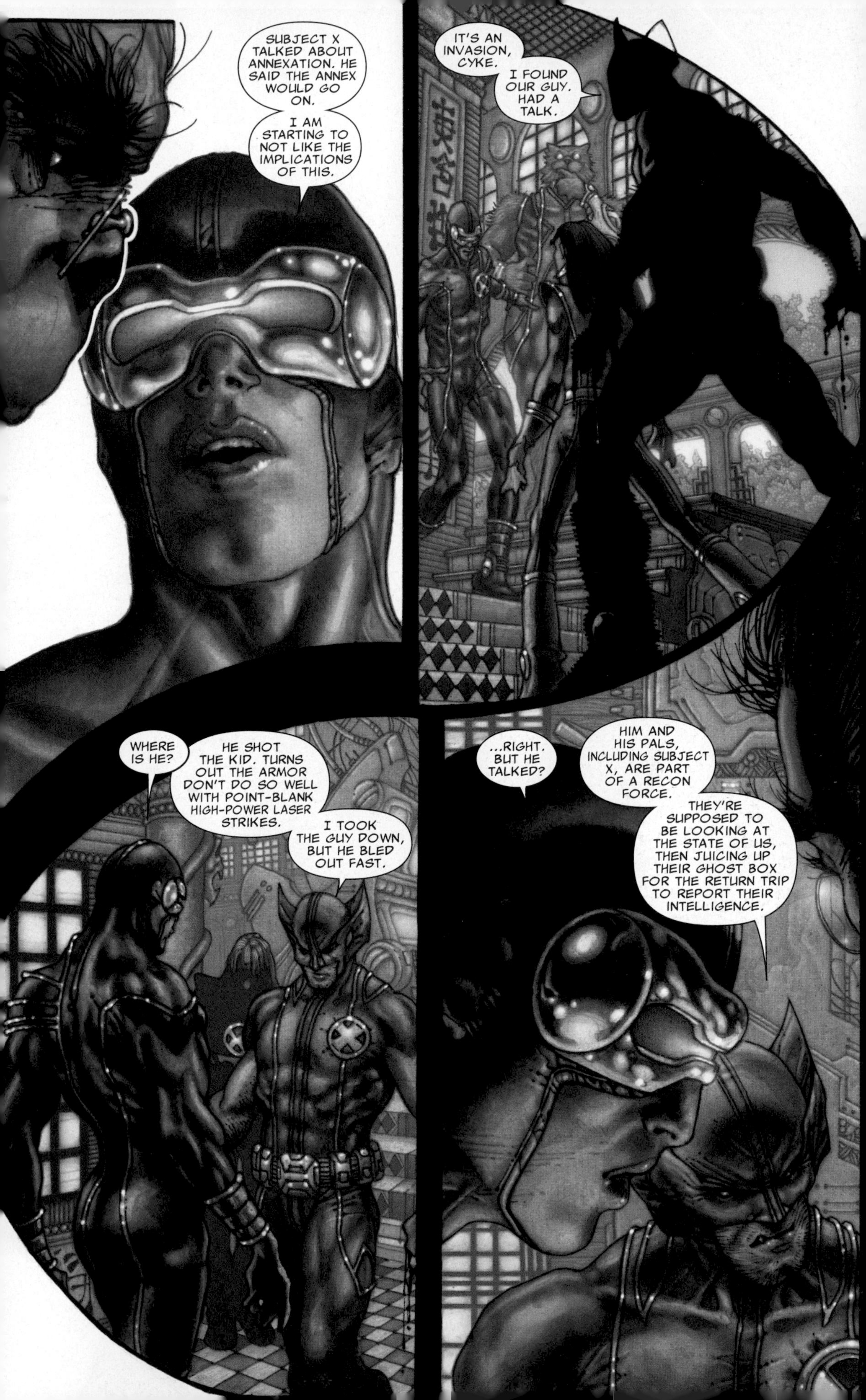
SUBJECT X TALKED ABOUT ANNEXATION. HE SAID THE ANNEX WOULD GO ON.
I AM STARTING TO NOT LIKE THE IMPLICATIONS OF THIS.
IT'S AN INVASION, CYKE.
I FOUND OUR GUY. HAD A TALK.
WHERE IS HE?
HE SHOT THE KID. TURNS OUT THE ARMOR DON'T DO SO WELL WITH POINT-BLANK HIGH-POWER LASER STRIKES.
I TOOK THE GUY DOWN, BUT HE BLED OUT FAST.
...RIGHT. BUT HE TALKED?
HIM AND HIS PALS, INCLUDING SUBJECT X, ARE PART OF A RECON FORCE.
THEY'RE SUPPOSED TO BE LOOKING AT THE STATE OF US, THEN JUICING UP THEIR GHOST BOX FOR THE RETURN TRIP TO REPORT THEIR INTELLIGENCE.

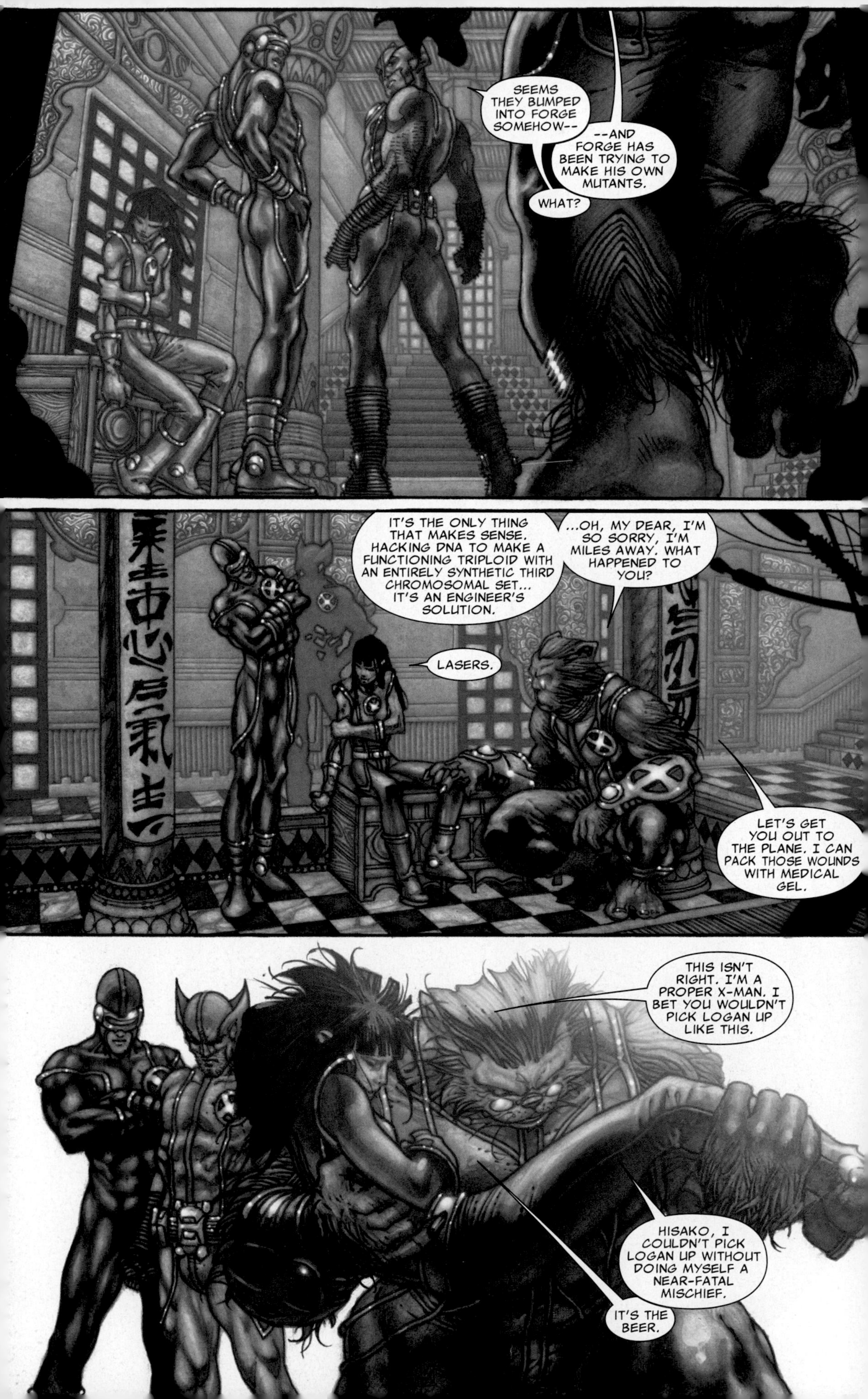
SEEMS THEY BUMPED INTO FORGE SOMEHOW--
--AND FORGE HAS BEEN TRYING TO MAKE HIS OWN MUTANTS.
WHAT?
IT'S THE ONLY THING THAT MAKES SENSE. HACKING DNA TO MAKE A FUNCTIONING TRIPLOID WITH AN ENTIRELY SYNTHETIC THIRD CHROMOSOMAL SET... IT'S AN ENGINEER'S SOLUTION.
...OH, MY DEAR, I'M SO SORRY, I'M MILES AWAY. WHAT HAPPENED TO YOU?
LASERS.
LET'S GET YOU OUT TO THE PLANE. I CAN PACK THOSE WOUNDS WITH MEDICAL GEL.
THIS ISN'T RIGHT. I'M A PROPER X-MAN. I BET YOU WOULDN'T PICK LOGAN UP LIKE THIS.
HISAKO, I COULDN'T PICK LOGAN UP WITHOUT DOING MYSELF A NEAR-FATAL MISCHIEF.
IT'S THE BEER.

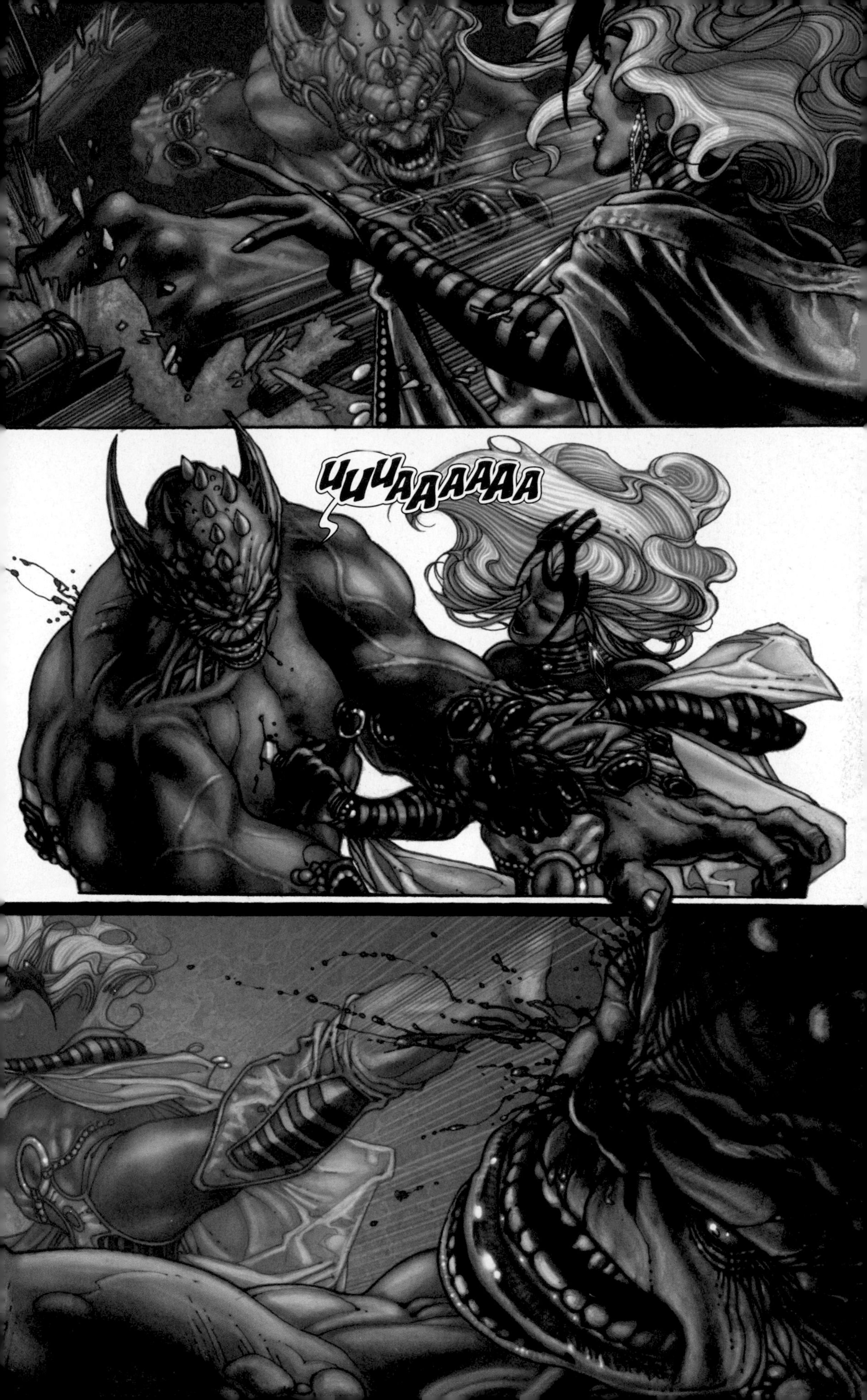
UUUAAAAAAA

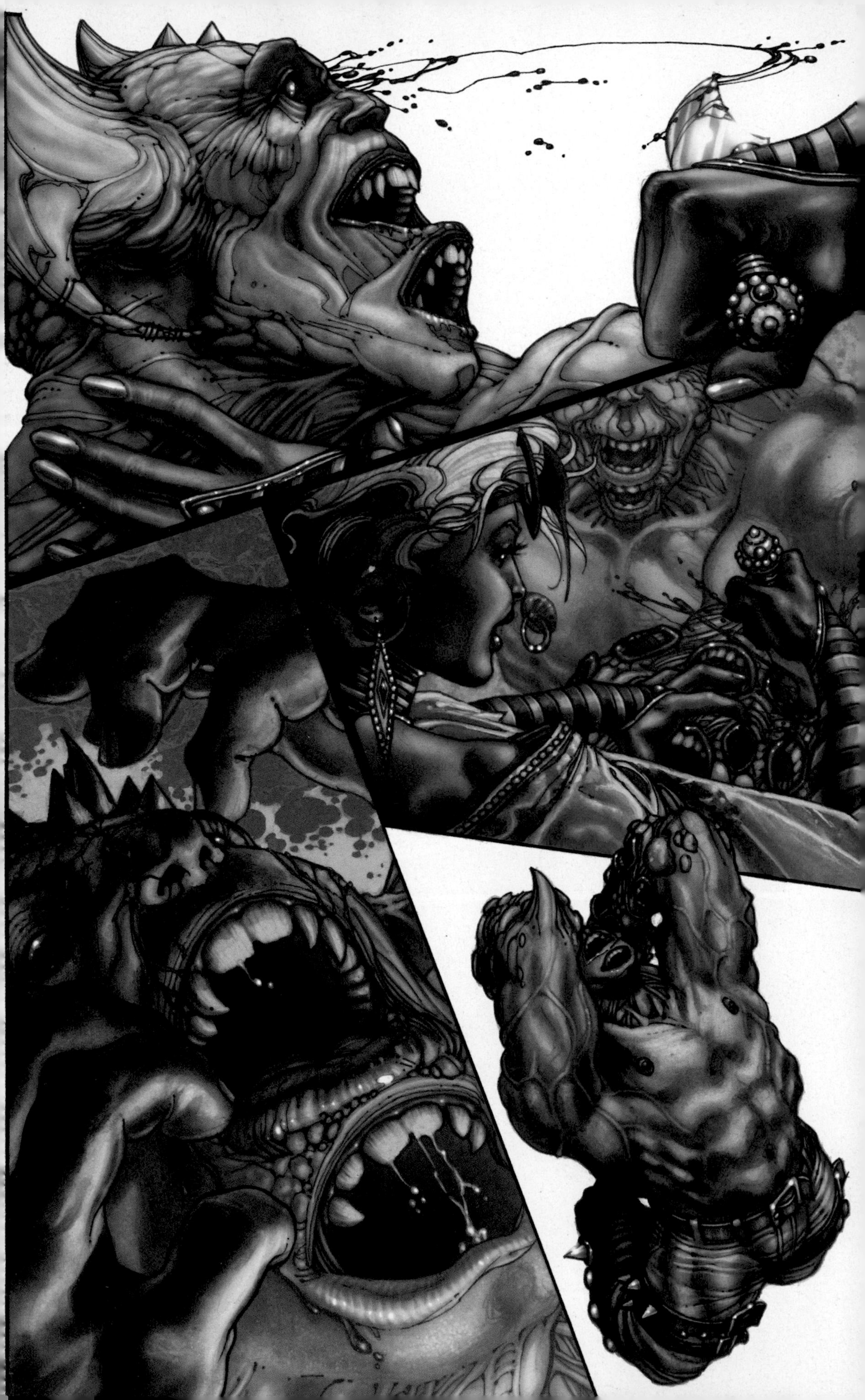

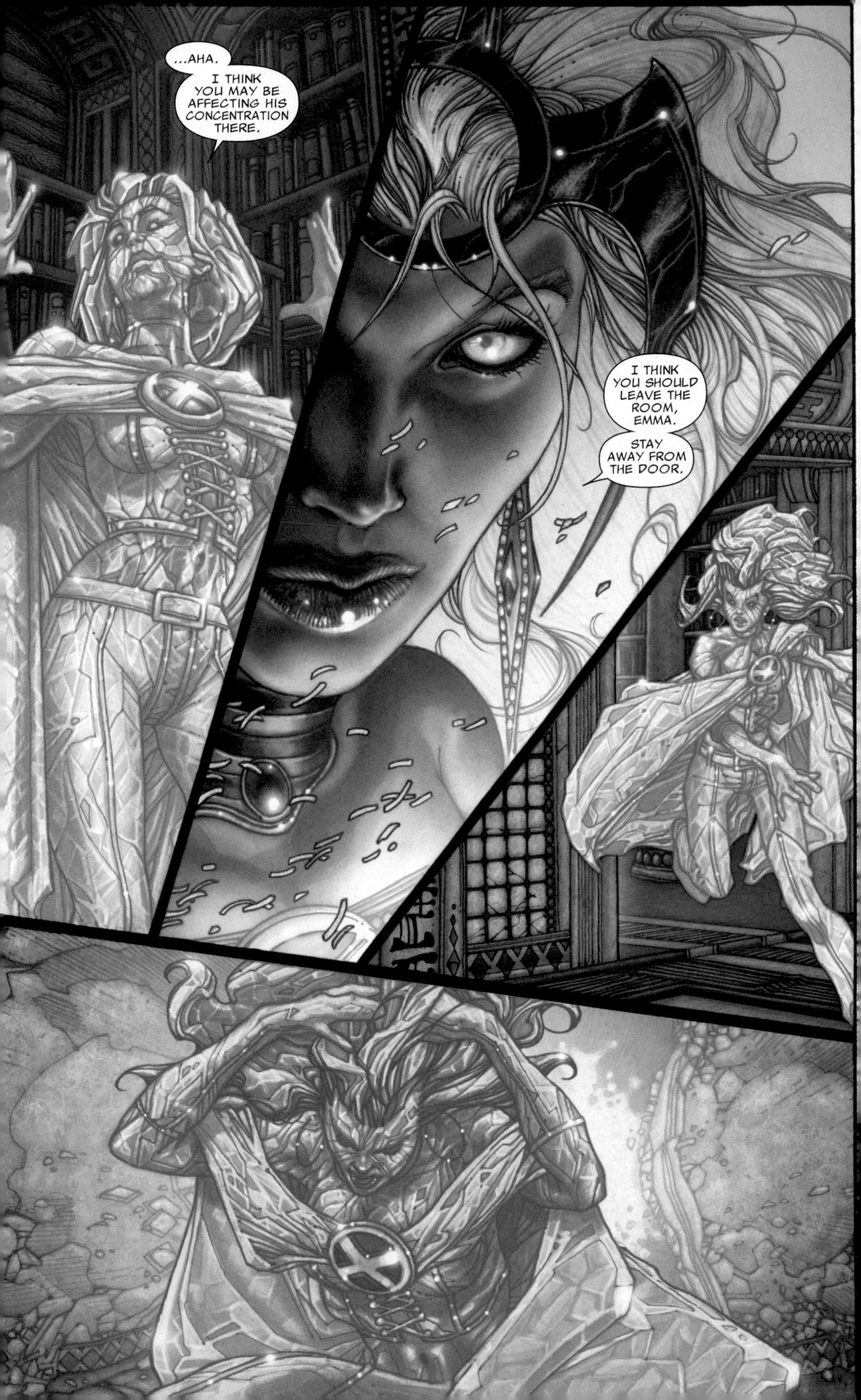
...AHA.
I THINK YOU MAY BE AFFECTING HIS CONCENTRATION THERE.
I THINK YOU SHOULD LEAVE THE ROOM, EMMA.
STAY AWAY FROM THE DOOR.

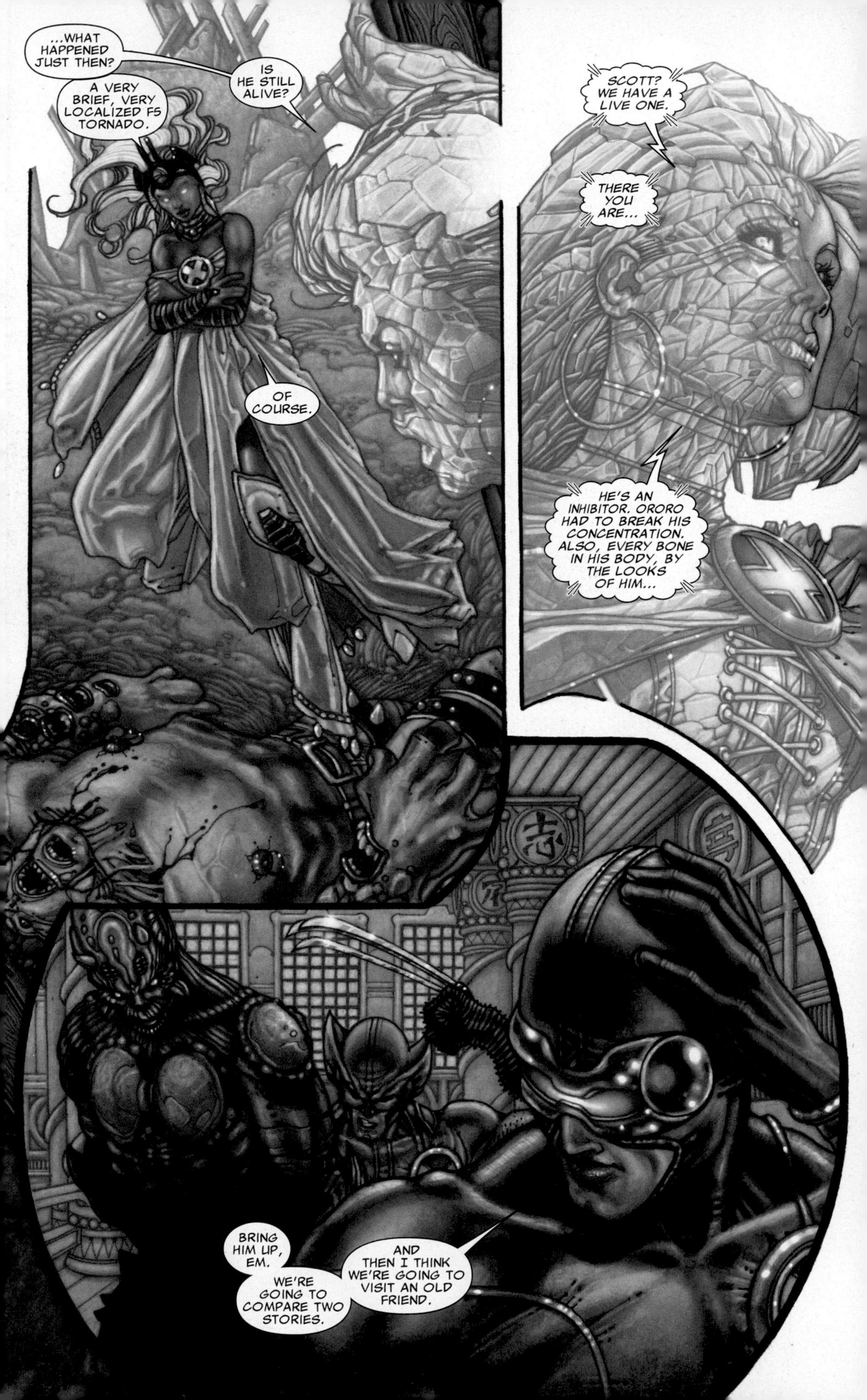
...WHAT HAPPENED JUST THEN?
IS HE STILL ALIVE?
A VERY BRIEF, VERY LOCALIZED F5 TORNADO.
OF COURSE.
SCOTT? WE HAVE A LIVE ONE.
THERE YOU ARE...
HE'S AN INHIBITOR. ORORO HAD TO BREAK HIS CONCENTRATION. ALSO, EVERY BONE IN HIS BODY, BY THE LOOKS OF HIM...
BRING HIM UP, EM.
WE'RE GOING TO COMPARE TWO STORIES.
AND THEN I THINK WE'RE GOING TO VISIT AN OLD FRIEND.

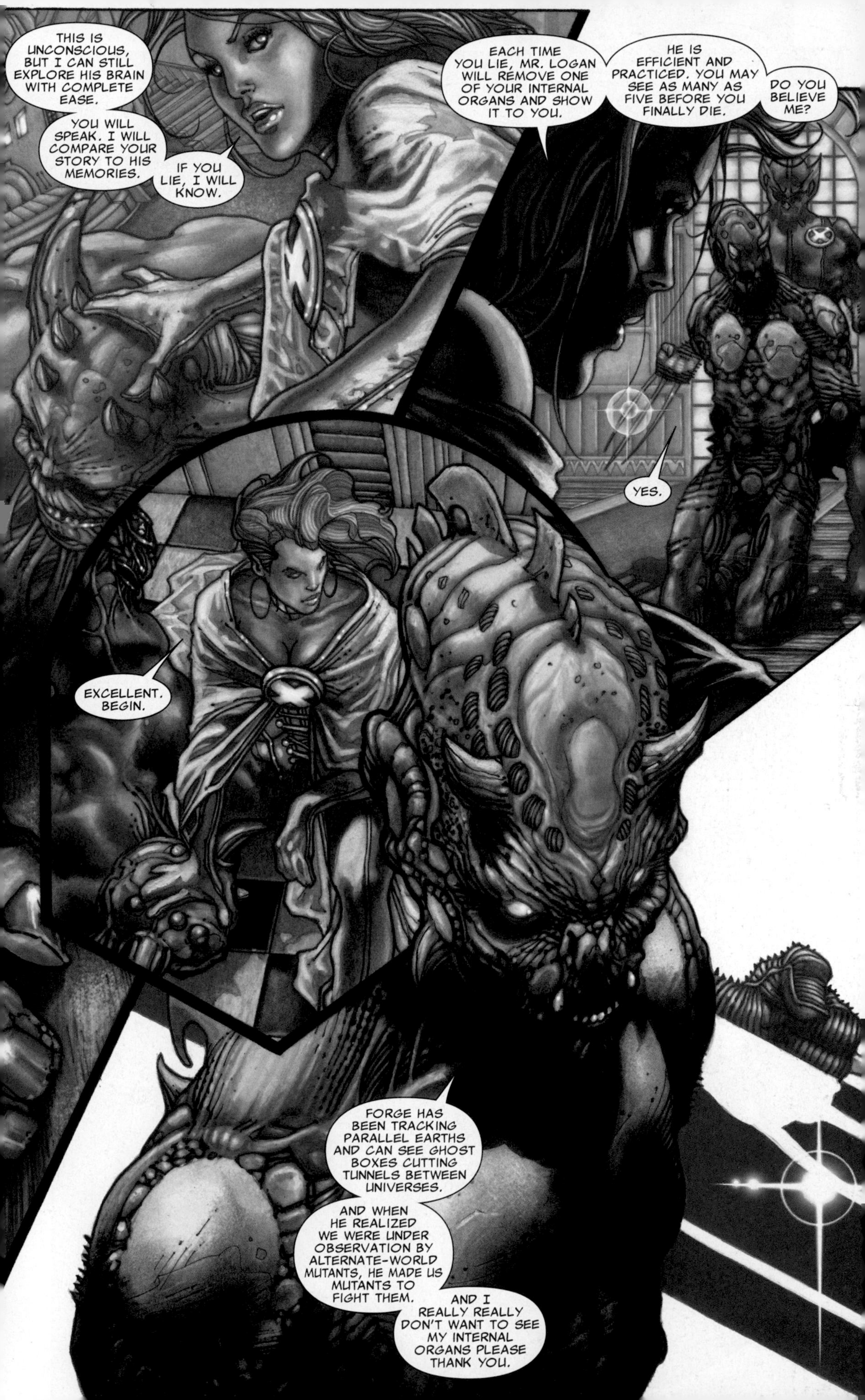
THIS IS UNCONSCIOUS, BUT I CAN STILL EXPLORE HIS BRAIN WITH COMPLETE EASE.
YOU WILL SPEAK. I WILL COMPARE YOUR STORY TO HIS MEMORIES.
IF YOU LIE, I WILL KNOW.
EACH TIME YOU LIE, MR. LOGAN WILL REMOVE ONE OF YOUR INTERNAL ORGANS AND SHOW IT TO YOU.
HE IS EFFICIENT AND PRACTICED. YOU MAY SEE AS MANY AS FIVE BEFORE YOU FINALLY DIE.
DO YOU BELIEVE ME?
YES.
EXCELLENT. BEGIN.
FORGE HAS BEEN TRACKING PARALLEL EARTHS AND CAN SEE GHOST BOXES CUTTING TUNNELS BETWEEN UNIVERSES.
AND WHEN HE REALIZED WE WERE UNDER OBSERVATION BY ALTERNATE-WORLD MUTANTS, HE MADE US MUTANTS TO FIGHT THEM.
AND I REALLY REALLY DON'T WANT TO SEE MY INTERNAL ORGANS PLEASE THANK YOU.

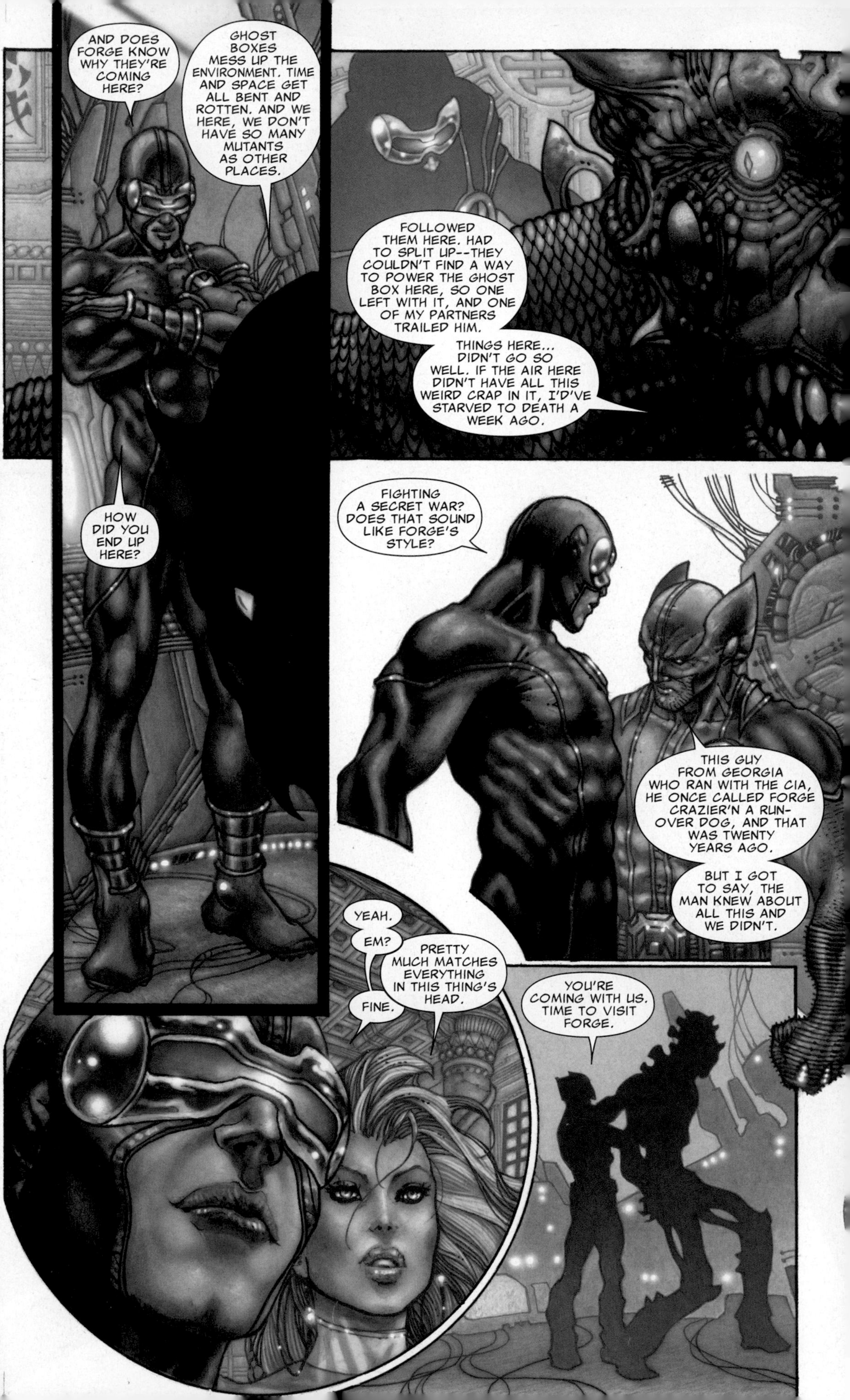
AND DOES FORGE KNOW WHY THEY'RE COMING HERE?
GHOST BOXES MESS UP THE ENVIRONMENT. TIME AND SPACE GET ALL BENT AND ROTTEN. AND WE HERE, WE DON'T HAVE SO MANY MUTANTS AS OTHER PLACES.
HOW DID YOU END UP HERE?
FOLLOWED THEM HERE. HAD TO SPLIT UP--THEY COULDN'T FIND A WAY TO POWER THE GHOST BOX HERE, SO ONE LEFT WITH IT, AND ONE OF MY PARTNERS TRAILED HIM.
THINGS HERE... DIDN'T GO SO WELL. IF THE AIR HERE DIDN'T HAVE ALL THIS WEIRD CRAP IN IT, I'D'VE STARVED TO DEATH A WEEK AGO.
FIGHTING A SECRET WAR? DOES THAT SOUND LIKE FORGE'S STYLE?
THIS GUY FROM GEORGIA WHO RAN WITH THE CIA, HE ONCE CALLED FORGE CRAZIER'N A RUN-OVER DOG, AND THAT WAS TWENTY YEARS AGO.
BUT I GOT TO SAY, THE MAN KNEW ABOUT ALL THIS AND WE DIDN'T.
YEAH.
EM?
PRETTY MUCH MATCHES EVERYTHING IN THIS THING'S HEAD.
FINE.
YOU'RE COMING WITH US. TIME TO VISIT FORGE.

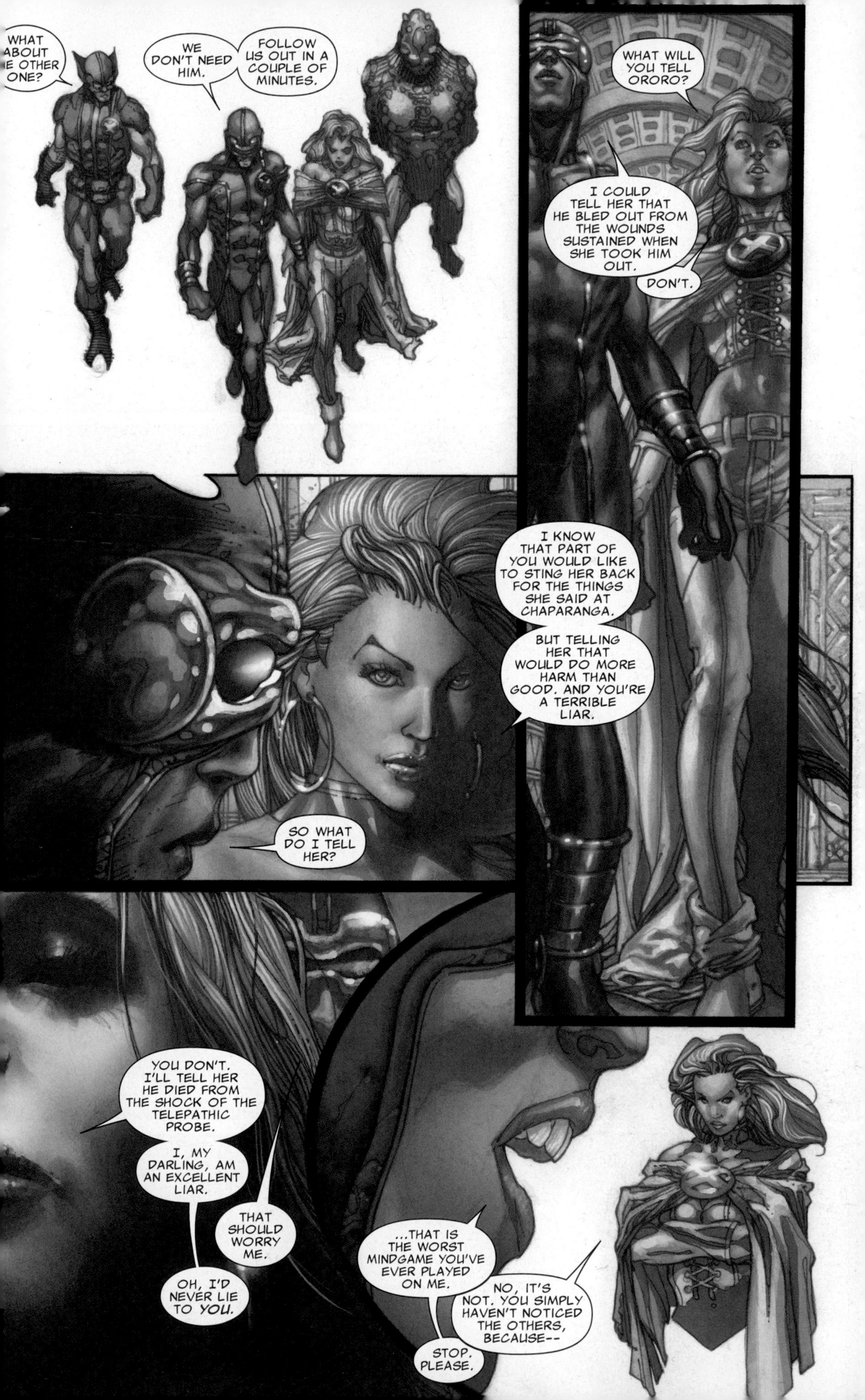
WHAT ABOUT THE OTHER ONE?
WE DON'T NEED HIM.
FOLLOW US OUT IN A COUPLE OF MINUTES.
WHAT WILL YOU TELL ORORO?
I COULD TELL HER THAT HE BLED OUT FROM THE WOUNDS SUSTAINED WHEN SHE TOOK HIM OUT.
DON'T.
I KNOW THAT PART OF YOU WOULD LIKE TO STING HER BACK FOR THE THINGS SHE SAID AT CHAPARANGA.
BUT TELLING HER THAT WOULD DO MORE HARM THAN GOOD. AND YOU'RE A TERRIBLE LIAR.
SO WHAT DO I TELL HER?
YOU DON'T. I'LL TELL HER HE DIED FROM THE SHOCK OF THE TELEPATHIC PROBE.
I, MY DARLING, AM AN EXCELLENT LIAR.
THAT SHOULD WORRY ME.
OH, I'D NEVER LIE TO YOU.
...THAT IS THE WORST MINDGAME YOU'VE EVER PLAYED ON ME.
NO, IT'S NOT. YOU SIMPLY HAVEN'T NOTICED THE OTHERS, BECAUSE--
STOP. PLEASE.

...HISAKO, FORGE IS A MAN WITH A MUTANT GENIUS FOR ENGINEERING WHO'S ALSO HAD ONE OR TWO MENTAL PROBLEMS IN THE PAST.

EVEN WITH HIS HEAD ON STRAIGHT, HE'S NEVER MADE THE BEST CHOICES IN THE WORLD.

REGARDLESS OF HOW LONG WE'VE KNOWN HIM, I DON'T THINK WE JUST DROP IN AND SAY HI.

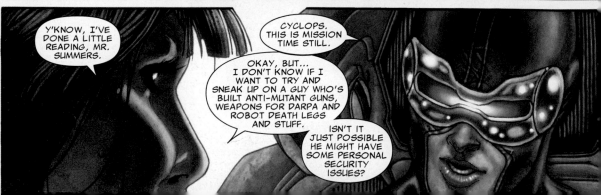

Y'KNOW, I'VE DONE A LITTLE READING, MR. SUMMERS.

CYCLOPS. THIS IS MISSION TIME STILL.

OKAY, BUT... I DON'T KNOW IF I WANT TO TRY AND SNEAK UP ON A GUY WHO'S BUILT ANTI-MUTANT GUNS, WEAPONS FOR DARPA AND ROBOT DEATH LEGS AND STUFF.

ISN'T IT JUST POSSIBLE HE MIGHT HAVE SOME PERSONAL SECURITY ISSUES?

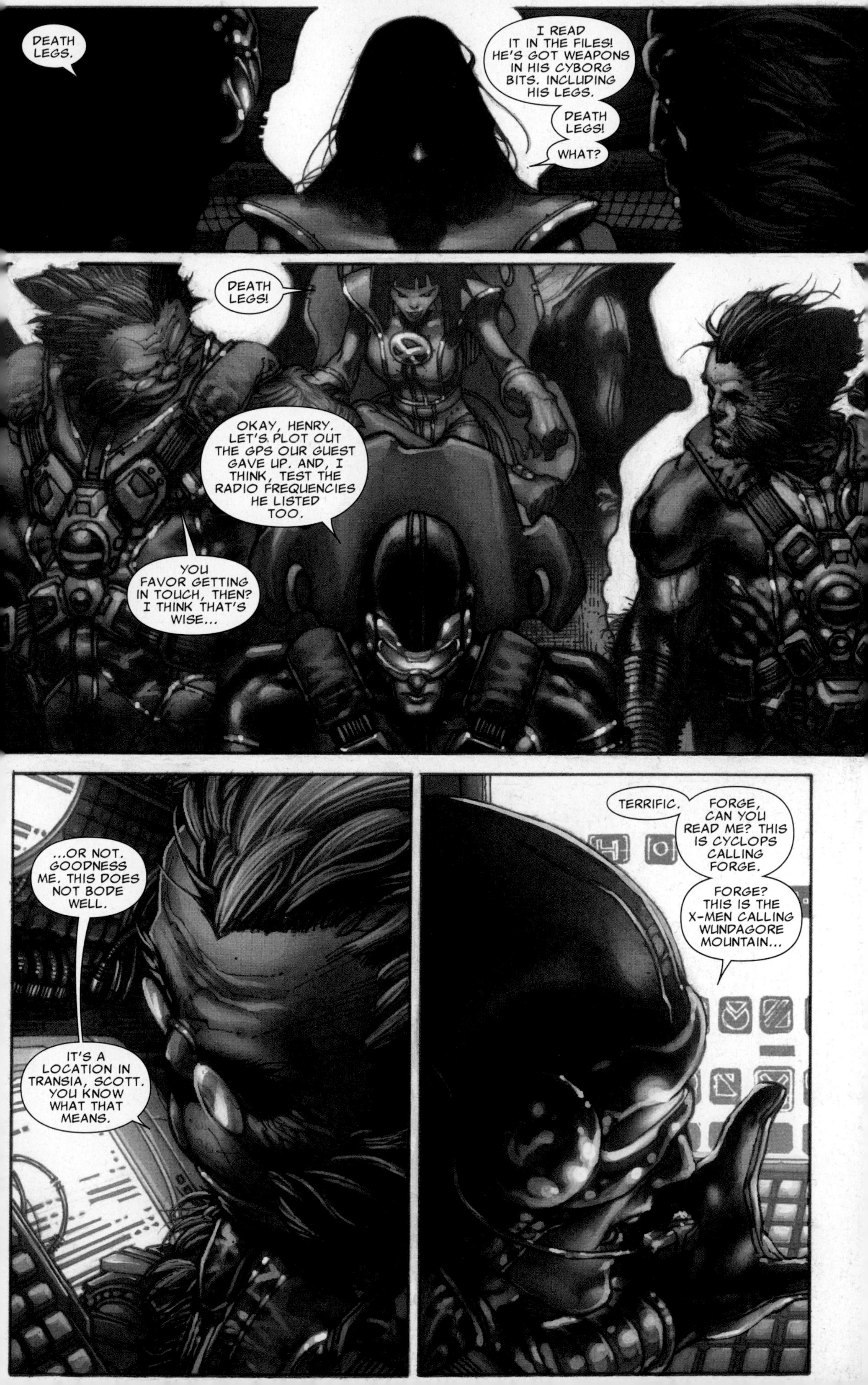
DEATH LEGS.
I READ IT IN THE FILES! HE'S GOT WEAPONS IN HIS CYBORG BITS. INCLUDING HIS LEGS.
DEATH LEGS!
WHAT?
DEATH LEGS!
OKAY, HENRY. LET'S PLOT OUT THE GPS OUR GUEST GAVE UP. AND, I THINK, TEST THE RADIO FREQUENCIES HE LISTED TOO.
YOU FAVOR GETTING IN TOUCH, THEN? I THINK THAT'S WISE...
...OR NOT. GOODNESS ME. THIS DOES NOT BODE WELL.
IT'S A LOCATION IN TRANSIA, SCOTT. YOU KNOW WHAT THAT MEANS.
TERRIFIC.
FORGE, CAN YOU READ ME? THIS IS CYCLOPS CALLING FORGE.
FORGE? THIS IS THE X-MEN CALLING WUNDAGORE MOUNTAIN...

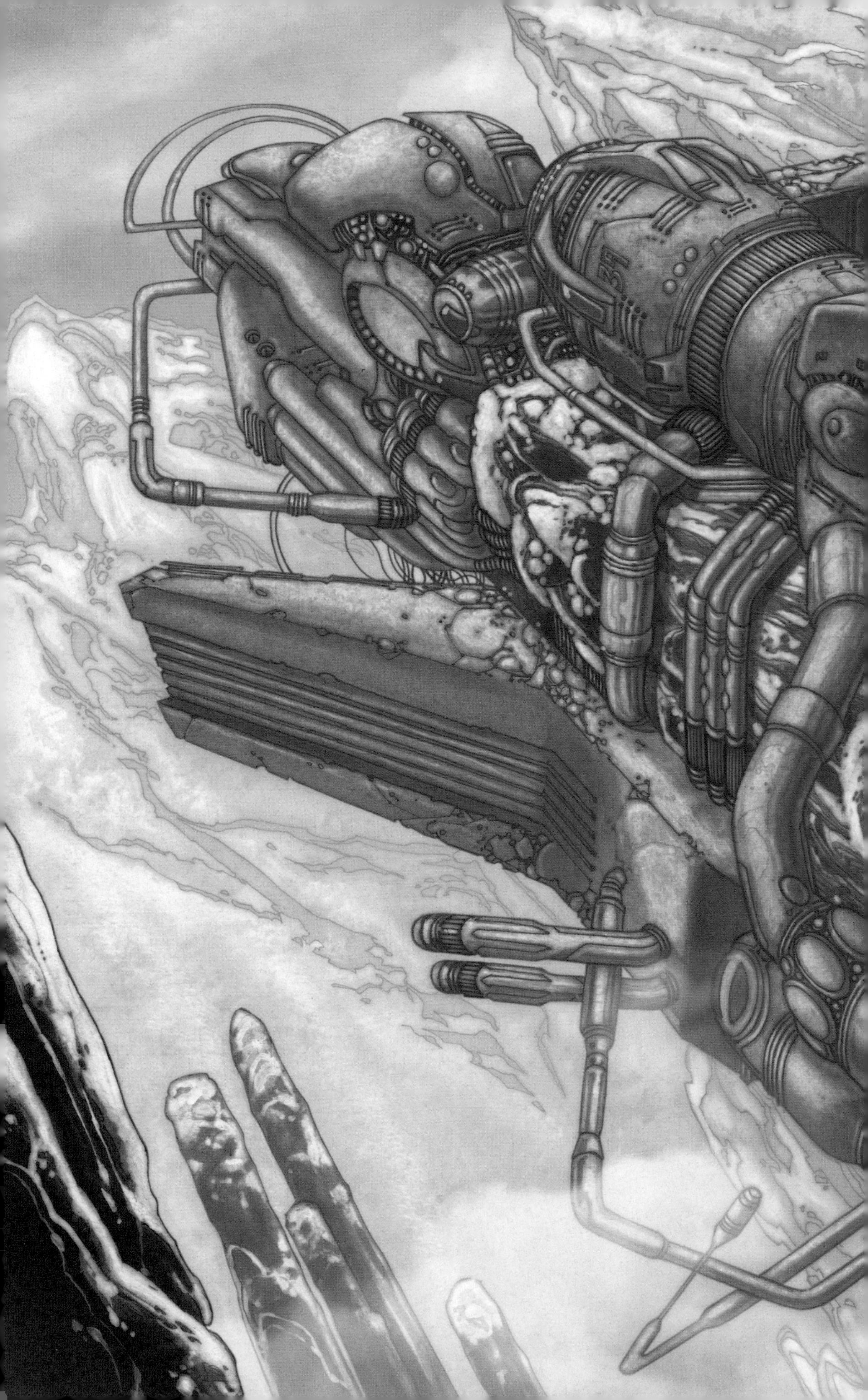

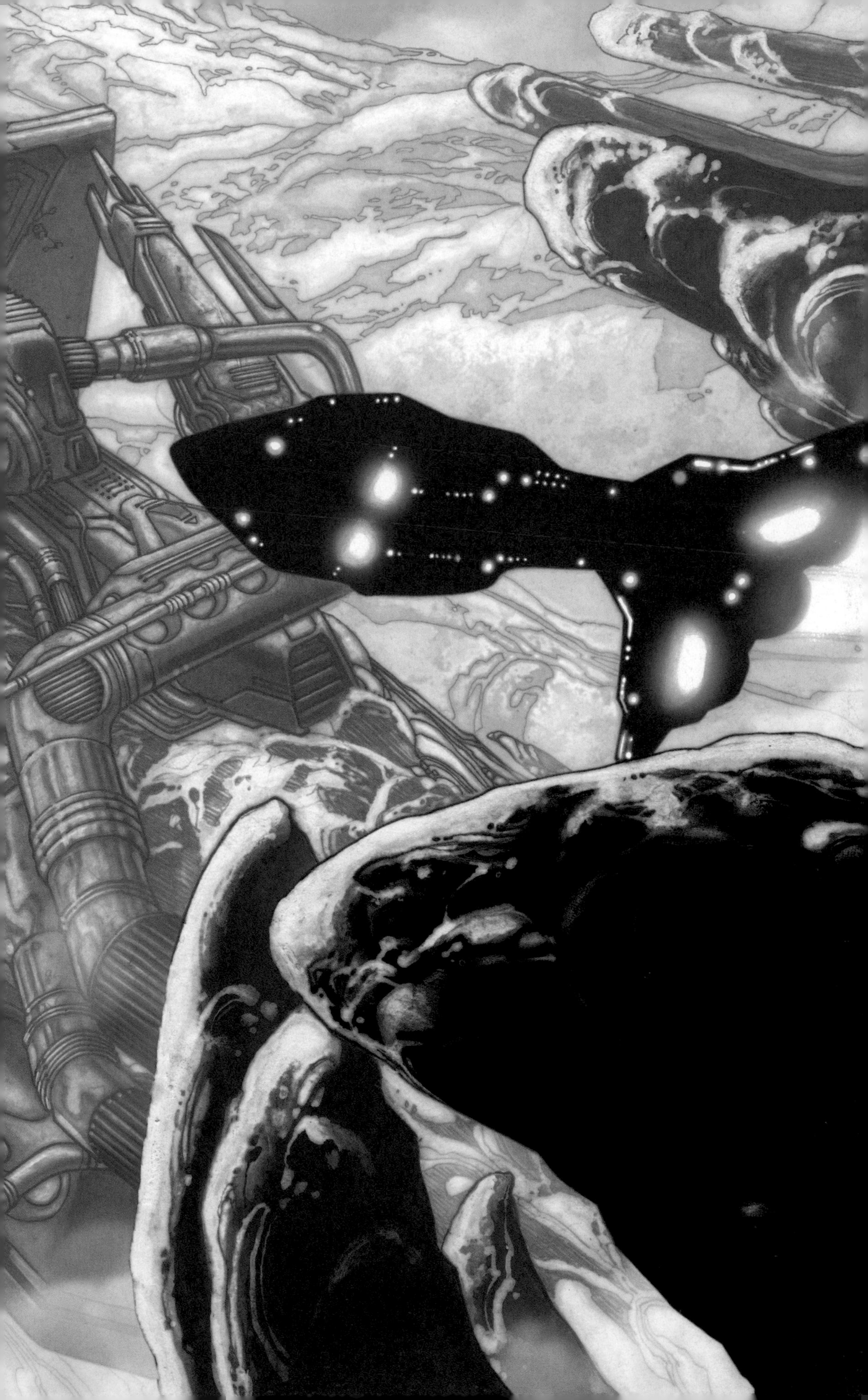

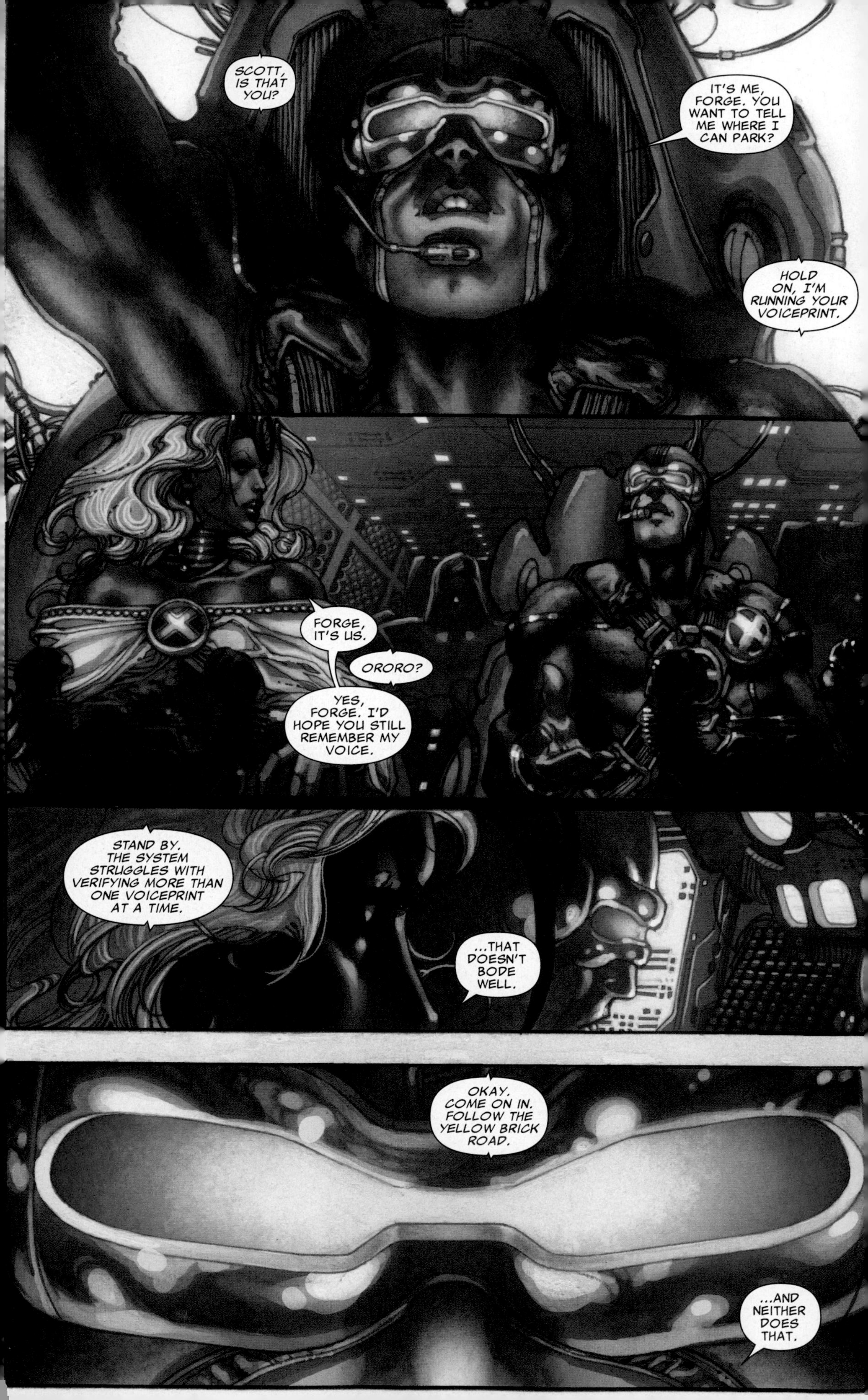
SCOTT, IS THAT YOU?
IT'S ME, FORGE. YOU WANT TO TELL ME WHERE I CAN PARK?
HOLD ON, I'M RUNNING YOUR VOICEPRINT.
FORGE, IT'S US.
ORORO?
YES, FORGE. I'D HOPE YOU STILL REMEMBER MY VOICE.
STAND BY. THE SYSTEM STRUGGLES WITH VERIFYING MORE THAN ONE VOICEPRINT AT A TIME.
...THAT DOESN'T BODE WELL.
OKAY. COME ON IN. FOLLOW THE YELLOW BRICK ROAD.
...AND NEITHER DOES THAT.

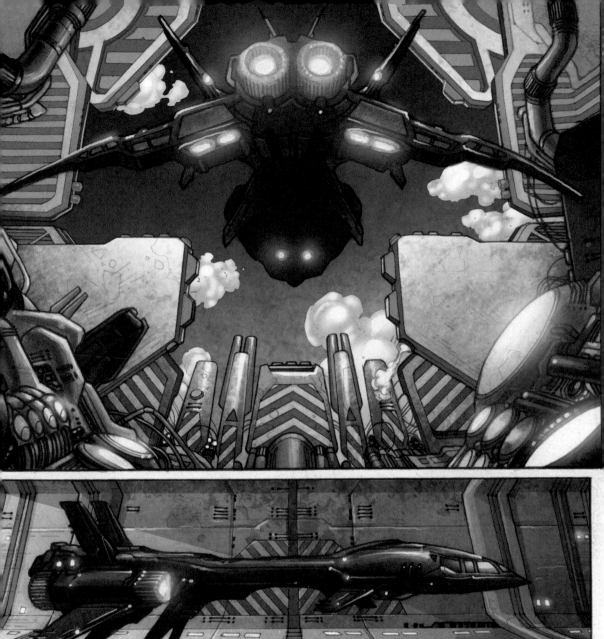
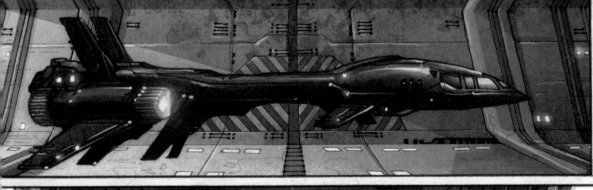

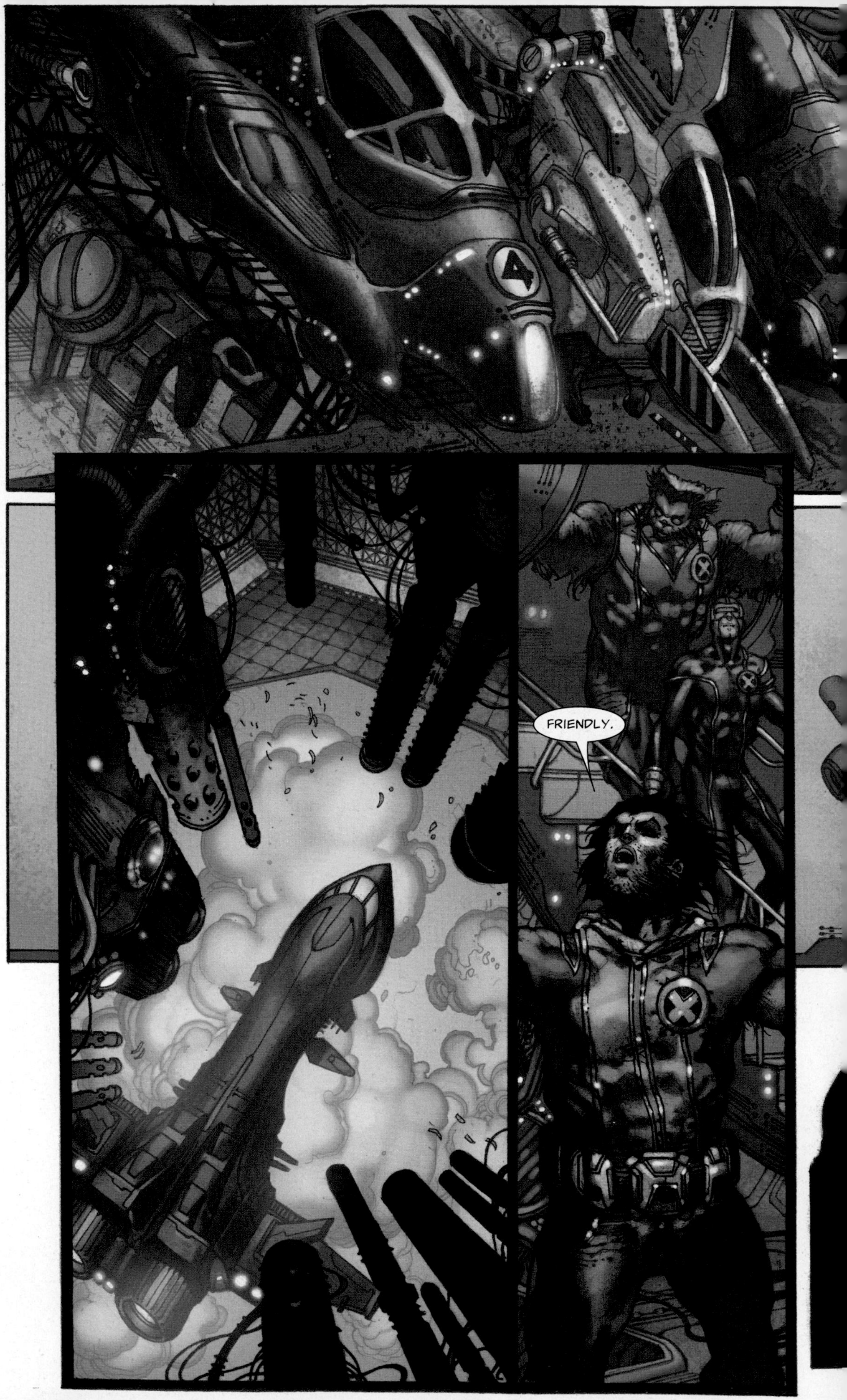
FRIENDLY.

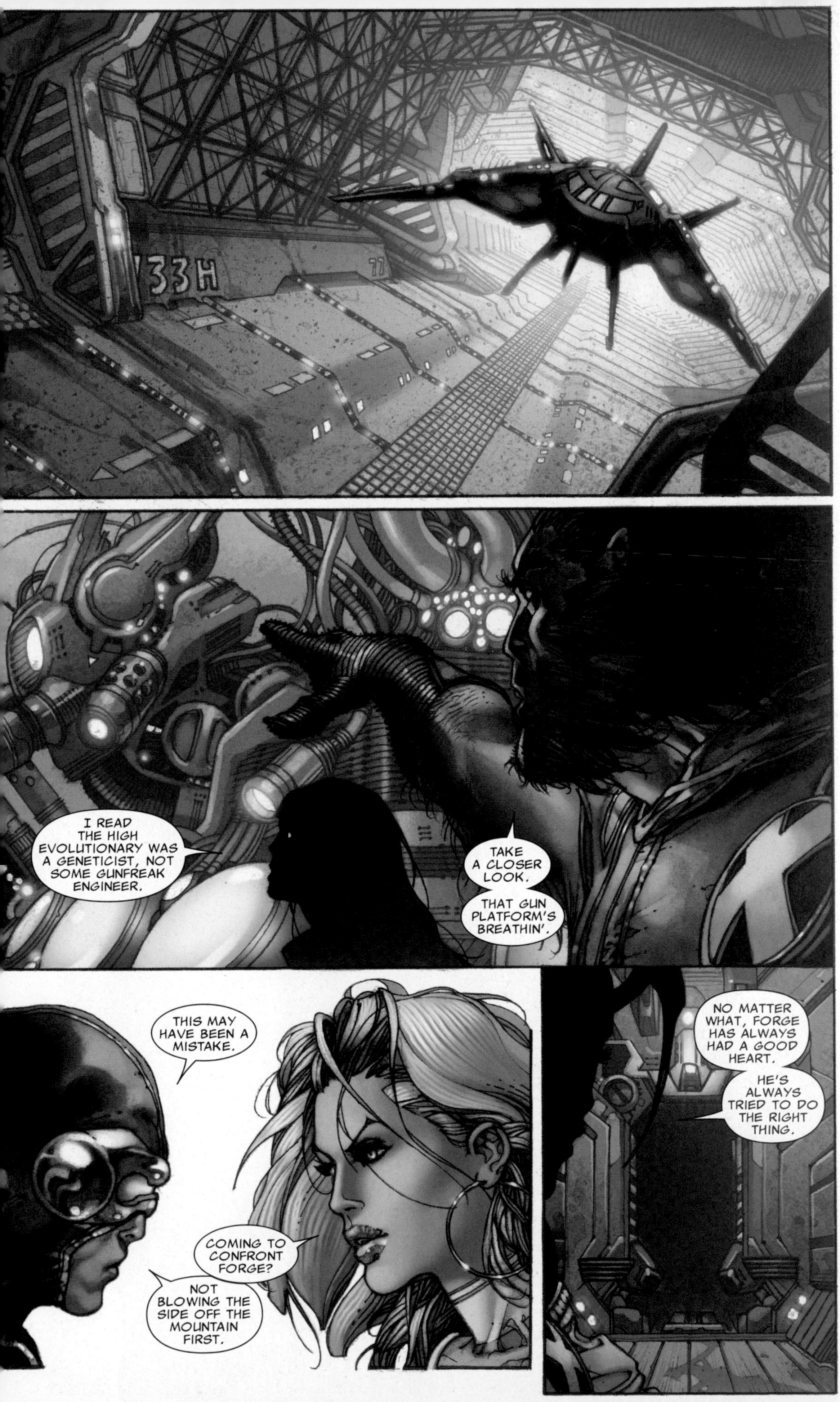
33H
I READ THE HIGH EVOLUTIONARY WAS A GENETICIST, NOT SOME GUNFREAK ENGINEER.
TAKE A CLOSER LOOK.
THAT GUN PLATFORM'S BREATHIN'.
THIS MAY HAVE BEEN A MISTAKE.
COMING TO CONFRONT FORGE?
NOT BLOWING THE SIDE OFF THE MOUNTAIN FIRST.
NO MATTER WHAT, FORGE HAS ALWAYS HAD A GOOD HEART.
HE'S ALWAYS TRIED TO DO THE RIGHT THING.

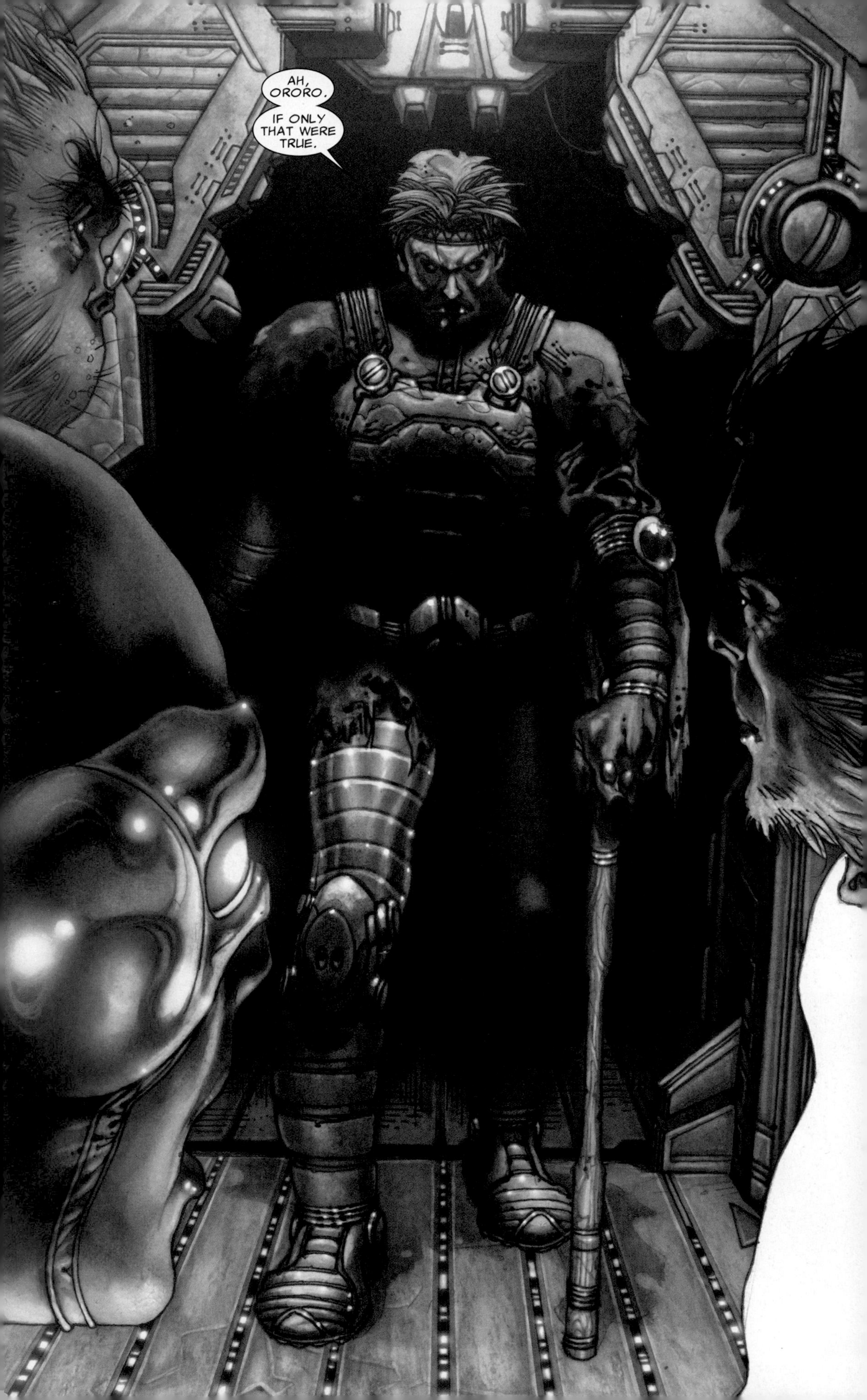
AH, ORORO.
IF ONLY THAT WERE TRUE.

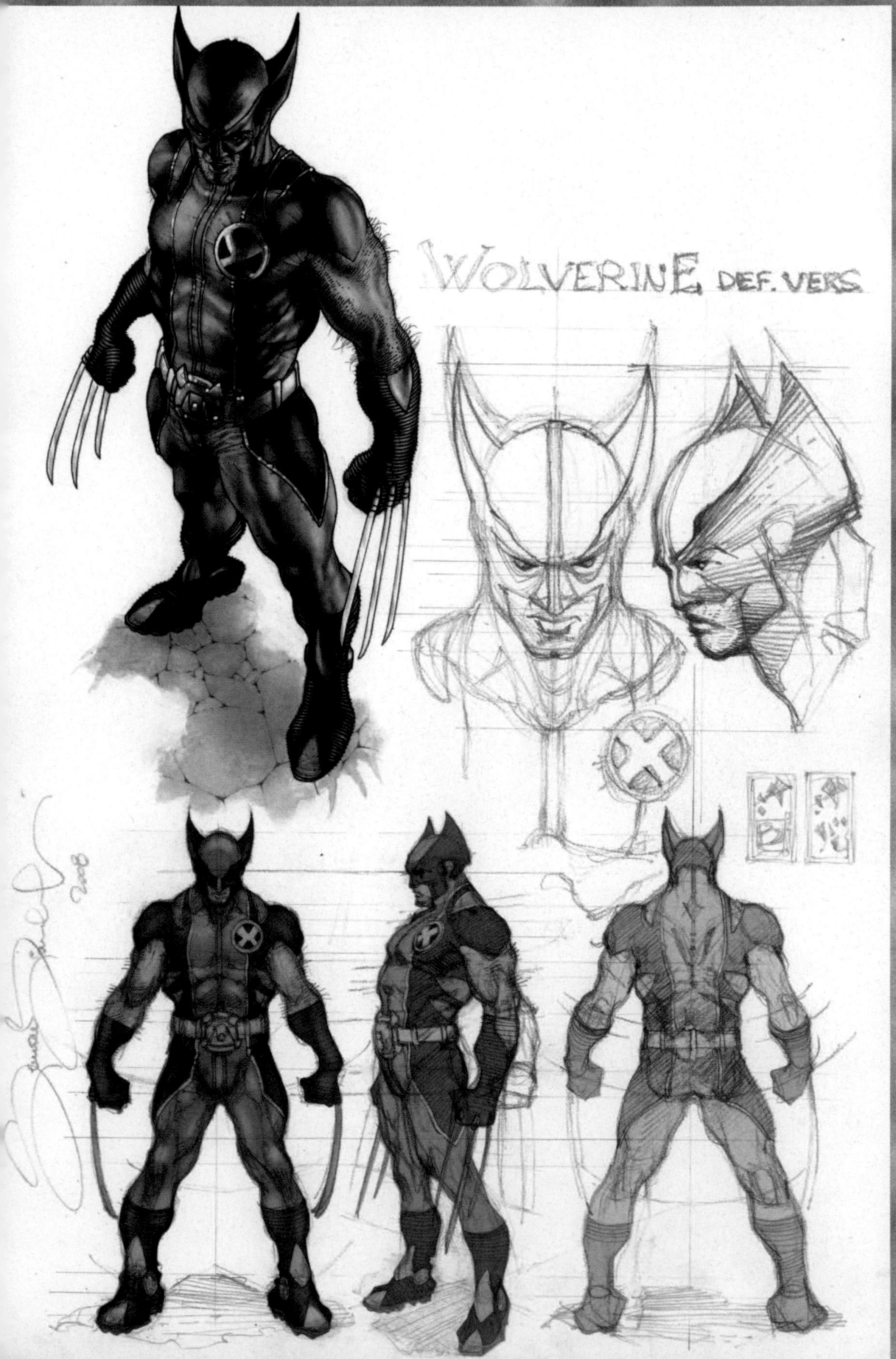
WOLVERINE DEF. VERS
2008

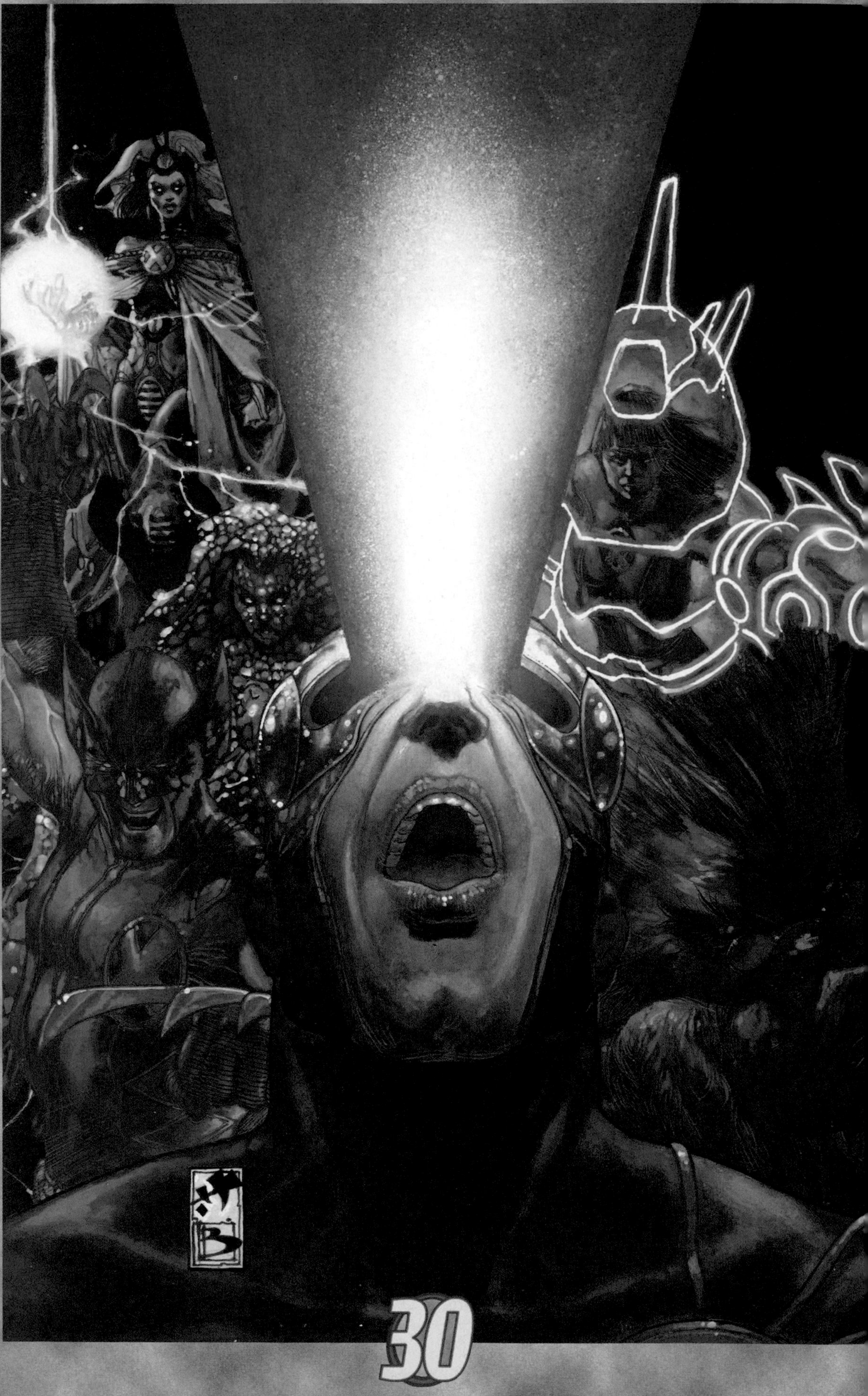
30

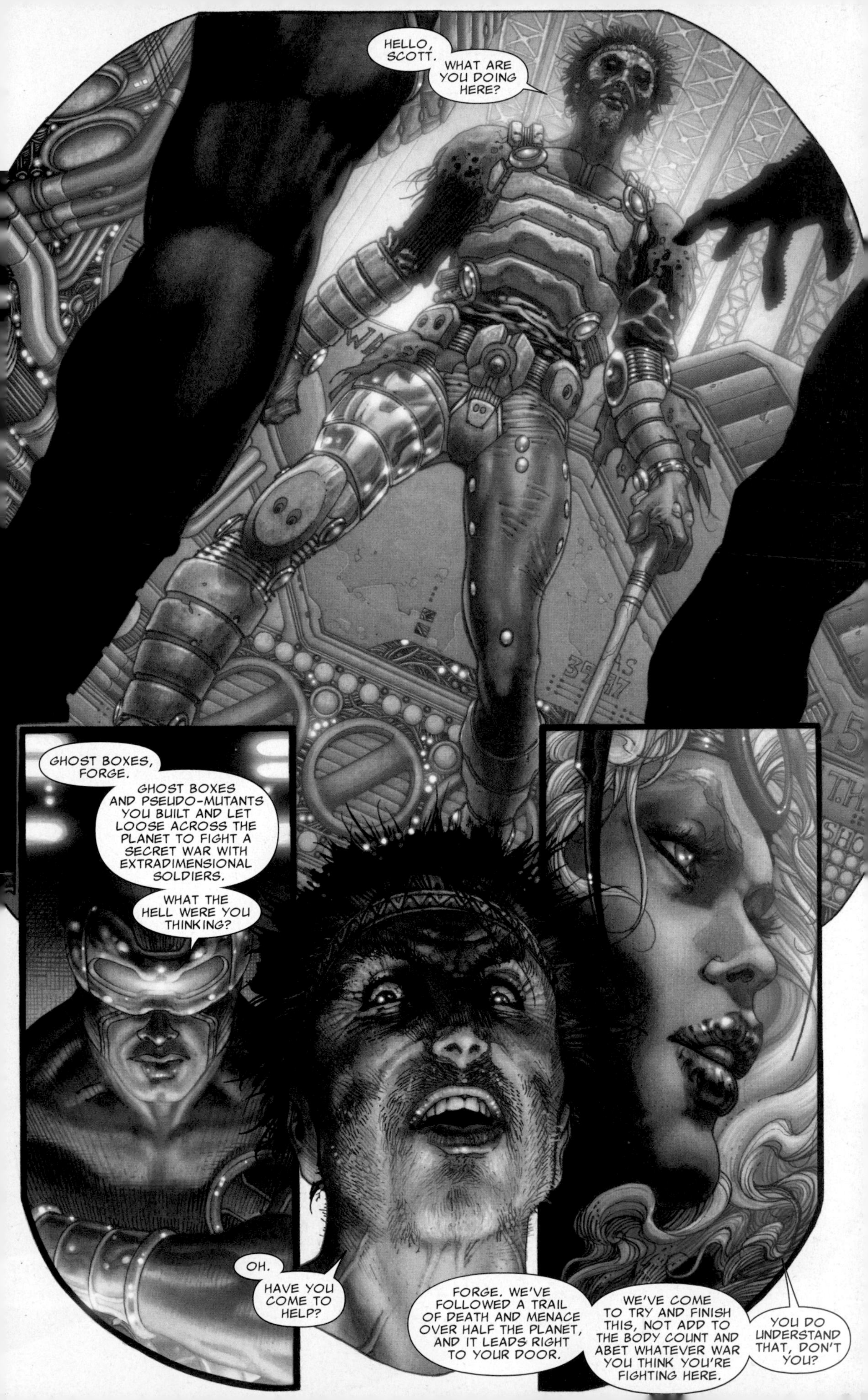
HELLO, SCOTT.
WHAT ARE YOU DOING HERE?
GHOST BOXES, FORGE.
GHOST BOXES AND PSEUDO-MUTANTS YOU BUILT AND LET LOOSE ACROSS THE PLANET TO FIGHT A SECRET WAR WITH EXTRADIMENSIONAL SOLDIERS.
WHAT THE HELL WERE YOU THINKING?
OH.
HAVE YOU COME TO HELP?
FORGE. WE'VE FOLLOWED A TRAIL OF DEATH AND MENACE OVER HALF THE PLANET, AND IT LEADS RIGHT TO YOUR DOOR.
WE'VE COME TO TRY AND FINISH THIS, NOT ADD TO THE BODY COUNT AND ABET WHATEVER WAR YOU THINK YOU'RE FIGHTING HERE.
YOU DO UNDERSTAND THAT, DON'T YOU?

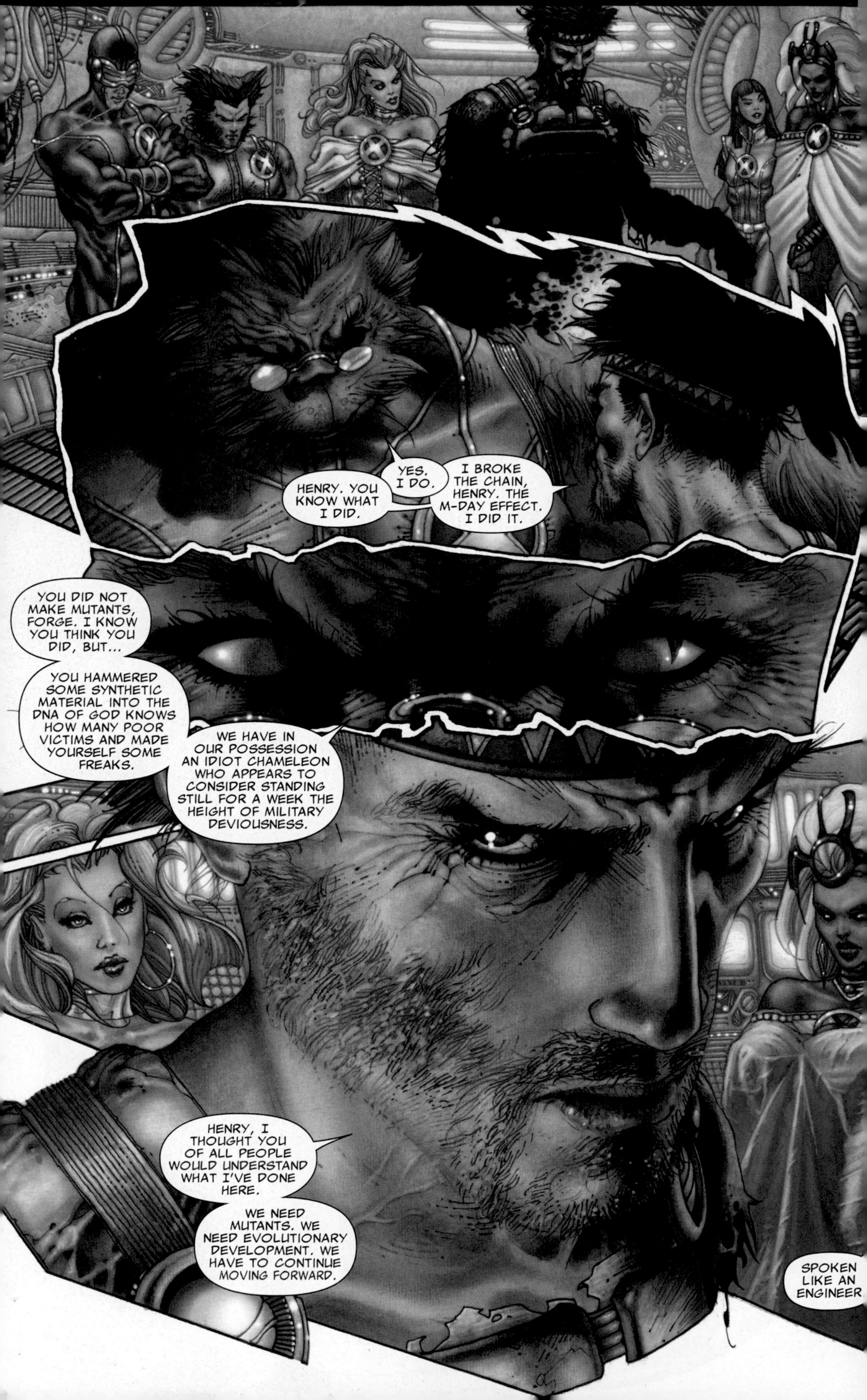
HENRY. YOU KNOW WHAT I DID.
YES. I DO.
I BROKE THE CHAIN, HENRY. THE M-DAY EFFECT. I DID IT.
YOU DID NOT MAKE MUTANTS, FORGE. I KNOW YOU THINK YOU DID, BUT...
YOU HAMMERED SOME SYNTHETIC MATERIAL INTO THE DNA OF GOD KNOWS HOW MANY POOR VICTIMS AND MADE YOURSELF SOME FREAKS.
WE HAVE IN OUR POSSESSION AN IDIOT CHAMELEON WHO APPEARS TO CONSIDER STANDING STILL FOR A WEEK THE HEIGHT OF MILITARY DEVIOUSNESS.
HENRY, I THOUGHT YOU OF ALL PEOPLE WOULD UNDERSTAND WHAT I'VE DONE HERE.
WE NEED MUTANTS. WE NEED EVOLUTIONARY DEVELOPMENT. WE HAVE TO CONTINUE MOVING FORWARD.
SPOKEN LIKE AN ENGINEER

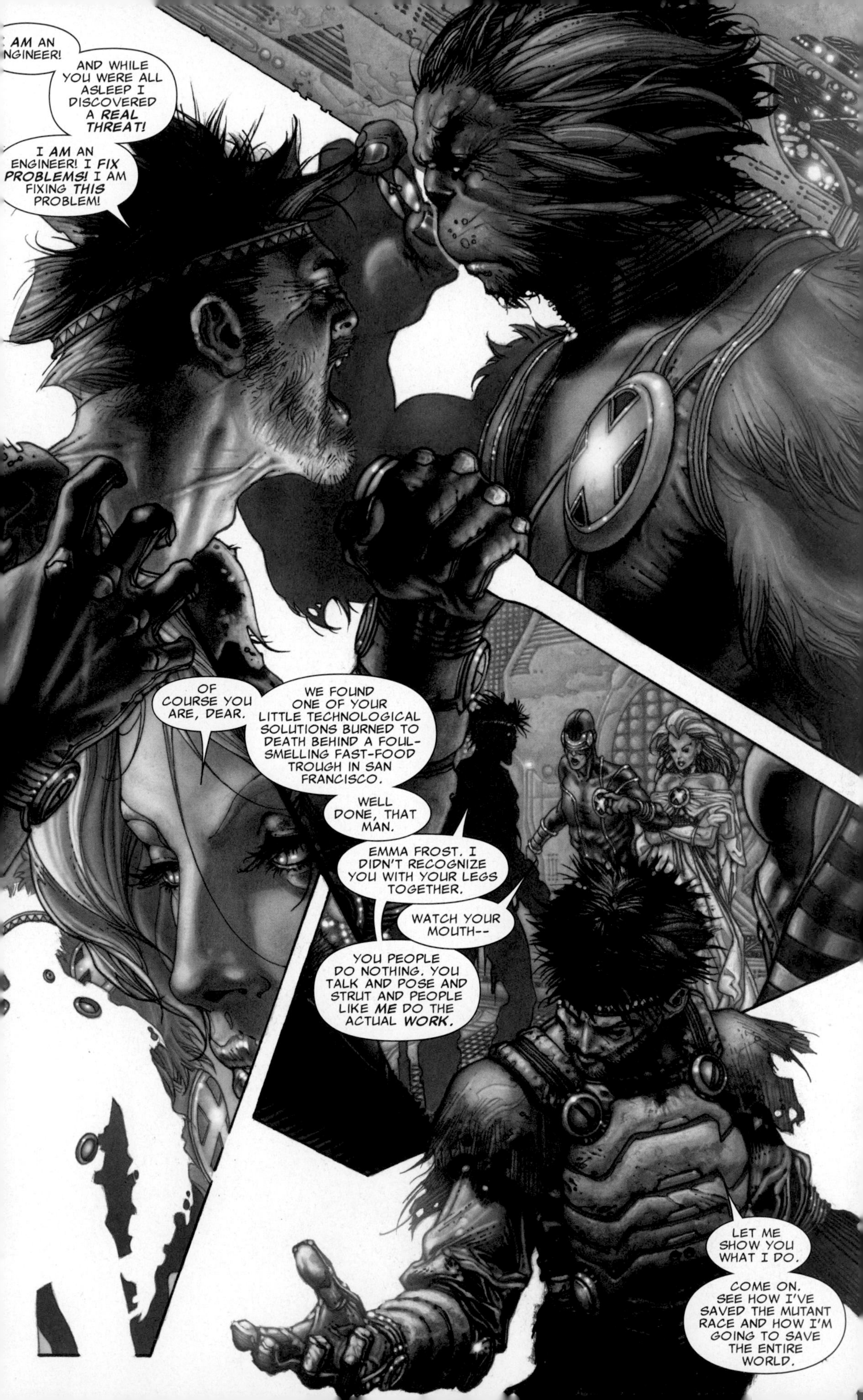

AM AN ENGINEER!
AND WHILE YOU WERE ALL ASLEEP I DISCOVERED A REAL THREAT!
I AM AN ENGINEER! I FIX PROBLEMS! I AM FIXING THIS PROBLEM!
OF COURSE YOU ARE, DEAR.
WE FOUND ONE OF YOUR LITTLE TECHNOLOGICAL SOLUTIONS BURNED TO DEATH BEHIND A FOUL-SMELLING FAST-FOOD TROUGH IN SAN FRANCISCO.
WELL DONE, THAT MAN.
EMMA FROST. I DIDN'T RECOGNIZE YOU WITH YOUR LEGS TOGETHER.
WATCH YOUR MOUTH--
YOU PEOPLE DO NOTHING. YOU TALK AND POSE AND STRUT AND PEOPLE LIKE ME DO THE ACTUAL WORK.
LET ME SHOW YOU WHAT I DO.
COME ON. SEE HOW I'VE SAVED THE MUTANT RACE AND HOW I'M GOING TO SAVE THE ENTIRE WORLD.

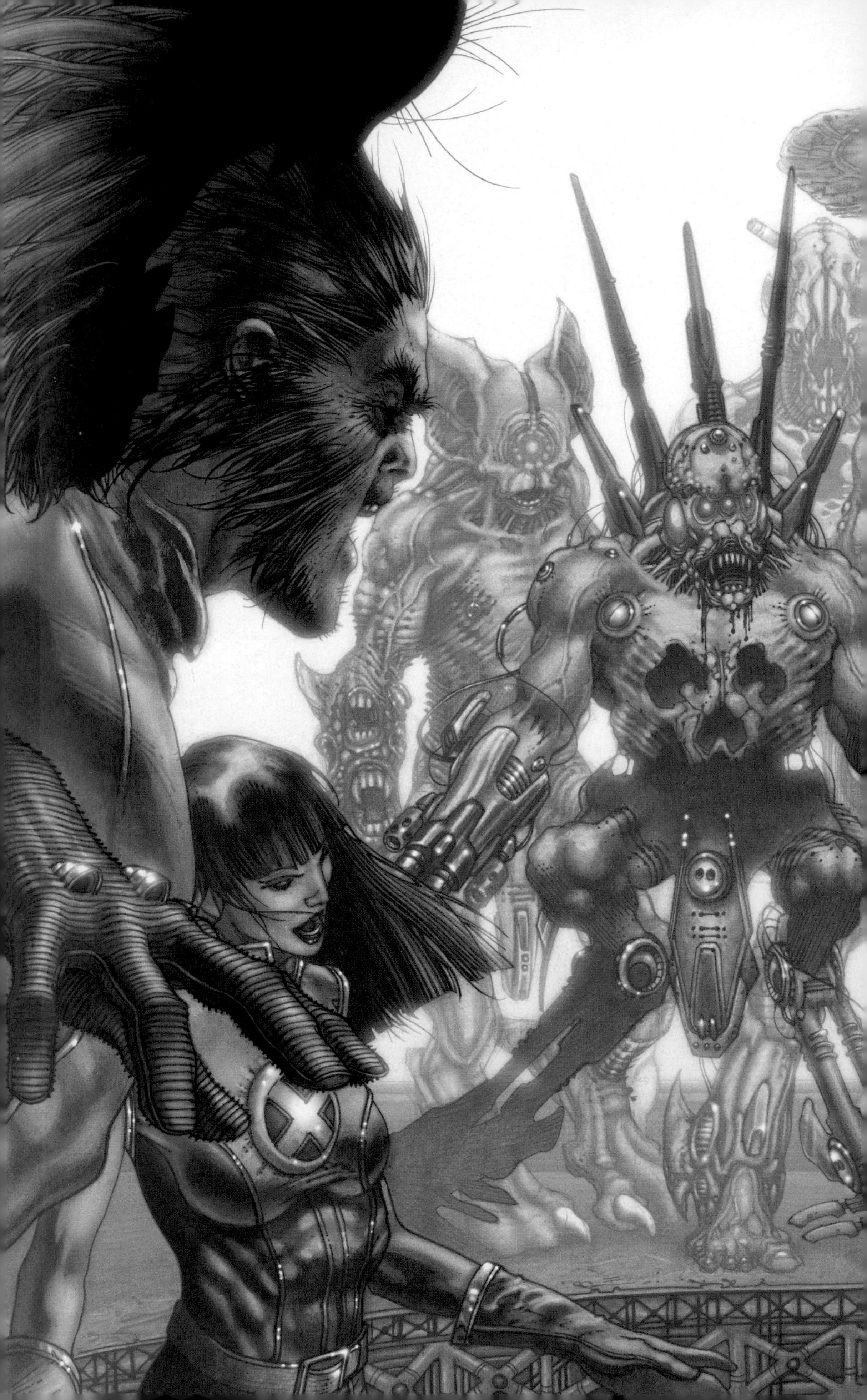

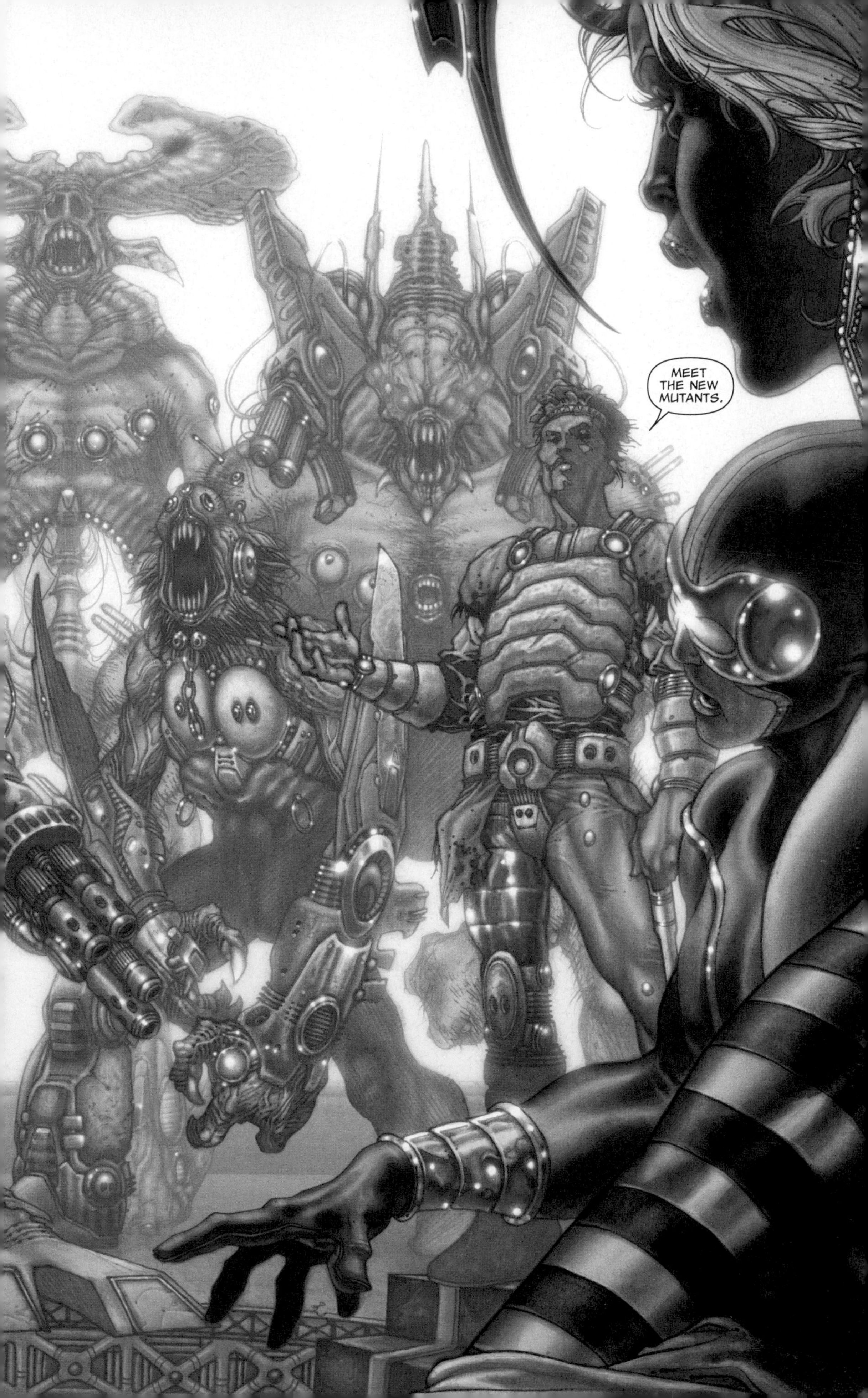
MEET THE NEW MUTANTS.

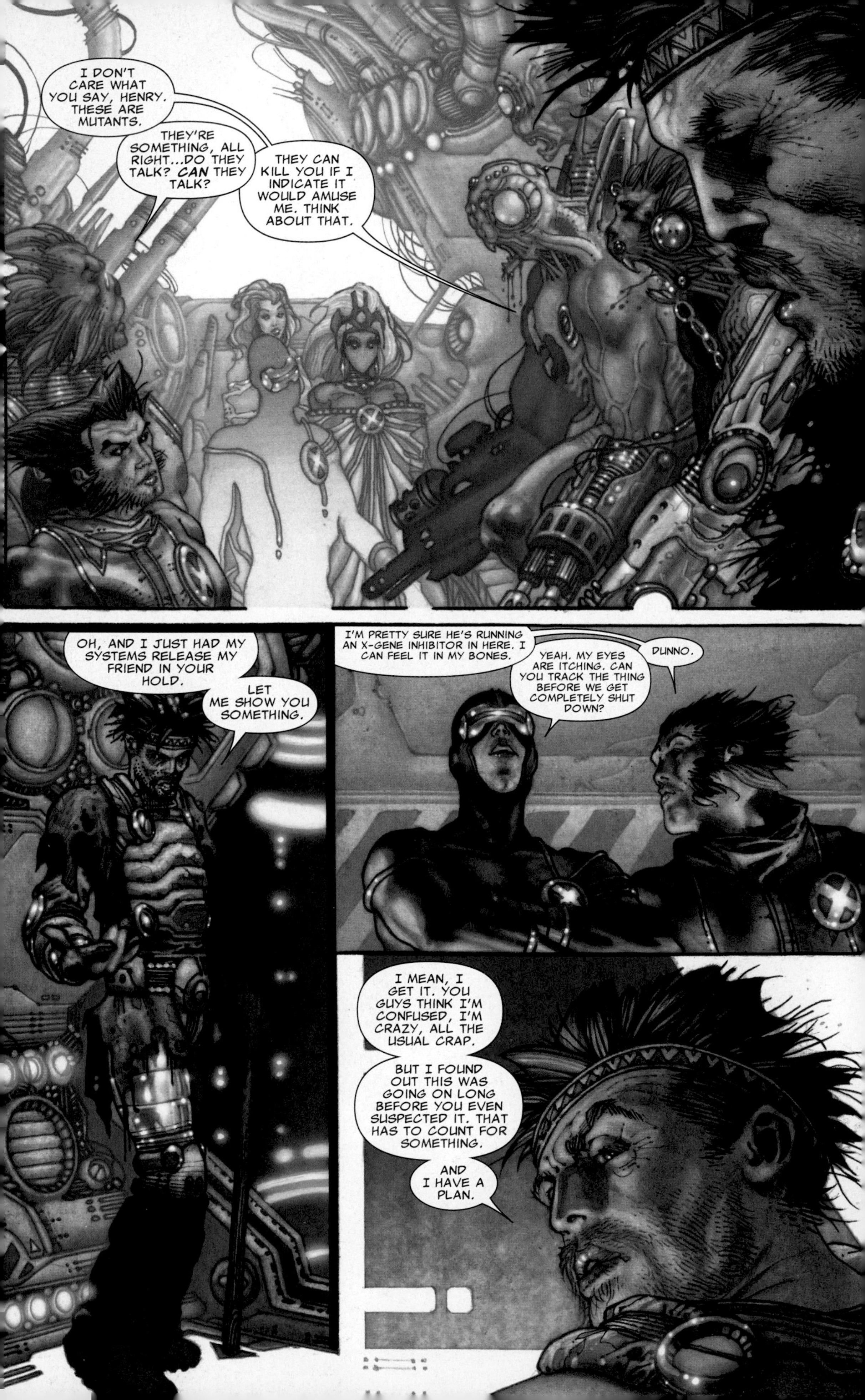
I DON'T CARE WHAT YOU SAY, HENRY. THESE ARE MUTANTS.
THEY'RE SOMETHING, ALL RIGHT...DO THEY TALK? CAN THEY TALK?
THEY CAN KILL YOU IF I INDICATE IT WOULD AMUSE ME. THINK ABOUT THAT.
OH, AND I JUST HAD MY SYSTEMS RELEASE MY FRIEND IN YOUR HOLD.
LET ME SHOW YOU SOMETHING.
I'M PRETTY SURE HE'S RUNNING AN X-GENE INHIBITOR IN HERE. I CAN FEEL IT IN MY BONES.
YEAH. MY EYES ARE ITCHING. CAN YOU TRACK THE THING BEFORE WE GET COMPLETELY SHUT DOWN?
DUNNO.
I MEAN, I GET IT. YOU GUYS THINK I'M CONFUSED, I'M CRAZY, ALL THE USUAL CRAP.
BUT I FOUND OUT THIS WAS GOING ON LONG BEFORE YOU EVEN SUSPECTED IT. THAT HAS TO COUNT FOR SOMETHING.
AND I HAVE A PLAN.

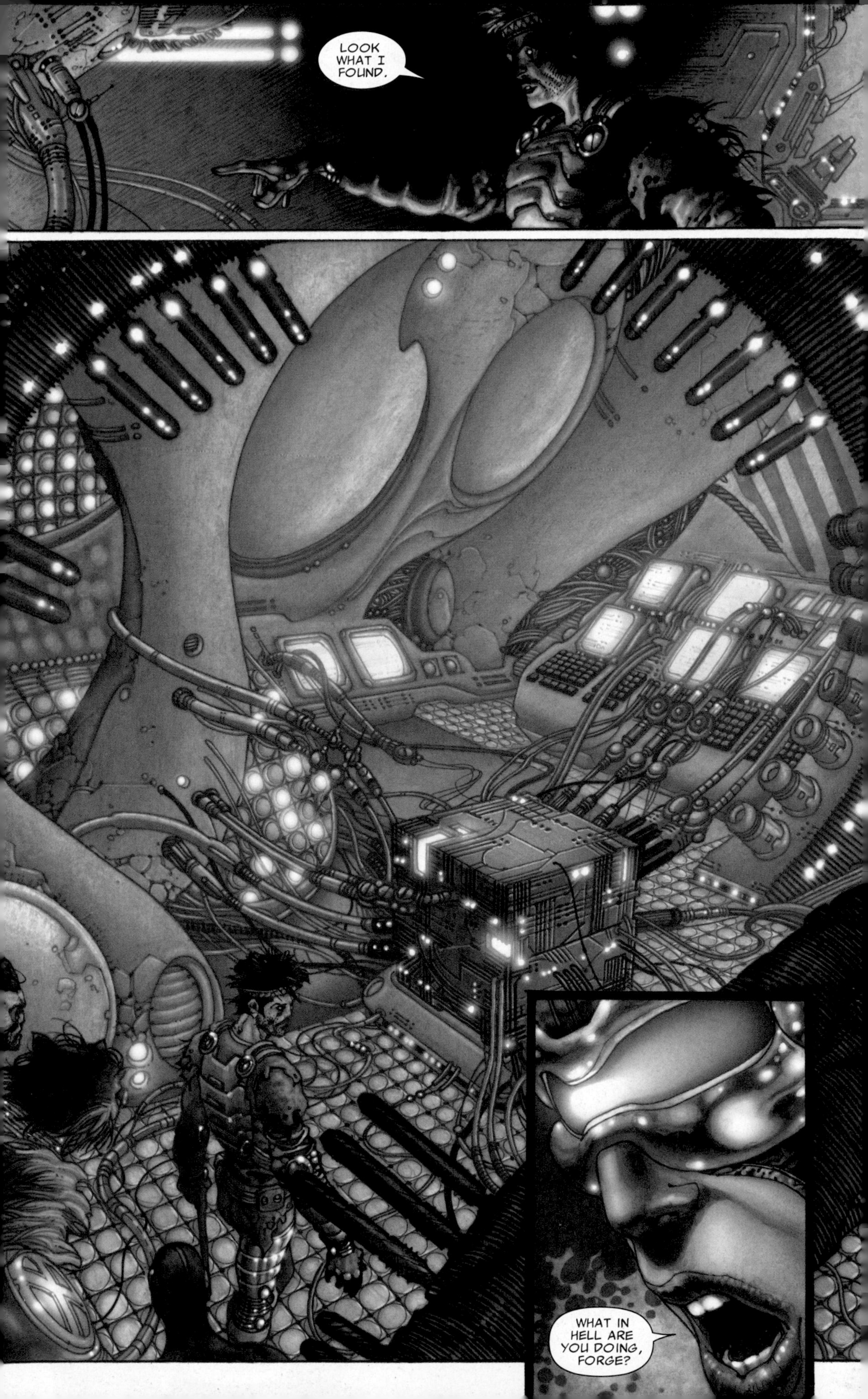
LOOK WHAT I FOUND.
WHAT IN HELL ARE YOU DOING, FORGE?

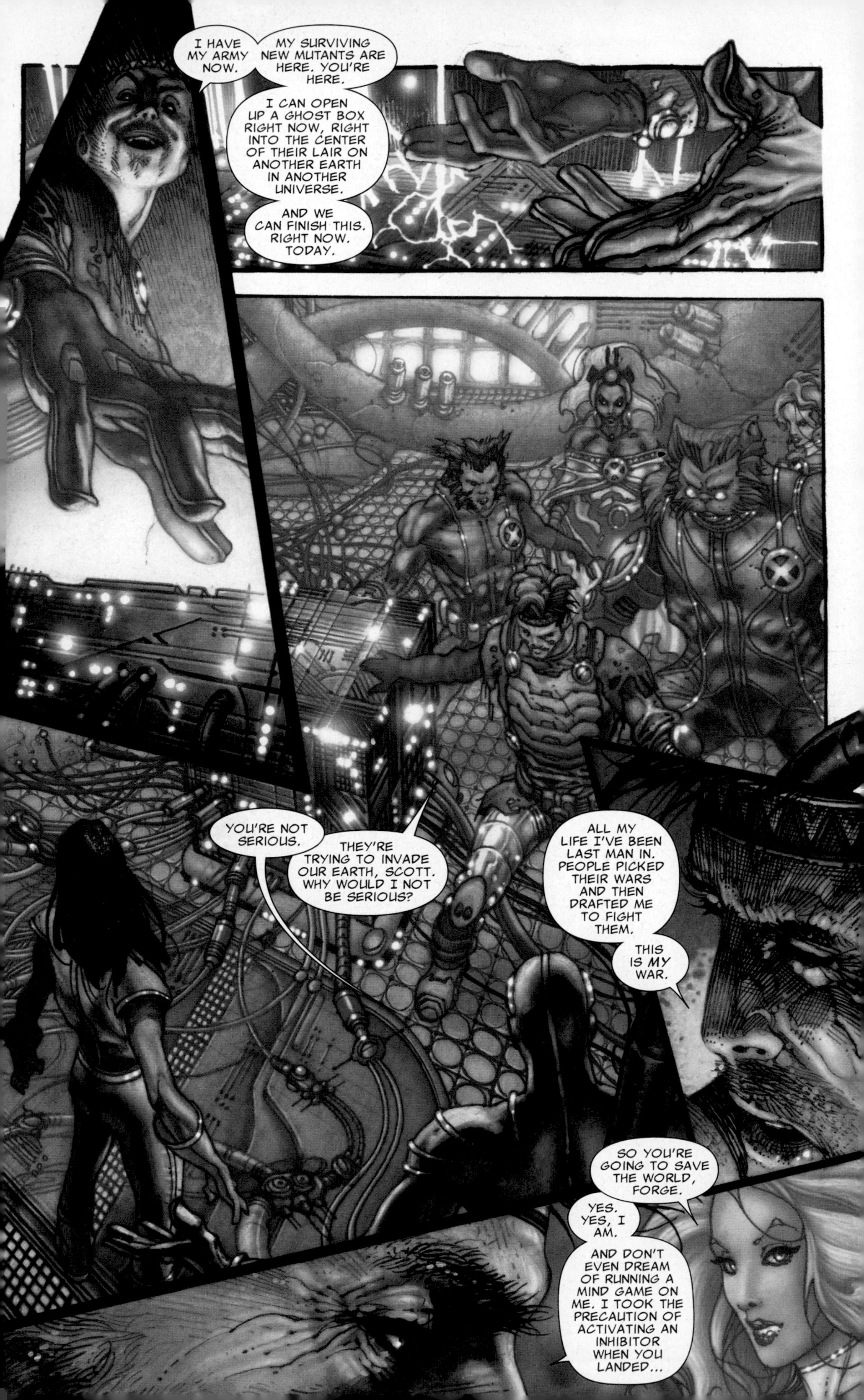
I HAVE MY ARMY NOW.
MY SURVIVING NEW MUTANTS ARE HERE. YOU'RE HERE.
I CAN OPEN UP A GHOST BOX RIGHT NOW, RIGHT INTO THE CENTER OF THEIR LAIR ON ANOTHER EARTH IN ANOTHER UNIVERSE.
AND WE CAN FINISH THIS. RIGHT NOW. TODAY.
YOU'RE NOT SERIOUS.
THEY'RE TRYING TO INVADE OUR EARTH, SCOTT. WHY WOULD I NOT BE SERIOUS?
ALL MY LIFE I'VE BEEN LAST MAN IN. PEOPLE PICKED THEIR WARS AND THEN DRAFTED ME TO FIGHT THEM.
THIS IS MY WAR.
SO YOU'RE GOING TO SAVE THE WORLD, FORGE.
YES. YES, I AM.
AND DON'T EVEN DREAM OF RUNNING A MIND GAME ON ME. I TOOK THE PRECAUTION OF ACTIVATING AN INHIBITOR WHEN YOU LANDED...

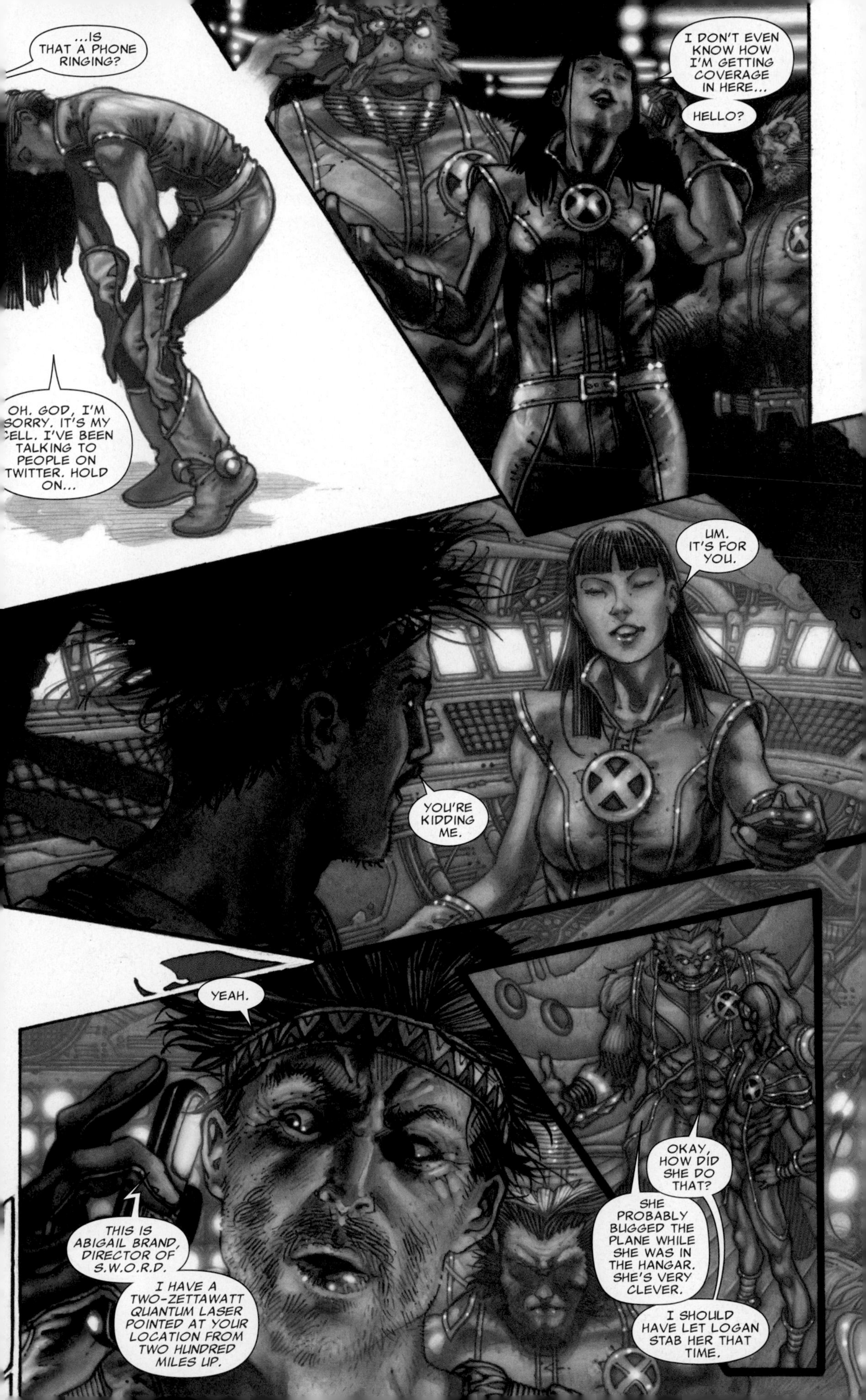
...IS THAT A PHONE RINGING?
I DON'T EVEN KNOW HOW I'M GETTING COVERAGE IN HERE...
HELLO?
OH. GOD, I'M SORRY. IT'S MY CELL. I'VE BEEN TALKING TO PEOPLE ON TWITTER. HOLD ON...
UM. IT'S FOR YOU.
YOU'RE KIDDING ME.
YEAH.
THIS IS ABIGAIL BRAND, DIRECTOR OF S.W.O.R.D.
I HAVE A TWO-ZETTAWATT QUANTUM LASER POINTED AT YOUR LOCATION FROM TWO HUNDRED MILES UP.
OKAY, HOW DID SHE DO THAT?
SHE PROBABLY BUGGED THE PLANE WHILE SHE WAS IN THE HANGAR. SHE'S VERY CLEVER.
I SHOULD HAVE LET LOGAN STAB HER THAT TIME.

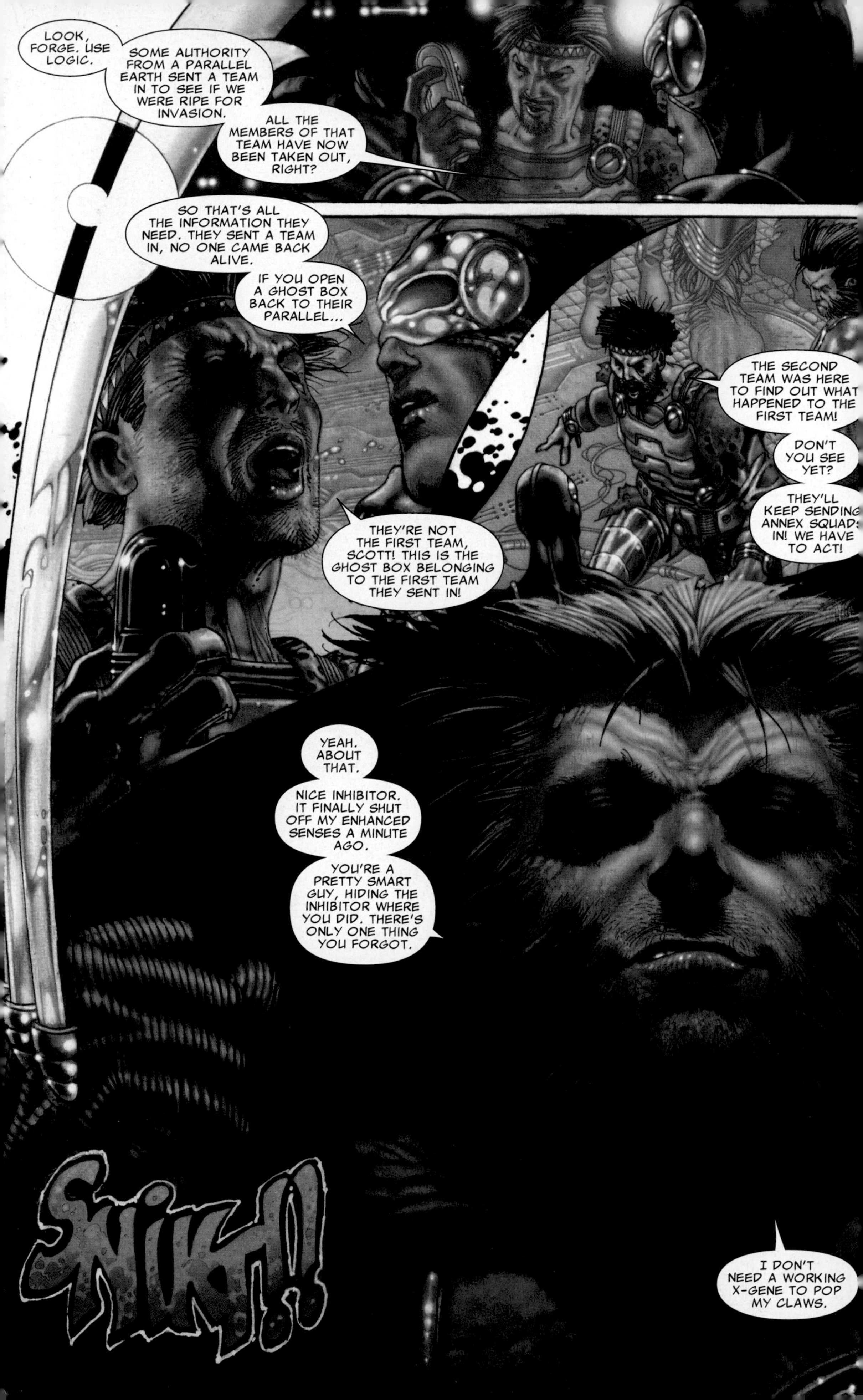
LOOK, FORGE. USE LOGIC.
SOME AUTHORITY FROM A PARALLEL EARTH SENT A TEAM IN TO SEE IF WE WERE RIPE FOR INVASION.
ALL THE MEMBERS OF THAT TEAM HAVE NOW BEEN TAKEN OUT, RIGHT?
SO THAT'S ALL THE INFORMATION THEY NEED. THEY SENT A TEAM IN, NO ONE CAME BACK ALIVE.
IF YOU OPEN A GHOST BOX BACK TO THEIR PARALLEL...
THEY'RE NOT THE FIRST TEAM, SCOTT! THIS IS THE GHOST BOX BELONGING TO THE FIRST TEAM THEY SENT IN!
THE SECOND TEAM WAS HERE TO FIND OUT WHAT HAPPENED TO THE FIRST TEAM!
DON'T YOU SEE YET?
THEY'LL KEEP SENDING ANNEX SQUADS IN! WE HAVE TO ACT!
YEAH. ABOUT THAT.
NICE INHIBITOR. IT FINALLY SHUT OFF MY ENHANCED SENSES A MINUTE AGO.
YOU'RE A PRETTY SMART GUY, HIDING THE INHIBITOR WHERE YOU DID. THERE'S ONLY ONE THING YOU FORGOT.
SNIKT!!
I DON'T NEED A WORKING X-GENE TO POP MY CLAWS.

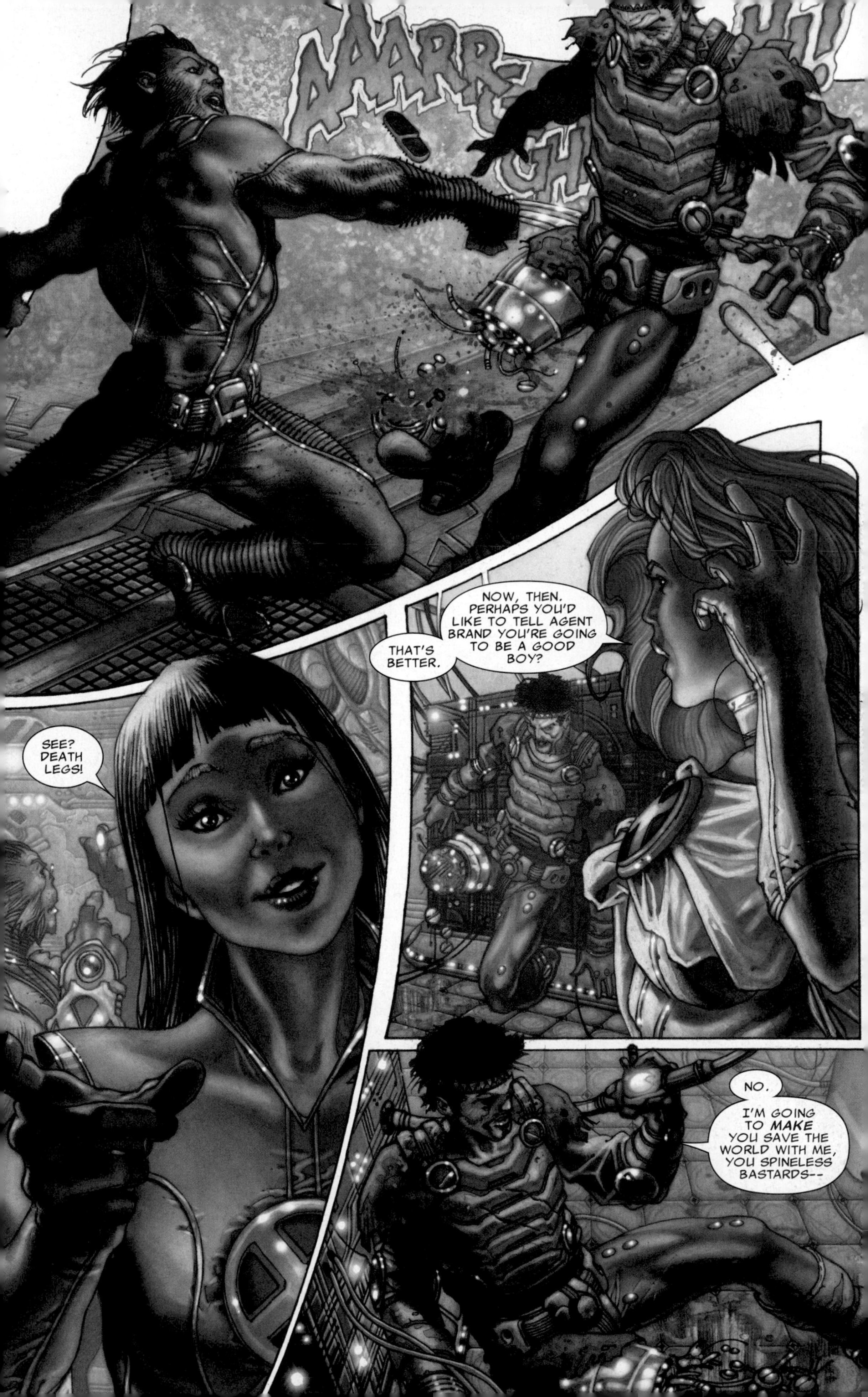
AAARR-GHHH!!
SEE? DEATH LEGS!
THAT'S BETTER.
NOW, THEN. PERHAPS YOU'D LIKE TO TELL AGENT BRAND YOU'RE GOING TO BE A GOOD BOY?
NO.
I'M GOING TO MAKE YOU SAVE THE WORLD WITH ME, YOU SPINELESS BASTARDS--

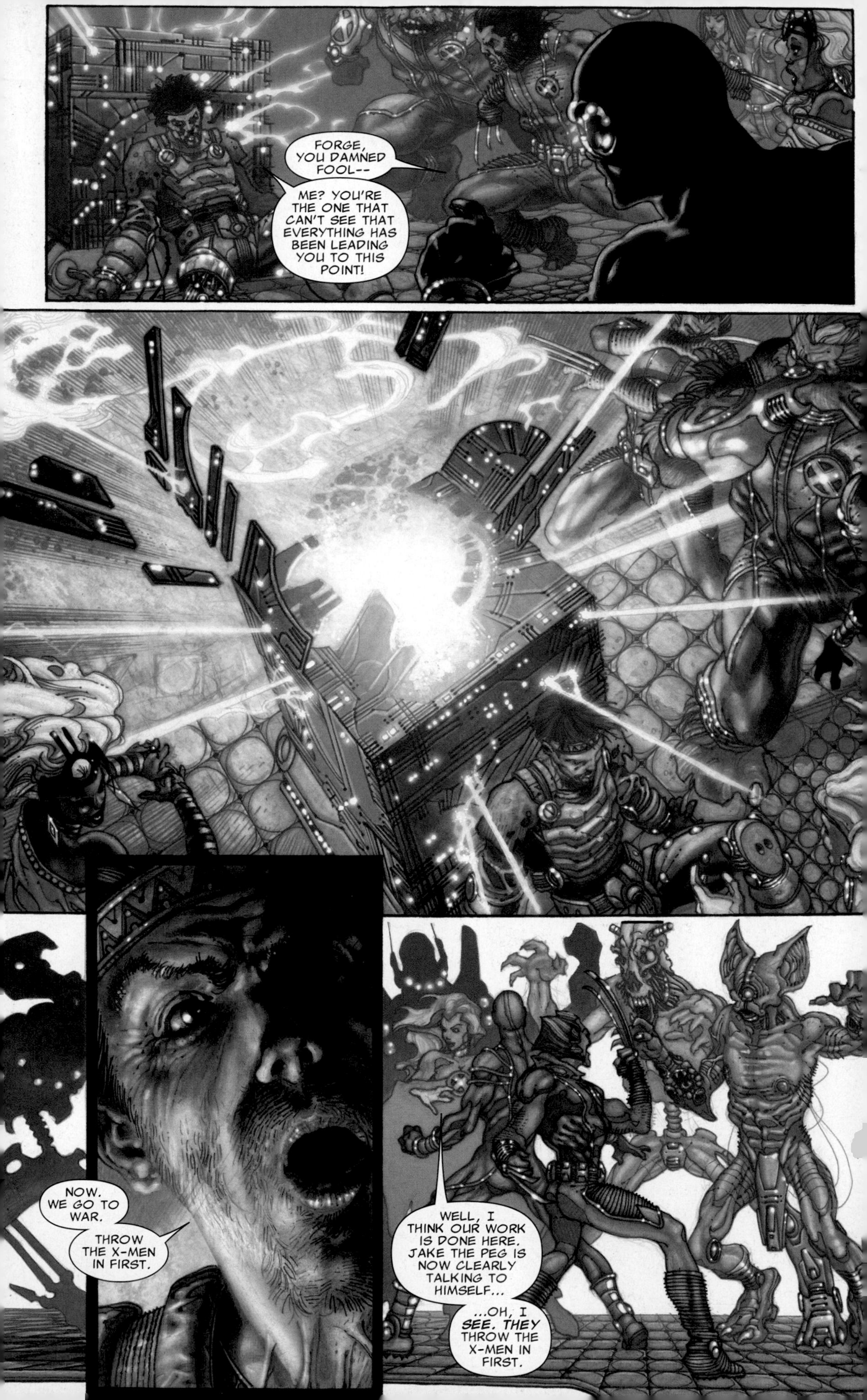
FORGE, YOU DAMNED FOOL--
ME? YOU'RE THE ONE THAT CAN'T SEE THAT EVERYTHING HAS BEEN LEADING YOU TO THIS POINT!
NOW. WE GO TO WAR.
THROW THE X-MEN IN FIRST.
WELL, I THINK OUR WORK IS DONE HERE. JAKE THE PEG IS NOW CLEARLY TALKING TO HIMSELF...
...OH, I SEE. THEY THROW THE X-MEN IN FIRST.

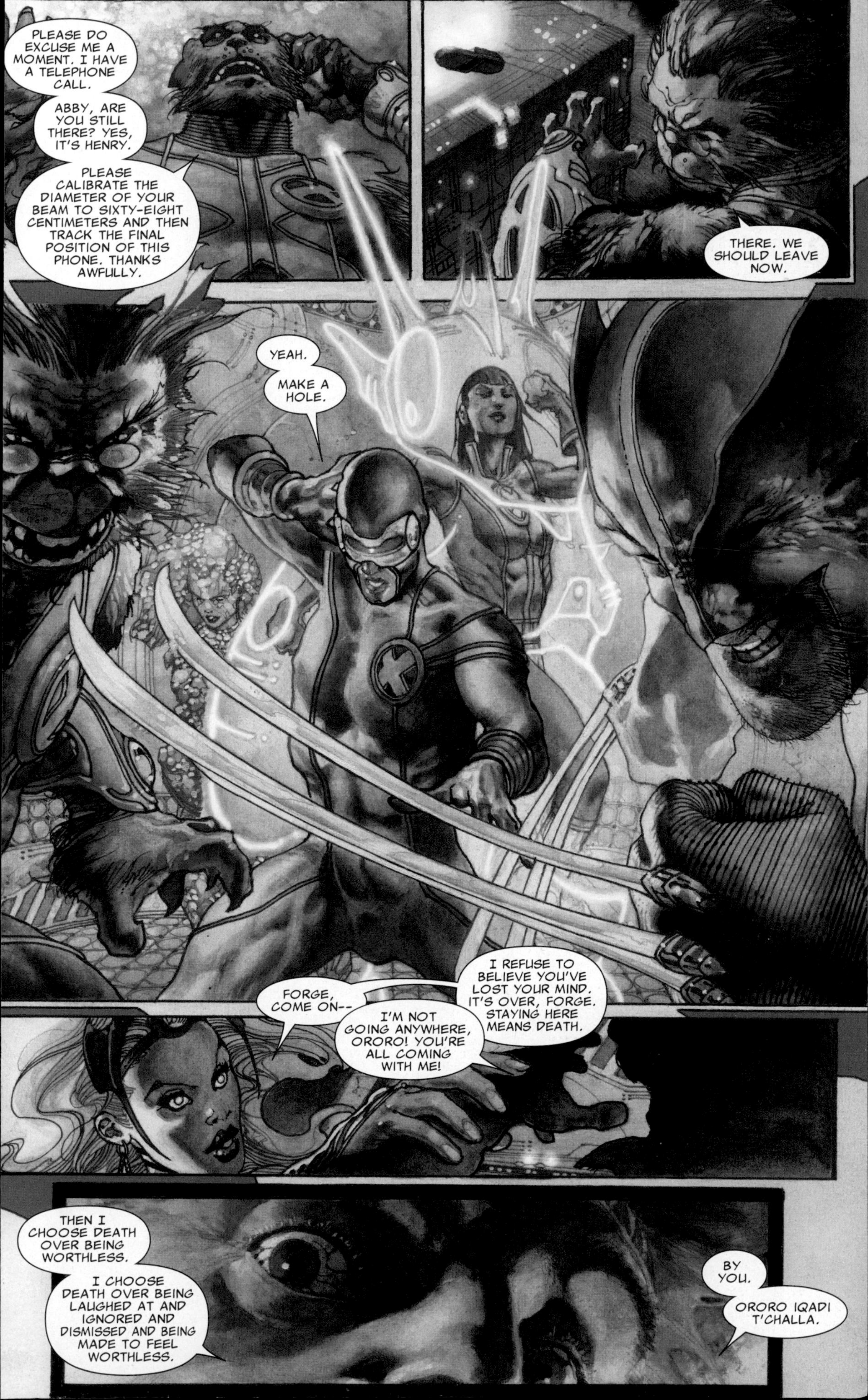
PLEASE DO EXCUSE ME A MOMENT. I HAVE A TELEPHONE CALL.
ABBY, ARE YOU STILL THERE? YES, IT'S HENRY.
PLEASE CALIBRATE THE DIAMETER OF YOUR BEAM TO SIXTY-EIGHT CENTIMETERS AND THEN TRACK THE FINAL POSITION OF THIS PHONE. THANKS AWFULLY.
THERE. WE SHOULD LEAVE NOW.
YEAH.
MAKE A HOLE.
FORGE, COME ON--
I REFUSE TO BELIEVE YOU'VE LOST YOUR MIND. IT'S OVER, FORGE. STAYING HERE MEANS DEATH.
I'M NOT GOING ANYWHERE, ORORO! YOU'RE ALL COMING WITH ME!
THEN I CHOOSE DEATH OVER BEING WORTHLESS.
I CHOOSE DEATH OVER BEING LAUGHED AT AND IGNORED AND DISMISSED AND BEING MADE TO FEEL WORTHLESS.
BY YOU.
ORORO IQADI T'CHALLA.

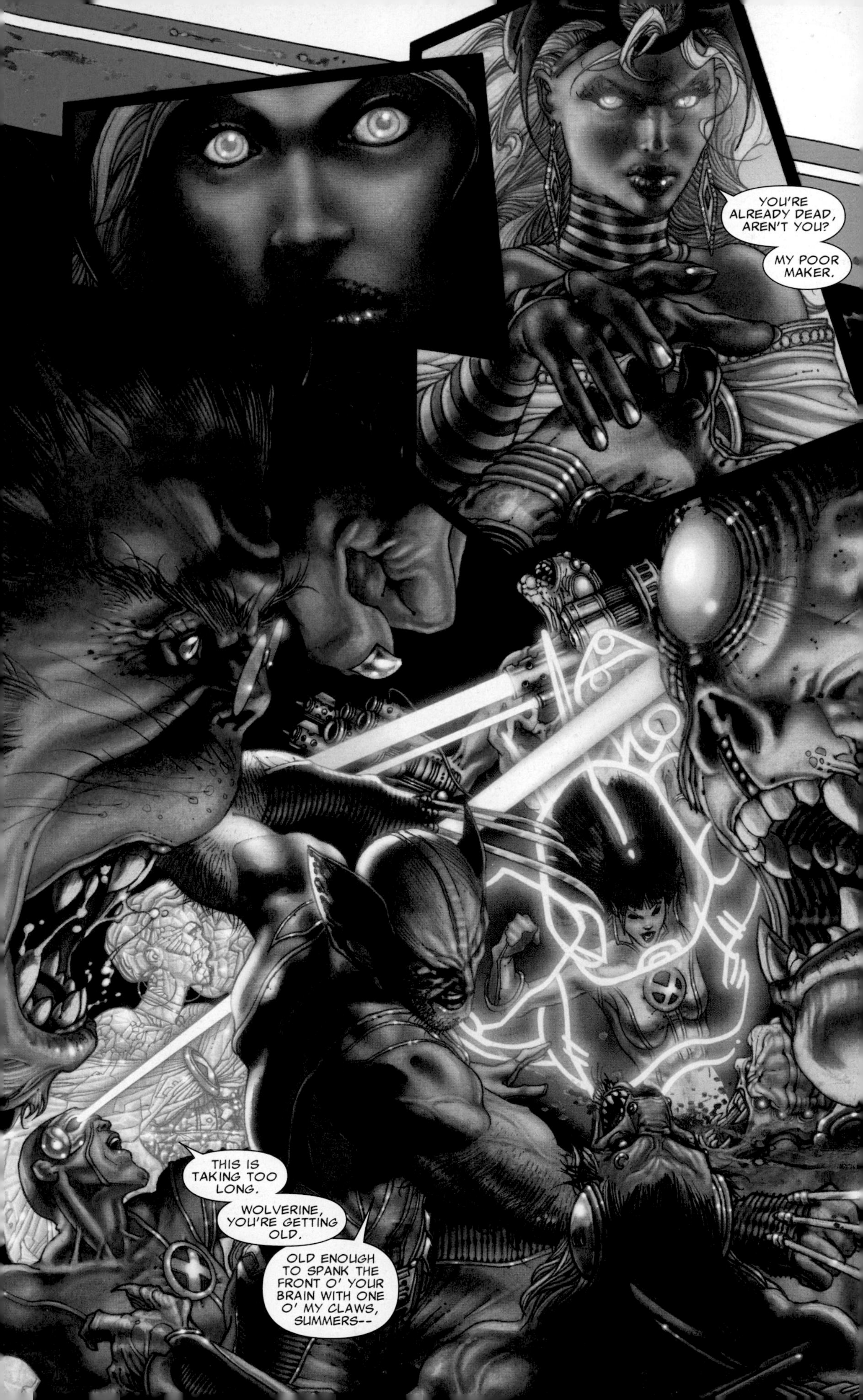
YOU'RE ALREADY DEAD, AREN'T YOU?
MY POOR MAKER.
THIS IS TAKING TOO LONG.
WOLVERINE, YOU'RE GETTING OLD.
OLD ENOUGH TO SPANK THE FRONT O' YOUR BRAIN WITH ONE O' MY CLAWS, SUMMERS--

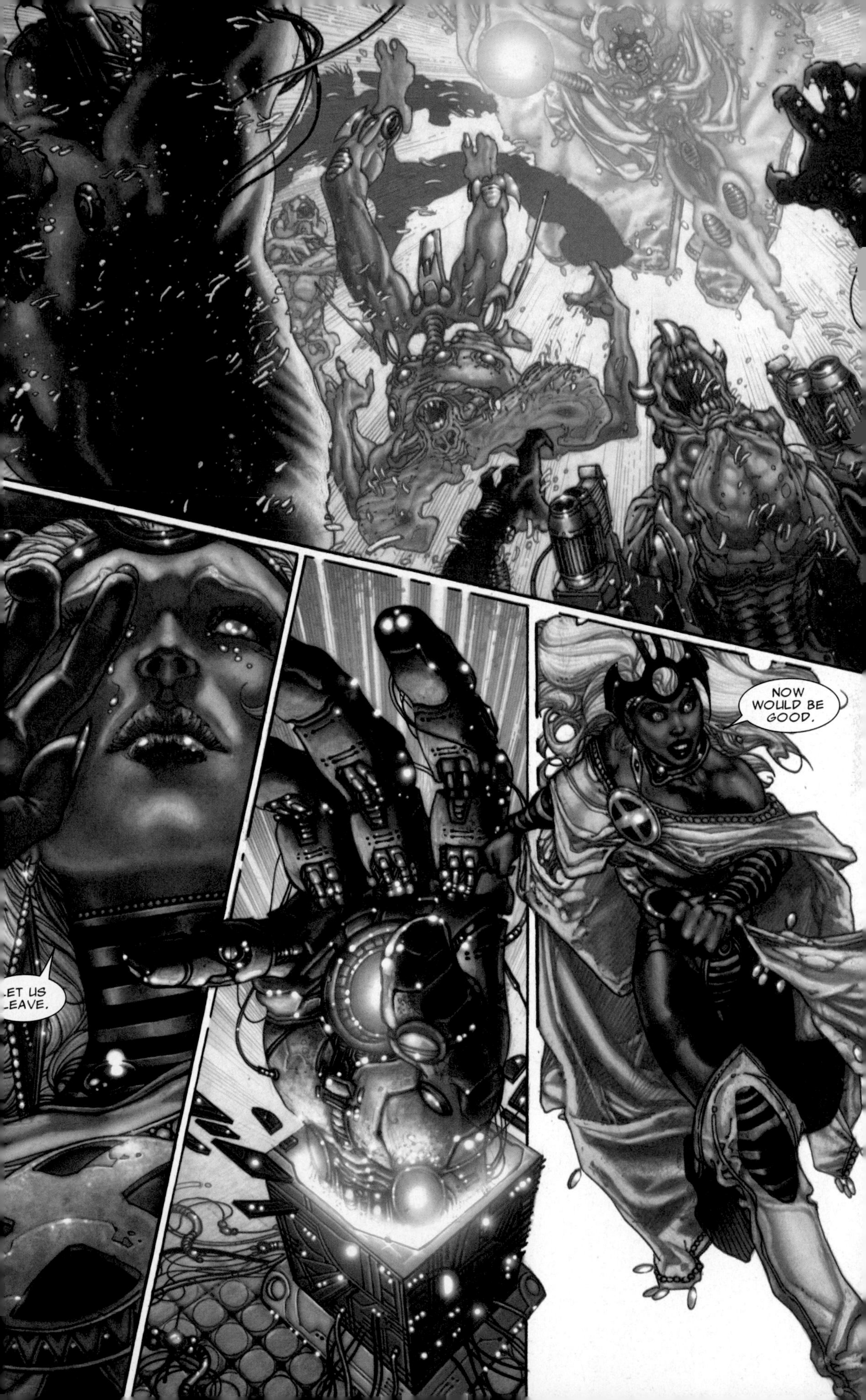

ET US
EAVE.
NOW
WOULD BE
GOOD.

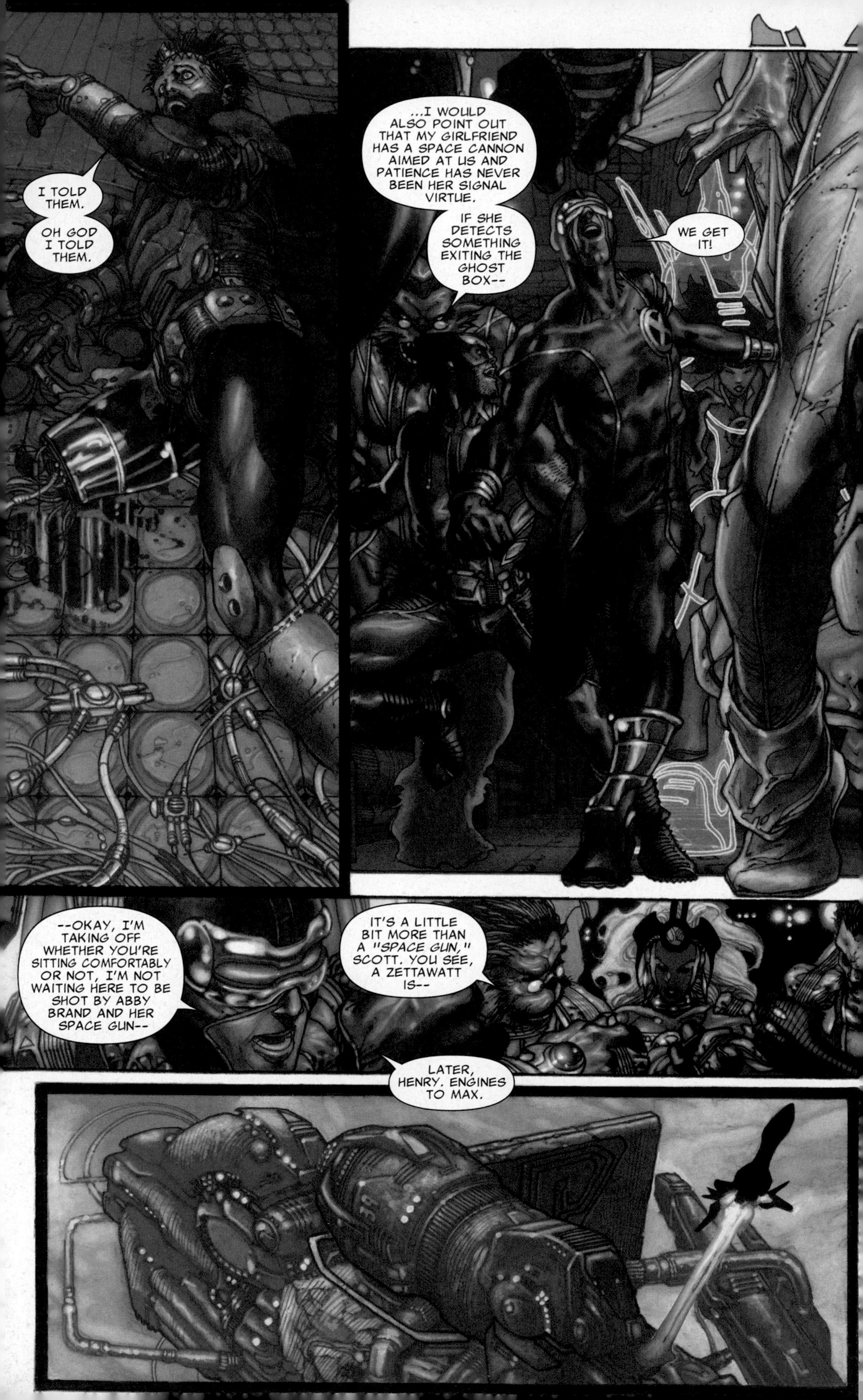
I TOLD THEM.
OH GOD I TOLD THEM.
...I WOULD ALSO POINT OUT THAT MY GIRLFRIEND HAS A SPACE CANNON AIMED AT US AND PATIENCE HAS NEVER BEEN HER SIGNAL VIRTUE.
IF SHE DETECTS SOMETHING EXITING THE GHOST BOX--
WE GET IT!
--OKAY, I'M TAKING OFF WHETHER YOU'RE SITTING COMFORTABLY OR NOT, I'M NOT WAITING HERE TO BE SHOT BY ABBY BRAND AND HER SPACE GUN--
IT'S A LITTLE BIT MORE THAN A "SPACE GUN," SCOTT. YOU SEE, A ZETTAWATT IS--
LATER, HENRY. ENGINES TO MAX.

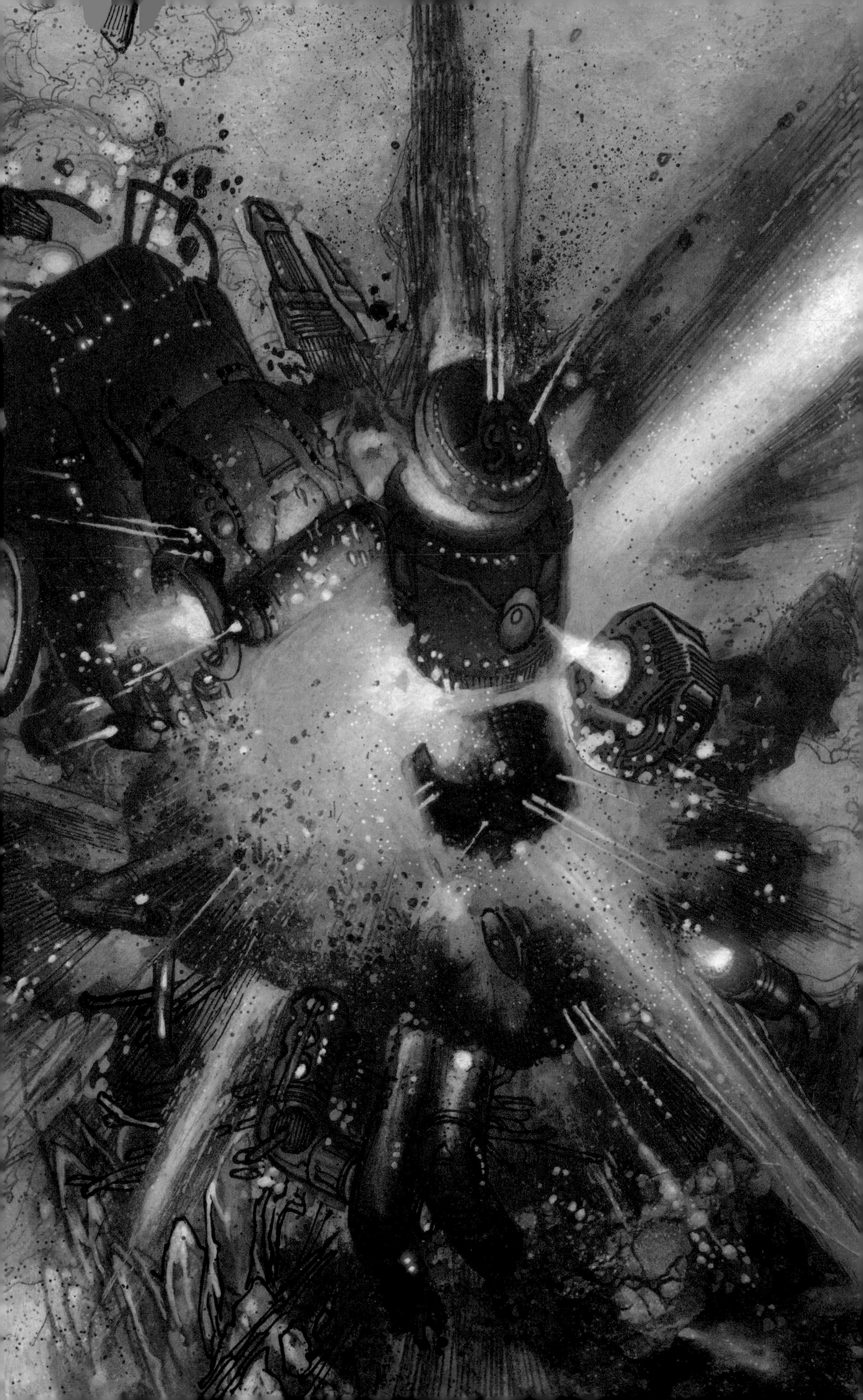

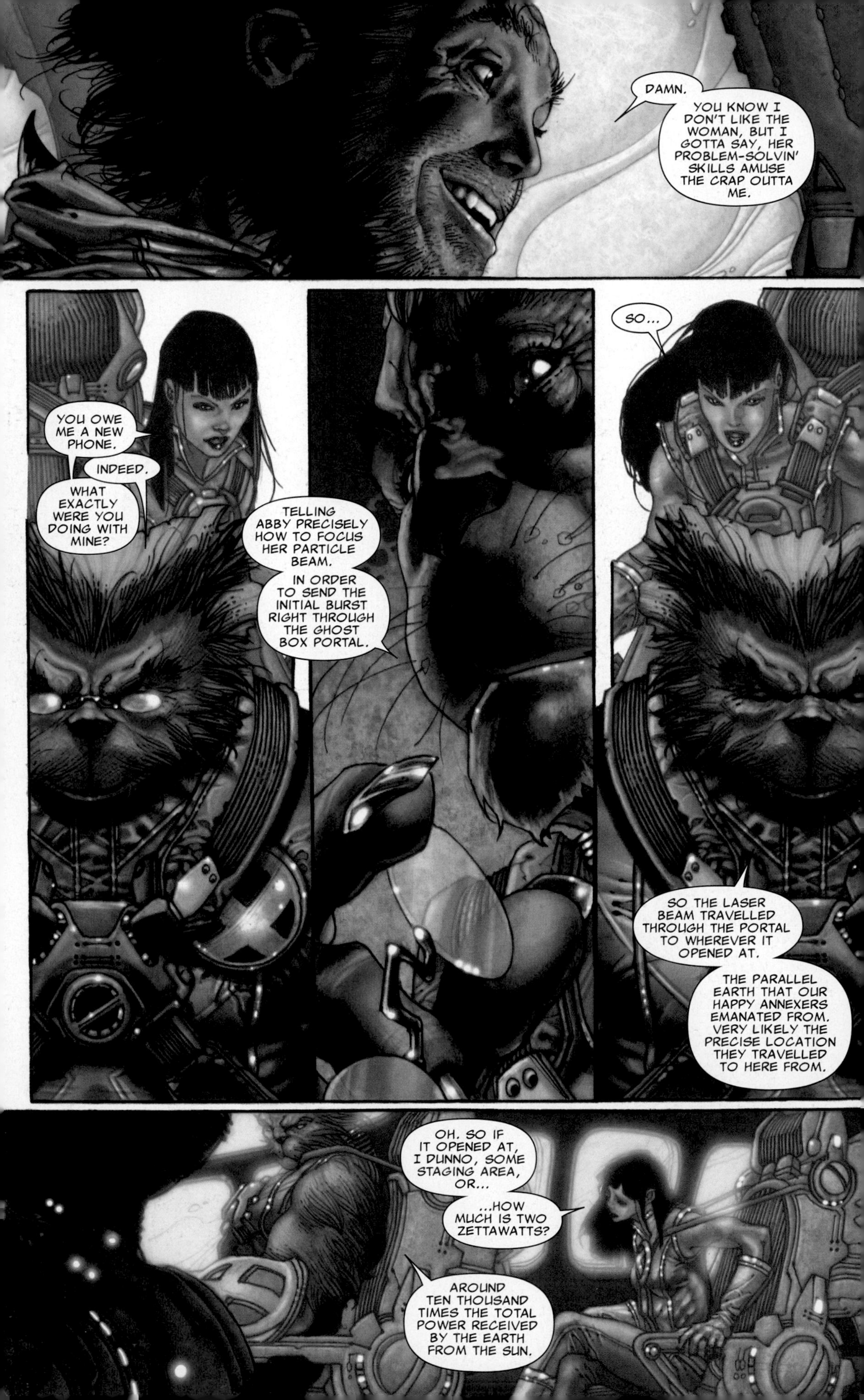
DAMN.
YOU KNOW I DON'T LIKE THE WOMAN, BUT I GOTTA SAY, HER PROBLEM-SOLVIN' SKILLS AMUSE THE CRAP OUTTA ME.
YOU OWE ME A NEW PHONE.
INDEED.
WHAT EXACTLY WERE YOU DOING WITH MINE?
TELLING ABBY PRECISELY HOW TO FOCUS HER PARTICLE BEAM.
IN ORDER TO SEND THE INITIAL BURST RIGHT THROUGH THE GHOST BOX PORTAL.
SO...
SO THE LASER BEAM TRAVELLED THROUGH THE PORTAL TO WHEREVER IT OPENED AT.
THE PARALLEL EARTH THAT OUR HAPPY ANNEXERS EMANATED FROM. VERY LIKELY THE PRECISE LOCATION THEY TRAVELLED TO HERE FROM.
OH. SO IF IT OPENED AT, I DUNNO, SOME STAGING AREA, OR...
...HOW MUCH IS TWO ZETTAWATTS?
AROUND TEN THOUSAND TIMES THE TOTAL POWER RECEIVED BY THE EARTH FROM THE SUN.

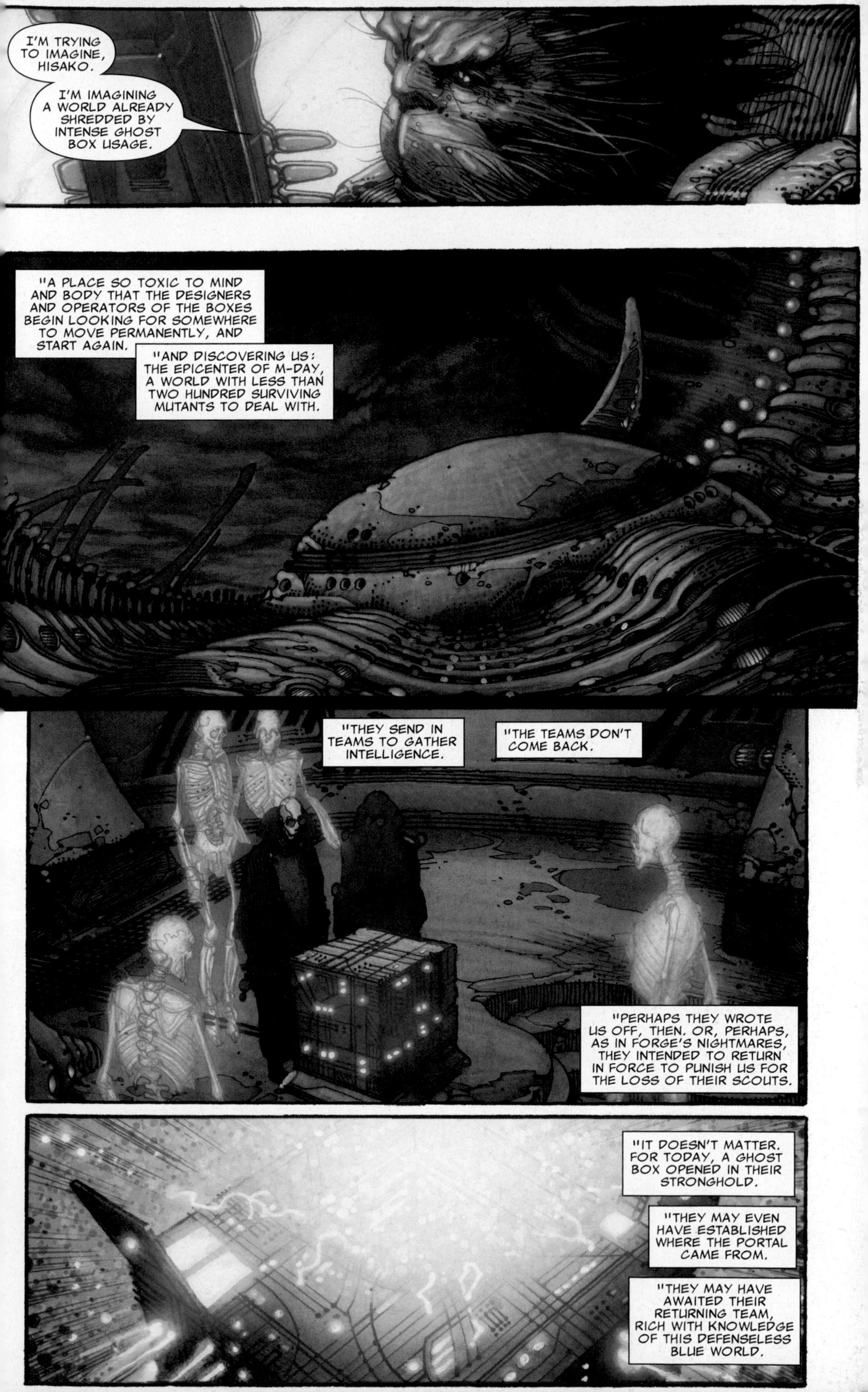
I'M TRYING TO IMAGINE, HISAKO.
I'M IMAGINING A WORLD ALREADY SHREDDED BY INTENSE GHOST BOX USAGE.
"A PLACE SO TOXIC TO MIND AND BODY THAT THE DESIGNERS AND OPERATORS OF THE BOXES BEGIN LOOKING FOR SOMEWHERE TO MOVE PERMANENTLY, AND START AGAIN.
"AND DISCOVERING US: THE EPICENTER OF M-DAY, A WORLD WITH LESS THAN TWO HUNDRED SURVIVING MUTANTS TO DEAL WITH.
"THEY SEND IN TEAMS TO GATHER INTELLIGENCE.
"THE TEAMS DON'T COME BACK.
"PERHAPS THEY WROTE US OFF, THEN. OR, PERHAPS, AS IN FORGE'S NIGHTMARES, THEY INTENDED TO RETURN IN FORCE TO PUNISH US FOR THE LOSS OF THEIR SCOUTS.
"IT DOESN'T MATTER. FOR TODAY, A GHOST BOX OPENED IN THEIR STRONGHOLD.
"THEY MAY EVEN HAVE ESTABLISHED WHERE THE PORTAL CAME FROM.
"THEY MAY HAVE AWAITED THEIR RETURNING TEAM, RICH WITH KNOWLEDGE OF THIS DEFENSELESS BLUE WORLD.

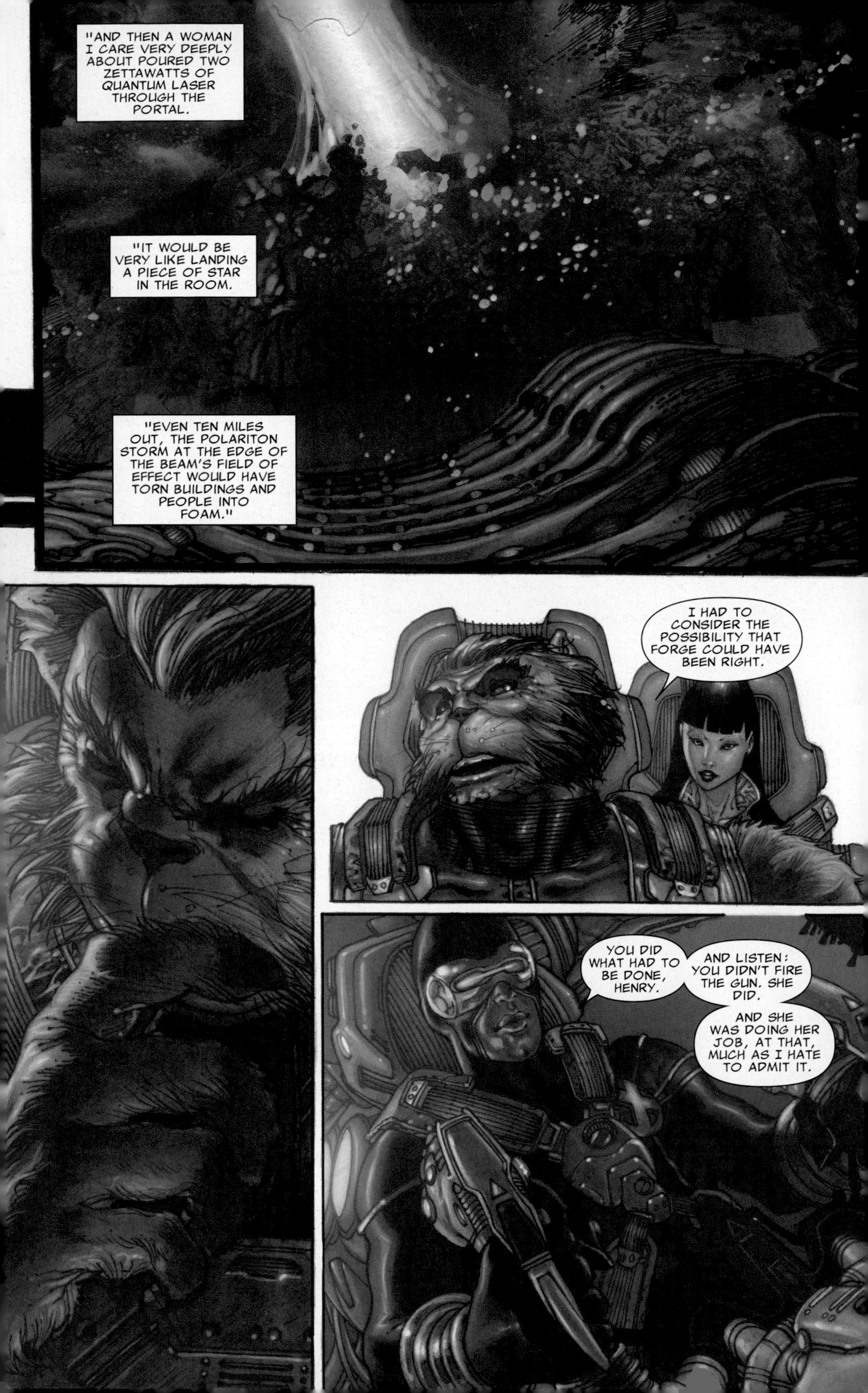
"AND THEN A WOMAN I CARE VERY DEEPLY ABOUT POURED TWO ZETTAWATTS OF QUANTUM LASER THROUGH THE PORTAL.
"IT WOULD BE VERY LIKE LANDING A PIECE OF STAR IN THE ROOM.
"EVEN TEN MILES OUT, THE POLARITON STORM AT THE EDGE OF THE BEAM'S FIELD OF EFFECT WOULD HAVE TORN BUILDINGS AND PEOPLE INTO FOAM."
I HAD TO CONSIDER THE POSSIBILITY THAT FORGE COULD HAVE BEEN RIGHT.
YOU DID WHAT HAD TO BE DONE, HENRY.
AND LISTEN: YOU DIDN'T FIRE THE GUN. SHE DID.
AND SHE WAS DOING HER JOB, AT THAT, MUCH AS I HATE TO ADMIT IT.

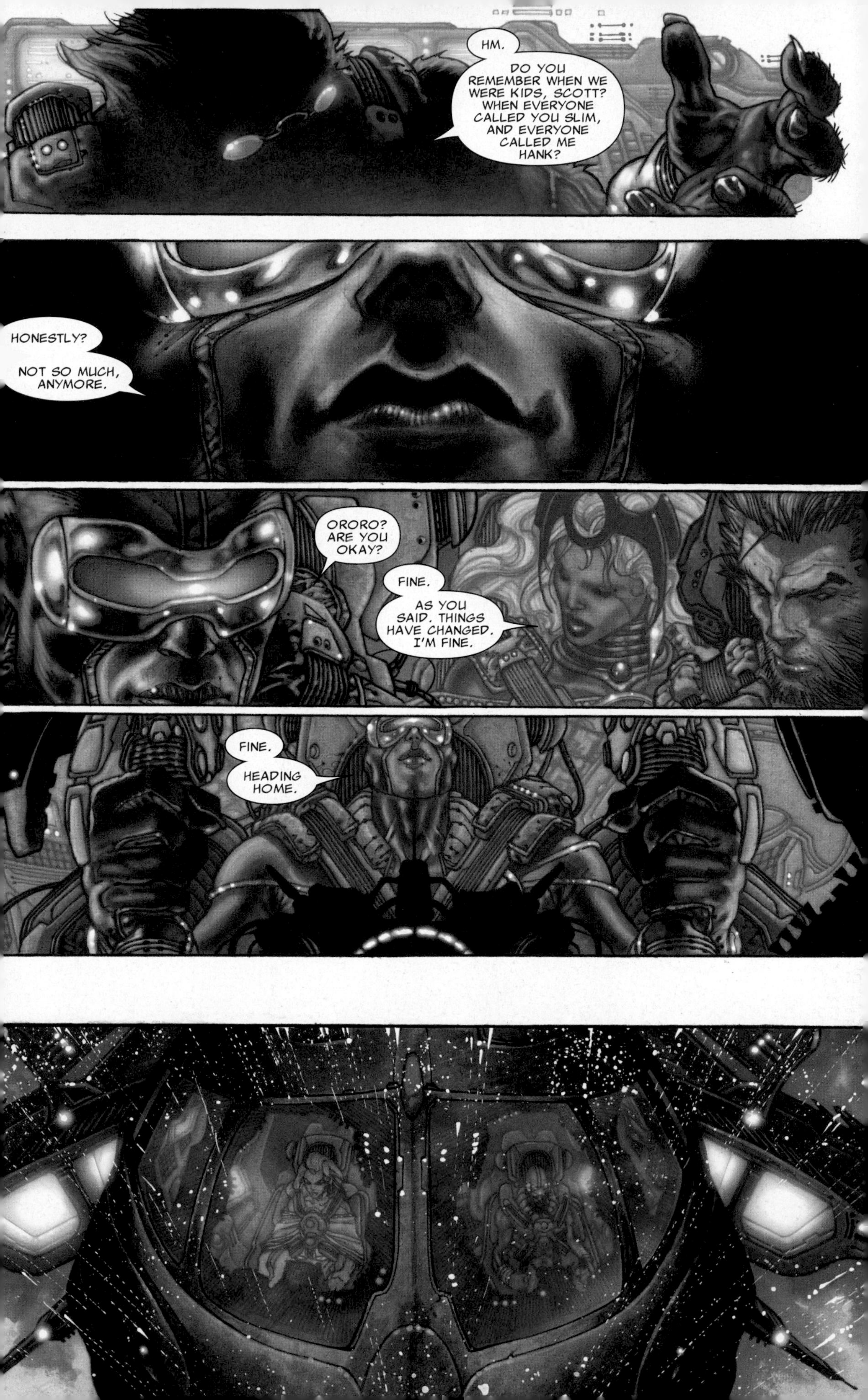
HM.
DO YOU REMEMBER WHEN WE WERE KIDS, SCOTT? WHEN EVERYONE CALLED YOU SLIM, AND EVERYONE CALLED ME HANK?
HONESTLY?
NOT SO MUCH, ANYMORE.
ORORO? ARE YOU OKAY?
FINE.
AS YOU SAID. THINGS HAVE CHANGED. I'M FINE.
FINE.
HEADING HOME.

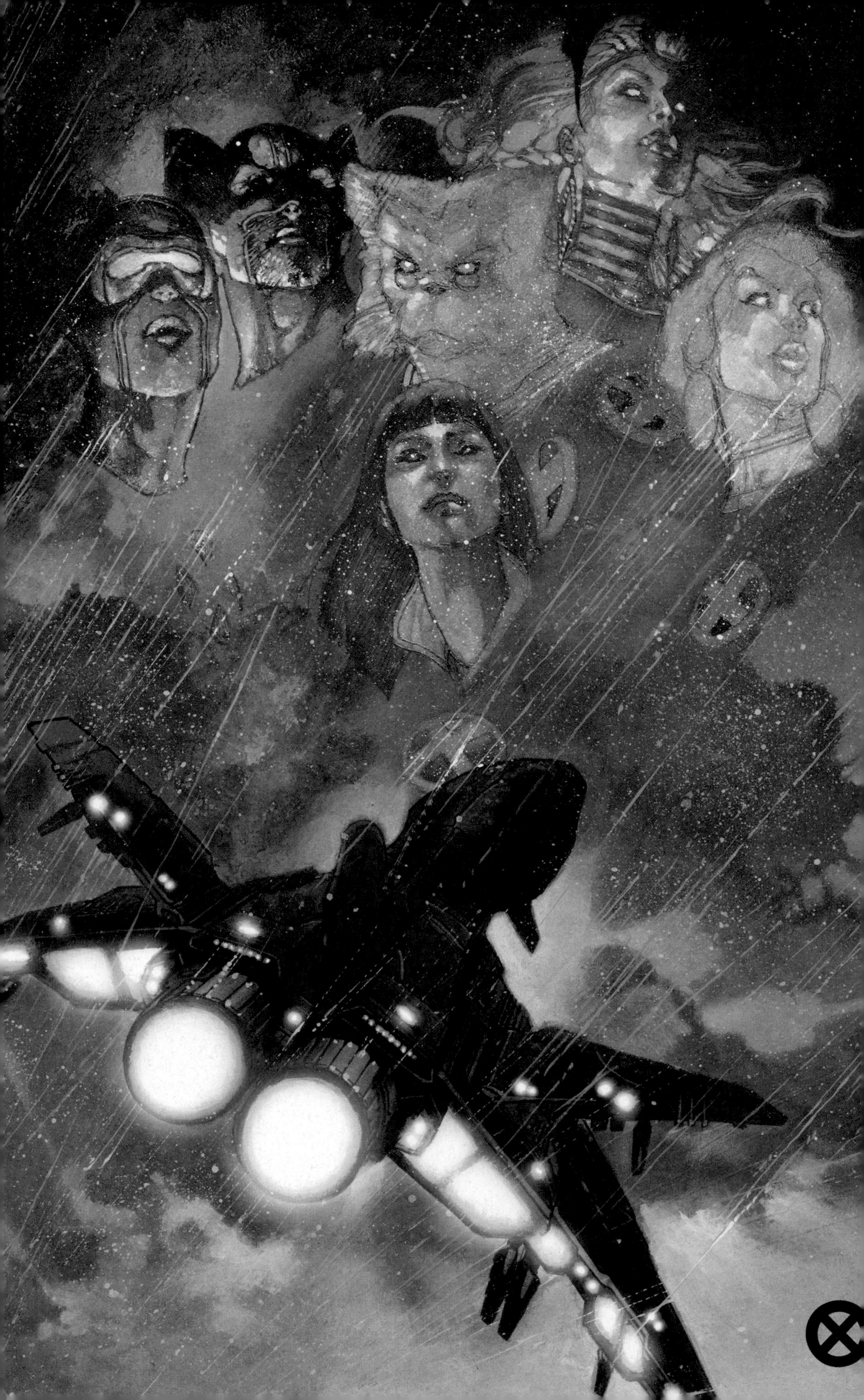

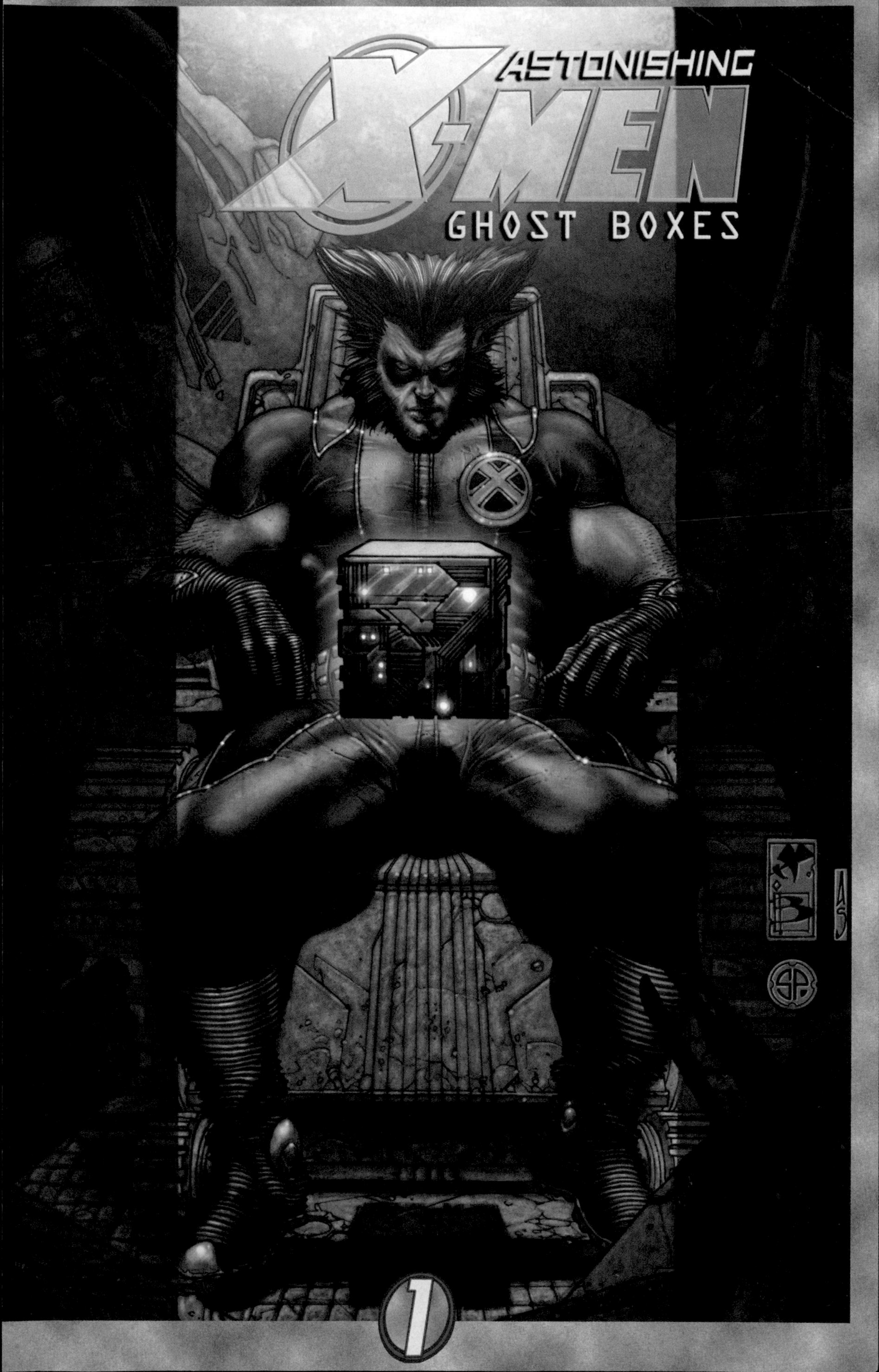
ASTONISHING
X-MEN
GHOST BOXES
1

AGENT X-13'S REPORT ON THE EMERGENCY ANNEXATION OF EARTH-616.

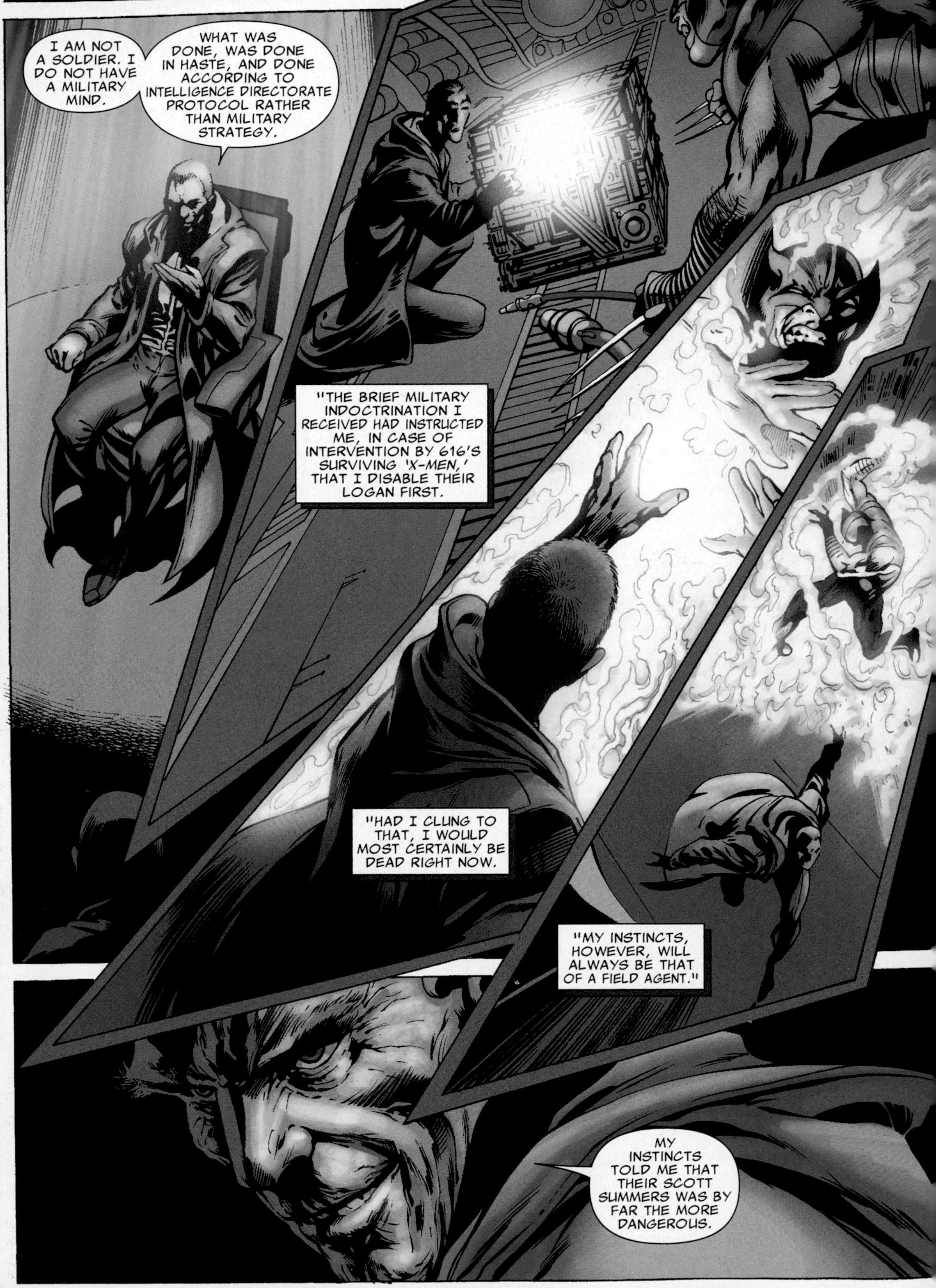
I AM NOT A SOLDIER. I DO NOT HAVE A MILITARY MIND.
WHAT WAS DONE, WAS DONE IN HASTE, AND DONE ACCORDING TO INTELLIGENCE DIRECTORATE PROTOCOL RATHER THAN MILITARY STRATEGY.
"THE BRIEF MILITARY INDOCTRINATION I RECEIVED HAD INSTRUCTED ME, IN CASE OF INTERVENTION BY 616'S SURVIVING 'X-MEN,' THAT I DISABLE THEIR LOGAN FIRST.
"HAD I CLUNG TO THAT, I WOULD MOST CERTAINLY BE DEAD RIGHT NOW.
"MY INSTINCTS, HOWEVER, WILL ALWAYS BE THAT OF A FIELD AGENT."
MY INSTINCTS TOLD ME THAT THEIR SCOTT SUMMERS WAS BY FAR THE MORE DANGEROUS.

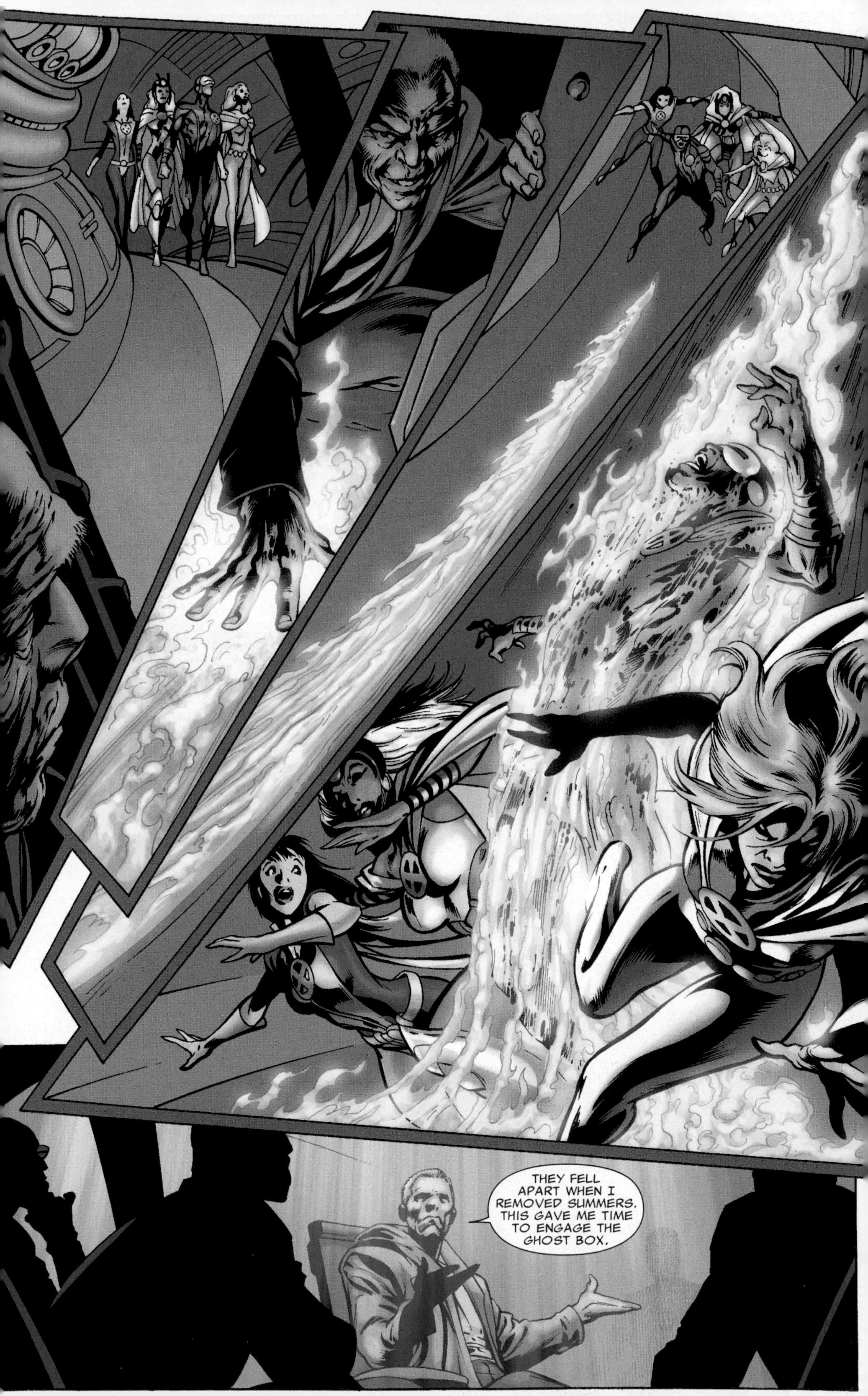
THEY FELL APART WHEN I REMOVED SUMMERS. THIS GAVE ME TIME TO ENGAGE THE GHOST BOX.

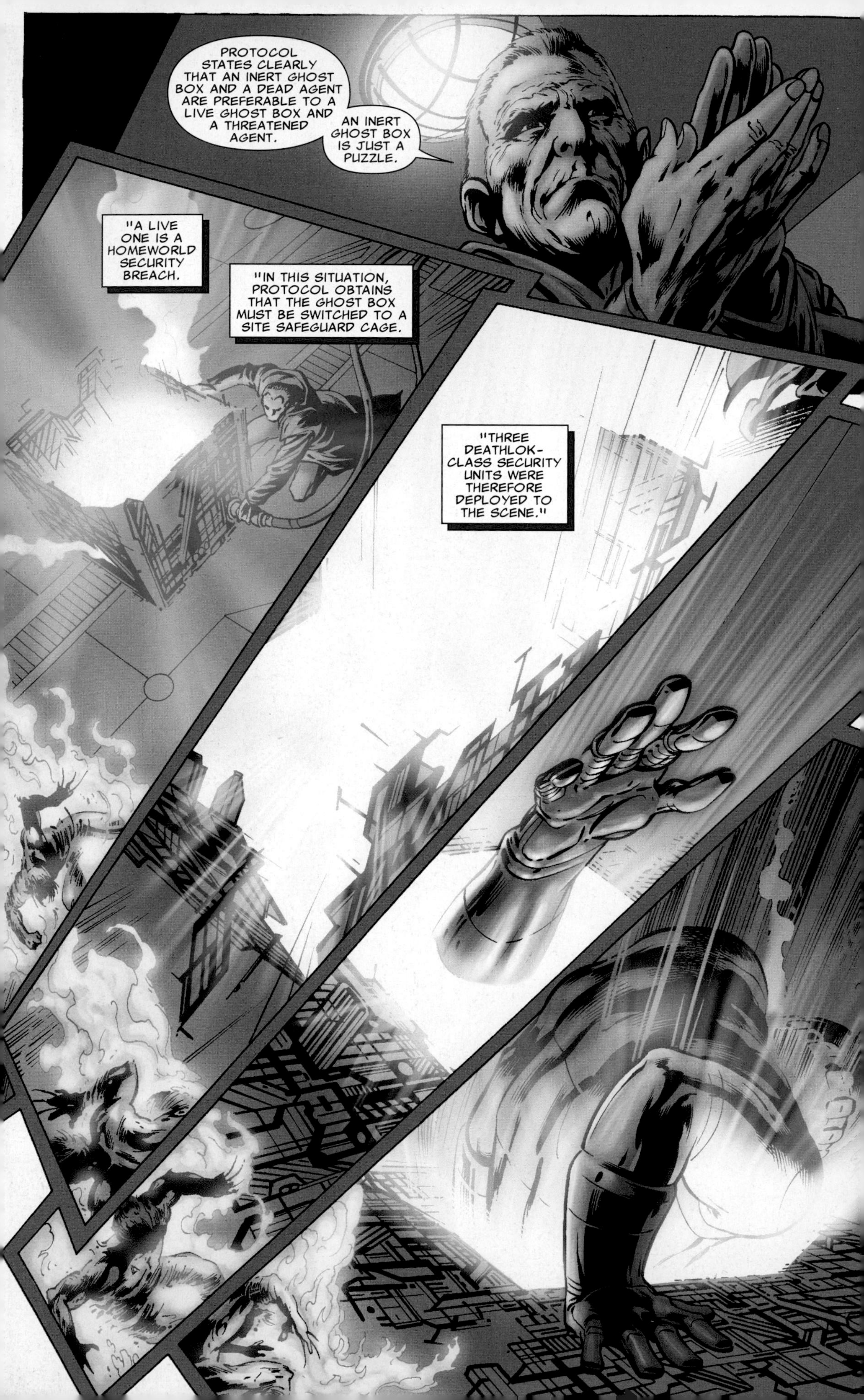
PROTOCOL STATES CLEARLY THAT AN INERT GHOST BOX AND A DEAD AGENT ARE PREFERABLE TO A LIVE GHOST BOX AND A THREATENED AGENT.
AN INERT GHOST BOX IS JUST A PUZZLE.
"A LIVE ONE IS A HOMEWORLD SECURITY BREACH.
"IN THIS SITUATION, PROTOCOL OBTAINS THAT THE GHOST BOX MUST BE SWITCHED TO A SITE SAFEGUARD CAGE.
"THREE DEATHLOK-CLASS SECURITY UNITS WERE THEREFORE DEPLOYED TO THE SCENE."

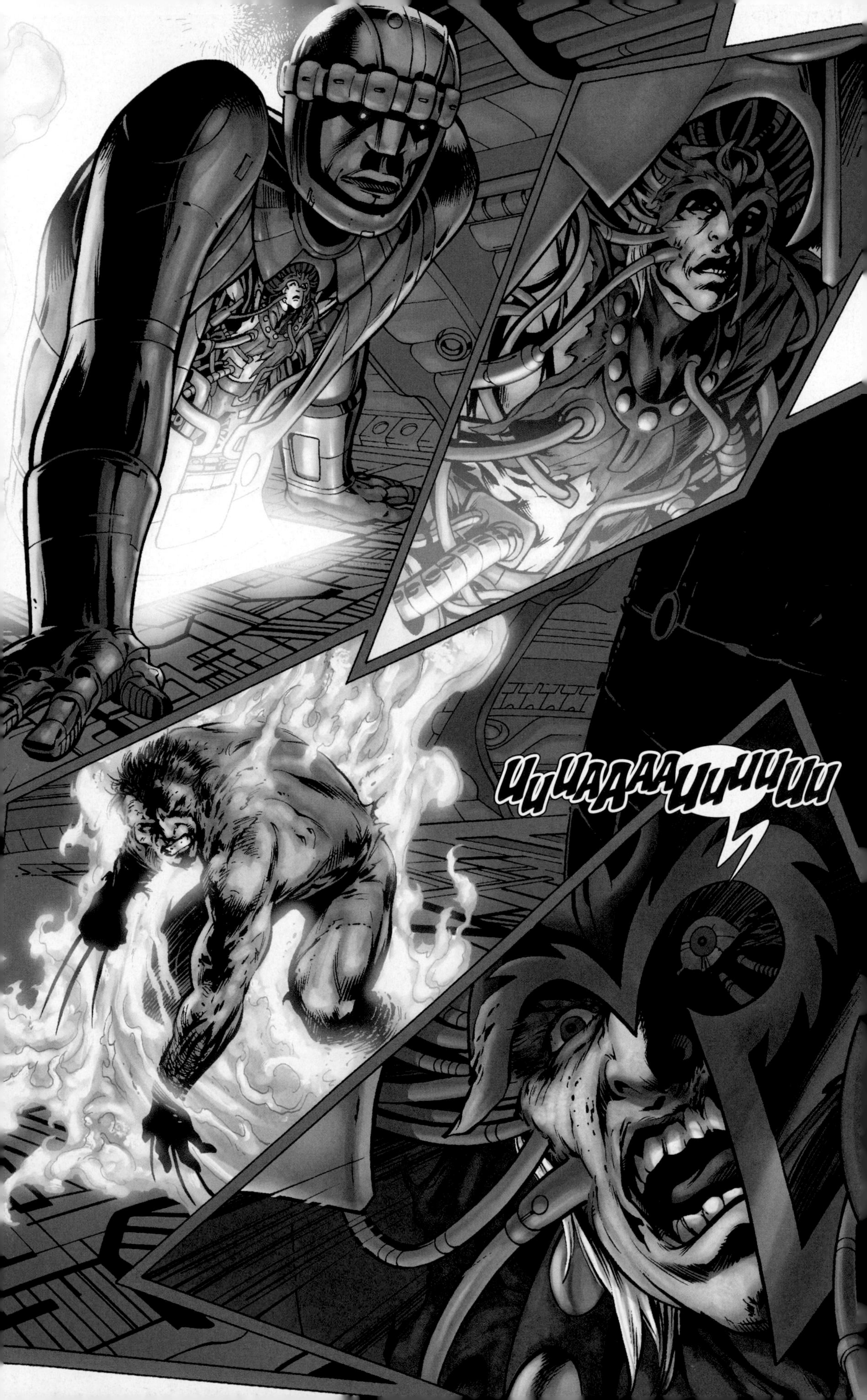
UUUAAAAUUUUUU

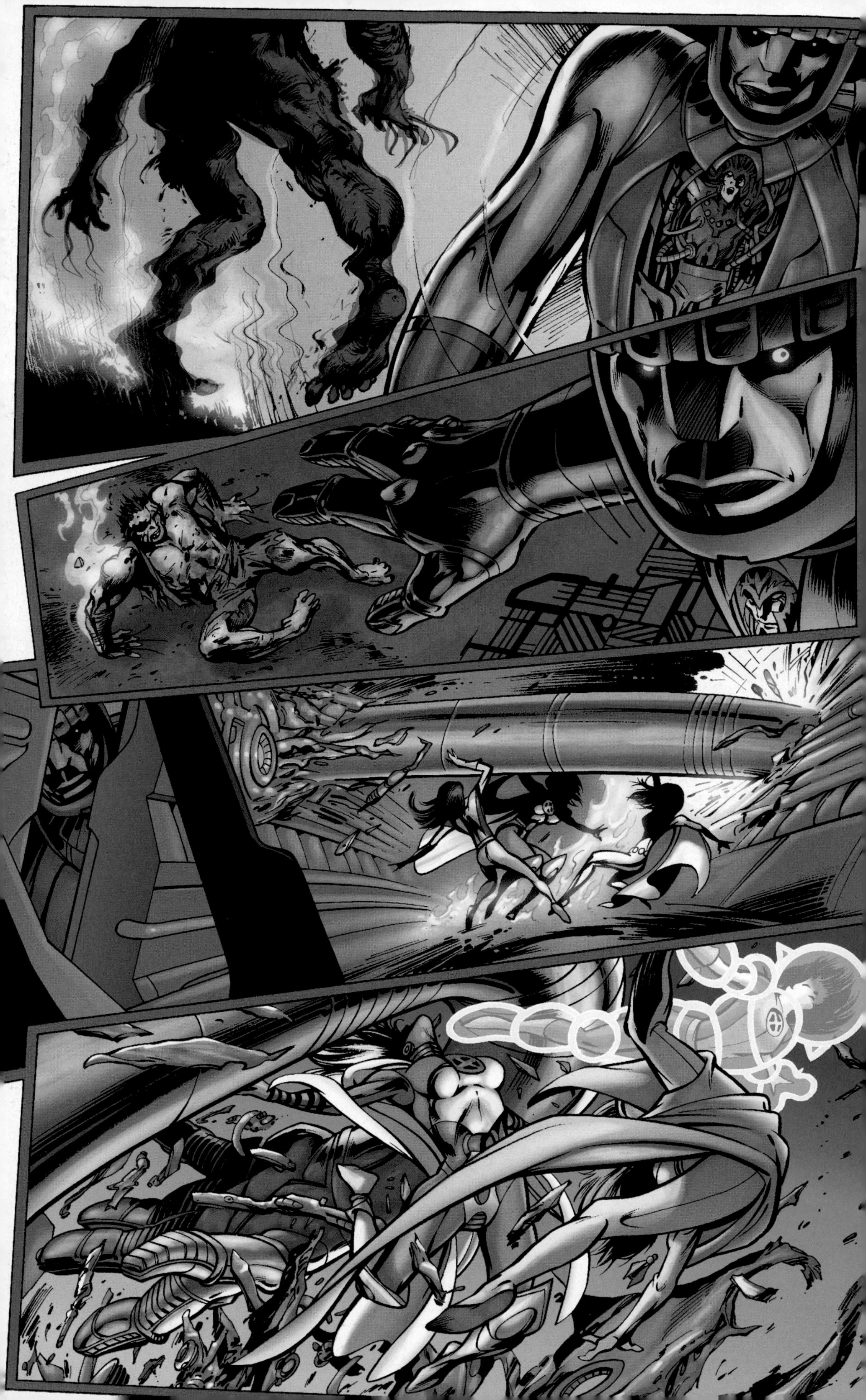

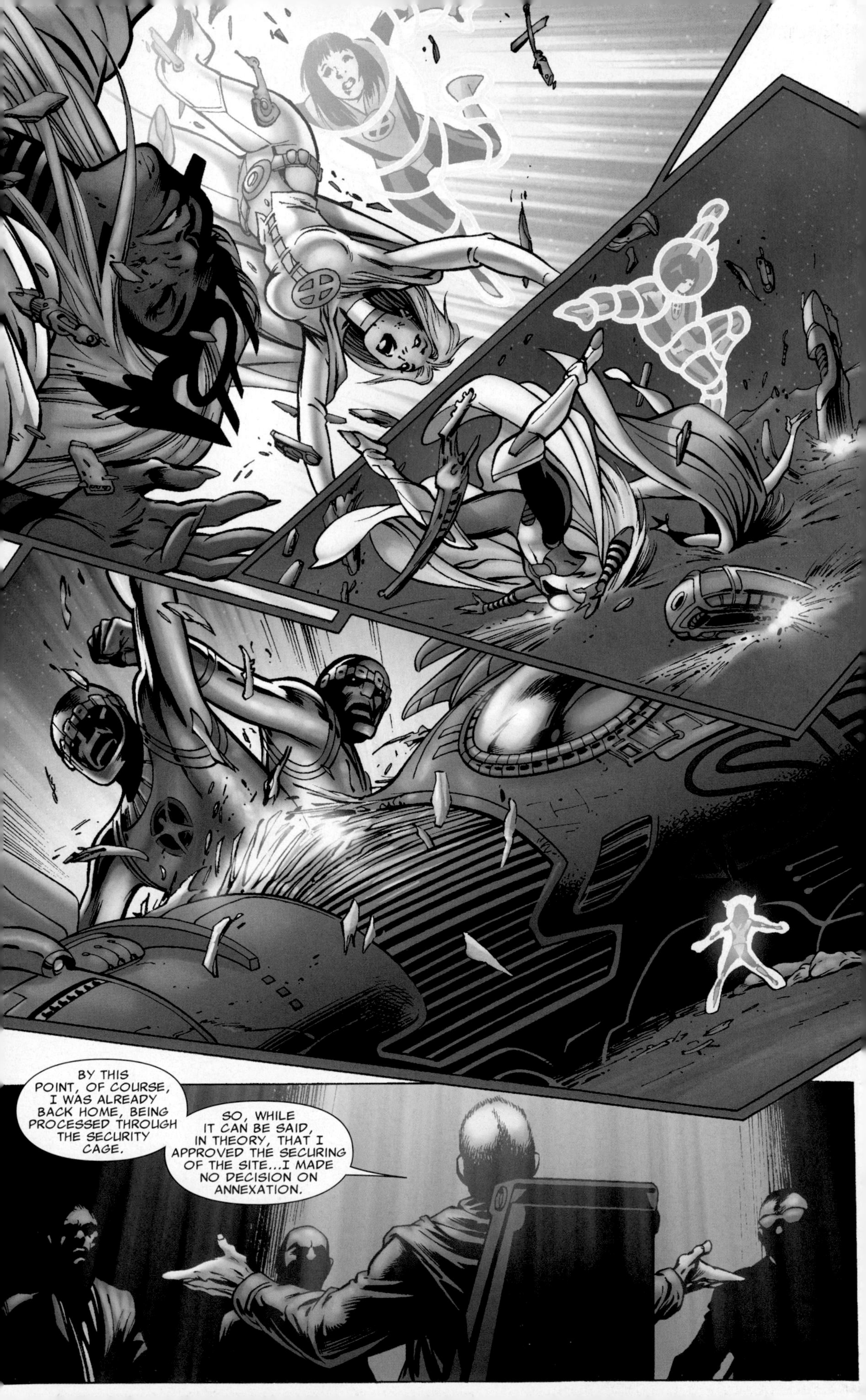
BY THIS POINT, OF COURSE, I WAS ALREADY BACK HOME, BEING PROCESSED THROUGH THE SECURITY CAGE.
SO, WHILE IT CAN BE SAID, IN THEORY, THAT I APPROVED THE SECURING OF THE SITE...I MADE NO DECISION ON ANNEXATION.

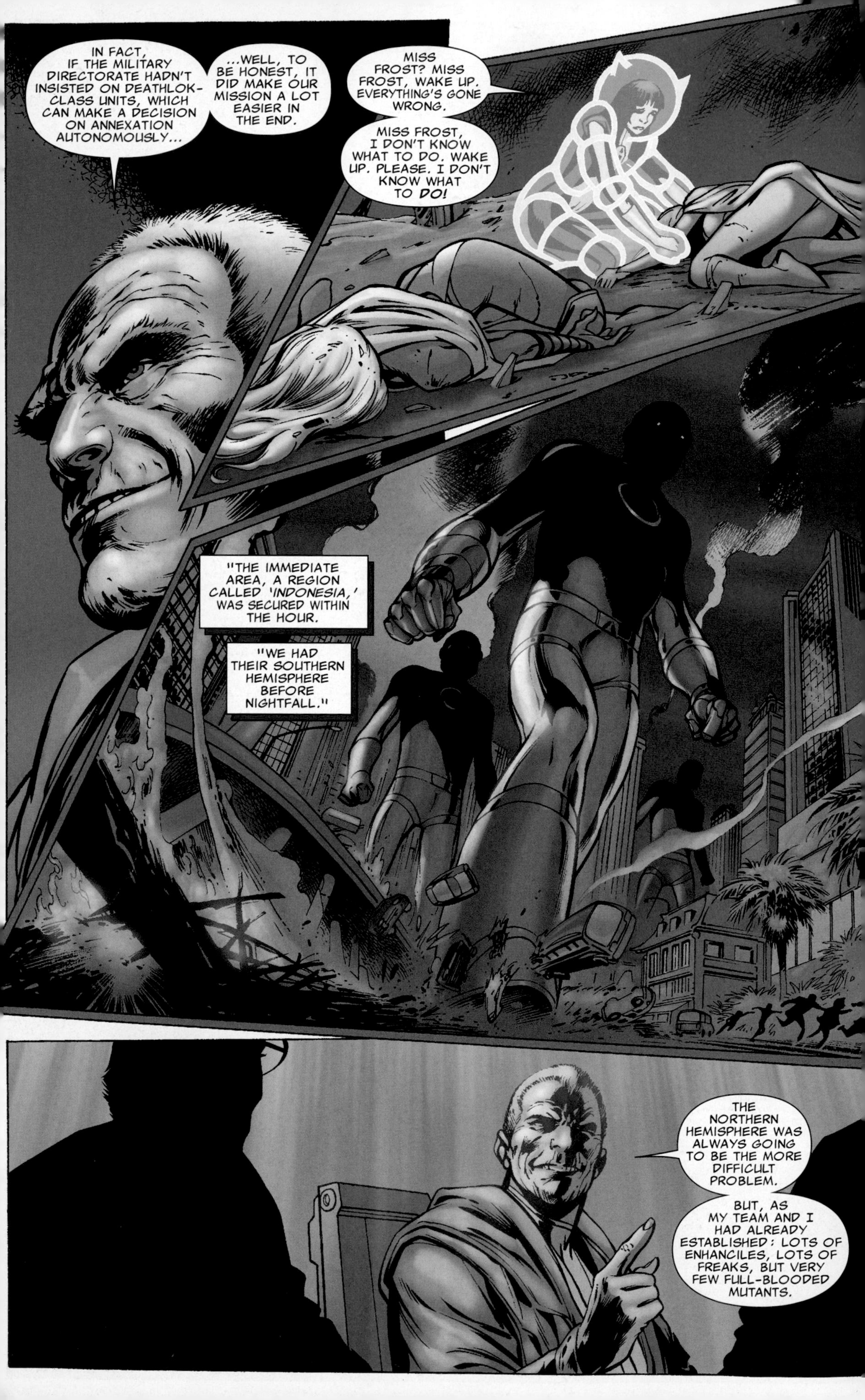
IN FACT, IF THE MILITARY DIRECTORATE HADN'T INSISTED ON DEATHLOK-CLASS UNITS, WHICH CAN MAKE A DECISION ON ANNEXATION AUTONOMOUSLY...
...WELL, TO BE HONEST, IT DID MAKE OUR MISSION A LOT EASIER IN THE END.
MISS FROST? MISS FROST, WAKE UP. EVERYTHING'S GONE WRONG.
MISS FROST, I DON'T KNOW WHAT TO DO. WAKE UP. PLEASE. I DON'T KNOW WHAT TO *DO!*
"THE IMMEDIATE AREA, A REGION CALLED '*INDONESIA,*' WAS SECURED WITHIN THE HOUR.
"WE HAD THEIR SOUTHERN HEMISPHERE BEFORE NIGHTFALL."
THE NORTHERN HEMISPHERE WAS ALWAYS GOING TO BE THE MORE DIFFICULT PROBLEM.
BUT, AS MY TEAM AND I HAD ALREADY ESTABLISHED: LOTS OF ENHANCILES, LOTS OF FREAKS, BUT VERY FEW FULL-BLOODED MUTANTS.

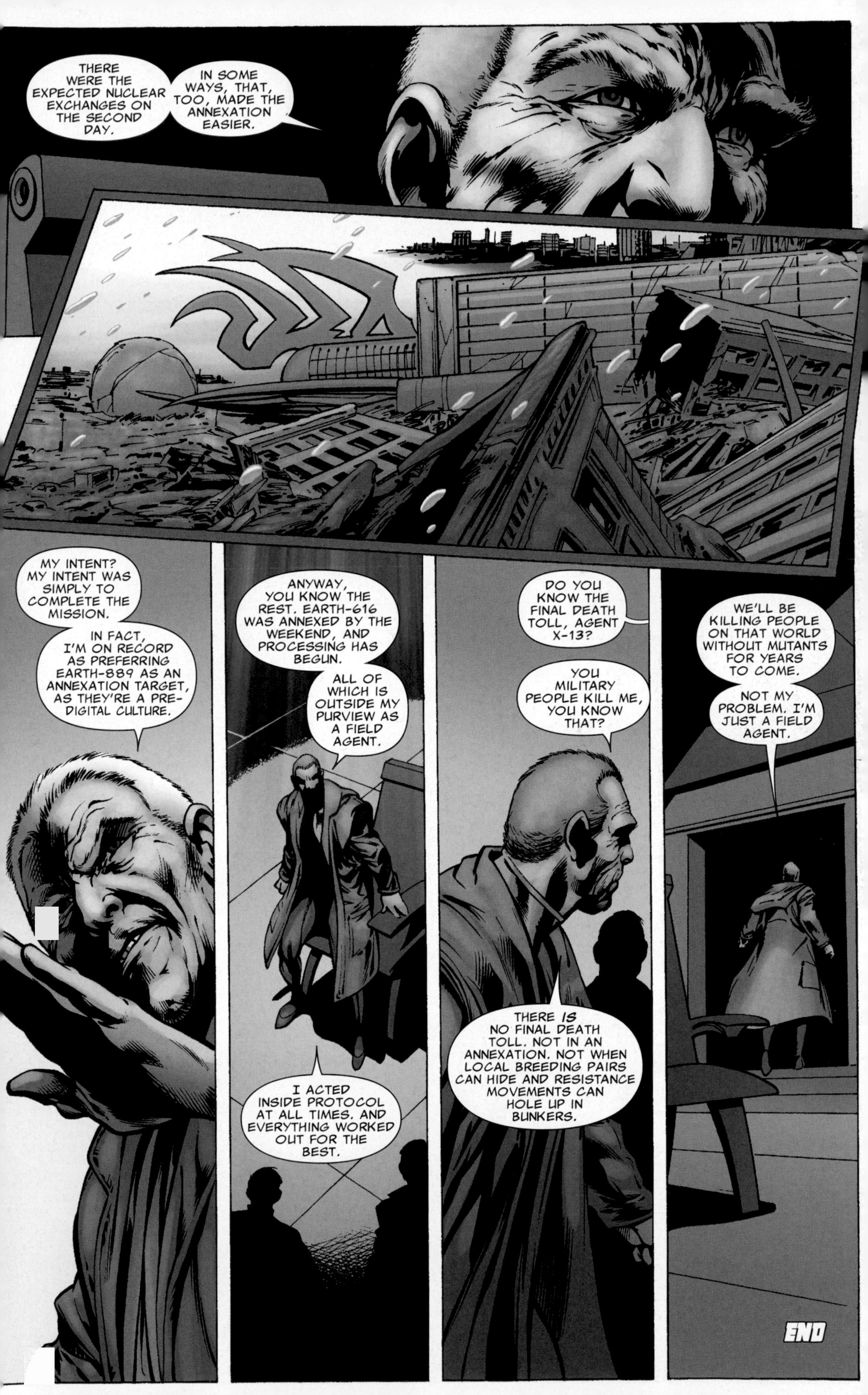
THERE WERE THE EXPECTED NUCLEAR EXCHANGES ON THE SECOND DAY.
IN SOME WAYS, THAT, TOO, MADE THE ANNEXATION EASIER.
MY INTENT? MY INTENT WAS SIMPLY TO COMPLETE THE MISSION.
IN FACT, I'M ON RECORD AS PREFERRING EARTH-889 AS AN ANNEXATION TARGET, AS THEY'RE A PRE-DIGITAL CULTURE.
ANYWAY, YOU KNOW THE REST. EARTH-616 WAS ANNEXED BY THE WEEKEND, AND PROCESSING HAS BEGUN.
ALL OF WHICH IS OUTSIDE MY PURVIEW AS A FIELD AGENT.
I ACTED INSIDE PROTOCOL AT ALL TIMES, AND EVERYTHING WORKED OUT FOR THE BEST.
DO YOU KNOW THE FINAL DEATH TOLL, AGENT X-13?
YOU MILITARY PEOPLE KILL ME, YOU KNOW THAT?
THERE IS NO FINAL DEATH TOLL. NOT IN AN ANNEXATION. NOT WHEN LOCAL BREEDING PAIRS CAN HIDE AND RESISTANCE MOVEMENTS CAN HOLE UP IN BUNKERS.
WE'LL BE KILLING PEOPLE ON THAT WORLD WITHOUT MUTANTS FOR YEARS TO COME.
NOT MY PROBLEM. I'M JUST A FIELD AGENT.
END

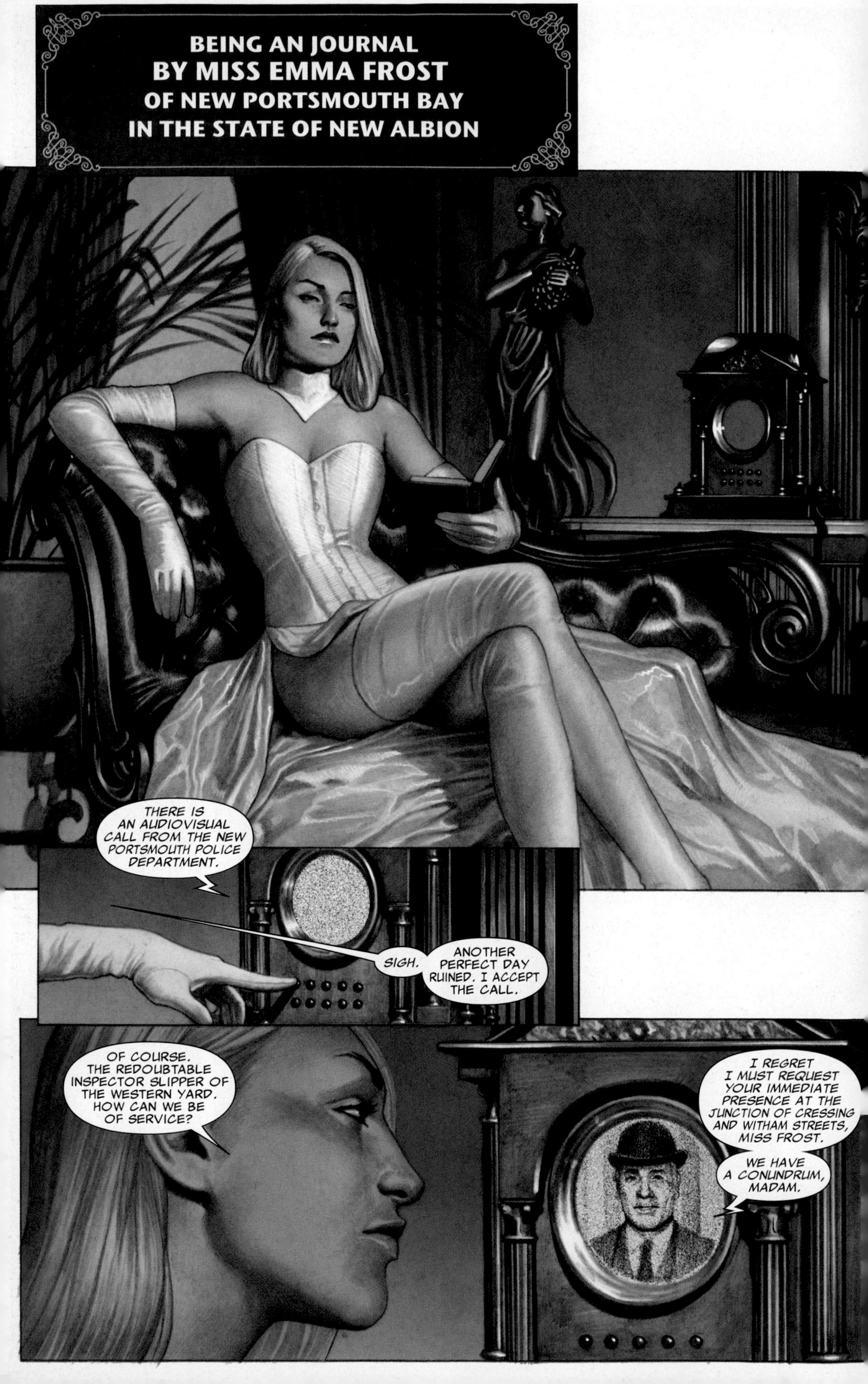
BEING AN JOURNAL
BY MISS EMMA FROST
OF NEW PORTSMOUTH BAY
IN THE STATE OF NEW ALBION
THERE IS AN AUDIOVISUAL CALL FROM THE NEW PORTSMOUTH POLICE DEPARTMENT.
SIGH.
ANOTHER PERFECT DAY RUINED. I ACCEPT THE CALL.
OF COURSE. THE REDOUBTABLE INSPECTOR SLIPPER OF THE WESTERN YARD. HOW CAN WE BE OF SERVICE?
I REGRET I MUST REQUEST YOUR IMMEDIATE PRESENCE AT THE JUNCTION OF CRESSING AND WITHAM STREETS, MISS FROST.
WE HAVE A CONUNDRUM, MADAM.

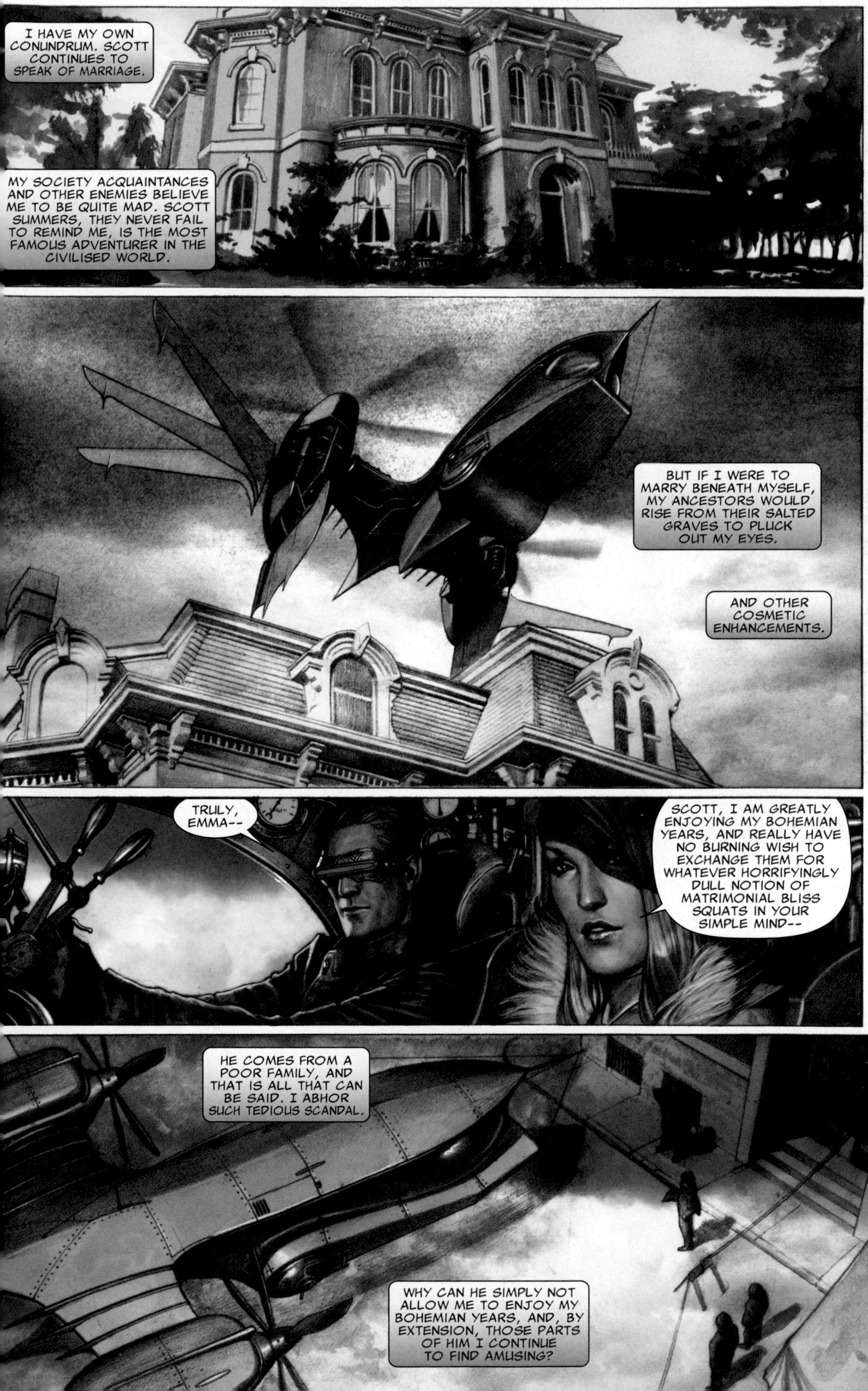
I HAVE MY OWN CONUNDRUM. SCOTT CONTINUES TO SPEAK OF MARRIAGE.
MY SOCIETY ACQUAINTANCES AND OTHER ENEMIES BELIEVE ME TO BE QUITE MAD. SCOTT SUMMERS, THEY NEVER FAIL TO REMIND ME, IS THE MOST FAMOUS ADVENTURER IN THE CIVILISED WORLD.
BUT IF I WERE TO MARRY BENEATH MYSELF, MY ANCESTORS WOULD RISE FROM THEIR SALTED GRAVES TO PLUCK OUT MY EYES.
AND OTHER COSMETIC ENHANCEMENTS.
TRULY, EMMA--
SCOTT, I AM GREATLY ENJOYING MY BOHEMIAN YEARS, AND REALLY HAVE NO BURNING WISH TO EXCHANGE THEM FOR WHATEVER HORRIFYINGLY DULL NOTION OF MATRIMONIAL BLISS SQUATS IN YOUR SIMPLE MIND--
HE COMES FROM A POOR FAMILY, AND THAT IS ALL THAT CAN BE SAID. I ABHOR SUCH TEDIOUS SCANDAL.
WHY CAN HE SIMPLY NOT ALLOW ME TO ENJOY MY BOHEMIAN YEARS, AND, BY EXTENSION, THOSE PARTS OF HIM I CONTINUE TO FIND AMUSING?

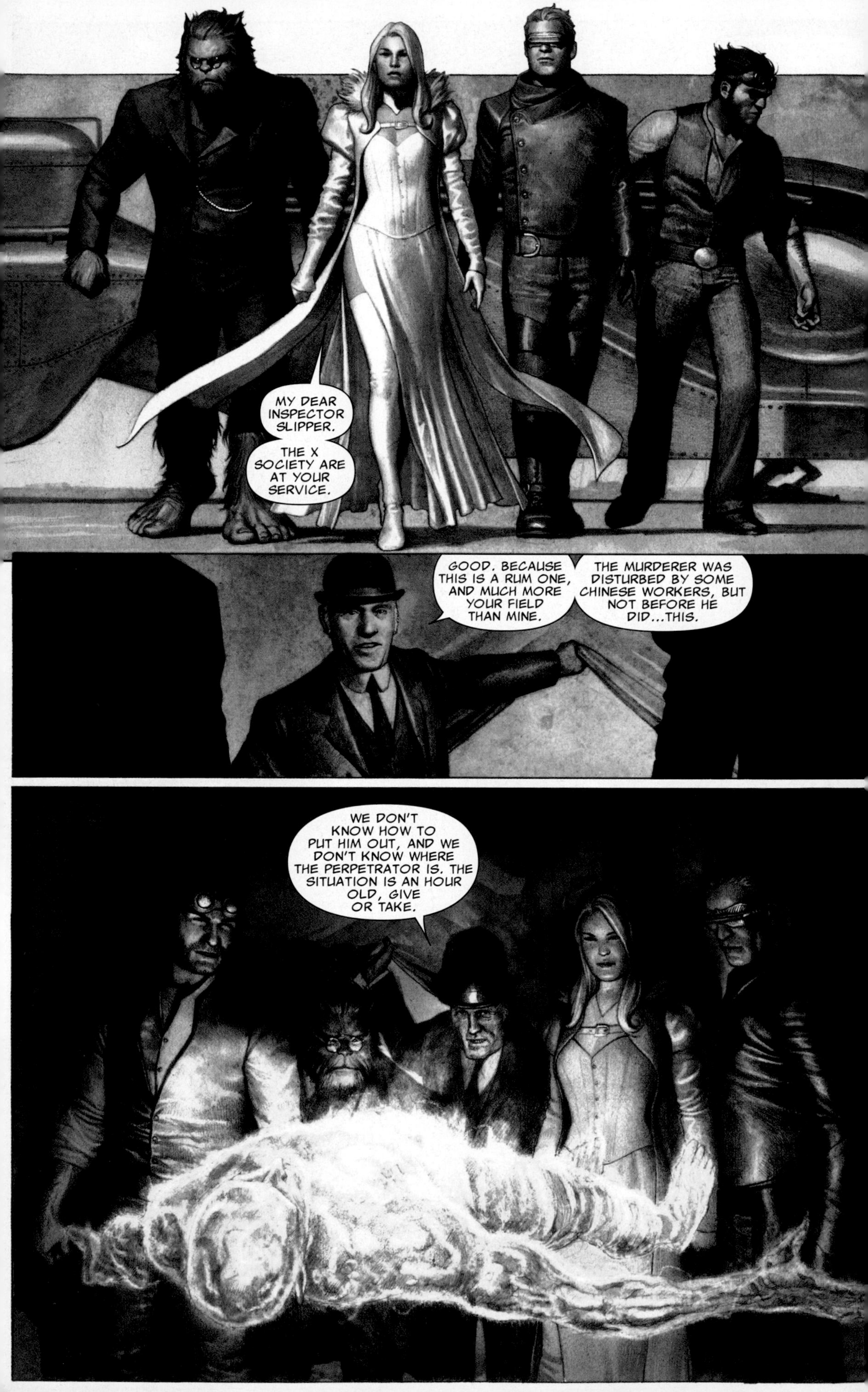
MY DEAR INSPECTOR SLIPPER.
THE X SOCIETY ARE AT YOUR SERVICE.
GOOD. BECAUSE THIS IS A RUM ONE, AND MUCH MORE YOUR FIELD THAN MINE.
THE MURDERER WAS DISTURBED BY SOME CHINESE WORKERS, BUT NOT BEFORE HE DID...THIS.
WE DON'T KNOW HOW TO PUT HIM OUT, AND WE DON'T KNOW WHERE THE PERPETRATOR IS. THE SITUATION IS AN HOUR OLD, GIVE OR TAKE.

DR. McCOY?

CLEARLY THE WORK OF HOMO MUTANDIS, MISS FROST.

HOMO MUTANDIS?

FROM THE LATIN, INSPECTOR. LITERALLY, "THE CHANGED HUMAN."

MISTER LOGAN. I BELIEVE WE'VE SPOKEN ABOUT YOUR BEHAVIOR IN PUBLIC.

CAN'T HELP IT, MISS EMMA. THERE'S A WRONG STINK 'ROUND THESE PARTS. 'ROUND...

...HERE.

SCOTT, TAKE THE BAG. I SEE A JOURNAL IN THERE--DON'T LET LOGAN TOUCH IT, HIS PAWS ARE ALWAYS FILTHY.

I FIGGER THE KILLER, HE WANTED TO TAKE THIS GUY'S GEAR, BUT HAD TO DUMP IT WHEN HE GOT HISSELF SPOTTED BY THE CHINEE.

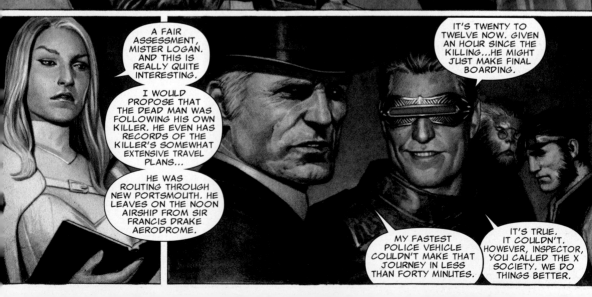

A FAIR ASSESSMENT, MISTER LOGAN. AND THIS IS REALLY QUITE INTERESTING.

I WOULD PROPOSE THAT THE DEAD MAN WAS FOLLOWING HIS OWN KILLER. HE EVEN HAS RECORDS OF THE KILLER'S SOMEWHAT EXTENSIVE TRAVEL PLANS...

HE WAS ROUTING THROUGH NEW PORTSMOUTH. HE LEAVES ON THE NOON AIRSHIP FROM SIR FRANCIS DRAKE AERODROME.

IT'S TWENTY TO TWELVE NOW. GIVEN AN HOUR SINCE THE KILLING...HE MIGHT JUST MAKE FINAL BOARDING.

MY FASTEST POLICE VEHICLE COULDN'T MAKE THAT JOURNEY IN LESS THAN FORTY MINUTES.

IT'S TRUE. IT COULDN'T. HOWEVER, INSPECTOR, YOU CALLED THE X SOCIETY. WE DO THINGS BETTER.

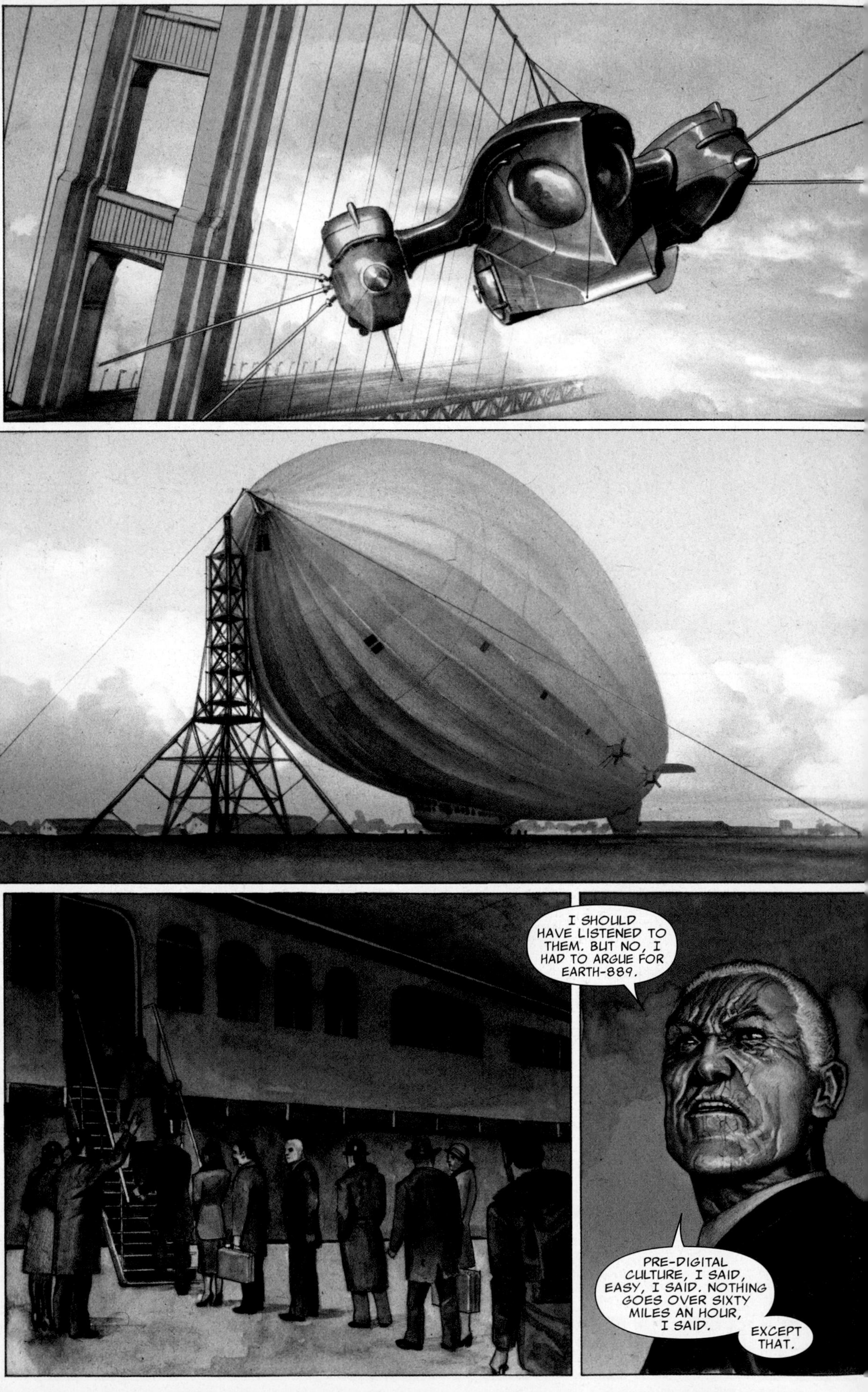
I SHOULD HAVE LISTENED TO THEM. BUT NO, I HAD TO ARGUE FOR EARTH-889.
PRE-DIGITAL CULTURE, I SAID, EASY, I SAID. NOTHING GOES OVER SIXTY MILES AN HOUR, I SAID.
EXCEPT THAT.

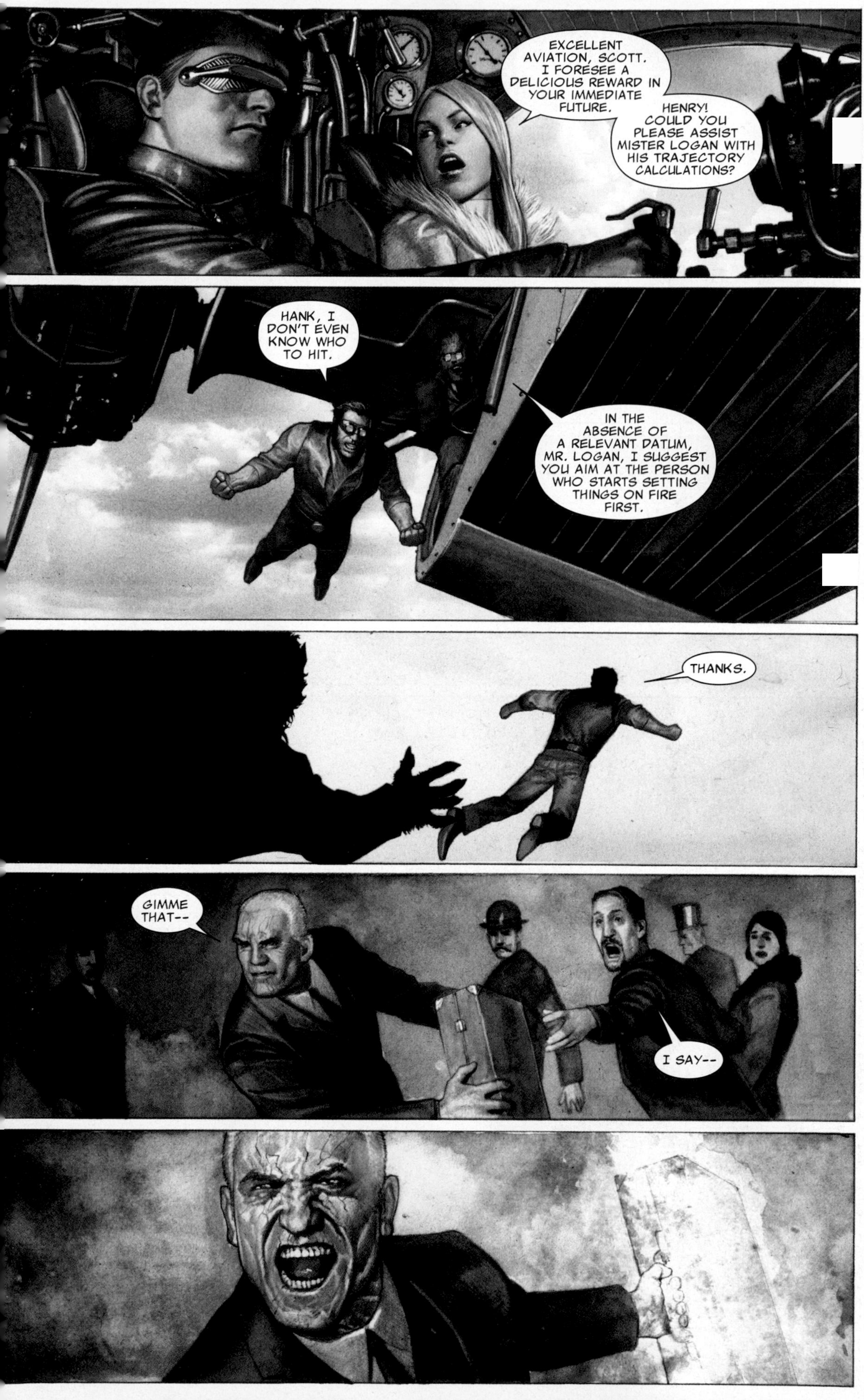
EXCELLENT AVIATION, SCOTT. I FORESEE A DELICIOUS REWARD IN YOUR IMMEDIATE FUTURE.
HENRY! COULD YOU PLEASE ASSIST MISTER LOGAN WITH HIS TRAJECTORY CALCULATIONS?
HANK, I DON'T EVEN KNOW WHO TO HIT.
IN THE ABSENCE OF A RELEVANT DATUM, MR. LOGAN, I SUGGEST YOU AIM AT THE PERSON WHO STARTS SETTING THINGS ON FIRE FIRST.
THANKS.
GIMME THAT--
I SAY--

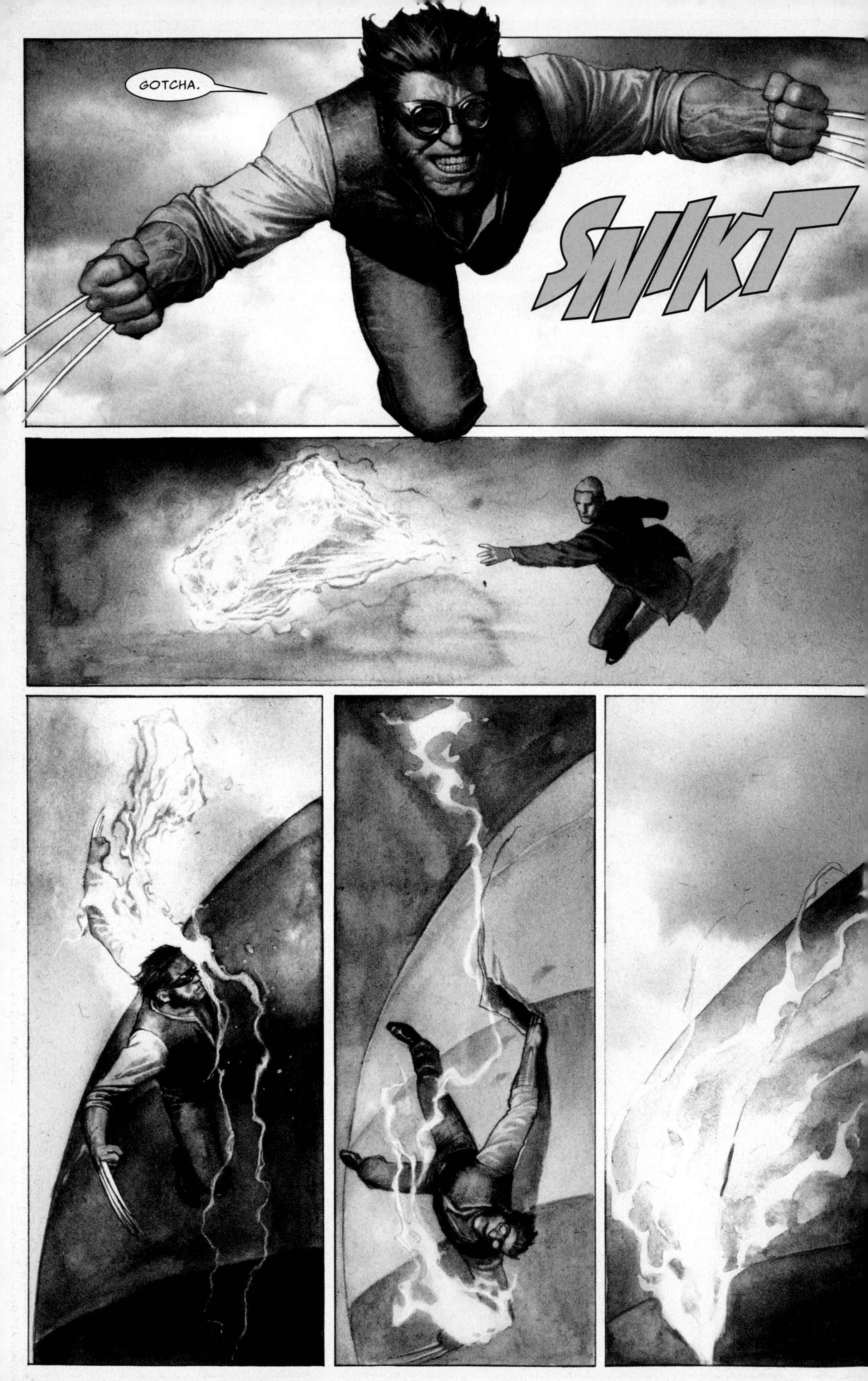
GOTCHA.
SNIKT

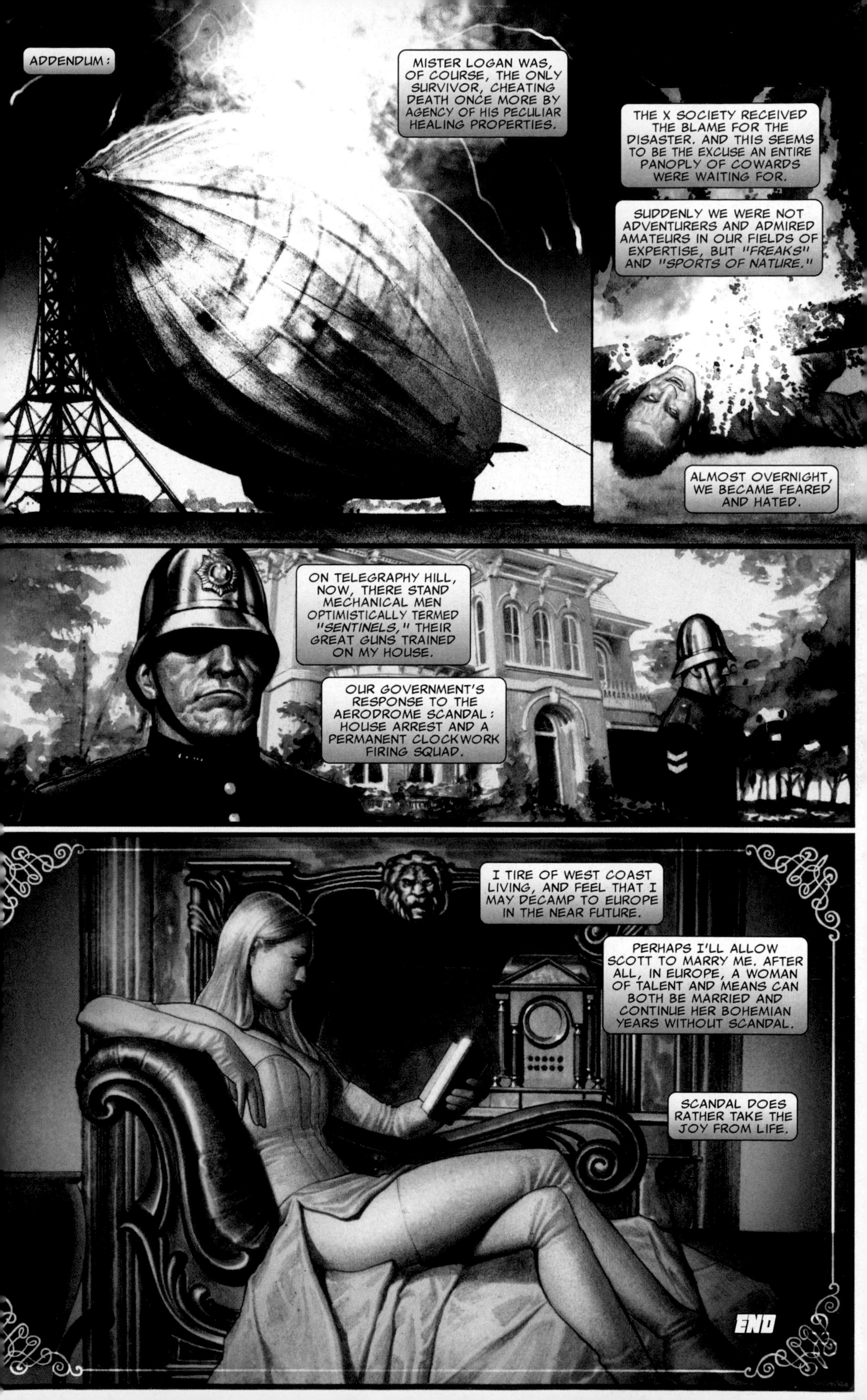
ADDENDUM:
MISTER LOGAN WAS, OF COURSE, THE ONLY SURVIVOR, CHEATING DEATH ONCE MORE BY AGENCY OF HIS PECULIAR HEALING PROPERTIES.
THE X SOCIETY RECEIVED THE BLAME FOR THE DISASTER. AND THIS SEEMS TO BE THE EXCUSE AN ENTIRE PANOPLY OF COWARDS WERE WAITING FOR.
SUDDENLY WE WERE NOT ADVENTURERS AND ADMIRED AMATEURS IN OUR FIELDS OF EXPERTISE, BUT "FREAKS" AND "SPORTS OF NATURE."
ALMOST OVERNIGHT, WE BECAME FEARED AND HATED.
ON TELEGRAPHY HILL, NOW, THERE STAND MECHANICAL MEN OPTIMISTICALLY TERMED "SENTINELS," THEIR GREAT GUNS TRAINED ON MY HOUSE.
OUR GOVERNMENT'S RESPONSE TO THE AERODROME SCANDAL: HOUSE ARREST AND A PERMANENT CLOCKWORK FIRING SQUAD.
I TIRE OF WEST COAST LIVING, AND FEEL THAT I MAY DECAMP TO EUROPE IN THE NEAR FUTURE.
PERHAPS I'LL ALLOW SCOTT TO MARRY ME. AFTER ALL, IN EUROPE, A WOMAN OF TALENT AND MEANS CAN BOTH BE MARRIED AND CONTINUE HER BOHEMIAN YEARS WITHOUT SCANDAL.
SCANDAL DOES RATHER TAKE THE JOY FROM LIFE.
END

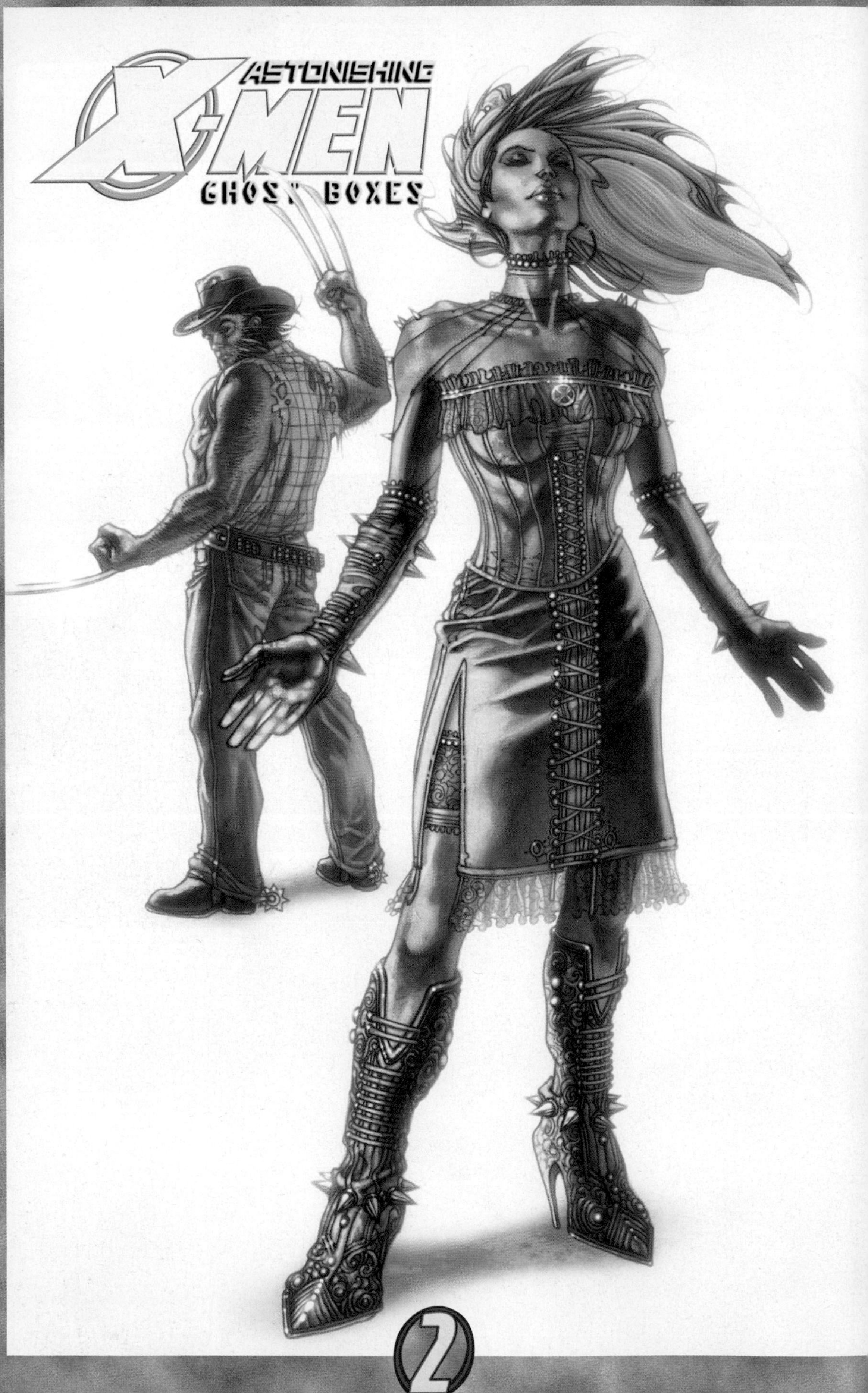
ASTONISHING
X-MEN
GHOST BOXES
2

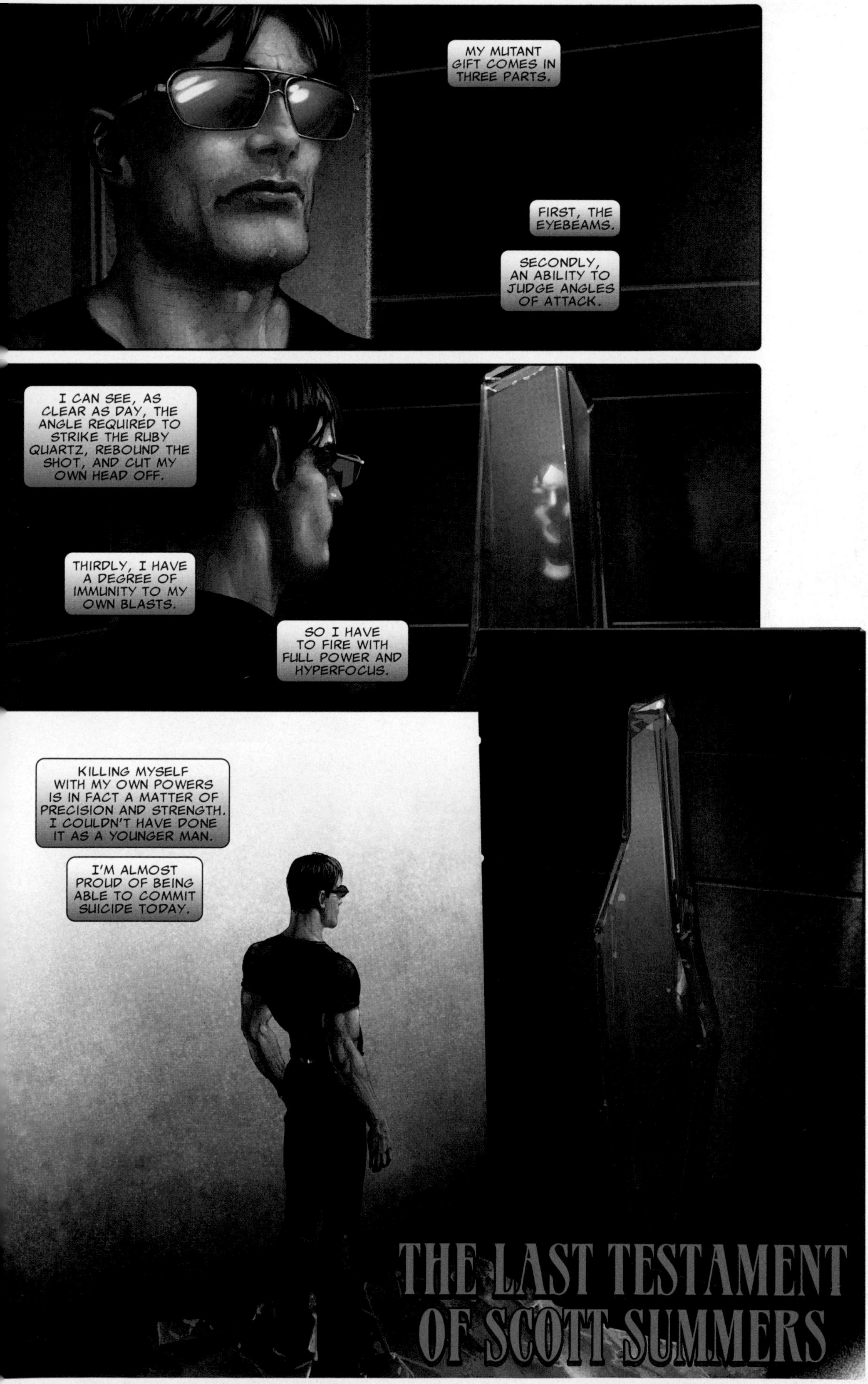
MY MUTANT GIFT COMES IN THREE PARTS.
FIRST, THE EYEBEAMS.
SECONDLY, AN ABILITY TO JUDGE ANGLES OF ATTACK.
I CAN SEE, AS CLEAR AS DAY, THE ANGLE REQUIRED TO STRIKE THE RUBY QUARTZ, REBOUND THE SHOT, AND CUT MY OWN HEAD OFF.
THIRDLY, I HAVE A DEGREE OF IMMUNITY TO MY OWN BLASTS.
SO I HAVE TO FIRE WITH FULL POWER AND HYPERFOCUS.
KILLING MYSELF WITH MY OWN POWERS IS IN FACT A MATTER OF PRECISION AND STRENGTH. I COULDN'T HAVE DONE IT AS A YOUNGER MAN.
I'M ALMOST PROUD OF BEING ABLE TO COMMIT SUICIDE TODAY.
THE LAST TESTAMENT OF SCOTT SUMMERS

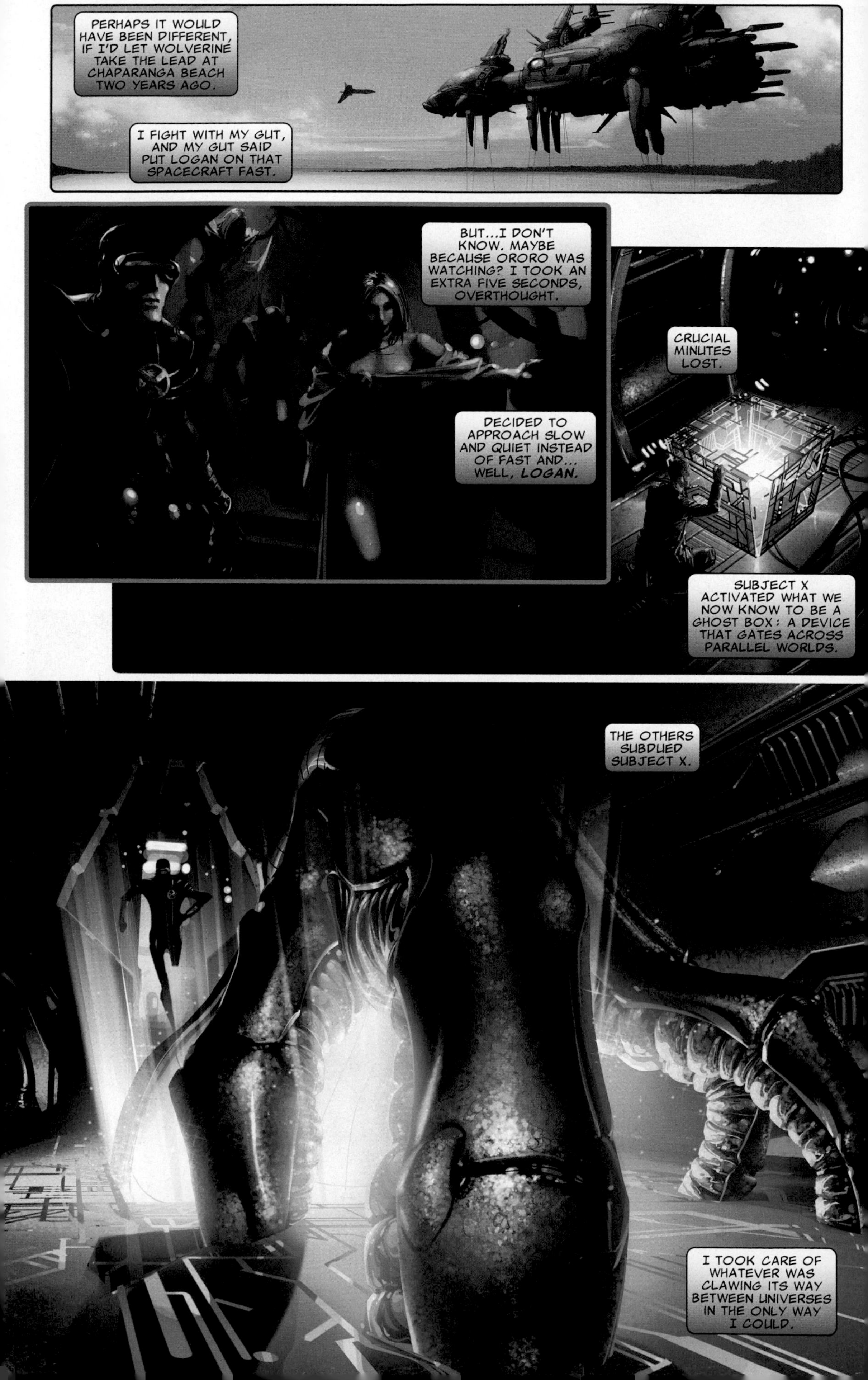
PERHAPS IT WOULD HAVE BEEN DIFFERENT, IF I'D LET WOLVERINE TAKE THE LEAD AT CHAPARANGA BEACH TWO YEARS AGO.
I FIGHT WITH MY GUT, AND MY GUT SAID PUT LOGAN ON THAT SPACECRAFT FAST.
BUT...I DON'T KNOW. MAYBE BECAUSE ORORO WAS WATCHING? I TOOK AN EXTRA FIVE SECONDS, OVERTHOUGHT.
DECIDED TO APPROACH SLOW AND QUIET INSTEAD OF FAST AND... WELL, LOGAN.
CRUCIAL MINUTES LOST.
SUBJECT X ACTIVATED WHAT WE NOW KNOW TO BE A GHOST BOX: A DEVICE THAT GATES ACROSS PARALLEL WORLDS.
THE OTHERS SUBDUED SUBJECT X.
I TOOK CARE OF WHATEVER WAS CLAWING ITS WAY BETWEEN UNIVERSES IN THE ONLY WAY I COULD.

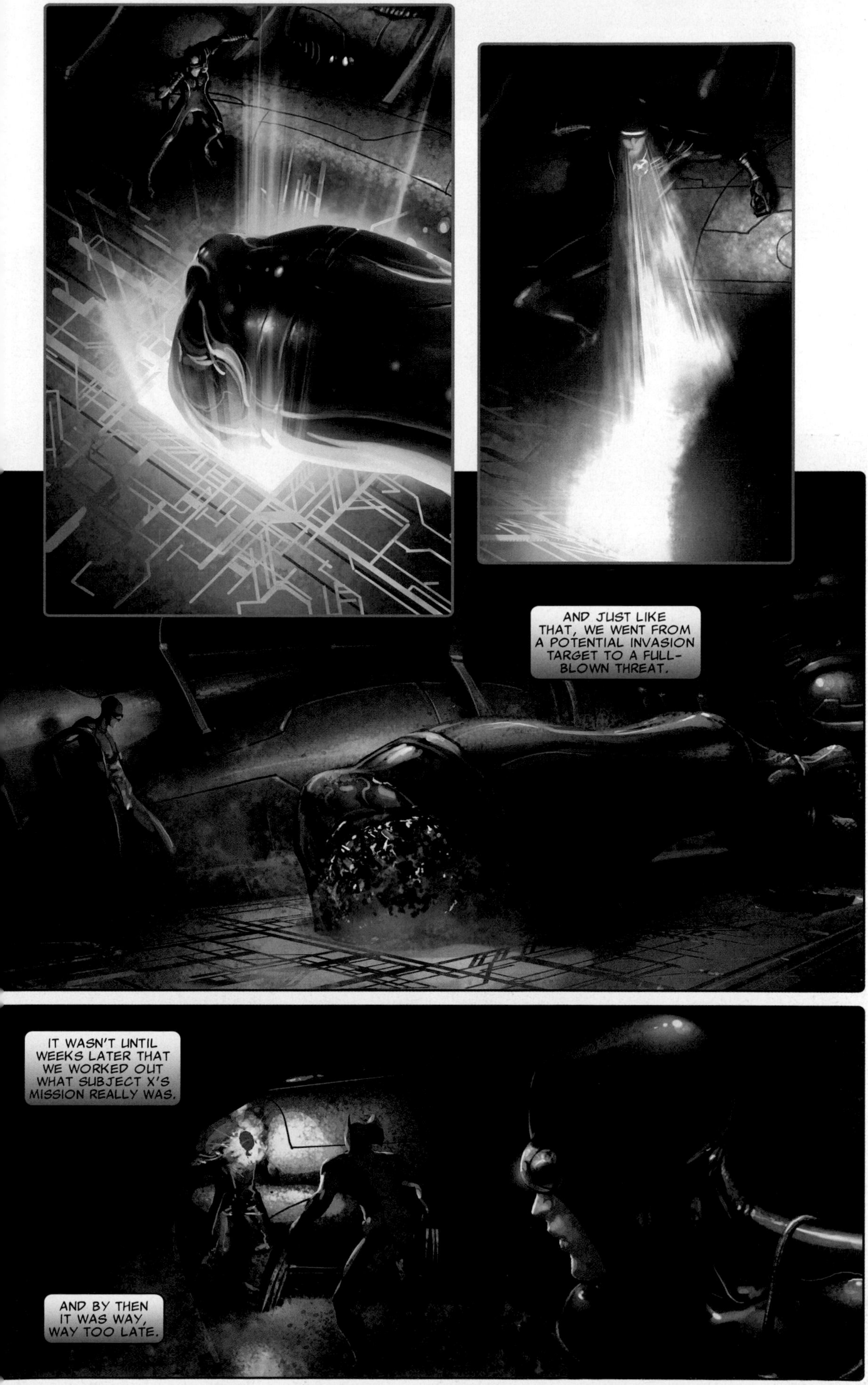
AND JUST LIKE THAT, WE WENT FROM A POTENTIAL INVASION TARGET TO A FULL-BLOWN THREAT.
IT WASN'T UNTIL WEEKS LATER THAT WE WORKED OUT WHAT SUBJECT X'S MISSION REALLY WAS.
AND BY THEN IT WAS WAY, WAY TOO LATE.

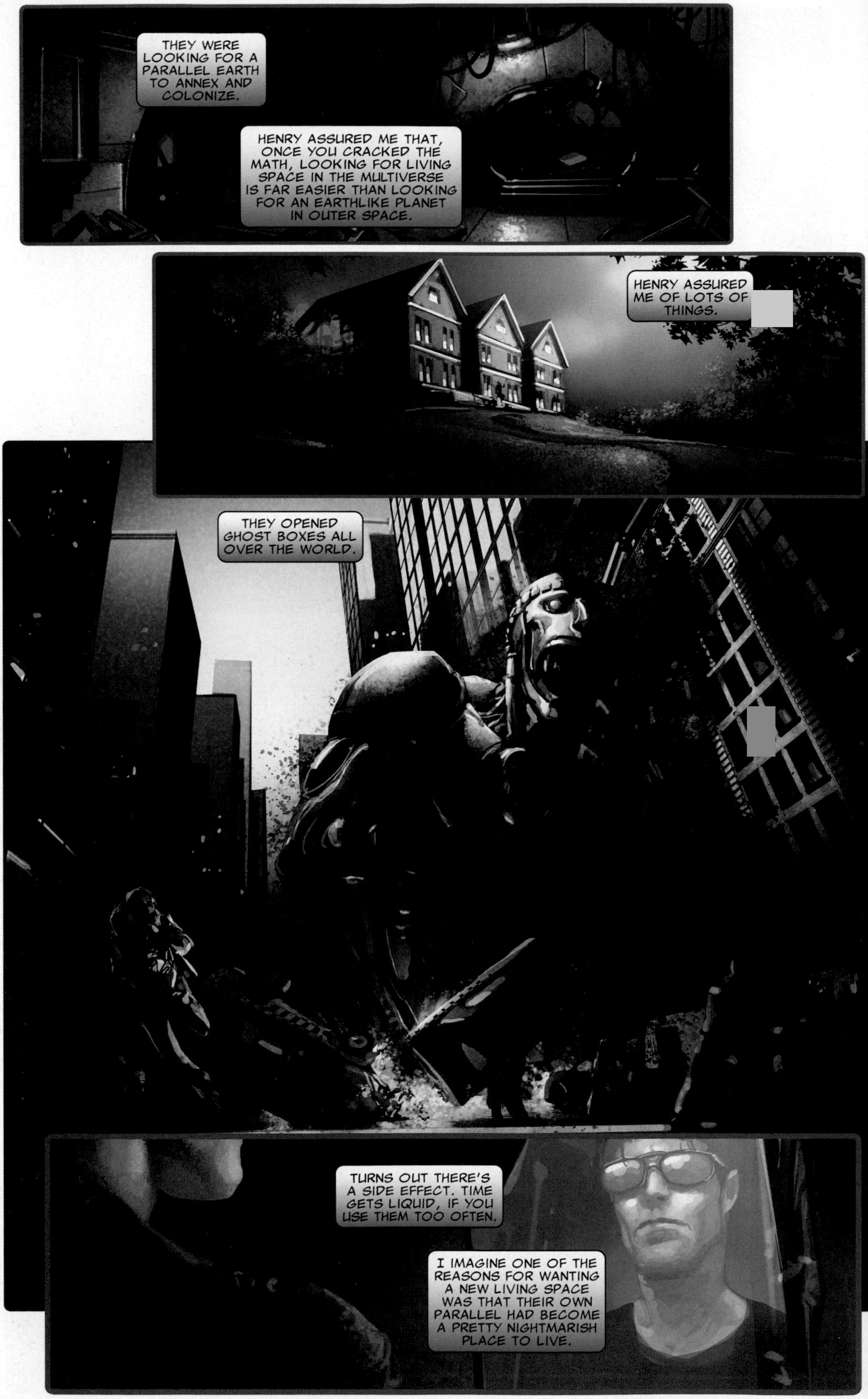
THEY WERE LOOKING FOR A PARALLEL EARTH TO ANNEX AND COLONIZE.
HENRY ASSURED ME THAT, ONCE YOU CRACKED THE MATH, LOOKING FOR LIVING SPACE IN THE MULTIVERSE IS FAR EASIER THAN LOOKING FOR AN EARTHLIKE PLANET IN OUTER SPACE.
HENRY ASSURED ME OF LOTS OF THINGS.
THEY OPENED GHOST BOXES ALL OVER THE WORLD.
TURNS OUT THERE'S A SIDE EFFECT. TIME GETS LIQUID, IF YOU USE THEM TOO OFTEN.
I IMAGINE ONE OF THE REASONS FOR WANTING A NEW LIVING SPACE WAS THAT THEIR OWN PARALLEL HAD BECOME A PRETTY NIGHTMARISH PLACE TO LIVE.

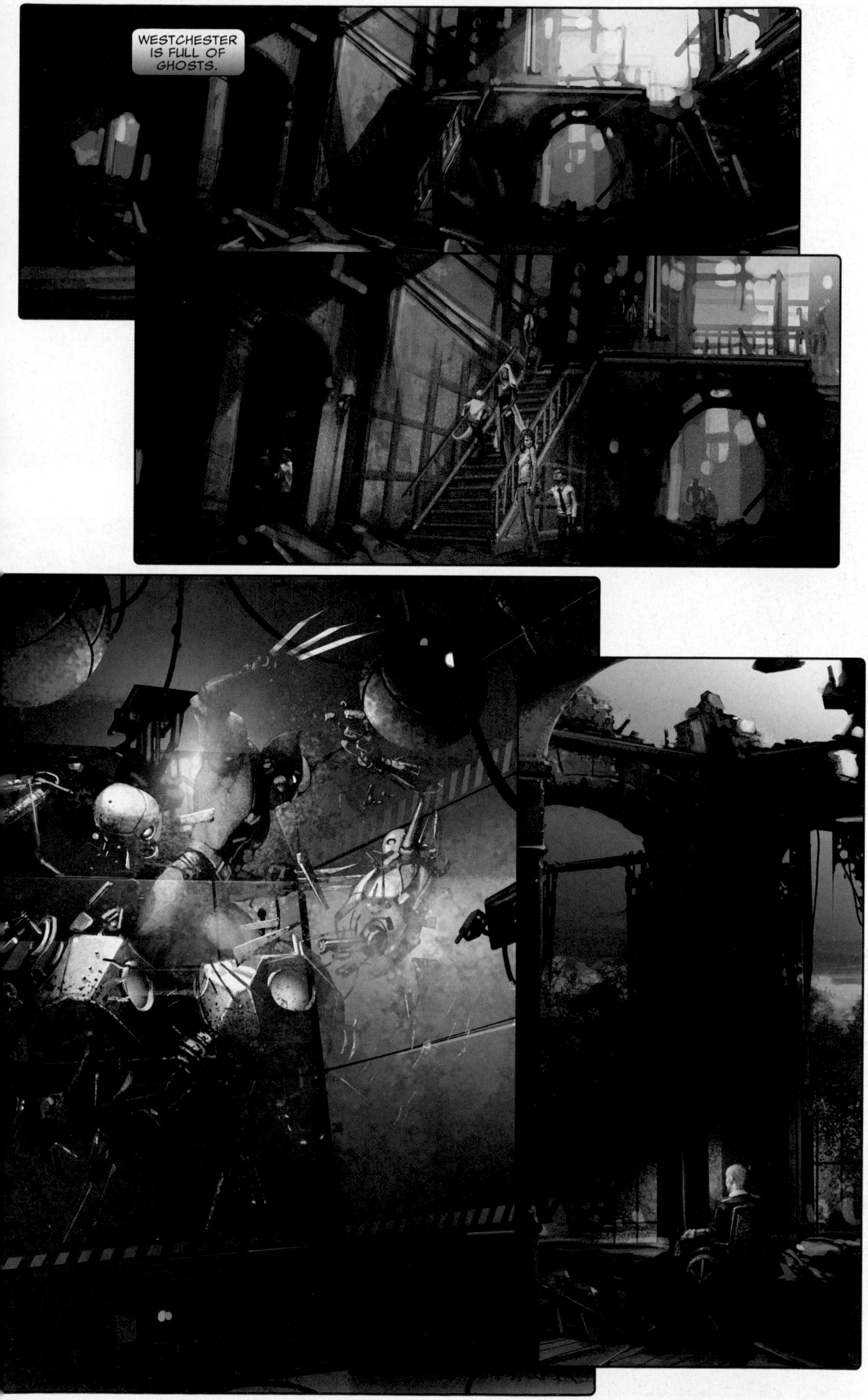
WESTCHESTER IS FULL OF GHOSTS.

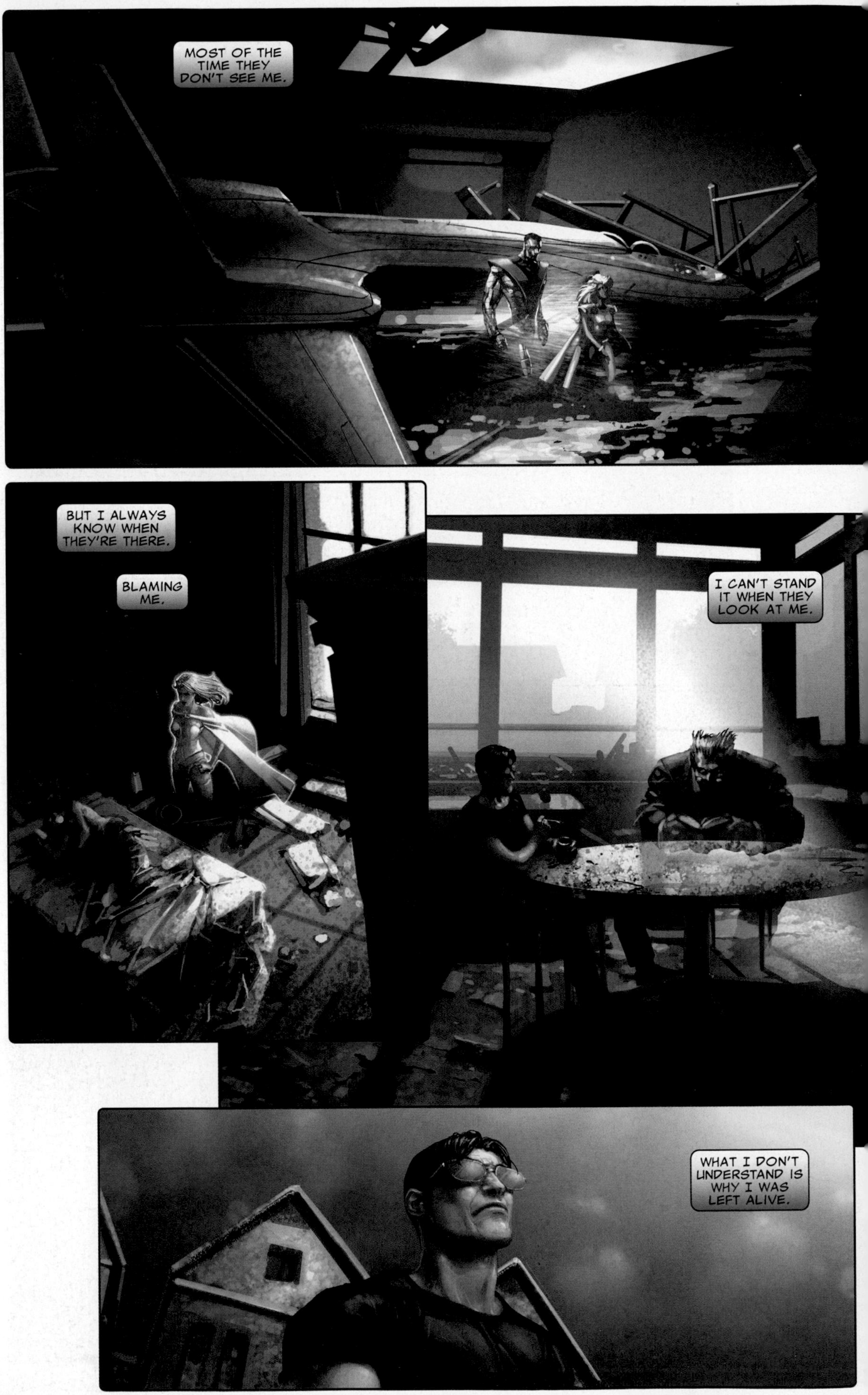
MOST OF THE TIME THEY DON'T SEE ME.
BUT I ALWAYS KNOW WHEN THEY'RE THERE.
BLAMING ME.
I CAN'T STAND IT WHEN THEY LOOK AT ME.
WHAT I DON'T UNDERSTAND IS WHY I WAS LEFT ALIVE.

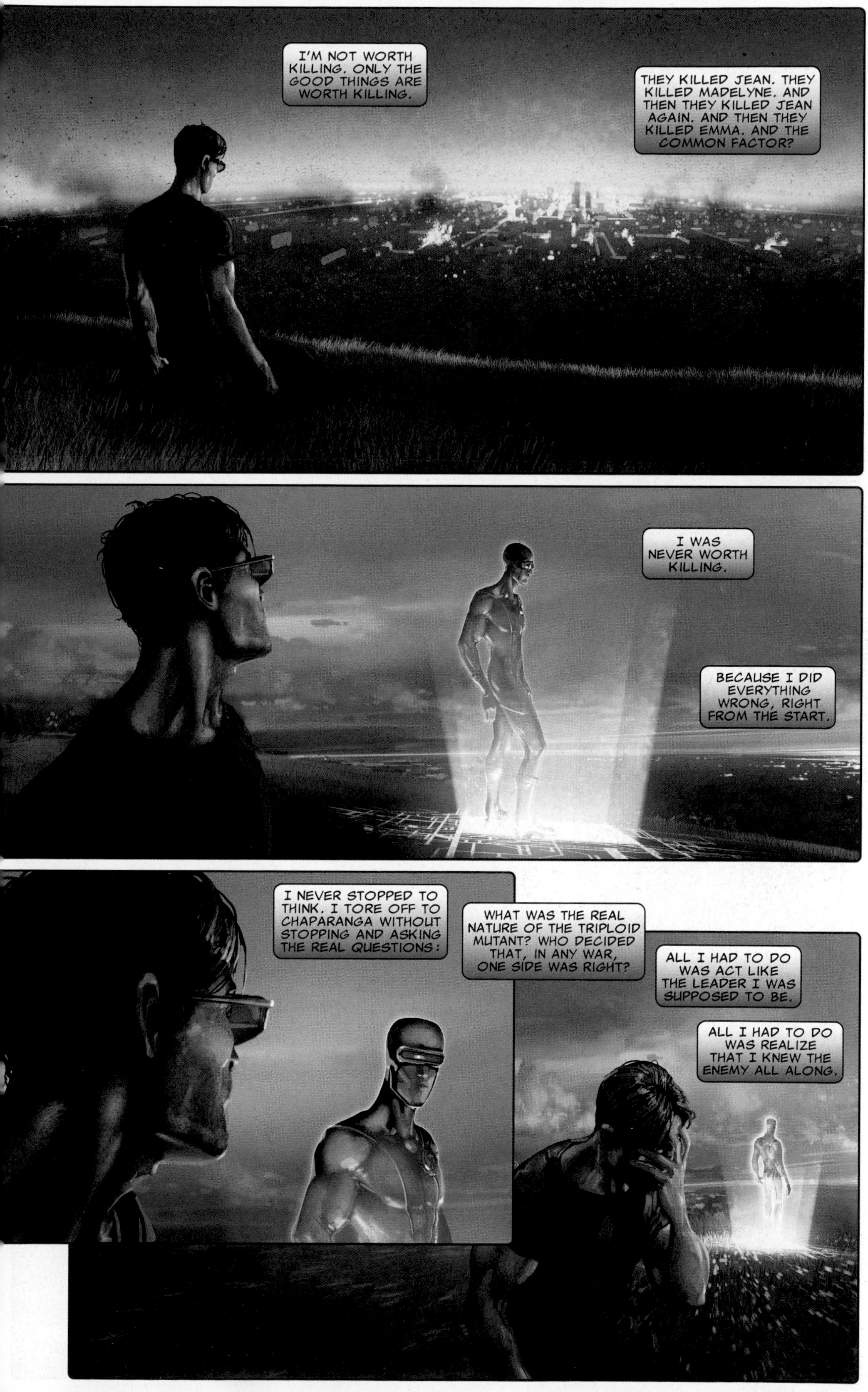
I'M NOT WORTH KILLING. ONLY THE GOOD THINGS ARE WORTH KILLING.
THEY KILLED JEAN. THEY KILLED MADELYNE. AND THEN THEY KILLED JEAN AGAIN. AND THEN THEY KILLED EMMA. AND THE COMMON FACTOR?
I WAS NEVER WORTH KILLING.
BECAUSE I DID EVERYTHING WRONG, RIGHT FROM THE START.
I NEVER STOPPED TO THINK. I TORE OFF TO CHAPARANGA WITHOUT STOPPING AND ASKING THE REAL QUESTIONS:
WHAT WAS THE REAL NATURE OF THE TRIPLOID MUTANT? WHO DECIDED THAT, IN ANY WAR, ONE SIDE WAS RIGHT?
ALL I HAD TO DO WAS ACT LIKE THE LEADER I WAS SUPPOSED TO BE.
ALL I HAD TO DO WAS REALIZE THAT I KNEW THE ENEMY ALL ALONG.

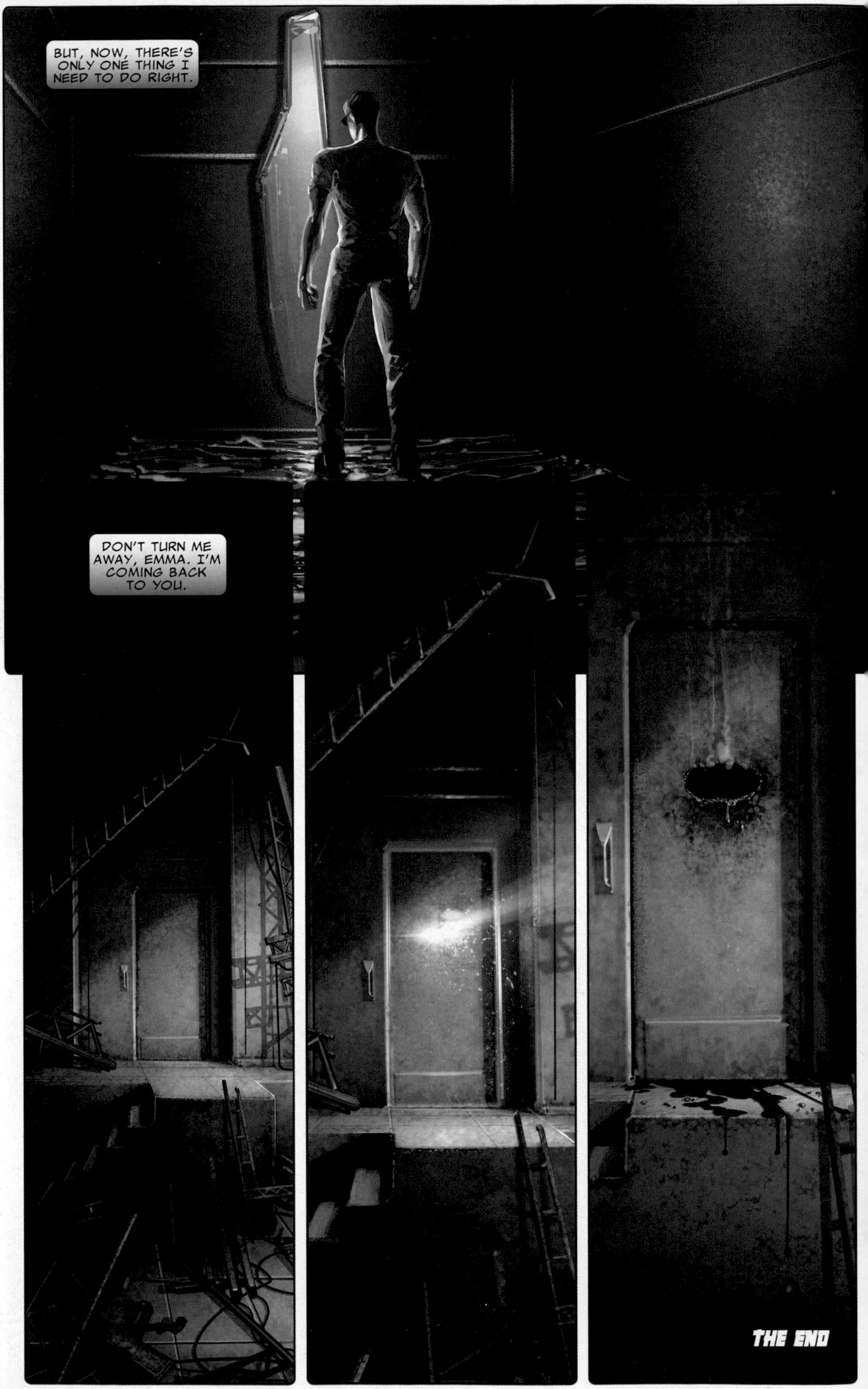
BUT, NOW, THERE'S ONLY ONE THING I NEED TO DO RIGHT.
DON'T TURN ME AWAY, EMMA. I'M COMING BACK TO YOU.
THE END

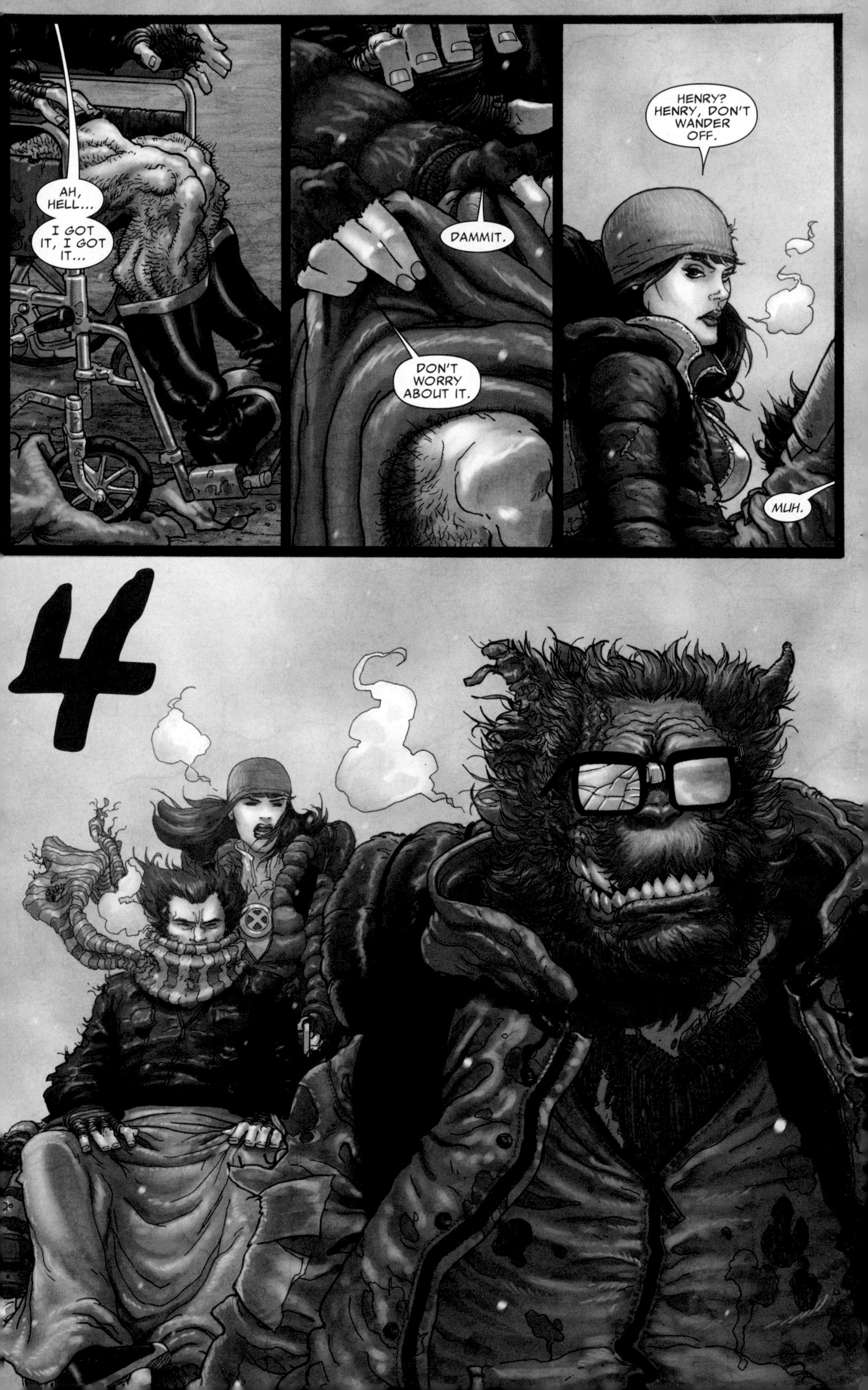
AH, HELL...
I GOT IT, I GOT IT...
DAMMIT.
DON'T WORRY ABOUT IT.
HENRY? HENRY, DON'T WANDER OFF.
MUH.
4

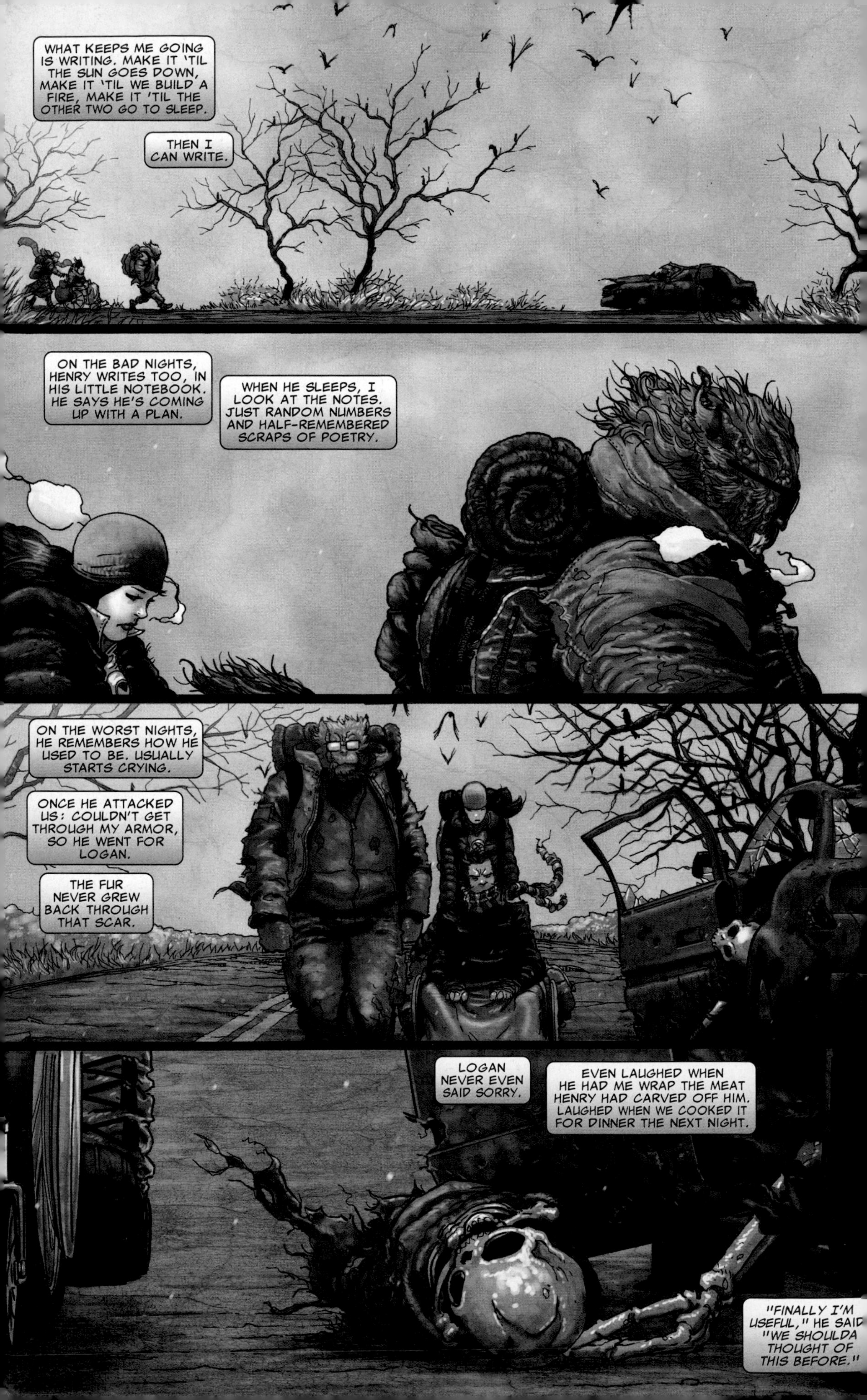
WHAT KEEPS ME GOING IS WRITING. MAKE IT 'TIL THE SUN GOES DOWN, MAKE IT 'TIL WE BUILD A FIRE, MAKE IT 'TIL THE OTHER TWO GO TO SLEEP.
THEN I CAN WRITE.
ON THE BAD NIGHTS, HENRY WRITES TOO, IN HIS LITTLE NOTEBOOK. HE SAYS HE'S COMING UP WITH A PLAN.
WHEN HE SLEEPS, I LOOK AT THE NOTES. JUST RANDOM NUMBERS AND HALF-REMEMBERED SCRAPS OF POETRY.
ON THE WORST NIGHTS, HE REMEMBERS HOW HE USED TO BE. USUALLY STARTS CRYING.
ONCE HE ATTACKED US: COULDN'T GET THROUGH MY ARMOR, SO HE WENT FOR LOGAN.
THE FUR NEVER GREW BACK THROUGH THAT SCAR.
LOGAN NEVER EVEN SAID SORRY.
EVEN LAUGHED WHEN HE HAD ME WRAP THE MEAT HENRY HAD CARVED OFF HIM. LAUGHED WHEN WE COOKED IT FOR DINNER THE NEXT NIGHT.
"FINALLY I'M USEFUL," HE SAID. "WE SHOULDA THOUGHT OF THIS BEFORE."

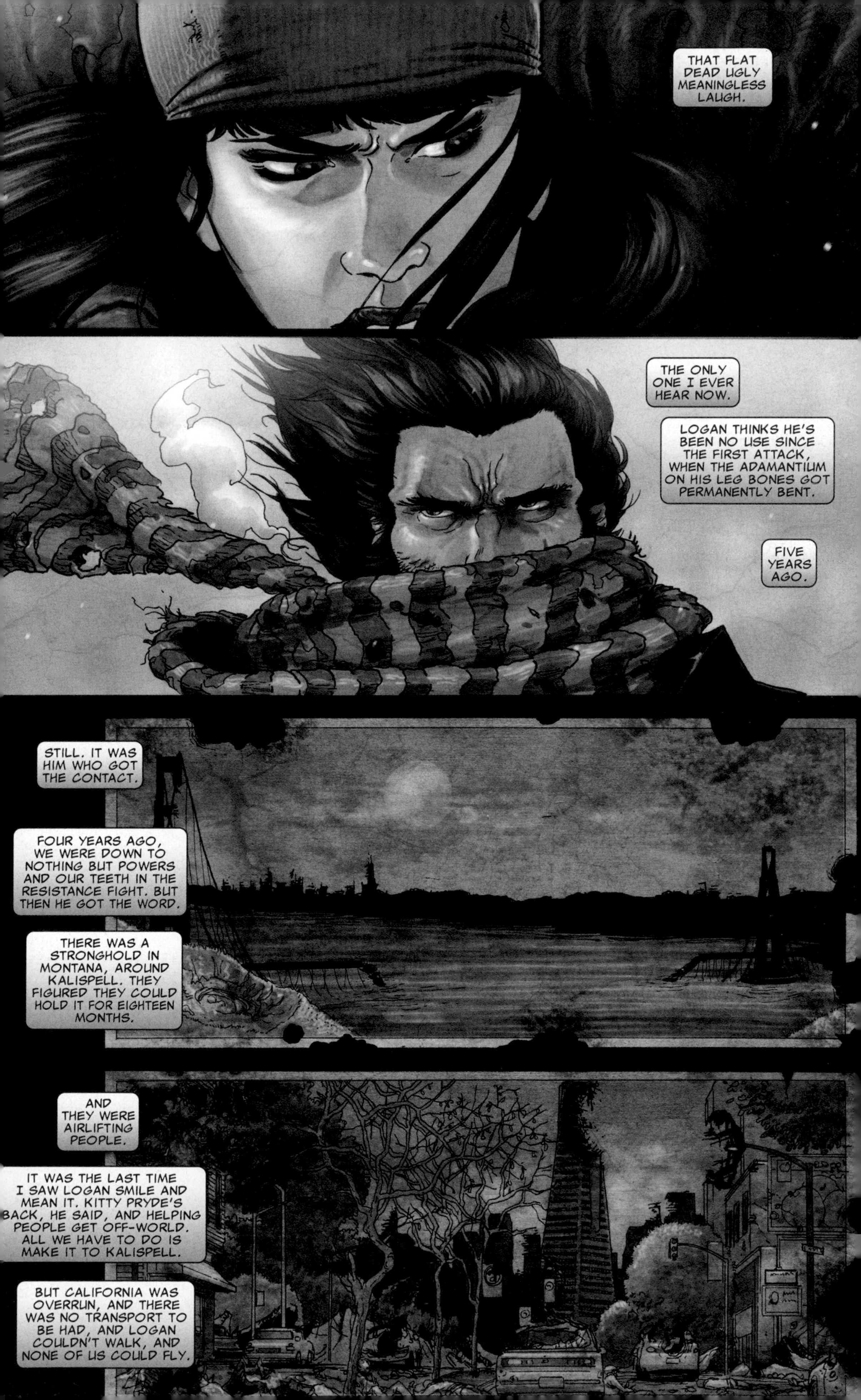
THAT FLAT DEAD UGLY MEANINGLESS LAUGH.
THE ONLY ONE I EVER HEAR NOW.
LOGAN THINKS HE'S BEEN NO USE SINCE THE FIRST ATTACK, WHEN THE ADAMANTIUM ON HIS LEG BONES GOT PERMANENTLY BENT.
FIVE YEARS AGO.
STILL. IT WAS HIM WHO GOT THE CONTACT.
FOUR YEARS AGO, WE WERE DOWN TO NOTHING BUT POWERS AND OUR TEETH IN THE RESISTANCE FIGHT. BUT THEN HE GOT THE WORD.
THERE WAS A STRONGHOLD IN MONTANA, AROUND KALISPELL. THEY FIGURED THEY COULD HOLD IT FOR EIGHTEEN MONTHS.
AND THEY WERE AIRLIFTING PEOPLE.
IT WAS THE LAST TIME I SAW LOGAN SMILE AND MEAN IT. KITTY PRYDE'S BACK, HE SAID, AND HELPING PEOPLE GET OFF-WORLD. ALL WE HAVE TO DO IS MAKE IT TO KALISPELL.
BUT CALIFORNIA WAS OVERRUN, AND THERE WAS NO TRANSPORT TO BE HAD, AND LOGAN COULDN'T WALK, AND NONE OF US COULD FLY.

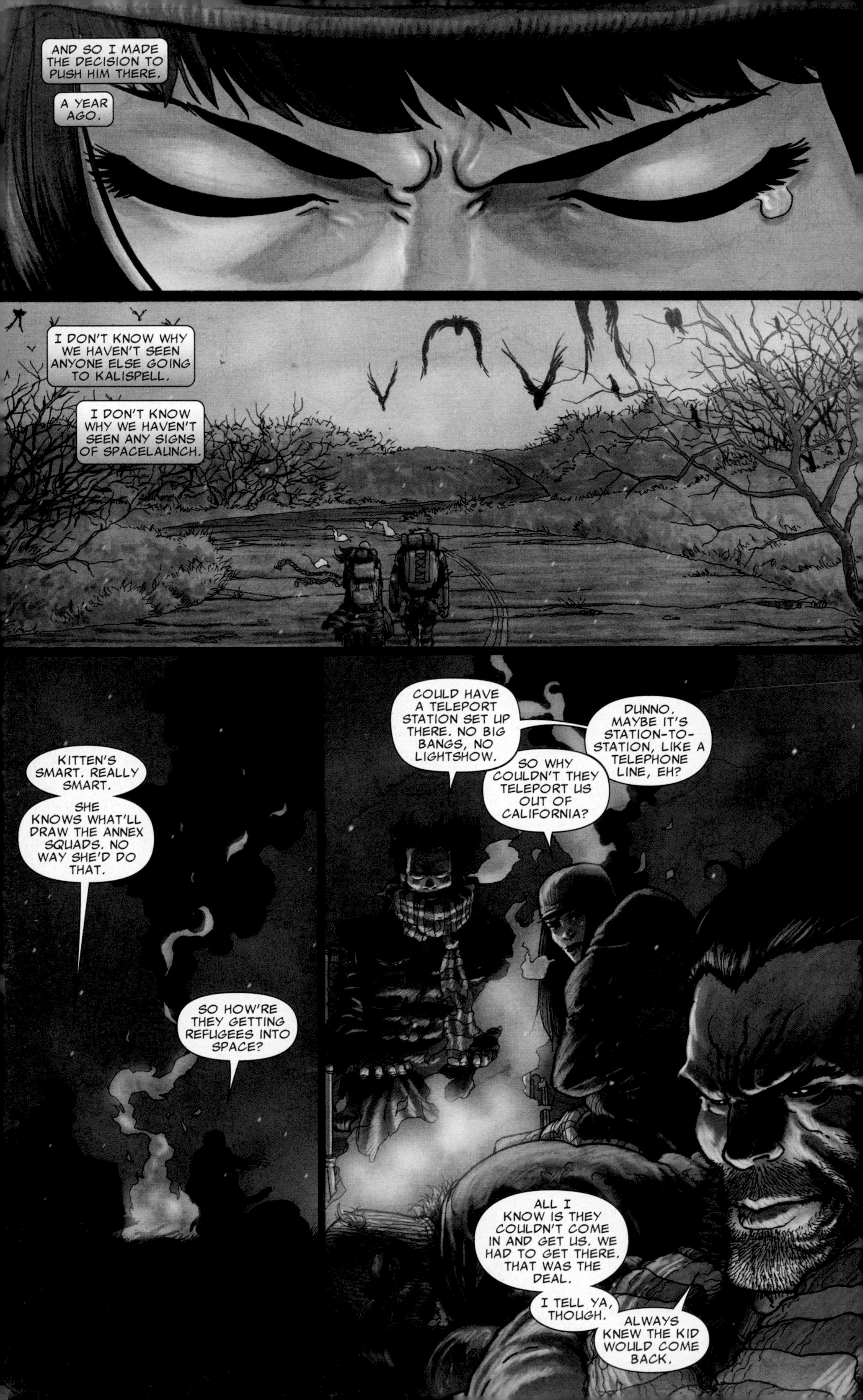
AND SO I MADE THE DECISION TO PUSH HIM THERE.
A YEAR AGO.
I DON'T KNOW WHY WE HAVEN'T SEEN ANYONE ELSE GOING TO KALISPELL.
I DON'T KNOW WHY WE HAVEN'T SEEN ANY SIGNS OF SPACELAUNCH.
KITTEN'S SMART. REALLY SMART.
SHE KNOWS WHAT'LL DRAW THE ANNEX SQUADS. NO WAY SHE'D DO THAT.
SO HOW'RE THEY GETTING REFUGEES INTO SPACE?
COULD HAVE A TELEPORT STATION SET UP THERE. NO BIG BANGS, NO LIGHTSHOW.
SO WHY COULDN'T THEY TELEPORT US OUT OF CALIFORNIA?
DUNNO. MAYBE IT'S STATION-TO-STATION, LIKE A TELEPHONE LINE, EH?
ALL I KNOW IS THEY COULDN'T COME IN AND GET US. WE HAD TO GET THERE. THAT WAS THE DEAL.
I TELL YA, THOUGH.
ALWAYS KNEW THE KID WOULD COME BACK.

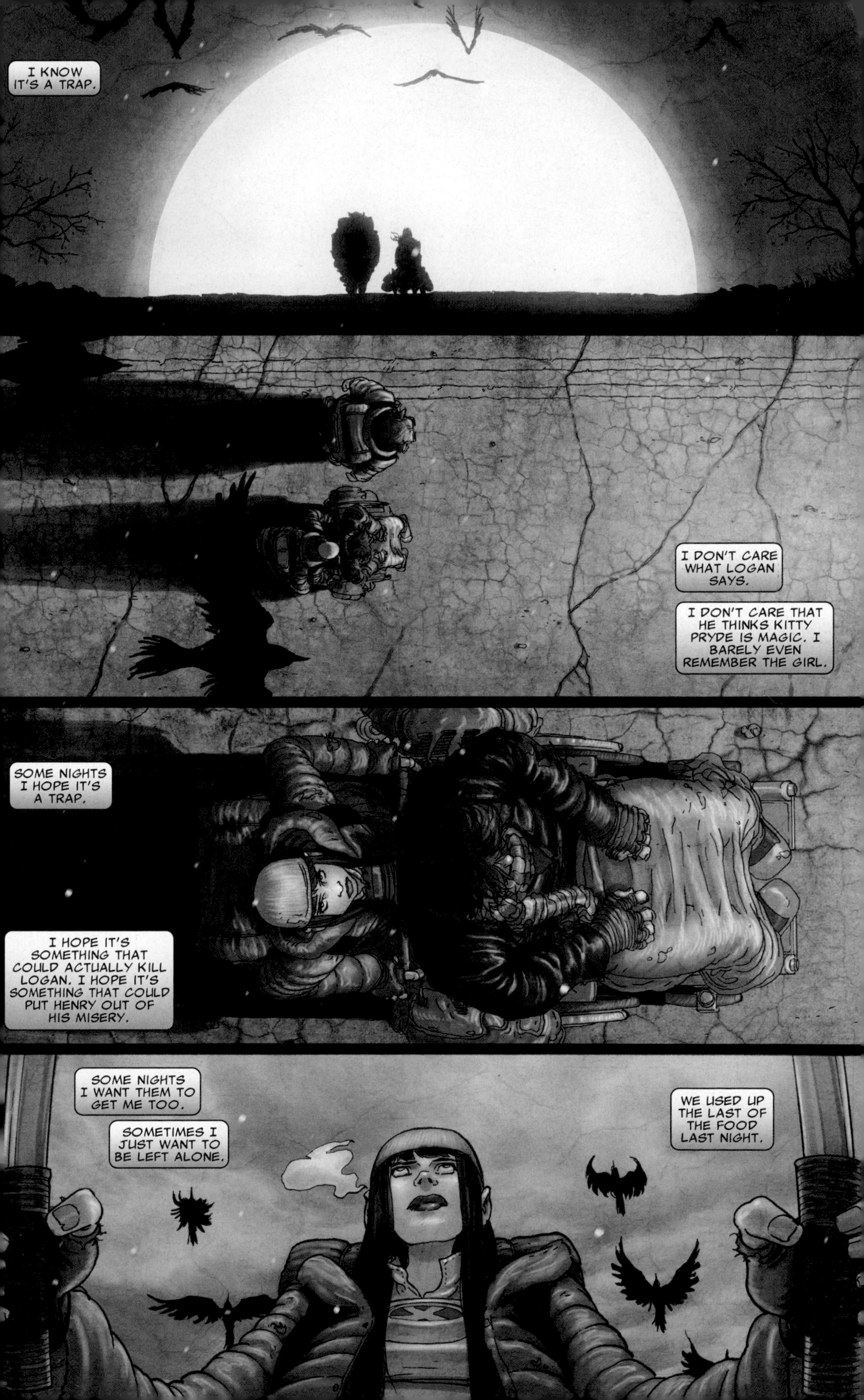

I KNOW IT'S A TRAP.
I DON'T CARE WHAT LOGAN SAYS.
I DON'T CARE THAT HE THINKS KITTY PRYDE IS MAGIC. I BARELY EVEN REMEMBER THE GIRL.
SOME NIGHTS I HOPE IT'S A TRAP.
I HOPE IT'S SOMETHING THAT COULD ACTUALLY KILL LOGAN. I HOPE IT'S SOMETHING THAT COULD PUT HENRY OUT OF HIS MISERY.
SOME NIGHTS I WANT THEM TO GET ME TOO.
SOMETIMES I JUST WANT TO BE LEFT ALONE.
WE USED UP THE LAST OF THE FOOD LAST NIGHT.

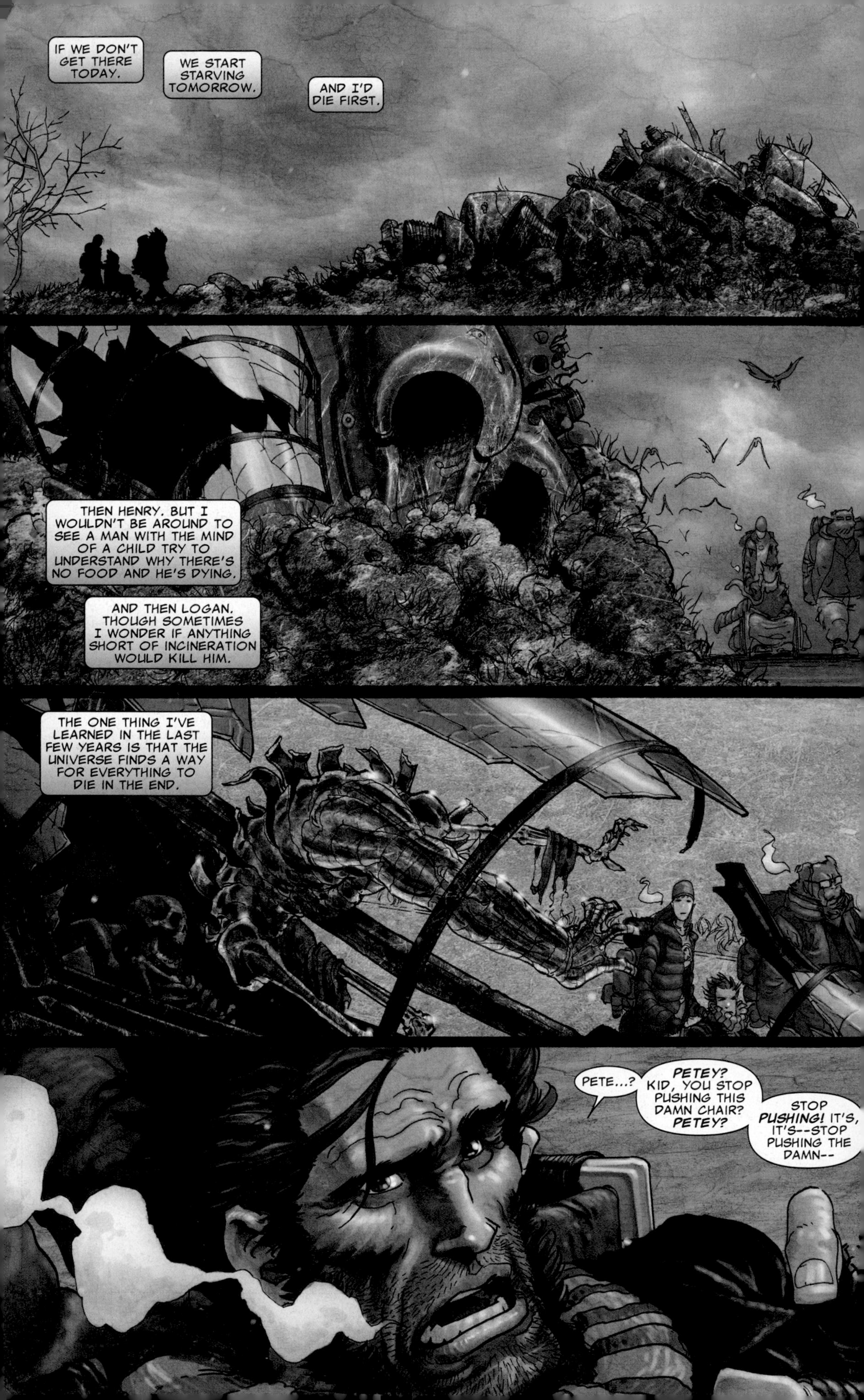
IF WE DON'T GET THERE TODAY.
WE START STARVING TOMORROW.
AND I'D DIE FIRST.
THEN HENRY. BUT I WOULDN'T BE AROUND TO SEE A MAN WITH THE MIND OF A CHILD TRY TO UNDERSTAND WHY THERE'S NO FOOD AND HE'S DYING.
AND THEN LOGAN. THOUGH SOMETIMES I WONDER IF ANYTHING SHORT OF INCINERATION WOULD KILL HIM.
THE ONE THING I'VE LEARNED IN THE LAST FEW YEARS IS THAT THE UNIVERSE FINDS A WAY FOR EVERYTHING TO DIE IN THE END.
PETE...?
PETEY? KID, YOU STOP PUSHING THIS DAMN CHAIR? *PETEY?*
STOP *PUSHING!* IT'S, IT'S--STOP PUSHING THE DAMN--

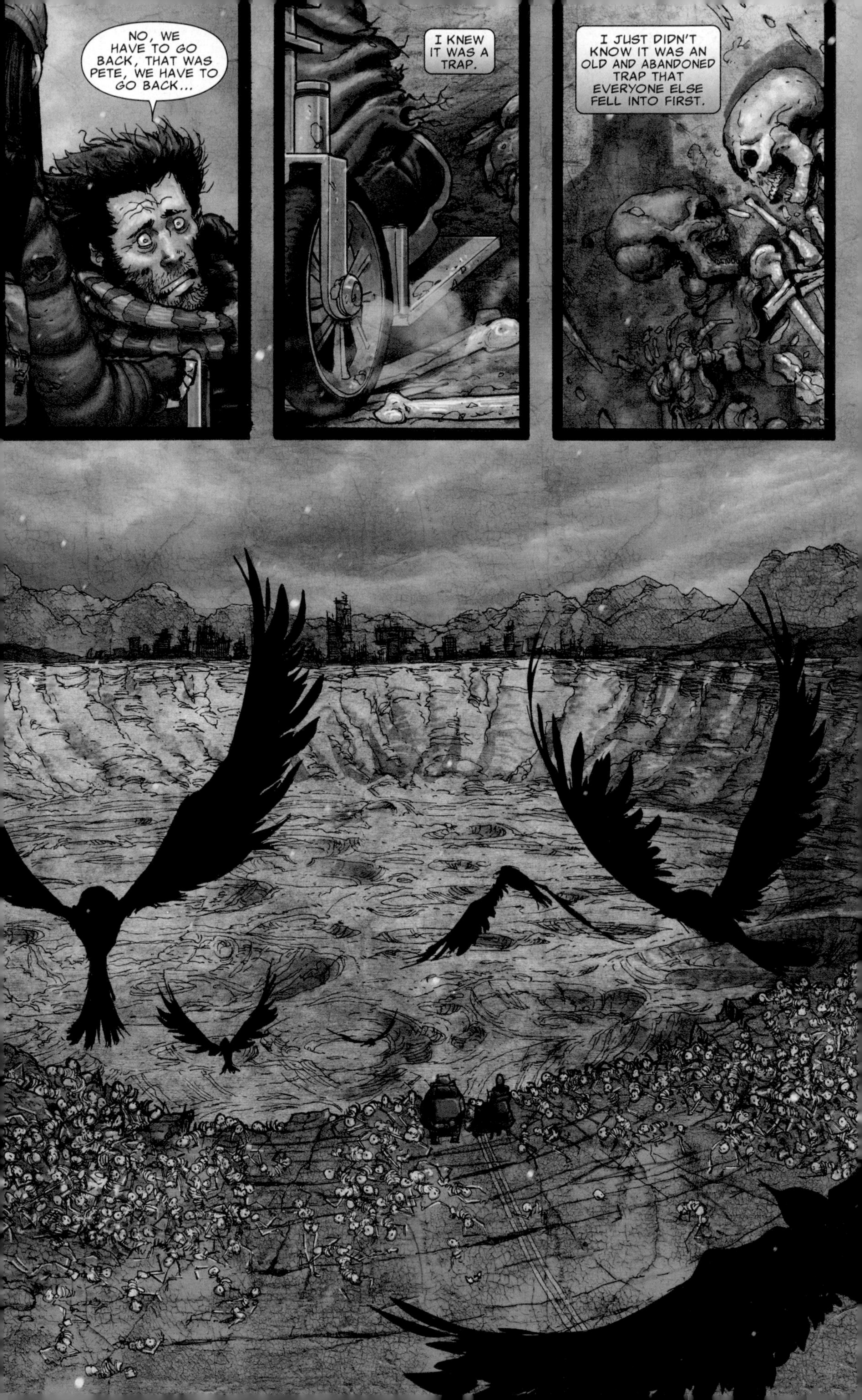
NO, WE HAVE TO GO BACK, THAT WAS PETE, WE HAVE TO GO BACK...
I KNEW IT WAS A TRAP.
I JUST DIDN'T KNOW IT WAS AN OLD AND ABANDONED TRAP THAT EVERYONE ELSE FELL INTO FIRST.

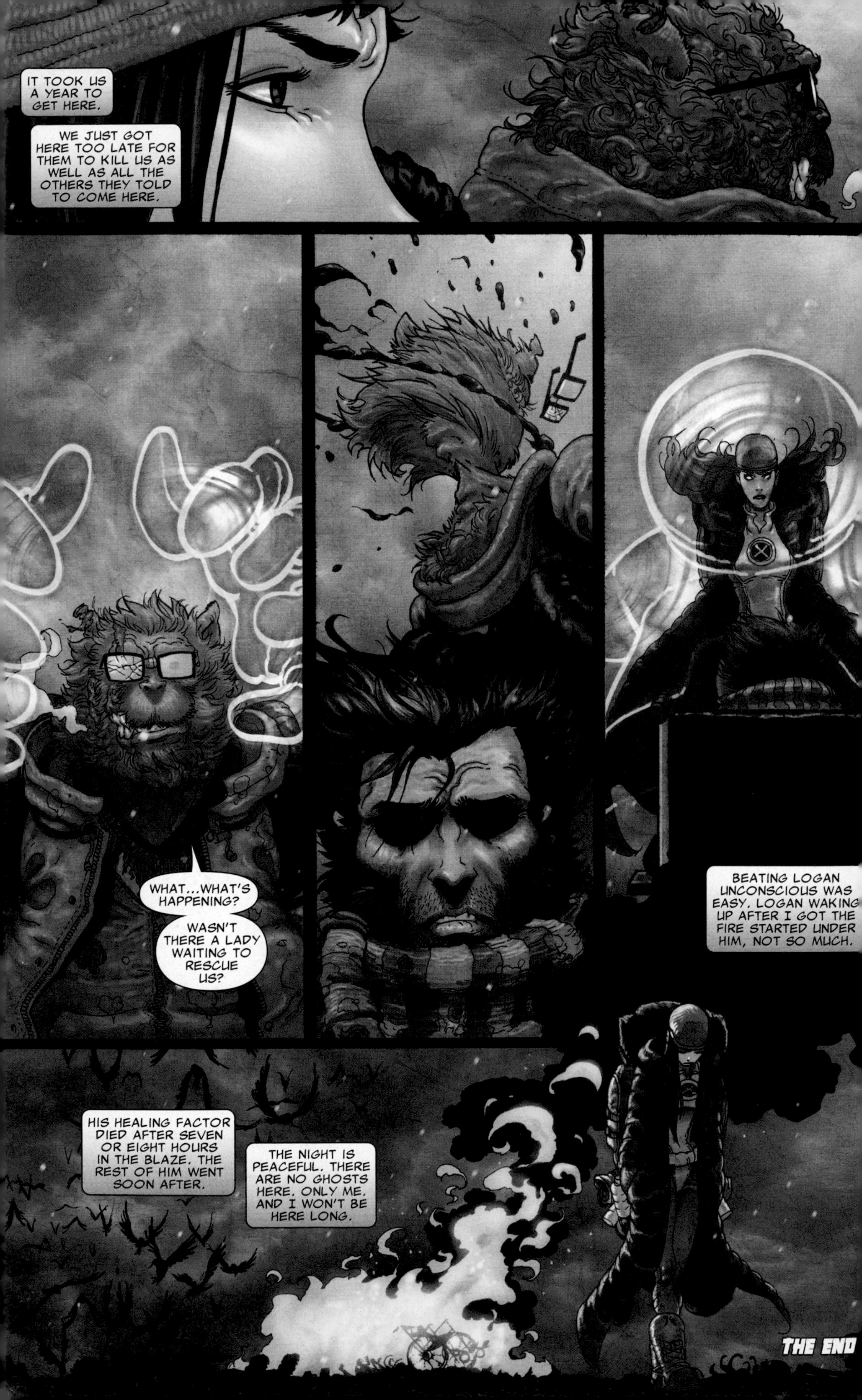
IT TOOK US A YEAR TO GET HERE.
WE JUST GOT HERE TOO LATE FOR THEM TO KILL US AS WELL AS ALL THE OTHERS THEY TOLD TO COME HERE.
WHAT...WHAT'S HAPPENING?
WASN'T THERE A LADY WAITING TO RESCUE US?
BEATING LOGAN UNCONSCIOUS WAS EASY. LOGAN WAKING UP AFTER I GOT THE FIRE STARTED UNDER HIM, NOT SO MUCH.
HIS HEALING FACTOR DIED AFTER SEVEN OR EIGHT HOURS IN THE BLAZE. THE REST OF HIM WENT SOON AFTER.
THE NIGHT IS PEACEFUL. THERE ARE NO GHOSTS HERE, ONLY ME. AND I WON'T BE HERE LONG.
THE END

Cyclops & Beast Designs by Simone Bianchi

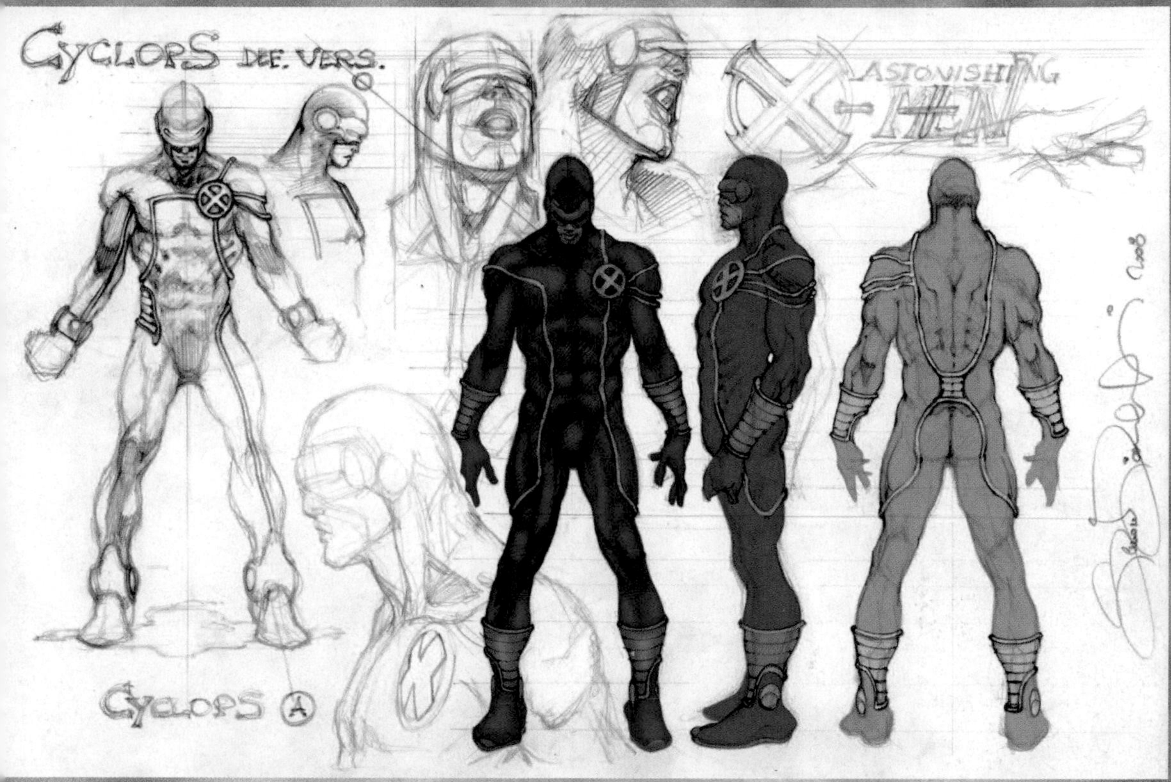
CYCLOPS DEF. VERS.
ASTONISHING X-MEN
CYCLOPS A

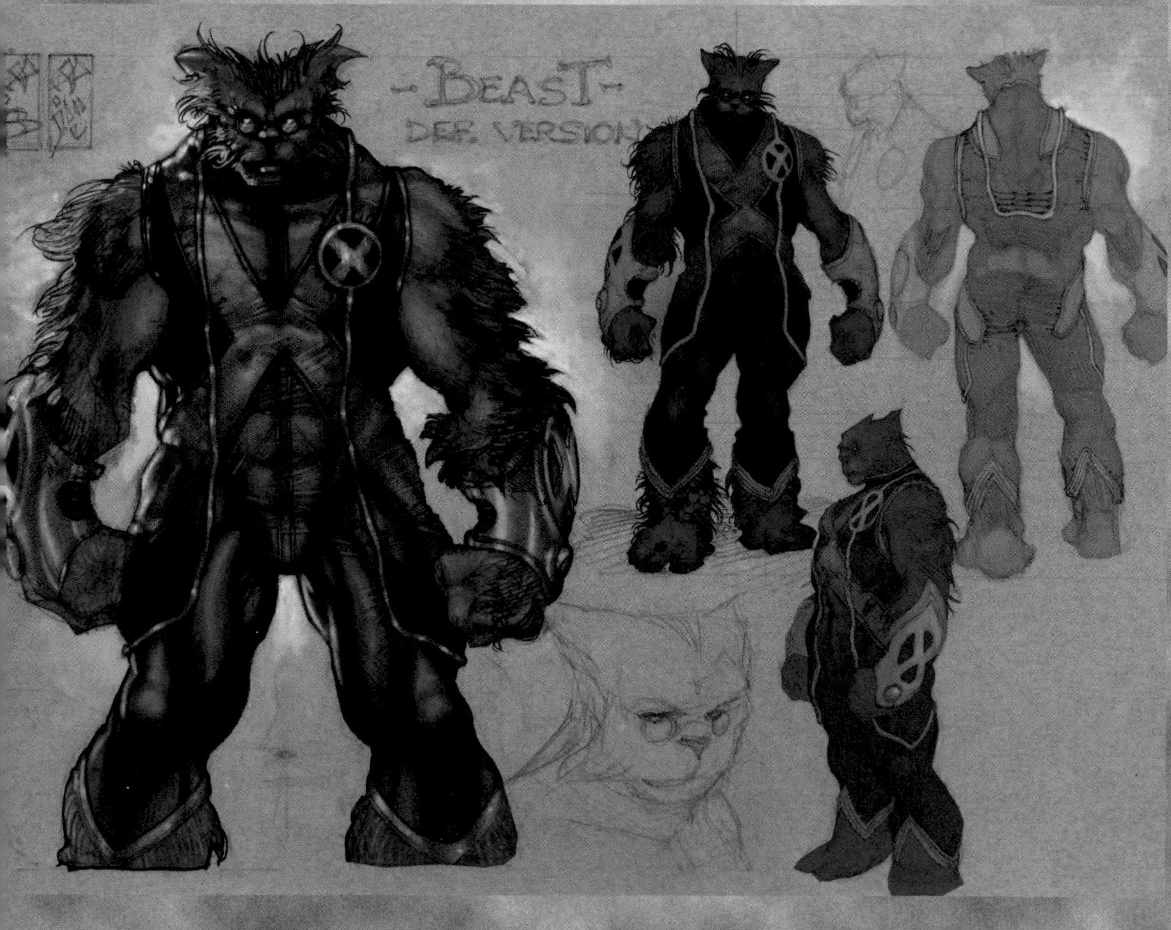
-BEAST-
DEF. VERSION

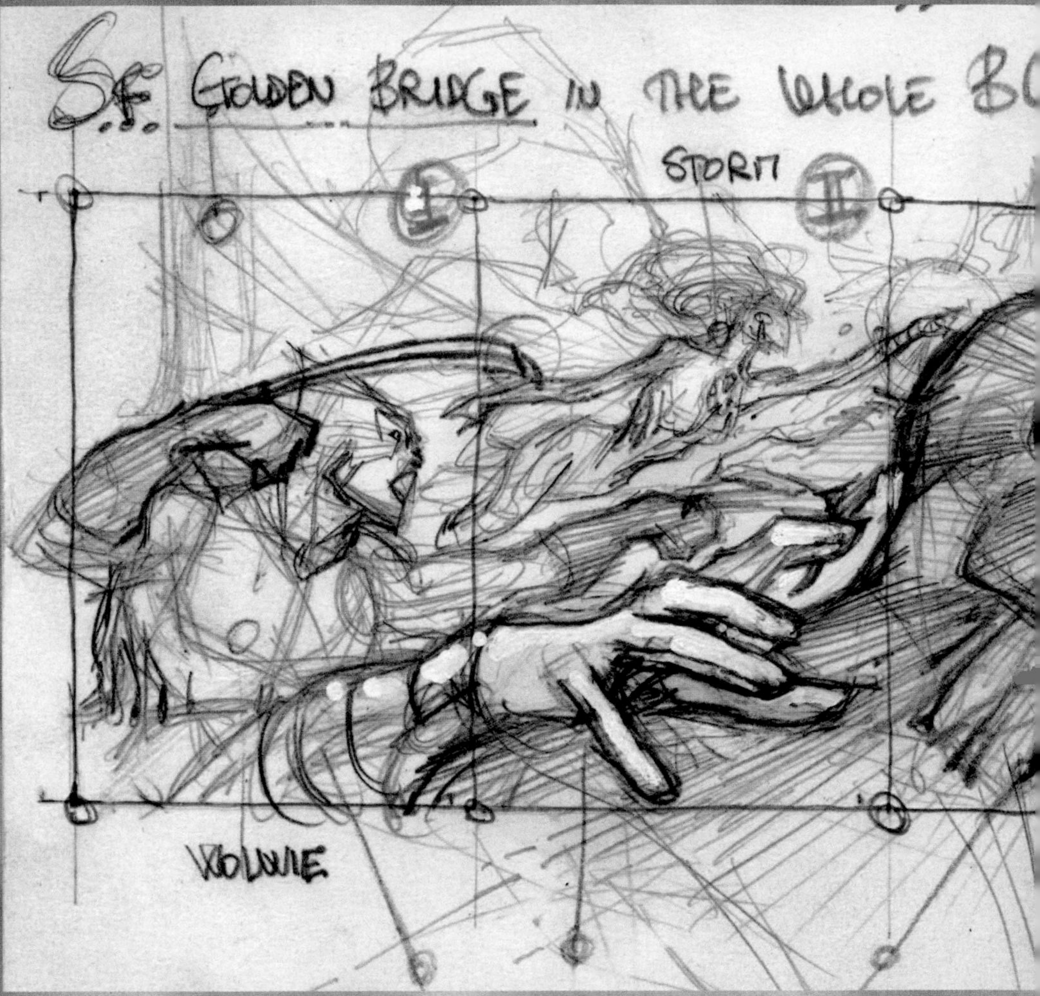
S.F. GOLDEN BRIDGE IN THE WHOLE
STORM
WOLVIE

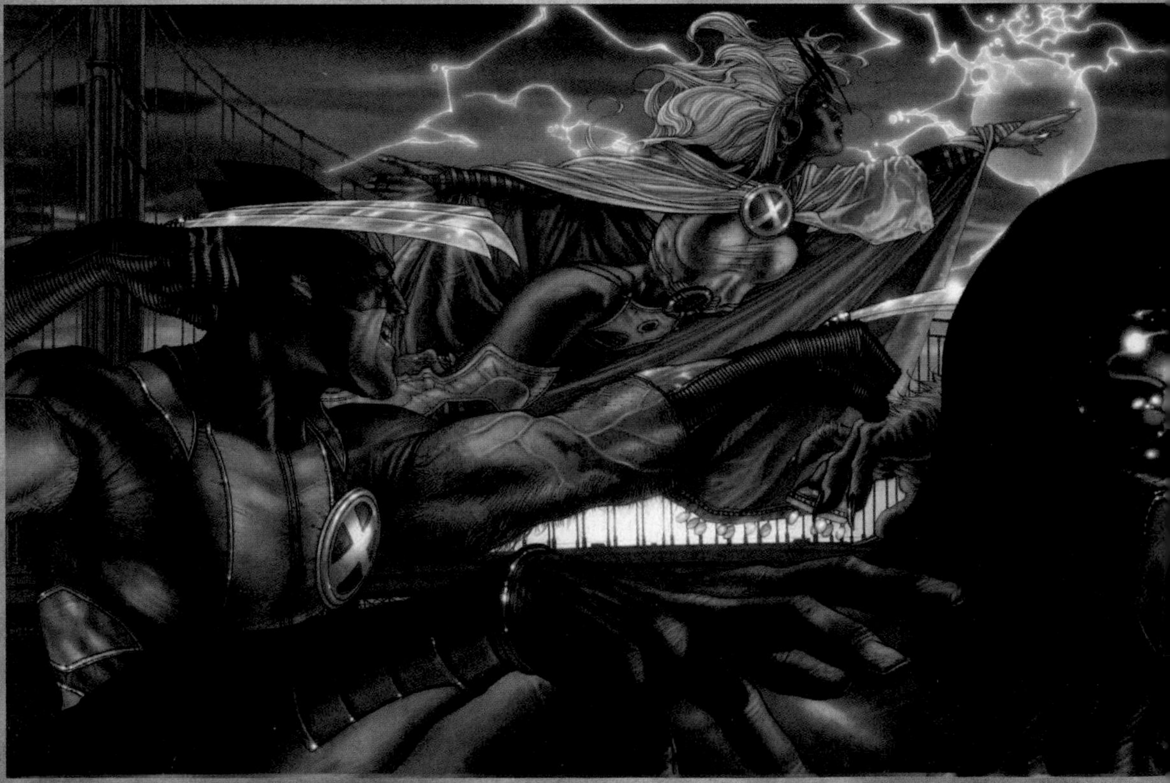

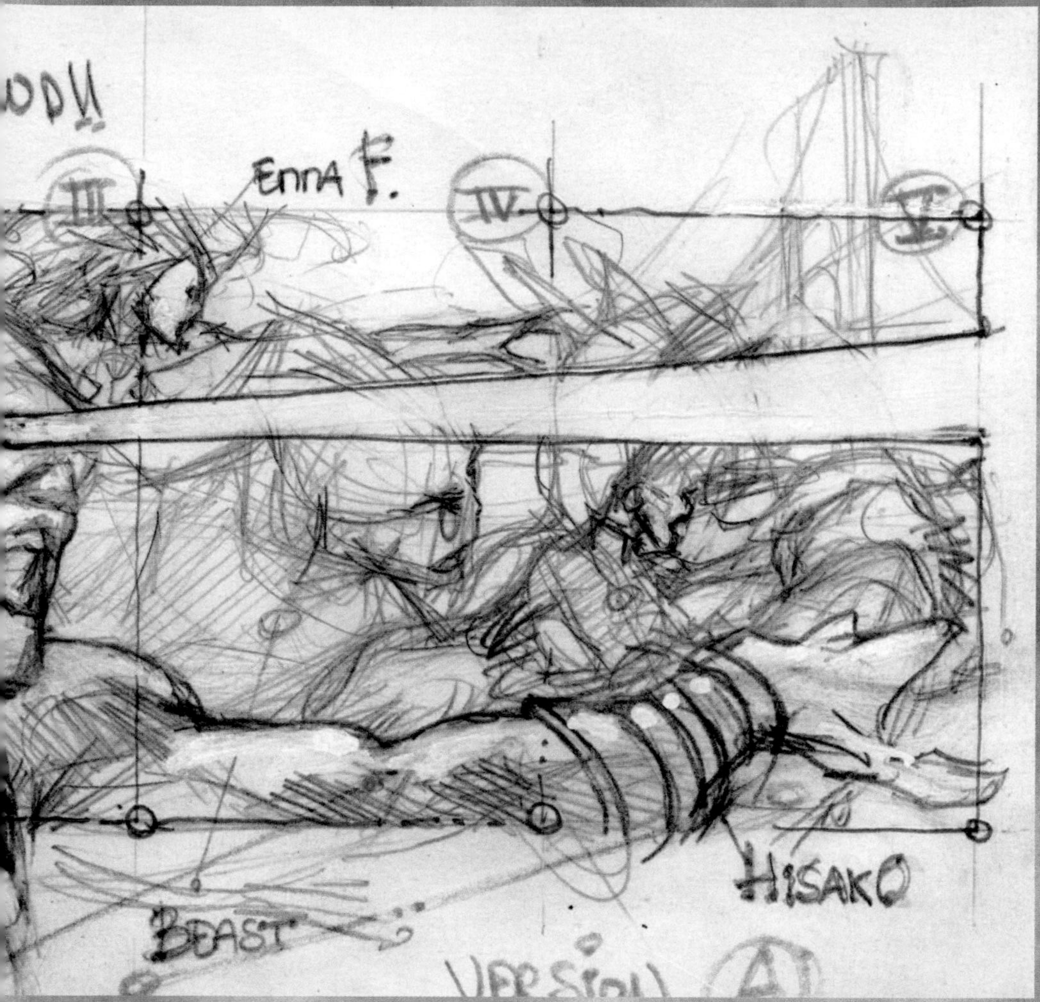
Emma F.
HISAKO
BEAST
VERSION A

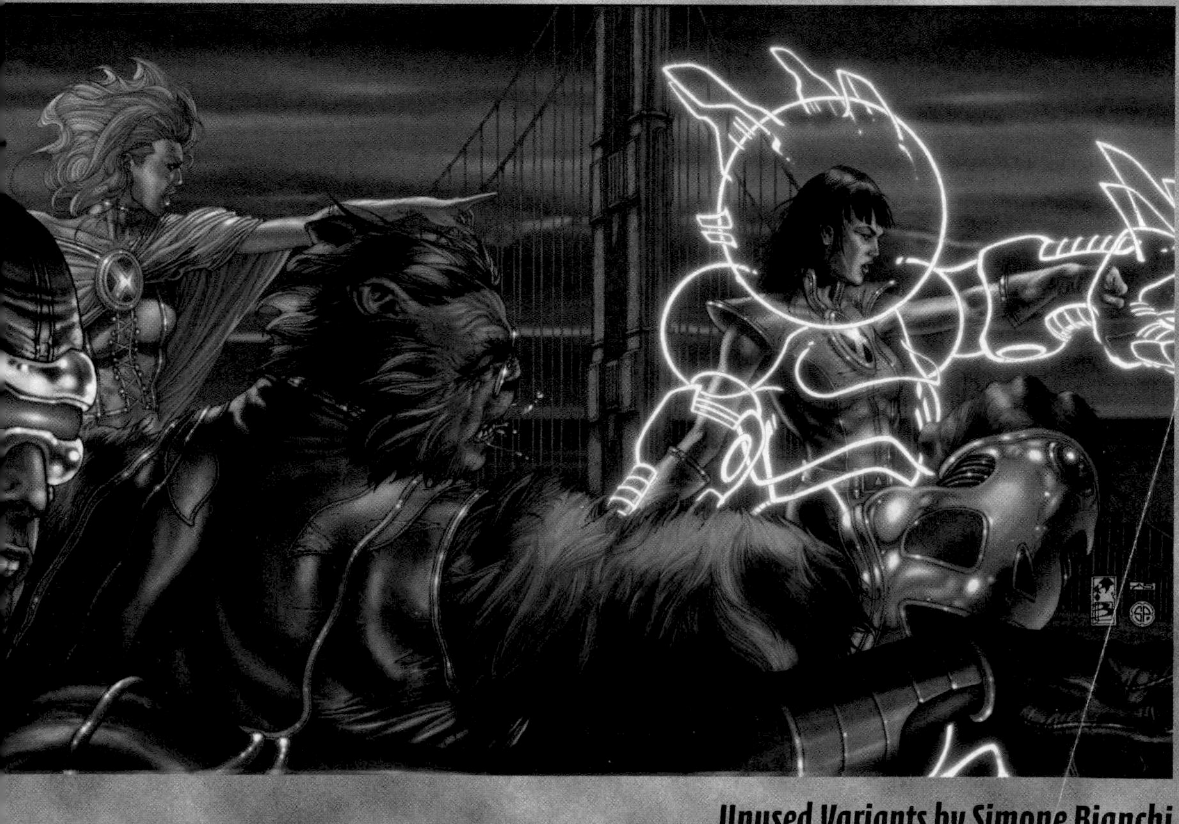

Unused Variants by Simone Bianchi

Storm Designs by Simone Bianchi

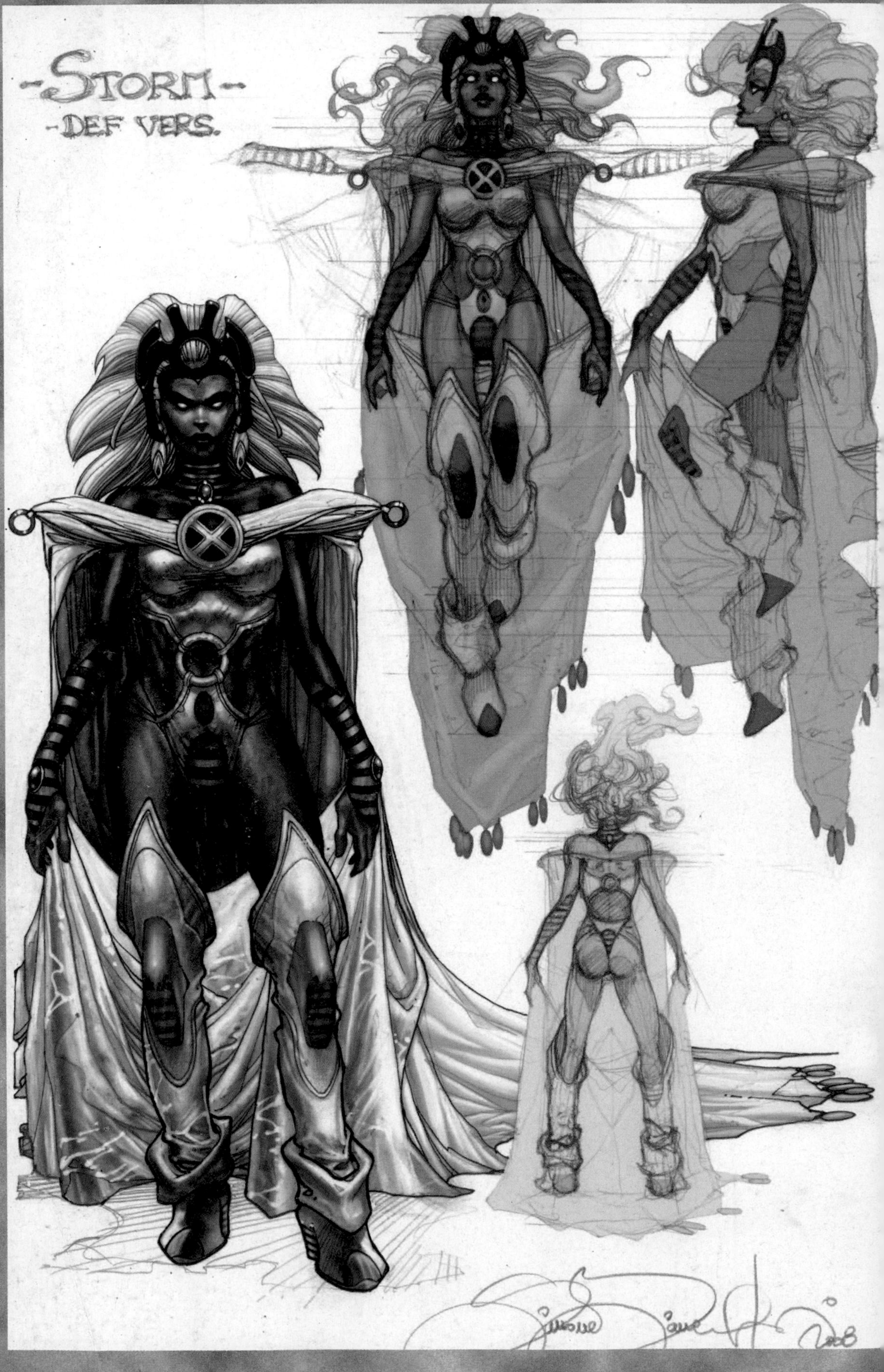

-STORM-
-DEF VERS.